MIT SORRELS and KEVIN SORRELS

Indispensable
Guide
to Clean Humor
and Wit

To order additional copies of this book, contact:
Xlibris Corporation
1-888-795-4274
www.Xlibris.com
Orders@Xlibris.com
58556

IIP will
never die
Wit and Kevin

Indispensable
Guide
to Clean Humor
and Wit

CONTENTS

PREFACE

My father Mit, entertained at public gatherings for approximately sixty years. He served as Master of Ceremonies, Roast master, guest speaker and lecturer at professional meetings, fraternal groups and private gatherings sometimes to the tune of seventy five appearances in a year. Mit, in the conduction of his day to day affairs also employed the use of philosophy and humor as businessman as well as with friends and family. He steadfastly intended this underlying message . . . that humor can heal.

Mit's original intention for this material was to aid the public speaker and also the individual in getting his message across, be it in front of a large group or between two individuals. Laughter and wisdom increase the affinity and thus the willingness to communicate and understand.

Through the years he amassed approximately twenty thousand philosophical and humorous entries in his repertoire. In this collection we have compiled over five thousand entries divided by topics. This volume is intended to be used as a reference text and entries can be easily located by number.

Mit successfully sprinkled his talks with both philosophical advice and humor. Of course humor is different to each individual and what may be funny to one individual may not necessarily be funny to another. When delivering a message there is usually no attempt to offend anyone but rather by the use of levity allow one to look at himself through the observation of the behavior and attitudes of others. In this volume we have hopefully removed the profanity and base innuendos in order to provide material that is suitably appropriate for a wide variety of general public and private gatherings.

The timing of the delivery and the appropriateness of the advice or humor is a talent which can be developed when one has the right tools. This material has been tested and proven successful time and again Whether you are an accomplished public speaker, comedian or novice you will find a treasure of material in this collection. In the spirit of fun, find what is enjoyable for you and that which you may wish to share with others. If you are a businessman, family member or just in the mood for a good laugh you too will enjoy the sage advice and outrageous hilarity of Mit's brand of "clean and philosophical" humor.

Kevin

Introduction

Since I was a small boy, I have enjoyed making people laugh. I knew if they laughed I was accepted and we could be friends. I also felt that no matter how difficult a problem seemed to be, if one could laugh, then the problem could be solved.

Many years ago, I became very involved in organizational work, which meant meetings, meetings, and meetings. I found I couldn't take the time to read novels, so I began collecting one-liner jokes and various quotes and sayings. The time in my life has come when I had to do something with them. So I have compiled them into what I will call a book. In doing this, I found a new appreciation for those who do this job for a living. There are many duplicates. As I would collect them, I found on occasions that everyone was a knee-slapper. Other nights I wondered why in the world I wasted my time, so I figured it was the mood I was in at that particular time that made the determination of whether or not an item was funny. Some I included because I knew I could change them for the better, but I have yet to get around to most of them.

If I have a joke about a drunk man in a bar with a dog, who eats some poisoned food and has to be taken to the vet, then how do I categorize it without duplicating? Drunk—bar—animal—food—vet? Where does it go? At this time I no longer care.

Well, I have compiled about twelve thousand of these things, and I believe they are all clean. At least I hope they are.

To all those whom I can identify, I have given credit for their material and also to my family who furnished the necessary encouragement.

I hope you enjoy them.

Mit

Advice, Philosophy and Wit—A

---

1. Never fight with ugly people, they've got nothing to lose.

2. Never wrestle with pigs, you both get dirty and they like it.

3. Never trust your wife's judgment, look who she married.

4. How do you get your wife's attention? Look comfortable.

5. When you've come to the end of a perfect day, the day probably isn't over.

6. If at first you don't succeed, destroy all evidence you ever tried.

7. If at first you don't succeed, quit.

8. I'd like to be a pessimist, but it probably wouldn't work.

9. Never argue with a fool, he may be doing the same thing.

10. When you think you've won an argument with your wife, the argument isn't over.

11. Never play poker with a man who has the first name of any city.

12. Never play golf with a man who has a suntan and carries a one iron.

13. Always be sincere, even if you have to fake it.

14. Develop a positive attitude like General Custer. When he saw the Indians, he said, "Men take no prisoners."

15. Women who seek to be equal with men lack ambition.

16. Americans will never be slaves. They are free to do whatever government and managed care allow them to do.

17. Every life is a work of art, shaped by the person who lives it.

18. It really doesn't matter whether you win or lose. What matters is whether I win or I lose.

19. Experience is not what happens to a man. It is what a man does with what happens to him.

20. He who lives in glasshouses better go out and buy some heavier draperies.

21. One robin doesn't make a spring, but a single lark is often responsible for a fall.

22. The longest odds in the world are those against "getting even."

23. As a country, we just can't give in to terrorists' demands. Anyone who has ever had children knows this.

24. Marriage is an institution, which either starts a beautiful friendship or ends one.

25. The hardest thing when you learn to skate is the ice when you come right down to it.

26. If you think it's better to have loved and lost, you probably would have had a better divorce lawyer.

27. One of the things you get along with free speech is cheap talk.

28. They all laughed at Isaac Newton. But he went right ahead and made us fig cookies.

29. You're never quite sure whether it's better to tell the truth or hire a lawyer.

30. Father to son: "Think of a marriage license as a hunting permit, son, that entitles you to only one dear at a time."

31. Some kinds of people come along only once in a generation . . . that's often enough.

32. Businessman to airline agency: "If possible, I want to go somewhere near my luggage.

33. Couple to marriage counselor: "It seems that the only thing keeping us together is neither one of us has AIDS.

34. Financial planner to client: "I've reviewed your financial picture, and if we manage your money properly, there should be plenty for both of us."

35. Self-Improvement Workshops: Creative Suffering, Guilt Without Sex, Overcoming Peace of Mind, the Primal Shrug, Whine Your Way to Alienation, Dealing with Post Self-Realization Depression, How to Overcome Self-Doubt through Pretense and Ostentation

    Home Economics Workshops: How You Can Convert Your Family Room into a Garage, Burglar-Proof Your Home with Concrete, Sinus Drainage at Home, 101 Other Uses for Your Vacuum Cleaner

    Health and Fitness Workshops: Creative Tooth Decay, the Joys of Hypochondria, Biofeedback and How to Stop It, Skate Your Way to Regularity, Tap-Dance Your Way to Social Ridicule, Using Burnout to Get Sympathy

    Business/Career Workshops: Money Can Make You Rich, Talking Good: How You Can Improve Speech and Get a Better Job, I Made $100 in Real Estate, Career Opportunities in Iran, How to Profit from Your Own Body, Underachievers' Guide to Very Small Business Opportunities, Filler Phrases for Thesis Writers

    Improving Your Effectiveness in the Classroom: Innovative Buffoonery, Prepared Scripts for Observation Day, Holding Your Students' Attention Through Guilt and Fear, Avoiding Teaching through Maximized Audiovisuals, Using Bad Breath and Body Odor to Reduce Class Size.

36. Leadership: When the best leader's work is done, the people will say, "We did it ourselves."

37. It's always easier to forgive an enemy after you've gotten even.

38. Treat the cause not the symptom—then try to prevent the cause.

39. Always owe your doctor; it gives him an incentive to keep you alive.

40. Tonsorial advice: When you go to get a haircut, always choose the barber with the worst haircut 'cause they cut each other's hair.

41. Have you ever noticed how people who can take it or leave it alone usually take it?

42. If you can keep your head when all others about you are losing theirs, maybe you just don't understand what's happening.

43. Conceit is a funny disease; it makes everyone sick but the person who has it.

44. Old Chinese proverb: "If thine enemy has wronged you, buy each of his children a drum."

45. Love maketh the heart light but the parlor dark.

46. Love may be blind, but it sure finds its way around in the dark.

47. I also know that familiarity breeds attempt and a bad girl means a good night.

48. Did you ever stop to think—sometimes a red light means just what a green light means?

49. Closed mouths gather no feet.

50. A smile is a gentle curved line that sets a lot of things straight.

51. Have you heard about those people who don't know nothing? Hell, he don't even expect nothing.

52. When you're rich you're rich on paper, but when you're broke, you're broke in cash.

53. It's sort of like a miracle that every day just enough happens to fill every newspaper in the world.

54. There is no one harder to shut up than the person who has nothing to say.

55. People who burn the candle at both ends aren't necessarily bright.

56. Nowadays, the guy who robs Peter to pay Paul is usually named Paul.

57. People in tin houses shouldn't throw can openers.

58. Isn't it funny that both Washington and Lincoln were born on holidays?

59. Have you ever noticed the way people who are easily shocked go out of their way to find things that shock them?

60. The main difference between genius and stupidity is that genius has its limits.

61. It's too late to agree with me. I've already changed my mind.

62. Coming to work doesn't hurt . . . it's the long wait to go home.

63. Nothing is impossible . . . if you don't have to do it yourself.

64. I've paid attention to your story . . . and drawn my own confusions.

65. You have to be a little crazy today . . . otherwise, you'll go nuts.

66. I like my job . . . it's the work I hate.

67. Please don't ask me for information . . . if I knew anything, I wouldn't be here.

68. No problem is too small to baffle this organization.

69. Money can't buy happiness, but it sure can make misery more enjoyable.

70. There's no reason for it . . . it's just our policy.

71. Be reasonable . . . do it my way.

72. Think! There must be a harder way to do this job.

73. Be original . . . at least make a different mistake each time.

74. Keep your eye on the ball, your shoulder to the wheel, your ear to the ground. Now try to work in that position.

75. Looking for someone with a little authority? I have as little as anyone.

76. It's better to give than to receive . . . now, what have you brought me?

77. Minds are like parachutes . . . they function only when opened.

78. I understand he is somewhat of a philosopher and is known for his sage advice. He once said to a struggling young lady, "Don't struggle."

79. It takes seventeen muscles to smile and forty-three to frown, so you can preserve your face value by smiling.

80. It usually takes me about three weeks to prepare a good impromptu speech.

81. Life is what happens when you have something else planned.

82. The trouble with the rat race is that even if you win, you're still a rat.

83. The world has achieved brilliance without wisdom, power without conscience. Ours is a world of nuclear giants and ethical infants. We know more about war than we do about peace, more about killing than we do about living.

84. For motivating humans, an ounce of recognition is worth a pound of complaints.

85. When you don't know who is in charge, you may be.

86. Death is not the greatest loss of life. The greatest loss is what dies inside us while we live.

87. Just because you are elected to the down-and-out club you don't have to become a life member.

88. Happiness consists of not getting the things we don't want.

89. An ounce of accomplishment is worth a ton of good intentions.

90. If people never made mistakes, there would be no rubber tips on lead pencils.

91. Greatness lies not in being strong, but in the right use of strength.

92. You can only be young once but immature all your life.

93. One of the things that she has taught me is that stress (failure, pain) is not an event. It is a perception of an event. We can't necessarily control events or people around us, but what we can control is our perception of them and, therefore, our response to them.

94. Judgment should be totally suspended while the creative process is flowing. I have discovered that my own creative work flowed most freely if I simply decided to delay judgmental decisions until a later stage, at which time I could function perfectly freely as editor of my earlier output. But if I were self-critical at the moment an idea was developing, I could inhibit the full expression of it. Even in group-think sessions, sometimes in the context of television production, I have often instructed my staff of people, "Let's just suggest any damn thing we think of at this stage. We can always throw something out later if it's not any good."

95. When opportunity knocks at the door, some people are out in the backyard looking for four-leaf clovers.

96. People are funny. They spend money they don't have to buy things they don't need to impress people they don't like.

97. The trouble with most people is that they work so hard for a living that they don't have any time to live.

98. It is more important to have fun than it is to be funny.

99. Never forget what a man says to you when he is angry.

100. So live that when your life shall end all men may say, "I've lost a friend."

101. I cannot give you the formula for success, but I can give you the formula for failure. Try to please everybody.

102. What you don't know won't hurt you. It's what you suspect that causes all of the trouble.

103. Six essential qualities that are the key to success: sincerity, personal integrity, humility, courtesy, wisdom, charity.

104. Where do people who live beyond their income get the money to live beyond their income?

105. If the going seems easy, you're going downhill.

106. A few choice olives at the top of the jar is the best way to sell the small ones.

107. When wine, women, and song become too much for you, stop singing.

108. If your wife wants to learn to drive your car, don't stand in her way!

109. Manager to employee: "When I want your advice, I'll give it to you!"

110. Never suffer future pain.

111. Today is the first day of the rest (or best) of your life.

112. Which one of us is the opposite sex?

113. One of the great mysteries and discoveries is that a human being can alter his life by altering his attitude.

114. Consider how hard it is to change yourself and you'll understand what little chance you have trying to change others.

115. Character is made by what you stand for; reputation by what you fall for.

116. Ability will enable a man to get to the top, but character is the only thing that keeps him from falling off.

117. Childhood is that wonderful time when all you need to do to lose weight is bathe.

118. As long as your conscience is your friend, never mind about your enemies.

119. It is not the load that breaks you down; it is the way you carry it.

120. Either do not attempt at all, or go through with it.

121. The harder you work, the harder it is to surrender.

122. Good judgment comes from experience, and experience comes from bad judgment.

123. A word of encouragement during a failure is worth more than a whole book of praise after a success.

124. Stranger—a friend you haven't met.

125. Failure is the greatest opportunity I have to know who I really am.

126. Failure is the only opportunity to begin again more intelligently.

127. In great attempts, it is glorious even to fail.

128. Our greatest glory is not in never failing, but in rising every time we fail.

129. It is hard to fail, but it is worse never to have tried to succeed.

130. People may fail many times, but they become failures only when they begin to blame someone else.

131. Success is never final, and failure is never fatal.

132. That which you cannot give away, you do not possess. It possesses you.

133. All progress is the result of change, but all change is not necessarily progress.

134. It is better to be silent and be considered a fool than to speak and remove all doubt.

135. Time wounds all heals.

136. If you cannot win, make the one ahead of you break the record.

137. Never mistake knowledge for wisdom. One helps you make a living; the other helps you make a life.

138. Don't be so concerned about making a living that you don't take the time to make a life.

139. Take your work seriously but yourself lightly.

140. The biggest mistake you can make is to believe you're working for someone else.

141. There is a fine difference of perspective between getting involved and being committed. In ham and eggs, the chicken is involved but the pig is committed.

142. There are only two lasting bequests we can hope to give our children. One of these is roots, the other, wings.

143. The pursuit of excellence is gratifying and healthy; the pursuit of perfection is frustrating, neurotic, and a terrible waste of time.

144. It takes both the sun and the rain to make a rainbow.

145. Don't ever be afraid to admit you were wrong. It's like saying you're wiser than you were yesterday.

146. The greatest mistake you can make in life is to be continually fearing you will make one.

147. An error doesn't become a mistake until you refuse to correct it.

148. We come into this world with nothing—and we leave it with nothing—which means that for all of our lives we have to work like hell just to break even.

149. If fifty million people say a foolish thing, it is still a foolish thing.

150. Love is not blind; it sees more, not less. But because it sees more, it is willing to see less.

151. You can't hope to be lucky. You have to prepare to be lucky.

152. Some people will believe anything if it's whispered to them.

153. A youth was questioning a lonely old man. "What is life's heaviest burden?" he asked. The old fellow answered sadly, "To have nothing to carry."

154. My idea of self-confidence is the guy who tries to pick up a girl who's already walking back from a ride.

155. What you have inherited from your fathers, earn over again for yourselves, or it will not be yours.

156. A person who follows the leader can never finish better than second.

157. Remember, no one can make you feel inferior without your consent.

158. The only thing of value we can give kids is what *we are*, not what *we have*.

159. "I must do something" will always solve more problems than "Something must be done." 160. Woody Allen says that 95 percent of success is showing up.

161. I must be OK because GOD don't make no junk!

162. There is no limit to what can be accomplished if it doesn't matter who gets the credit.

163. You can hire people to work for you, but you must win their hearts to have them work with you.

164. Never tell people how to do things. Tell them what to do, and they will surprise you with the ingenuity.

165. A smile is a gentle curved line that sets a lot of things straight.

166. We do not stop playing when we grow old. We grow old when we stop playing.

167. When you talk, you only hear what you know. When you listen, you hear what someone else knows.

168. He who laughs last thinks slowest.

169. Pride is what we have. Vanity is what others have.

170. Pain is inevitable, but suffering is optional.

171. Best thing about being imperfect is the joy it gives to others.

172. Be like a postage stamp and stick to one thing until you get there.

173. The only thing wrong with doing nothing is that you never know when you're finished.

174. Have you noticed that as soon as you find the key to success they change the locks?

175. The ax forgets—the tree remembers.

176. If buttercups are yellow, what color are hiccups? Burple.

177. They say a fool and his money are soon parted. What bothers me is, how did they ever get together in the first place?

178. It's funny when something bends, but not when it breaks.

179. People laugh when they see somebody fall down, but if he doesn't get up, they stop laughing.

180. Slogan for Laxative: "Don't just sit there—do something!"

181. Man stayed up all night wondering where the sun went. It finally dawned on him.

182. I have abandoned my search for truth and am now looking for a good fantasy.

183. Things are never as bad as they turn out to be.

184. The one good thing about being pessimistic is at least it shows you understand the situation.

185. If astronauts are so smart, why do they count backward?

186. No one ever injured their eyesight looking on the bright side of things.

187. Real friends are those who, when you've make a fool of yourself, don't feel that you've done a permanent job.

188. All people smile in the same language.

189. It's bad to suppress laughter; it goes back down and spreads your hips. (F. Allen)

190. I feel much better now that I've given up hope.

191. Dependable Precepts:

1. The more popular something is, the more likely some religious person will object to it.
2. Something not worth doing well is something not worth doing.
3. The thing about being a celebrity is that when you bore people, they think it's their fault.

192. We gather here today to consider one of the most pressing issues of our time: Who wears the pants in a nudist family?

193. Sometimes I wonder . . . If all the world's a stage, why did I audition for this part?

194. Tonight we will try to answer one of the great and burning questions of our time: What is the Christian science attitude toward Dr. Pepper?

195. Don't give till it hurts. Give till it feels good!

196. A person is measured by his accomplishments, not the time spent.

197. I never worry about the future. I'm too busy worrying about the present.

198. Remember, you can lead a horse to water, but wouldn't it be smarter to ride the horse there?

199. Humor is a valuable business and personal success asset to anyone who applies it. Use it to relieve stress, to resolve conflict, to blunt anger, to prevent reckless action, and to calm anxiety so that one can think constructively in high-pressure situations. To motivate: humor seems to energize, thereby inducing a creative, problem-solving state of mind. To gain attention: people remember more of what is said because the communications have greater impact. To adjust to the insoluble problems in life, to survive until conditions change and problems can be solved, to relieve and to prevent negative emotional stress.

200. Don't put your trust in an infectious disease specialist who is always scratching.

201. Think twice before checking into a hospital where all the nurses wear uniforms made by Gucci.

202. Don't allow anyone with fangs to draw your blood.

203. Beware of hospitals that run summer specials or offer green stamps.

204. To err is human, but to really screw up requires a computer.

205. Life's Little Lies:

> Sorry, but our budget is made out for the year.
> I'd say the same thing to his face.
> I was just about to return your call.
> As soon as we get settled in, we're going to have you over.

206. Truisms:

> The class yell of the school of experience is "Ouch"
> In snowy weather, watch out for the slide streets
> General Custer wore Arrow shirts
> An auction house is a place to get something for nodding.
> If you don't learn to laugh at trouble, you won't have anything to laugh at when you get old.
> The only thing some people learn from experience is that they made a mistake.
> Fruitless; like rearranging the deck chairs on the titanic
> Inevitable; like a freight train—you can hear the whistle
> Plan your crisis early each morning so you can enjoy the rest of the day.
> Love enables you to give.
> Love—caring profoundly about what happens to someone else.
> Friend—someone who stabs you in the front.
> From sameness comes stagnation—from diversity and imagination comes progress.
> It's been said that a civilization can be judged by its humor.
> Leadership—ability to hide your pain from others.
> Stress is not an event; it is a perception of an event.
> Pain is inevitable but suffering is optional.
> Stranger—a friend you haven't met.
> The head never begins to swell until the mind stops growing.
> Like trying to wear out a crowbar.
> Treat the cause not the symptom—then try to prevent the cause.
> Mark Twain: "Wrinkles should only indicate where the smiles have been."

Statistics are like a loose woman—once you put them down, you can do anything you want with them.
Know it about the right people.

223. Man learns in two ways—by doing and by being done.

224. Pound for pound, the amoeba is the most vicious animal on earth.

225. Sex is hereditary; if your parents never had it, chances are you won't either.

226. He who fears to suffer suffers from fear.

227. When throwing grass clippings into the air to get the wind direction in golf, remember to take into account the earth is rotating at one thousand miles per hour.

228. No matter how much you accomplish in life, always remember the size of your funeral still will be determined by the weather.

229. A man never gets so rich that he can afford to lose a friend.

230. It is better to give than to lend, and it costs about the same.

231. What people really need to succeed in life is someone who expects them to.

232. The good times that family members have together aren't as important or as much fun as the years of recalling them.

233. Live your life so that you would not be ashamed to sell the family parrot to the town gossip.

234. The fellow that apologizes when there isn't a need to knows something that you don't.

235. Never approach a bull from the front, a horse from the rear, or a fool from any direction.

236. There's a connection between laughter and play. You need play to let your body loosen up. You need humor to let your mind loosen up. Life presents us with a lot of sadness, so we have to find in ourselves

the ability to laugh. I don't mean we laugh at life and say everything silly. Rather, we're laughing in a way that celebrates life. Laughter is a celebration of the human spirit.

237. Folks are more apt to swallow what you say, if you serve it with a spoon instead of a pitchfork.

238. When a friend needs you, listen with your heart.

239. Money isn't everything; it isn't even a lot of things it used to be.

240. He who looketh with lust on women joggers denteth his fender.

241. Perhaps the finest aphorism on the human condition was coined by Walpole when he observed, "Imagination was given to man to compensate him for what he is not, and a sense of humor was provided to console him for what he is."

242. All some guys leave behind is seat prints on the sands of time.

243. There's only a little difference between being in a rut and being in the groove.

244. It makes you humble to attend a dinner where you're the only one you never heard of.

245. Sometimes fame is just a matter of dying at the right time.

246. May you have the hindsight to know where you've been, the foresight to know where you're going, and the insight to know when you're going too far.

247. When the going gets tough, the smart get lost.

248. For years he thought he was a failure. They told him to be positive. Now he's positive he's a failure.

249. What happens to the hole when the cheese is gone?

250. What's the sense in being an early bird if you don't like worms?

251. If her lips are on fire and she trembles in your arms, forget her—she's probably got malaria.

252. Is it progress if a cannibal eats with a fork?

253. It's funny that all the people who hate the rich are the first ones to buy lottery tickets.

254. The problem with an hourglass figure is that the sands of time always end up in the lower half.

255. The nice thing about heredity—it allows us to share the blame.

256. Free speech is a right, not a continuous obligation.

257. The best time to study human nature is when no one else is present.

258. Be suspicious of any restaurant which advertises same-day service.

259. Our final decision is not necessarily the same as the one we make later.

260. One of the worst irritations in life is the fact that by the time you get it all together, you're too old to lift it.

261. If diamonds are forever, then next in line would be potholes.

262. That halo only has to slip twelve inches, and it's a hangman's noose.

263. Who determines whether or not dog food tastes good?

264. If you think it is hard living within your income, try living without it.

265. Some hairdos look like they are trying to retaliate for all of the teasing.

266. If dresses get any shorter, women will have two more cheeks to powder.

267. Nothing is impossible to the man who doesn't have to do it.

268. Only Irish coffee provides in a single cup all four essential food groups—alcohol, caffeine, sugar, and fat.

269. Oxymoron—Rush hour

270. It's not change that bothers people—it's the unknown.

271. I'd rather be a could-be if I cannot be an are because a could-be is a may-be who might be reaching for a star. I'd rather be a has-been than a might-of-been by far, for a might-of-been has never been, but a has-been was once an are.

272. Have you ever wondered how they described tornadoes before they had trains? Or how they described hail before they had golf balls? Or how they described the size of tumors before we had fruit?

273. Optimists are never surprised by trouble. Optimists look for partial solutions. Optimists allow for regular renewal. Optimists are cheerful even when they can't be happy. Optimists accept what cannot be changed.

274. If you are one of those who don't like wasting anything, try peeling onions the same time you fill out your income tax.

275. When you mix flour and water together, you get glue. When you add eggs and sugar, you get a cake. Where does the glue go?

276. Why do kamikaze pilots wear helmets?

277. If at first you don't succeed, you are running about average.

278. A patch of ground, an old gray mule, enough to eat, his kids in school. A faithful wife, a song to sing. It doesn't take much to make a king.

279. If you don't learn to laugh at trouble, you won't have anything to laugh at when you get old.

280. Life is what happens when you have something else planned.

281. Advice: never go to a dentist who's had his office soundproofed.

282 The darkest hour is just before the dawn.

283. Fruitless—like rearranging the deck chairs on the *Titanic*.

284. Inevitable; like a freight train, you can hear the whistle.

285. Plan your crisis early each morning so you can enjoy the rest of the day.

286. My kid beat up your honor student.

287. Get revenge, live long enough to be a problem to your child.

288. Success is getting what you want—happiness is wanting what you get.

289. Love enables you to give.

290. Love—caring profoundly about what happens to someone else.

291. Friend—someone who stabs you in the front.

292. Man convinced against his will is of the same opinion still.

293. From sameness comes stagnation, from diversity and imagination comes progress.

294. It's been said that a civilization can be judged by its humor.

295. Optimism indicates that the situation has not been clearly understood.

296. A rolling stone gathers no moss, and a closed mouth gathers no foot.

297. When opportunity knocks, you still have to get up off your butt and answer the door.

298. The trouble with the future is that it keeps getting closer and closer.

299. John Steinbeck in his book *Of Mice and Men* pointed out the decline in moral *values* when one of his characters commented, "There's nothing wrong anymore."

300. Be fanatics. When it comes to being and doing and dreaming the best, be maniacs.

301. If at first you don't succeed, don't take any more stupid chances.

302. If it is to be, it is up to me.

303. Honesty is the best policy—there's less competition.

304. When you starve with a tiger, the tiger starves last.

305. Never date a woman whose father calls her "Princess." Chances are, she believes it.

306. Laughter is not just a pleasure; it is a necessity.

307. It's a fowl thought, but are ornithologists really birdbrains?

308. If there were no difficulties, there would be no triumphs.

309. He who angers you controls you.

310. Wallpapering is easy, once you get the hang of it.

311. Don't take yourself so seriously that you forget how to laugh. Some people don't laugh because they somehow think it's unbecoming. They have this idea of what they should and shouldn't do. Take a look at yourself and accept what you find. We are what we are, so why not enjoy it? Become aware of what actually makes other people laugh. If you give yourself a chance, your sense of humor will improve, and you'll find that you'll be enjoying yourself as you make others laugh at the same time.

312. If you want to drive your wife crazy, don't talk in your sleep, just grin.

313. There's as much love today as there used to be. There's just a different bunch doing it.

314. When he says he wants to make a long story short, it's already too late.

315. With all the problems we have in the world today, it's good to read Dear Abby and find there are some people whose biggest worry is how they should acknowledge a wedding present.

316. After every note, does a tuba player have to say, "Excuse me"?

317. Casey Stengel: The secret of managing is to keep the guys who hate you away from the guys who are undecided.

318. The hymn "Onward Christian Solders" sung to the fight tune and not to brisk tempo makes a very good egg timer. If you put the egg into boiling water and sing all five verses and chorus, the egg will be just right when you come to the Amen.

319. I used to say I'll take all the help I can get. Now I'd just as soon you do it all.

320. It doesn't make sense—like a eunuch taking Vitamin E.

321. Show me a voice crying in the wilderness, and I'll show you a backpacker with sunburn!

322. "*Education* is to be aware of the uniqueness of each individual and to treat that uniqueness with loving concern. To provide each student with the opportunities appropriate to his or her abilities and interests. To encourage each to develop an 'I will, I can' attitude. To help kids go a step above and beyond what they, themselves, or others, might expect of them."

323. Whatever your years, there is in every being's heart the love of wonder, the undaunted challenge of events, and an unfailing, childlike appeal for "what next" on the job and in the game of life. You are as young as your faith, as old as your doubts, as young as your self-confidence, as old as your fear, as young as your hope, as old as your despair. In the central place of your heart, there is a recording chamber—so long as it received messages of beauty, hope, cheer, and courage, so long you are *young*.

324. He who never walks except where he sees other men's tracks will make no discoveries.

325. There is no speed limit on the pursuit of excellence.

326. The Chinese word for "crisis" is composed of two picture characters . . . the one meaning "danger" and the other meaning "opportunity."

327. You never get a second chance to make a first impression.

328. I saw a sign. Keep Door Closed at All Times. Why have a door?

329. We appreciate your advice and criticism. We will rush it through the proper channel. One flush usually does it.

330. One thing better than enjoying your own personal pleasure is watching someone else's misery.

331. To Whom It May Concern:

> I hereby officially tender my resignation as an adult. I have decided I would like to accept the responsibilities of a six-year-old again.
> I want to go to McDonald's and think that it's a four-star restaurant. I want to sail sticks across a fresh mud puddle and make ripples with rocks. I want to think M&Ms are better than money because you can eat them. I want to play kickball during recess and paint with watercolors in art. I want to lie under a big oak tree and run a lemonade stand with my friends on a hot summer's day.
> I want to return to a time when life was simple. When all you knew were colors, addition tables, and simple nursery rhymes, but that didn't bother you because you didn't know what you didn't know and you didn't care. When all you knew was to be happy because you didn't know all the things that should make you worried and upset. I want to think that the world is fair. That everyone in it is honest and good. I want to believe that anything is possible.
> Somewhere in my youth . . . I matured and I learned too much.
> I want to live simply again. I don't want my day to consist of computer crashes, mountains of paperwork, depressing news, how to survive more days in the month than there is money in the bank, doctor bills, gossip, illness, and loss of loved ones. I want to believe in the power of smiles, hugs, a kind word, truth, justice, peace, dreams, the imagination, mankind and making angels in the snow.
> I want to be six all over again.

332. There is little chance for people to get together as long as most of us want to be in front of the bus, the back of the church, and the middle of the road.

333. How much more grievous are the consequences of anger than the causes of it? (Marcus Aurelius)

334. If you pick up a starving dog and make him prosperous, he will not bite you. This is the principal difference between a man and a dog. (Mark Twain)

335. To my wife, double parking means on top of another car. (Dave Barry)

336. One of the great mysteries and discoveries is that a human being can alter his life by altering his attitude.

337. The six phases of project development: (1) wild enthusiasm (2) disillusionment (3) total confusion (4) search for the guilty (5) punishment of the innocent and (6) promotion of nonparticipants.

338. Consider how hard it is to change yourself and you'll understand what little chance you have of trying to change others.

339. Everyone thinks of changing humanity, but no one thinks of changing himself. (Leo Tolstoy)

340. I am more of a sponge than an inventor. I absorb ideas from every source. I take half-matured schemes for mechanical development and make them practical. I am sort of a middleman between the long-haired and impractical inventor and the hardheaded businessman who measures all things in terms of dollars and cents. My principal business is giving commercial value to the brilliant but misdirected ideas of others. (Thomas Edison)

341. Character is made by what you stand for; reputation by what you fall for.

342. Ability will enable a man to get to the top, but character is the only thing that keeps him from falling off.

343. The best index to a man's character is one, how he treats people who can't do him any good, and two, how he treats people who can't fight back. (Abigail Van Buren)

344. A patient who complains is doing you a great service.

345. As long as your conscience is your friend, never worry about your enemies.

346. Let no one suppose that the words *doctor* and *patient* can disguise from the parties that they are employer and employee. (George Bernard Shaw)

347. Its not the load that breaks you down; it's the way you carry it.

348. Either do not attempt at all, or go through with it. (Ovid)

349. The harder you work, the harder it is to surrender. (Vince Lombardi)

350. It's not whether you are knocked down, it's whether you get up. (V. Lombardi)

351. Stanley Baldwin said to the House of Commons: "The halls of fame are open wide, and they are always full. Some go in the door called 'push' and some by the door called 'pull.'"

352. I have but one lamp by which my feet are guided, and that is the lamp of experience. I know of no way of judging the future but by the past. (Patrick Henry)

353. We should be careful to get out of an experience only the wisdom that is in it and stop there, lest we be like the cat who sits down on the hot stove lid. She will never sit down on a hot stove lid again, and that is well, but she will also never sit down on a cold one. (Mark Twain)

354. Good judgment comes from experience, and experience comes from bad judgment.

355. Experience does not err; it's only your judgment that errs in expecting from her what is not in her power. (Leonardo da Vinci)

356. Facts do not cease to exist because they are ignored. (Aldous Huxley)

357. A word of encouragement during a failure is worth more than a whole book of praise after a success.

358. Failure is the greatest opportunity I have to really know who I am. (J. Killinger)

359. Failure is the only opportunity to begin more intelligently. (Henry Ford)

360. In great attempts it is glorious even to fail. (V. Lombardi)

361. Our greatest glory is not in never failing, but in rising every time we fall. (Confucius)

362. It is hard to fail, but it is worse never to have tried to succeed. (T. Roosevelt)

363. To women—if you want your husband to show more interest in you, wear the sports pages to bed.

364. Sorrow looks back, worry looks around, faith looks up.

365. All the darkness in the world can't put out the light of one candle. (Confucius)

366. The greatest of faults is to be conscious of none. (Thomas Carlyle)

367. That is about as easy as stacking greased b-bs.

368. Am I not destroying my enemies when I make friends of them? (A. Lincoln)

AGE

---

1. I went to a funeral one hot July afternoon. I dreaded the long traffic wait outside, so I decided I would just stay in the funeral home until the crowd was more manageable. Things were working as planned. The funeral director came over, and we started small talking. Nothing important. Then he asked my age. I said, "I'm eighty years old." He said, "It's hardly worth the trip home, is it?"

2. I'm at the age where happy hour is taking a nap.

3. Sign of old age—you like being in a crowd 'cause they keep you from falling down.

4. Old age is when a woman buys a sheer nightie and doesn't know anyone who can see through it.

5. Old age is where your clothes go in the overnight bag so there will be room in the suitcase for the pills.

6. One good thing about being my age—I don't have to worry about dying young.

7. I'm at the point in life where I'm beyond resentment, beyond hatred—I'm really into revenge.

8. Ninety-year-old couple got married, spent their entire honeymoon trying to get out of the car.

9. George Burns—every time he stoops over, he looks around to see if anything needs to be picked up.

10. You know you're getting old when you don't care where your wife goes as long as you don't have to go with her.

11. Spinster insisted on six-women pallbearers. She said, "The men wouldn't take me out when I was alive, so I don't want them to take me out when I am dead."

12. George Burns said you can enjoy the fruits of marriage after ninety—of course that doesn't mean as a participant.

13. Old-timer to friend: "What I don't understand is how I got over the hill without ever being on top."

14. Old people smile so much because their teeth are the only thing they have that isn't wrinkled.

15. Old age is when you don't have to own an antique chair to sit down on something that's seventy years old.

16. I knew I was getting old when I took my dog out for a walk and I couldn't keep up with him. I swapped him for a turtle.

17. Trapped in humors past is Bob Hope, who said about Phyllis Diller in a radio interview: "Her bra size is a thirty-four long."

18. Ninety-five-year old man was interviewed by a reporter. "I can't understand why anyone would want to live to be ninety-five. Answer: That's because you are not ninety-four.

19. With our aging population, this time it could be called the Gray '90s.

20. You know you are getting old when you tell your wife you are having an affair, and she wants to know who's catering it.

21. Women live longer than men because they have closets full of dresses they wouldn't be caught dead in.

22. I am now recalling the '70s and how many miniskirted women looked like matrons in tutus. Not all women in miniskirts looked like that, of course. Some resembled a pair of pliers with a Band-Aid wrapped around it.

23. Her mouth is so big that when she yawns her whole face disappears.

24. I'm getting to the stage in life when I'm glad when my nose runs since nothing else does. 25. Why, she was so old she knew Madame Butterfly when she was a caterpillar.

26. This movie is so old, Gabby Hayes got the girl.

27. Old? She remembers Baskin Robbins when he only had three flavors.

28. I was talking to a guy you claimed that when he was born they threw away the mold. I didn't have the heart to tell him it grew back.

29. We do not stop playing when we grow old; we grow old when we stop playing.

30. When he was younger, he was called a boy wonder. A millionaire by the time he was thirty. The problem though, he was born a multimillionaire.

31. My house and I are getting more alike—we both suffer from a thinning roof, a sagging foundation, and clogged pipes.

32. You should have caught the first show. Laughs? There wasn't a dry seat in the room.

33. The only time he respected age was when it was bottled.

34. An elderly Broadway star went to a psychiatrist and complained about her husband's impotency. "How old are you?" asked the doctor. "It's none of your business," she said, "but if you must know, I'm eighty-four.
    "And how old is your husband?"
    "He's ninety-three."
    "And when did you first notice his disinterest in you physically?"
    "Well," she said, "the first time was last night and again this morning."

35. You're living proof that wisdom doesn't come with age.

36. "You should be ashamed of yourself," said Dad to his lazy son. "When Abe Lincoln was your age, he chopped wood for a living." "Sure," said the son, "and when he was your age he was president."

37. Growing older has convinced me you just can't win. I'm now getting wrinkles in the same places I used to have pimples.

38. Retirement is always a time for reflection—particularly when your fellow workers throw a big going-away party the day after you leave.

39. I've thought of retiring early, but my wife convinced me she still isn't strong enough, talented enough, and mature enough to handle the responsibility of having me on her hands full time.

40. You know you're old when you discover that your children are learning in history class what you studied in current events.

41. Middle age is when you wish you could have some of the naps you refused to take as a kid.

42. Maturity is the ability to do a job whether or not you are supervised, to carry money without spending it, and bear an injustice without wanting to get even.

43. Maturing begins when we're content to feel we're right about something, without feeling the necessity to prove someone else wrong.

44. And when you're retired, you really don't get all that much sympathy from your spouse. This morning I told my wife I felt old, fat, bald, useless, and neglected. She said she didn't see why I felt neglected.

45. Personally, I look forward to retirement. Right now I just don't have the time to really enjoy all my aches and pains.

46. The harder you work, the luckier you get.

47. There is no one luckier than he who thinks himself so.

48. Sixty is that wonderful age when you suddenly realize that all those wonderful things you didn't have as a child, didn't have as an adolescent, and didn't have as an adult—you now won't have in retirement as well.

49. George Burns was sitting next to a young beauty at a New York dinner: "What keeps that dress on you?" he asked. "Only your age," she said

50. You know you're getting old when your candles cost more than the cake.

51. Old? He can remember when a Citizens' Band was a posse.

52. My grandfather always used to ask me, "What's more important, your money or your health?" I'd say, "My health." He'd say, "Great, can you lend me twenty bucks?"

53. George Washington had wooden teeth. He brushed after every meal and saw his carpenter twice a year.

54. Spring really gets the vital juices flowing. I just saw two senior citizens standing in front of an X-rated moving singing, "Memories! Memories!

55. I wasn't born of the wrong side of the tracks, but I may have to retire there.

56. I asked by grandfather if he watched *Saturday Night Live*. He said, "So far."

57. When you reach the age of 98.6, you'll be exactly as old as you feel.

58. When they're young, they sit close together because they're in love. When they're old, they sit close together so they can hear each other.

59. A wealthy seventy-two-year-old man married a shapely twenty-one-year-old blonde. "How did a seventy-two-year old codger like you manage to marry such a young woman? he was asked. "I told her I was ninety," he replied.

60. An eighty-seven-year-old fellow at the nursing home hobbles over to the nurse and asks, "Bet you can't tell me how old I am." The nurse says, "Drop your drawers." Oldster complies. "Eighty-seven," says the nurse, looking at the oldster's posterior. "Amazing," says the old man. "How'd you know?" "You told me last night," says the nurse.

61. Old is not being able to find anybody who's ten years older than you are.

62. You know you're getting old when someone says, "Come here, old boy," and faithful Fido doesn't budge because he thinks it's you they want.

63. The first sign of old age is when you hear "Snap, crackle, pop" in the morning, and it isn't your cereal.

64. One of the worst irritations in life is that by the time you get it all together, you're too old to lift it.

65. George Burns: sex is exciting after reaching eighty. Imagine having her blow in your hearing aid.

66. "Everything is a point of view. Gray hair doesn't bother the person who's bald."

67. An eighty-one-year-old man was in the hospital whose wife was bedside holding his hand. The old man said, "You know, Sara, I've been thinking. You've stayed with me through thick and thin all of our married life. I remember when the Depression came and times were so hard, you were with me. And when the war came and I had to join the army, you became a nurse. And when I was wounded, you came to my side. You were with me. I think of the many problems we've had through our lives together and that you've always been there. You know, Sara, I've been thinking. You're bad luck."

68. Phone conversation in a retirement center:

Voice: "How do you feel this morning?"
Second Voice: "Great!"
Voice: "I guess I have the wrong number."

69. Good timing is when you get the mortgage paid off before entering a nursing home.

70. Overheard: "Just once I'd like to see an article on retirement that says it's all right to sit around and enjoy it.

71. There's a story about an eighty-eight-year-old woman who threw her ninety-year-old husband out the window of their eighteenth-floor apartment on the fashionable side of town. When she was brought before the district attorney, he wanted to know why in the world she do that to her husband of so many years. "Well, I came home the other afternoon and found him in our bedroom with an eighteen-year-old girl," she said. "And I figured if he could do that, he could fly too."

72. You know you are over forty when your new winter salon tan prompts people to ask not whether you've been to Bermuda, but whether your liver is acting up.

73. You never let us down since we never expected much from you.

74. And remember, you are always welcome to visit your old desk and catch up on your sleep.

75. I hope we can carry on without you since you're the one who did all the carrying-on.

76. You make us laugh, you made us cry, but enough about your work.

77. When we heard you were retiring, a bunch of us took up a collection to buy new locks so you can't get back in.

78. When there was a problem, we always knew we could come to you and ask what you did to cause it.

79. For a retirement gift, I wanted to give you the clock on the office wall. I know you admire it because you were always looking at it.

80. Why do retiring employees receive gold watches? They no longer have anything to be on time for.

81. She was talking to a friend whose husband recently retired. She asked how things were going for the two of them. She replied, "Well, it's all right, I suppose, but every time I want to open a kitchen drawer, he's leaning against it.

82. I can't believe all the sex and violence in the movies nowadays—of course, at my age, sex and violence are the same thing. (George Burns)

83. Grandmother is recovering from a serious surgery. A letter came from her eleven-year-old grandson who contributed to her recovery. "Dear Grandma," the youngster wrote. "I'm glad you made it. We don't have any black clothes to wear."

84. Life begins at forty. Begins to what?

85. On a T-shirt of an aging gent sitting on a bench: "Cruel, nasty, neurotic, paranoid, mean, and antisocial but basically happy."

86. He was at a meeting of some senior citizens recently, a fellow says, and someone complimented another member of the group, saying, "You're growing old gracefully." "Might as well do it gracefully," the lady sighed. "Kicking and screaming doesn't do any good."

87. One of the problems with growing old, a senior citizen informed me, is that "after you get it all together, you forget where you left it."

88. The authors retell the story about the funeral of Harry Cohn, the much-disliked boss of Columbia studios. A large crowd was present at the service, and Red Skelton, counting the house, commented, "It just goes to show you—give the people what they want and they'll turn out."

89. Here's a piece of good news/bad news for males who read it in a woman's magazine. The good news is that college girls find middle-aged men attractive. The bad news is that they think thirty is middle-aged.

90. He is so old that when he went to school they didn't even have history.

91. The older I get, the better I used to be.

92. A man at the office mentioned it was his birthday, so I asked him his age. "I'm fifty-three, but I prefer to think of myself as eleven Celsius.

93. A guy says he was worried about old age creeping up on him. Then he discovered it was just cheap underwear.

94. Everybody else was doing it, so he got some weights in order to go into training.

    "I should have gone into hiding," he says. "I couldn't pick them up down at the freight office."

    "This smart young kid had to show off and throw them in the back of the pickup for me. I hate people like her."

95. I don't tan, I don't burn. But you'll never hear me complain about the sun. It's about the only thing left I know of that's still hot for my body.

96. You know you're getting older when "scoring" has to do with Ping-Pong.

97. At my age when a girl smiles at me, I look to see who is behind me or what is unbuttoned.

98. He's so old I hear he was a waiter at the last supper.

99. We no longer call them graveyards; today they are called homes for the permanently still.

100. Now when I drop a dime I have to give someone a nickel to pick it up for me.

101. I went to a rest home to see my aunt; I asked the lady at the desk, "Do you know who I am?" She said, "No, honey, but if you'll ask in the business office, they'll tell you."

102. I don't eat health foods anymore. I need all the preservatives I can get.

103. When you reach the age of 98.6 you will be exactly as old as you feel.

104. You're getting old if you don't understand the message on a teenager's T-shirt.

105. You're middle-aged when your clothes no longer fit and it's you who needs the alterations.

106. A fellow who just celebrated his fifty-fifth birthday says he realized that I have come to that stage of life when it is harder to find temptation than it is to resist it.

107. An aged husband and wife are sitting on the porch.

    Wife: "I certainly could go for a vanilla ice cream cone."

    Husband: "I'll hobble right down to the drugstore and get you one."

    Wife: "Now remember, I want vanilla. You always get chocolate. Write it down."

    Husband: "I don't have to write it down. I can remember. The drugstore's only two blocks away." The husband comes back with a hamburger and hands it to his wife. She looks at it disgustedly. "I knew you'd forget the mustard," she said.

108. Even South Irish Catholic. "Being fat," he said, "is all in where you come from. If I took this body to India, people would worship it."

109. Age doesn't matter unless you are a cheese.

110. Sex is better than ever after you reach seventy, especially the one in the winter.

111. Three years since I retired—don't have to take my treatments anymore.

112. Since I retired I've developed insomnia. I can sleep okay at night, but I just toss and turn in the mornings and afternoons.

113. You know you're getting old when you stoop to tie your shoelaces and ask yourself, what else can I do while I'm down here.

114. I hope we can still call on you as a consultant. We may forget how to use the coffeemaker.

115. Old age is like your underwear. It creeps up on you.

116. As a token of our appreciation, we have created this special gold watch to serve as a constant reminder of your many years with our company. It needs a lot of winding up—is always a little late—and every day, at a quarter to five, it stops working.

117. Middle age is when the only pants you're trying to get into are your own.

118. Fascinated by an ancient mummy in the Smithsonian, I asked the guard how old it was. He said, "Two thousand years and eight months." Amazed, I asked, "How are you able to date it so accurately?" He said, "It was two thousand years old when I was hired, and I've been working here eight months."

119. Retirement is having to get used to working part of the time while being supervised all the time.

120. Middle age is when you whistle at a pretty girl, and she turns to see where your dog is.

121. I am at the age when putting on evening clothes means putting on pajamas.

122. One of my grandfather's brothers died in Oklahoma while attending a public ceremony when the flooring collapsed. He was hanged as a horse thief.

123. Am I forgetful? Last night I forgot the Alamo. (Henny Youngman)

124. You're getting old when you don't care where your wife goes as long as you don't have to go with her.

125. It's terrible to grow old alone. My wife hasn't had a birthday in six years.

126. Old age is when you can't decide whether you've saved too little or stayed too long.

127. At my age when I drop $10 in the collection plate, it's not a contribution—it's an investment.

128. He is so old he was a waiter at the last supper.

129. There must be something wrong in this world where you have to die in order to get perpetual care.

130. I'm not young enough to know everything.

131. Age is a very high price to pay for maturity.

132. Graveyard epitaph: Once I wasn't. Then I was. Now I ain't again

133. Forty is the old age of youth. Fifty is the youth of old age. (Victor Hugo)

134. Old men are only walking hospitals. (Horace)

135. When a man's friends begin to compliment him about looking young, he may be sure that they think he is growing old. (W. Irving)

136. The reason that grandparents and grandchildren get along so well is that they have a common enemy. (Sam Levenson)

137. Old people shouldn't eat health foods. They need all the preservatives they can get. (R. Orben)

138. You're as old as you feel. If you don't feel anything, you're old.

139. When I feel like exercising, I lie down until the feeling passes.

140. I get my exercise acting as a pallbearer for my friends who exercise. (Chauncey Depew)

141. If you are over the hill, why not enjoy the view?

142. Sixty is when the biological urge slowly turns into an occasional nudge.

143. You know you're getting old. There are certain signs. I walked past a cemetery, and two guys ran after me with shovels. (R. Daingerfield)

144. Failing eyesight is Mother Nature's way of telling us to slow down as we grow older. She would say, "Why spend so much time reading when you won't remember most of it tomorrow anyway."

145. As a retired couple, we don't have all those piddly little quarrels anymore. We just have one big one that starts at seven in the morning and lasts till bedtime.

146. Now that I'm over sixty, I'm veering toward respectability. (Shelly Winters)

147. They tell you that you'll lose your mind when you grow older. What they don't tell you is that you won't miss it very much.

148. One nice thing about old age, you can whistle while you brush your teeth.

149. An octogenarian felt it necessary to resist the determined advances of a widow of thirty-two. He said, "Mother and Father would be against it." She said, "Your mother and father? Are they still alive?" He said, "I'm referring to Mother Nature and Father Time."

150. I'm at the age where I have to find my hearing aid to ask where my glasses are.

151. Middle age is when your glasses and your waistline get thicker and your hair and wallet get thinner. When you don't give much thought to exercise and entirely too much to dinner.

152. An old gentleman was telling another how much his memory had improved since he had been treated by this new doctor. Interested the man asked him the doctor's name. Old man said, "Well, you are going to have to help me with this. Give me the name of a flower that has a long stem and thorns." The young man said, "Rose?" The old man said, "That's it." "Hey, Rose, what's the name of that doctor?"

153. Old man went to the club, and the members were asking him about his new wife. "Was she rich and now you have inherited a fortune?" No, not that."
"Was she a beauty queen in college?"
"No, not that."

"Well, she has to be a great cook then."
"No, not that either."
"Then why did you marry her?"
"Because she can drive at night."

154. The lady was visiting with Mable Jones, her neighbor down at the end of the block. Mabel said, "Well, I never thought it would happen to me at this time of my life, but I am in love again. I know he's sloppy, drinks too much beer, thinks only of himself and watches TV day and night and he never helps me at all, but I love him." The neighbor went on home, and later her husband came in. She said, "What's this I hear about you and Mabel Jones?"

155. I guess I am getting old. I took the dog out for a walk, but I couldn't keep up with him, so I traded him in for a turtle.

156. Middle age is when you whistle at a pretty girl, and she turns to see where your dog is.

157. Middle age is when you stop having emotions and start having symptoms.

158. At middle age, you can no longer plead innocence or ignorance. You are either stupid or guilty.

159. I was worried about old age creeping up on me then I found out it was just cheap underwear.

160. I'm at the awkward stage; too young to junk and too old to repair.

161. I felt pretty good when I got up this morning, but I got over it.

162. I can always find my car in the parking lot. It's the one with the lights on.

163. As I grow older, I find it is harder and harder for sexual harassment charges to stick.

164. Your back goes out but you stay home.

165. It takes longer to get into your clothes than to wash them.

166. How to deal with a nervous wife. Tell her it is a symptom of old age.

167. Suggestion: before you retire stay home a week and watch daytime TV shows.

168. Just once I'd like to see an article on retirement that says it is all right to sit around and enjoy it.

169. Your secrets are safe with your friends 'cause they can't remember them either.

170. George Burns: "You know you are getting old when the first candle on your cake burns out before you can light the last one."

171. I'm at the age where I have to find my hearing aid to ask where my glasses are.

172. Phyllis Diller: "Different parts of me are different ages."

173. I asked my grandpa if he watched *Saturday Night Live*. He said, "So far."

174. My grandfather is ninety-three and my grandmother is ninety. They never argue. They can't hear each other.

175. You are getting old when you don't understand the message on a teenager's T-shirt.

176. When someone asked Red Skelton to shake hands, he said, "Just hold it. It will shake by itself."

177. There's nothing left to learn the hard way.

178. I'm the first one to find the bathroom wherever I go.

179. Retirement is overrated. You never get a vacation and how much fun is it to drink coffee on your own time?

180. If life begins at forty just what ended at thirty-nine?

181. For Sale: Secondhand tombstone. Excellent buy for someone named Murphy.

AGGIE (MIT IS AN AGGIE)

1. Aggie smoke alarm, lets you sleep an extra ten minutes.

2. Female Aggies are called Maggies

3. Thursday—Visual—Make a circle with thumb and forefinger. Touch little finger with thumb—that is Monday. Thumb to next fingertip is Tuesday and finally thumb with forefinger is Thursday.

4. Aggie thought high cholesterol was a religious holiday.

5. The Aggie farmer was lifting hogs, one by one up to his apple trees to graze on the apples. A friend asked him, "Doesn't that take a lot of time?" The Aggie replied, "What's time to a hog?"

6. Aggie saw a sign that said, "All the worms you want for $1." He said, "Give me $2 worth."

7. Aggie was asked if he preferred red or white wine for dinner. He said, "It doesn't matter I'm color-blind."

8. So Tight—had mother tattooed across his stomach so he could use the *o*.

9. What do you say when you see an Aggie with a pretty girl on his arm?—"Where did you get the tattoo?"

10. Man asked an insurance agent if he sold fire insurance. The insurance agent said that he didn't, but he sold flood insurance. First man said, "No thanks, I don't know how to start a flood."

11. Aggie was too tight to buy a burglar alarm, so he taught his kids to bark.

12. In math class, an Aggie was asked, "How much is two by two?" His answer was four. The class, in unison, yelled, "Give him another chance."

13. Aggie, UT, and Baylor men on construction job building a new building brought their own lunches. First man: "If my wife makes another peanut butter sandwich tomorrow, I'll jump. Second man: "Me too." Aggie: "Me too." Next day all had peanut butter sandwiches—all jumped. First man's wife: "If I had only known, all he had to do was tell me." Second wife said same thing. Aggie wife said, "I just don't understand. He always made his own lunch."

14. Where did you get the callous on your nose? Aggie said, "Glasses." Did you ever try contacts? Aggie said, "They don't hold enough beer."

15. Call 1-800-AGGIE—IQ for the latest Aggie joke

16. Did you hear about the Aggie who thought a topless restaurant was a restaurant without a roof?

17. Aggie seven-course dinner is a hamburger and a six-pack.

18. Sergeant Preston said, "It is only the lead dog that sees a change in the scenery.

19. Did you hear about the Aggie who was so filthy his door chimes went ding dung?

20. A T-Sipper riding a cross-country train got into a poker game in the club car. An Aggie stopped by to watch. The T-Sipper said, "Aggie, get me a glass of water." The Aggie left, returning after a few minutes with a glass of water. Fifteen minutes later, the T-Sipper again ordered, "Aggie, get me a glass of water." The Aggie left, but this time returned with an empty glass. The T-Sipper asked, "Aggie, where is my glass of water?" The Aggie answered, "I can't get any. There is a man sitting on the well."

21. The Aggie was hospitalized in a contagious ward. The doctor asked, "When were you last exposed?" The Aggie answered, "The last time my zipper stuck."

22. Aggie thought the epistles were the wives of the apostles.

23. Then there was the Aggie who thought diarrhea was hereditary because it runs in your jeans.

24. T-Sipper: What do you think of the abortion bill? Aggie: Pay it.

25. What do you call an intellectual on the College Station campus? A visitor.

26. Did you hear about the Aggie who enrolled in night school so he could learn to read in the dark?

27. The first Aggie to ever takes a bath was called a ringleader.

28. And then there was the Aggie who was learning how to drive. He was so terrible he got three tickets on the written test.

29. Thought a carnation was a land of automobiles.

30. An obstetrician received a phone call at two in the morning from an Aggie. "Doc," the frantic male voice said, "the pains are coming every five minutes." "Is this her first baby?" the doctor asked. "No," the Aggie replied, "this is her husband."

31. An Aggie married a Puerto Rican. They named their baby Retardo.

32. As the general procession came down the street in Bryan, a bystander asked an Aggie, "Who died?" The Aggie replied, "The fellow in the first car."

33. Dear son: Just a few lines to let you know I'm still alive. I'm writing this letter slowly because I know you cannot read fast. You won't know the house when you come home. We've moved. About your father, he has a lovely new job. He has five hundred men under him. He is cutting grass at the cemetery. There was a washing machine in the new house when we moved in, but it isn't working too good. Last week I put fourteen shirts into it, pulled the chain, and I haven't seen the shirts since. Your sister Mary had a baby this morning, but I haven't heard whether it is a boy or girl, so I don't know whether you'll be an aunt or uncle. Your Uncle Dick drowned last week in a vat of whiskey in a distillery. Some

of his fellow workers dived in to save him, but he was able to fight them off. We cremated his body, and it took three days to put out the fire. Your father didn't have much to drink on Christmas. I put a bottle of castor oil in his pint of beer. It kept him going until New Year's Day. I went to the doctor the other day, and your father came with me. The doctor put a tube in my mouth and told me not to open it for ten minutes. Your father tried to buy it from him. It rained twice last week, first for three days and then for four days. Monday was so windy that one of our chickens laid the same egg four times. We had a letter from the undertaker. He said that if the last installment wasn't paid on your grandmother with seven day, up she comes. Your loving mother. PS: I was going to send you $10, but I had already sealed the envelope.

34. A Red Raider, a T-Sipper, and an Aggie were drinking together in a bar.

The Red Raider ordered a VT. "That's easy," said the bartender, "Vodka tonic." The T-Sipper ordered a WW. "Okay," said the bartender, "I know that one too. Whiskey and water." Then the Aggie ordered, "Gimme a fifteen." "Fifteen," bellowed the bartender. "I know all the nicknames for drinks, but I've never heard of a fifteen. What the !@#$%^&*! is a fifteen?" Answered the Aggie, "A seven and seven, of course."

35. A T-Sipper, a Baylor Bear, and an Aggie started on a trip across the desert.

The T-Sipper carried a canteen of water, the Baylor Bear took a loaf of bread, and the Aggie a Ford truck door. They met a stranger who asked the T-Sipper what he was going to do with the water. "When I get thirsty I'll drink it," he answered. The stranger asked the Baylor Bear what he was going to do with the bread. "When I get hungry I'll eat it," he answered. The stranger asked the Aggie what he was going to do with the Ford truck door. The Aggie answered, "When it gets hot, I'm going to roll down the window.

36. A drunken Aggie staggered through the park early one morning and spied a man doing push-ups. "Pardon me," ventured the Aggie, "I hate to be the bearer of bad news, but I think your girl has already gone."

37. An Aggie and a T-Sipper were applying for a job, for which they had to take a written test. When the boss had graded the tests, he told

them, "Well, you both got the same grade, but I'm hiring the T-Sipper." "Why?" asked the Aggie. The boss replied, "His answer to question 9 was "I don't know, yours was 'Neither do I.'"

38. Did you hear about the Aggie who got it all together and couldn't figure out what it was?

39. Most Aggie jokes portray the Aggie as being stupid. How about the smart Aggie who never lost a bet? He was on an ocean cruise and had won every bet he makes with the ship captain. Finally he bet the captain $1,000 that he could draw a two-feet circle on the top deck and a seagull would bomb in the circle within two minutes. There wasn't a seagull in sight, so the captain covered the bet. Just as the Aggie finished drawing the circle, a seagull flew out of one of the stacks and bombed in the circle. The captain paid off but radioed a nearby tanker to come alongside. He put the Aggie off the liner and on the tanker and told the captain of the tanker not to make any bets with this Aggie because he never lost a bet. As the tanker pulled away, the Aggie told the taker captain he would bet him $10 he had piles. The captain knew he could win this bet, so he asked the Aggie how he intended to determine who won. The Aggie said, "With a candle. If it comes out red, I win brown, you win." Sure enough it was brown, and the Aggie lost $10. The tanker captain was so elated he wired the liner captain the details on how he won a bet from the Aggie. The liner captain wired back, "Drown the SOB. He bet me $10,000 he would have a candle up your rear within ten minutes after he boarded the tanker."

40. The friend asked the Aggie, "Why is your face plastered with bandages?" "I was just trying to learn to eat with a fork," the Aggie replied.

41. The Aggie's brother was explaining the plot of *Lolita* to him. "There's plenty of hot stuff in that book," he told the Aggie. "It's all about a love affair between a middle-aged man and a twelve-year-old." "A twelve-year-old what?" asked the Aggie.

42. The first prize at the high school science contest was a five-dollar bill. The second prize was a four-year scholarship to A&M.

43. Did you hear about the Aggie who thinks the English Channel is the station that shows British movies?

44. Then there was the Aggie who thought "vice versa" meant dirty poems.

45. The Aggie who bragged to all his friends after spring vacation of spending the entire holiday in a house of ill-fame. "Got kind of expensive, didn't it?" one friend commented. "Naw," was the reply, "kin folks."

46. An Aggie usually describes A&P shopping bags as matched luggage.

47. Did you hear about the Aggie who claimed to be the world's greatest lover?

   The fifty-third entry in his little black book is Alice Aaronson.

48. Aggie ham radio operator hooked his antenna up to a pig.

49. Did you hear about the two Aggies who were a shooting craps? They shot a hole in the commode.

50. An Aggie went to a drugstore and asked the clerk for a package of condoms. The clerk said, "They are packaged three for $1." The Aggie handed him a dollar bill, and the clerk said, "That will be $1.05." "What's the five cents for?" asked the Aggie. "Tax," the clerk replied. "Why?" the Aggie said. "I thought you just rolled them on."

51. Did you hear about the Aggie who was so dumb he thought a bar stool was something Davy Crockett stepped in.

52. A well-plastered Aggie was driving along merrily the wrong way down a one-way street until stopped by a patrolman. "Didn't you see the arrows?" asked the cop. "The arrows?" answered the inebriated Aggie. "I didn't even see the Indians."

53. Did you hear about the Aggie who thought it was unlucky to be superstitious?

54. Did you hear about the Aggie who worked at General Dynamics and thought tail assembly was the company picnic?

55. Did you hear about the Aggie who thought bacteria were the rear entrance to a cafe?

56. Did you hear about the Aggie who jumped out of bed and broke one of his socks?

57. "Take these pills two days running, then skip a day," the doctor told the Aggie. "Follow this routine for two weeks, then report back to me." At the end of one week, the Aggie went back to the doctor. "I'm tired, Doctor," he complained. "That skipping wore me out."

58. Did you hear about the Aggie who said he'd give his right arm to be ambidextrous?

ANIMALS

1. If you cross a pit bull with Lassie, you get a dog that will chew your arm off and run for help.

2. We have a very large family dog. He doesn't permit us to sit on the sofa.

3. "Is it true," a reporter asked a safari guide, "that jungle animals won't harm you if you carry a torch?" "That depends," replied the guide, "on how fast you carry it."

4. The American farmer has produced a sow so wholesome virtually every part of it can be used for something. All but the squeal. And a caller then phoned in to say now even that has a use. They are making "oinkment" out of it.

5. One afternoon, several firemen were sitting in front of the fire station playing with the company dog, a mascot of Dalmatian breed. Just about that time, a woman with a small boy walked by. They stopped. "Why is it that most fire departments have dogs?" the woman asked.

   "That's a tradition that goes way back," one of the men said. "They find the hydrants for us at night."

6. Sign—Lost: Small apricot poodle. Reward: Neutered. Like one of the family.

7. One speaker was telling everyone how to try to make the best of every bad situation. He offered an example.

"There's a veterinarian in my hometown with the right outlook," he said. "A sign in front of his home listed his profession followed by another that also advertised his taxidermy skills."

He said a lot of people wondered about that outlook for a beloved pet, that it seemed a bit macabre. The veterinarian didn't agree with that. His response was, "Either way, you get to take your dog home with you."

8.   A crazy crow is a raven maniac.

9.   Myra was always rescuing winter birds from the cold. One day her hubby, Frank, charged into the dining room where Myra was toweling a cold wren and loudly began a vicious tirade about all of the fowl recuperating here and there in the room. "Please, Frank," Myra said reprovingly. "Not in front of the chilled wren."

10. Two men encounter a bear in the forest. One of the men pulls his running shoes out of his knapsack and put them on. The other man says, incredulously, "You don't think those running shoes are going to help you outrun that bear?" The other man replies, "I don't have to outrun the bear. I only have to outrun you!"

11. Have you heard why you shouldn't kiss a canary? You might get "chirpees" disease and there is no "tweetment."

12. A reader has sent me a copy of a letter to the editor of the *National Geographic*. The letter concerned a geographic story about the praying mantis. "You might be interested to know," wrote the letter writer, "that unconfirmed reports state that the University of Florida entomologists have succeeded in mating a praying mantis with a termite, thereby producing a bug that says grace before starting to eat your house."

13. His cat won't leave anything alone. Three days ago it swallowed a ball of yarn, and yesterday it had mittens.

14. The man had his dog on a leash in a crowded store. The critter appeared rather benign, but one person quickly moved away, pushing and bumping into other people. "My dog doesn't bite," assured the owner. "I know," said the departing person, "but I observed he was raising his hind leg, and I was afraid he was going to kick me."

15. A lady buys a parrot, a parrot with a gutter vocabulary. After a day of listening to the parrot's swearing, she took it back to the pet shop, insisting she couldn't keep him. "Don't worry about that," the shop owner said. "Be firm and use discipline and he'll straighten up."

   She took the parrot home again, put him on his perch, and the cussing began. That's when she got an idea.

   "You're going into the freezer for five minutes each time you swear," she told the parrot.

   After five minutes in the freezer, the parrot was quiet and subdued. No more vulgarities at least for a week. Then he started again, and it was awful. This time the sentence was fifteen minutes in the freezer.

   As the parrot shivered in the freezer and ice formed on his feathers, he happened to look over at a frozen turkey his owner had brought home for a big family dinner.

   "Wow! I know it's none of my business," the parrot said, "but what the heck did you say, anyway?"

16. Two young male dinosaurs happened upon a female. One of them said, "I'd like to make lover to her." The other one said, "I don't think so. She's having her century."

19. One dog asks another, "What's your name?" The other answers, "I'm not sure, but I think it's 'Down, boy.'"

17. A man's pit bull had chewed up half the neighborhood and the neighbors.

   The court gave the owner two ways of resolving the continued destruction of life and limb. The dog could be put to sleep or, failing that, be castrated. Castration would remove all the anger and venom. The dog would become as docile as a lamb.

   Loving the dog very much, the owner chose the surgery. On the day of the appointment at the vet, the owner started to walk the dog to its destiny. A block from the animal hospital, the dog saw an old man walking. Roaring, the dog pulled away from the owner and jumped on the old man. He had just about chewed up the old man when the owner managed to get the leash on again. The owner tied the savage animal to a pole and went to the old man. Helping the old man up, he begged, "Don't make this a police matter, I beg you. I implore you. I'll take care of any costs you may have—medical bills, clothing. I'll get you a new crutch! Whatever you want for your agony, I'll pay anything. And you don't have to worry about my dog. He's on the way to the vet to be castrated. He'll be like a lamb!"

The old man said, "Forget the castration. Better get his teeth pulled out. I knew one second after he came at me that he didn't want to mate!"

18. A furrier recently crossed a mink with a gorilla. He got a fur coat, but the sleeves were too long.

19. Seems the salesman was lost on a country road late at night and stopped at a lighted house for directions. He knocked on the front door, and a voice said, "Come on in, come on in."

So he opened the door, and the voice kept saying, "Come on in."

He followed the voice through the living room and dining room and entered the kitchen. There he saw a parrot repeated, "Come on in."

Suddenly a Doberman with slashing teeth jumped at him. The salesman backed against the wall with hands up high as the dog growled, jumped about, slashed his teeth. Meanwhile, the parrot repeated, "Come on in."

Deathly afraid, the salesman said, "You blasted parrot, is that all you can say, come on in?"

The parrot said, "Sic him!"

20. The idea of defining objectives and setting priorities:

If you are indeed going to do the fight things right, it's important to start by figuring out just what the fight things are. And that reminds me of a story—true, by the way—that came to my attention recently on a trip to Canada.

It seems that in some of the outlying areas of British Columbia, the farmers have been plagued by wolves killing their livestock. There were meetings of environmentalists, farmers, and concerned citizens. Most of the local people were in favor of shooting or poisoning the wolves. But a one meeting, a lady took the microphone, listed her credentials, which were impressive, and explained her solution.

"Vasectomy," she said, "is the answer. Simply trap the wolves humanely, neuter the males, and release them."

At that point, a grizzled old sheep farmer rose to his feet. "Ma'am," he said, "I don't mean no disrespect, you going an expert . . . but them wolves is killing my sheep, not making love to them."

21. We had a dog with no legs. We didn't name him 'cause if you called him he couldn't come.

22. Bumper sticker: Help preserve our forests—shoot a woodpecker.

23. Man went into a bar, saw dog and sign that read Beware of Vicious Dog. He told the bartender the dog didn't look too vicious to him. The bartender said, "He's not. We just put the sign up to keep people from tripping over him."

24. "Have you ever noticed that one line of geese in formation is always longer than the other one?"
"Yes, why?"
"It has more geese in it."

25. During an auction of exotic pets, a woman who had placed the winning bid told the auctioneer, "I'm paying a fortune for that parrot. I hope he talks as well as you say he does." Auctioneer, "I guarantee it, madam. Who do you think was bidding against you?"

26. Man told the pet store owner his bird wasn't eating well. The pet store owner told him to file the bird's beak. Next day he reported to the pet store owner that he probably filed it too much because the bird was dead when he took it out of the vice.

27. The difference between a regular zoo and a Cajun zoo—Regular zoo gives scientific and common names. Cajun zoo gives scientific names, common names, and the recipe.

28. "My cat can say its own name," said the drunk. "What's his name?" asked the bartender. "Meow."

29. "I have nothing against dogs. I just hate rugs that go *squish-squish*." (Phyllis Diller)

30. My husband, Fang, is so dumb I once said, "There's a dead bird," and he looked up. (Phyllis Diller)

31. Cats are intended to teach us that not everything in nature has a function. (Garrison Keeler)

32. Can you name an animal that has eyes and cannot see, has legs and cannot walk, but can jump as high as the Empire State Building? Give up? The answer is a wooden horse. But how does it jump as high as the Empire State Building? The Empire State Building can't jump.

33. A man and a dog were standing on the street corner. Another man walked up and said, "My, that is a pretty dog. Will your dog bite?" First man said no. So the guy bent down to pet him and the dog almost tore him apart. He said, "I thought you said your dog wouldn't bite." The man answered, "That ain't my dog."

34. The lion and the calf shall lie down together, but the calf won't get much sleep. (Woody Allen)

35. We have a cat named Ben Hur. We called it Ben till it had kittens.

36. When the insects take over the world, I hope they will remember with gratitude how we took them along on all our picnics.

37. I just heard a sad story. It's about this turtle that fell in love with a German helmet.

38. I have the most frustrated pet in the world. It's a turtle that chases cars.

39. In my aquarium is a very aristocratic fish. His folks swam over under the mayflower.

40. Lady walking to work one morning passes a pet store. A parrot in the window says, "Lady, you are the ugliest person I have ever seen." This annoyed the lady, but she continued on. Then on the way home that night again the parrot says, "Lady you are really ugly." This was too much, so she went in to the owner and told him if the parrot said that again she would sue him. The owner apologized and promised it would not happen again.

   The next morning as she passed the pet store again the parrot yelled out, "Lady." She spun around in anticipation and the parrot said, "You know."

41. Do incubator chickens love their mother?

42. The only difference in a pit bull and a cheer leader's mother is the lipstick.

43. A Pekinese married a tomcat. Now they have a Peeking tom.

44. Two kittens were watching a tennis match. One said, "My dad's in that racket."

45. What kind of dog is that? He's a police dog. He doesn't look like a police dog. Of course not. He's in the secret service.

46. There once was a dachshund so long that he didn't have any notion of how long it took to notify his tail of an emotion. And so it happened, while his eyes were full of woe and sadness his little went wagging on because of previous gladness.

47. We got so disgusted going to the MD we now go to a vet. It's really no problem except in the waiting room. Sometimes they mistake your leg for a fireplug and if you don't mind being examined on all fours. At least they rub your stomach and give you some cookies. You have to be careful though in that squeeze chute—you can be wormed, dipped, and tagged in nothing flat. Our vet is also a taxidermist. He has a sign over his door that reads, "Either way you get your loved one back."

Bumper Snickers

1. I HATE HOUSEWORK—the only thing domestic about me is that I live in a house

2. Clinton Happens

3. If you think I drive bad, you ought to see me putt.

4. "God is dead"—Nietzschke 1886

5. "Nietzschke is dead"—God 1900

6. To die poor is unfortunate, but to die rich is just plain stupid.

7. If you don't like my driving, stay off the sidewalk.

8. Humpty Dumpty was pushed

9. Support mental health or I'll kill you

10. If you can read this, you're doing better than 42 percent of our high school graduates.

11. I may be slow, but I'm ahead of you.

12. My son beat up your honor student.

13. Did you see the army drill sergeant who's riding around with license plates: HUP 234?

14. To err is human. To really goof, form a committee!

15. For sale: LAWN MOWER, push type. Used very little. When used, pushed very slowly!"

16. Ad for ballpoint pens: EQUAL WRITES FOR WOMEN

17. I love my country, but fear my government.

18. If you want to burn our flag, wrap yourself in it first.

19. World's Shortest Books

    My Plan to Find the Real Killers by O. J. Simpson
    To All the Men I've Loved Before by Ellen DeGeneres
    Human Rights Advances in China
    Things I Wouldn't Do for Money by Dennis Rodman
    Amelia Earhart's Guide to the Pacific Ocean
    America's Most Popular Lawyers
    Dr. Kevorkian's Collection of Motivational Speeches
    French Hospitality
    George Foreman's Big Book of Baby Names
    Mike Tyson's Guide to Dating Etiquette
    One Hundred and One Spotted Owl Recipes by the EPA
    The Electrician's Guide to Fashion

20. Driver under the Influence of Children.

21. Like to be a member of a minority group? Try putting in an honest day's work.

22. Remember Jonah was down in the mouth once too.

23. Help stamp out, eliminate, and abolish redundancy.

24. Sorry. My karma just ran over your dogma.

25. If You Never Had a Wreck, I'll Sell You This One.

26. The Keys Are on the Seat Next to the Doberman.

27. Honk if you're against noise pollution.

28. Disarm Rapists.

29. Growing Old Isn't for Sissies.

30. Yesterday Is a Memory, Tomorrow Is a Vision, but Today Is a Bitch!

31. On My Salary I Can't Pay Attention.

32. Does the name Pavlov ring a bell?

33. Happiness is seeing your boss's face on a milk carton.

34. I'm So Far Behind, I Think I'm in First Place.

35. Concrete People Are Mixed Up and Set in Their Ways.

36. Don't Worry About My Dog, Beware of My Wife!

37. SIGN IN HANDICAPPED PARKING SPACE: If you're not handicapped when you park here, you will be when you leave.

38. Without Plumbers You Wouldn't Have Any Place to Go.

39. Support the Crisis of your Choice.

40. Congress Happens.

41. Honk Softly—I've Had a Lousy Day

42. If your cup runneth over, let someone else runneth the car.

43. Bumper sticker on mobile home: Howard's pad when Adeline's mad.

44. Texans think the motto "The Friendship State" on their license plates is too wimpy. How about "Get laid back in Texas"?

45. Evangelists do more than *lay* people.

46. If there's a will, I want to be in it.

47. Women Love the Simple Things: Men.

48. BUMPER STICKER in Arkansas: To hell with the snail darter—save the Democrats.

49. If you don't trust my driving stay off the sidewalk.

50. BUMPER STICKER spotted on a plumbing truck: Take us to your leaker.

51. Put our Congressman to Work. Don't Reelect Him.

52. Kamikaze pilots do it once.

53. Be kind to animals: hug a hockey player.

54. BUMPER STICKER in Washington in view of the sex scandal: Have you hugged your congressman today?

55. Firemen are always in heat.

56. If you drink, don't drive; you may hit a pothole and spill it.

57. Save the wetlands, drown a developer.

58. I brake for reloading.

59. Don't shoot, I'll move over.

60. Don't shoot, I'm going as fast as I can.

61. Spotted on a streetwalker's T-shirt: Not all the pros are on strike!

62. Sign on a fire hydrant: Park Now, Pay Later.
    Sign on beauty shop: "We can give you the new look if you have the old parts."
    Sign in singles bar: "Men: no shirts, no serve. Women: no shirts, no check."
    Sign in office: Do it tomorrow. We've made enough mistakes today.
    Sign in IRS office: "In God we trust, everyone else, we audit."

63. Rabbits Die for Your Sins

64. Make War Not Love—It's Safer

65. Billboard: Learn to read. I wonder who their intended audience is.

66. Lorena Bobbit for White House Intern

67. Make love not war or do both—get married

68. Starve with Dignity—Be a Teacher.

69. I Have No Enemies. My Friends Just Don't Like Me.

70. Don't Tell Me What Kind of Day to Have.

71. Pushing Forty Is Exercise Enough.

72. Nonsmokers Do It without Puffing.

73. Let an Electrician Check Your Shorts.

74. I Still Miss My Ex-Husband But My Aim Is Getting Better.

75. On hippie car: Fight Mental Health

76. On wedding party limousine: Letter writing caused this.

77. Sign in ski shop: Help stamp out summer

78. Sex Appeal—Give Generously

79. Sign in a Xmas gift shop—Ho, Ho, Ho spoken here

80. Sign in a consultant's office: We charge $200 per hour. If you want brains cheap, go to a butcher.

81. I took an IQ test, and the results were negative.

82. Don't tell me what kind of day to have!

83. Be kind to animals. Hug a hockey player

84. The world is proof that God is a committee.

85. Jesus is coming. Everyone look busy.

86. Honk if you love peace and quiet.

87. Honk if you have never seen a UZI fired from a car window.

88. Without plumbers you wouldn't have any place to go.

89. Horn Broken: Watch for Finger

90. If you have never had a wreck, I will sell you this one

91. Humpty Dumpty was pushed.

92. Ask me about microwaving cats for fun and profit

93. Disarm rapists

94. Stamp out conceit. You will love yourself for it

95. Honk if you have ever been married to Zsa Zsa Gabor

96. On a plumbing truck: Take us to your leaker

97. Save the wetlands. Drown a developer

98. On back of boat: I brake for whales

99. I wish my wife was this dirty (on back of car)

100. Constipated people don't give a crap

101. Practice safe sex, go screw yourself.

102. I brake for tailgaters

103. When the chips are down, the buffalo is empty.

104. Ever since I took the Houston Texans bumper sticker off, the car has been running and passing better

105. The most important sex organ is the brain.

106. We have enough youth—How about a fountain of smart?

107. Regarding a quiet man: He never really says anything. Even his bumper sticker is blank

108. Spotted in a parking lot. The keys are on the seat next to the Doberman.

109. On the side of a plumbing truck: A flush beats a full house

110. Women who seek to be equal to men lack ambition.

111. Avoid hangovers—Stay drunk

112. Keep honking—I'm reloading

113. As long as there are tests there will be prayer in public schools

114. I want to die in my sleep like my grandfather—not screaming and yelling like the passengers in his car

115. Bill Clinton: Commander in Heat

116. Only a plastic surgeon will let you pick your nose.

117. Support a Lawyer: Send Your Son to Medical School

118. Honk if you have had sex with Bill Clinton

119. Jail to the Chief

120. Save Clinton: Legalize Perjury

121. Clinton—Our Nation's Fondling Father

122. If Clinton's private life doesn't matter, let him date your daughter.

123. If you are heading in the wrong direction, God allows U-turns

124. Fight Crime—Shoot Back

125. Stamp out conceit—You'll love yourself for it.

126. Honk if you've never seen a UZI fired from a car window.

Business

1. We can honestly say that our boss is about a year away from being an exceptional leader. Next year he'll be about two years away.

2. College commencement speaker to professor, "How can I tell them the future of the world is in their hands without frightening the rest of the guests?"

3. Don't be awed at all my degrees. Thermometers also have degrees, and you know where the doctors put them.

4. Staff makes inexcusable errors; we make justifiable mistakes.

5. Sign in a man's office: "My job gives me what I need—an excuse to drink."

6. He's what you might call an ethical businessman. Never distorts the truth unless it's absolutely convenient.

7. I won't say I feel insecure, but the boss just gave me this year's calendar, and it only goes as far as January 15!

8. Some of those commercials are fantastic. I was watching TV this morning that starts off with a huge picture of Venus de Milo followed by the announcer saying, "See what happens when you use too strong a detergent?"

9. It doesn't make sense, like a falsie manufacturer saying, "Beware of imitations!"

10. Would you like to turn cash flow constipation into a veritable diarrhea of prosperity?

11. Use our easy credit plan . . . 100 percent down, no payments.

12. I was a masseuse, but I got fired—rubbed a customer the wrong way.

13. Recessions and depressions don't bother me. I was a failure even when things were good.

14. "Tell me, Mr. Wright," said the personnel manager, "why did you leave your last job?" "It was because of illness, sir," answered Wright. "The boss got sick of me!"

15. I would have been . . .

    a mother, but who was I kidding?
    a butcher, but I got a bum steer.
    a mechanic, but the idea sounded nuts.
    a roofer, but I got a bad case of the shingles.
    a belly dancer, but I had no stomach for it.
    a stocking salesperson, but it didn't work out in the long run.
    a milkman, but I found an udder job.
    a race car driver, but it was just the pits.
    a forester, but I couldn't hack it.
    a greeting card store manager, but it was too stationary.
    a movie star, but I couldn't get the picture.
    a tobacco heiress, it was just a pipe dream.
    a ballerina, but it was tutu much.

16. A confident applicant for a job presented his credentials to a personnel manager. The manager looked them over and said, "I see you've got recommendations from your church minister and Sunday school teacher. That's good. And I must admit, you look honest and appear to be of good character. Nevertheless, I'd like to see a recommendation from someone who knows you on weekdays."

17. An employer interviewing an applicant remarked, "You ask high wages for a man with no experience." "Well," the prospect replied, "it's so much harder to work when you don't know anything about it."

18. Success is a journey, not a destination.

19. Boss went in for open-heart surgery and they're still looking

20. Asked why he was no longer at the firm: Man said, "I wouldn't work for a boss who said 'Get out and stay out.'"

21. Tax Accountant: "I have got terrible news for you. Last year was the best year you ever had."

22. It is important to remember that figures and statistics can be misleading. We all know about the man who drowned trying to walk across a lake with an average depth of three feet.

23. I'm known as Old Bedspread at our friendly neighborhood bank. Every time I come in for a loan, they turn me down.

24. If you think athletes exaggerate the importance of the home-field advantage, ask yourself this question: "How many times have you won in the boss's office?"

25. I believe in the truthful approach. Yesterday I called my office and said I wouldn't be coming in because my arm was in a sling. And it was—the one on my golf bag.

26. In any organization, there is always one person who really knows what's going on. That person must be fired.

27. I lost my job at the orange juice factory. I got squeezed out.

28. The secret of managing is to keep the guys, who hate you, away from the guys who are undecided. (Casey Stengal)

29. Survey—slogans that best sum up the spirit of the Christmas season

    1. Peace on Earth Good Will to Men
    2. Joy to the World
    3. Attention K-Mart shoppers

30. When you go to a bank, why do you find the doors of the vault open and the pens chained to the desk?

31. A man received a letter appealing for funds. It was addressed to "Occupant." He sat right down and wrote out a check for $1,000 and mailed it back in the postpaid envelope, which was enclosed. The fund-raisers were delighted to open the envelope and find the check for $1,000 until they noticed the signature, "Occupant."

32. We let go of frustration just by thinking of including the following note with statements to our past-due clients: "Please let us be your pallbearer when you die. We've carried you this long, and we'd like the privilege of doing so to the end!"

33. I upped my income—up yours!

34. Truth in advertising comes to the street corner: I saw a guy standing there at rush hour yesterday holding a sign that said, "Will work for beer!"

35. The trouble with giving someone the title of associate editor is you have to be very careful when you abbreviate it.

36. To impress my friends, I speak of my salary in millions. I make .035 million a year.

37. I'm called into my boss's office so often, I keep a picture of my family on his desk.

38. We need a fence along the Mexican border. To keep illegal aliens out? No, to keep American industries in!

39. The boss told me I was in line for a promotion. The end of the line, to be precise.

40. I received a piece of junk mail asking me to list other people who might be interested in getting junk mail from that same company. I gave them some names: occupant resident, homeowner, consumer . . .

41. When asked how to go bankrupt: "Two ways. Gradually and then suddenly."

42. Remember: when banks offer you credit cards, they have your interest at heart.

43. Many retail stores are now offering courteous, efficient self-service.

44. Our boss is very tough. At this morning's board meeting, she said, "All opposed to this plan of mine will signify by saying, 'I resign.'"

45. The boss has a sign hanging on the wall in this office: "If at first you don't succeed, you're through!"

46. We're a two-income family. Unfortunately, we're also a five-expense family.

47. A lot of people in this company are lazy and disorganized. Their left hand doesn't know what the right hand isn't doing.

48. Americans are living beyond their means . . . but they're saving the rest.

49. I lost my job at the orange juice factory. The boss said I couldn't concentrate.

50. When I asked the bank manager for instant, low-interest credit, he requested to see my gun.

51. When I applied for a bank loan, I knew right away I was in trouble. All the employees were wearing "Just Say No" buttons.

52. I invested in one of those treasure ship salvage companies. So far, their most profitable discovery was me.

53. I'm not at all happy with my small new office. It's confining, the walls are a dull grey, and the seat is too low . . . and I keep getting jabbed in the side by that toilet paper dispenser.

54. I don't have my money in blue chip stocks. They're more like the buffalo chip variety.

55. Spring is the boss's favorite season. He loves stepping on things just starting to grow.

56. "Boss, I just called in to say that I won't be in for work for a few days. My wife broke an arm." "Oh that's too bad," replied the employer, but

that doesn't seem serious enough to keep you away from work." "Well," came the answer, "it was my arm she broke."

57. You can always find one person to take on a job . . . if you make him a chairman.

58. A Dallas bank swears that its vault is the best little hoard house in Texas.

59. Teaching is a strange profession in which you keep after school the student you are most eager to send home.

60. Lady to man: "I think bankers get a lot of unfair criticism. My bank is very generous with me. They guaranteed me maximum interest for the next five years, which is more than my husband can do!

61. Three men had adjacent businesses in the same building. The guy who ran the store on one end put up a sign reading Year-End Clearance. The businessman at the other end followed with a sign Closing-Out Sale. The fellow in the middle was hurting so he put up this sign Main Entrance.

62. Maybe you read where Toyota and Chevrolet are considering a joint venture to produce a small American car. Word is that it will be called the Toylet.

63. It's always interesting to read the resumes of June graduates. My son has put together a five-page resume, and the most important item in it is his pulse.

64. This is the land of opportunity. Where else is it possible to grow up, lose a job, and go on unemployment?

65. "I think you are the laziest person I've ever met," said the boss to the young office clerk. "I doubt you do an hours work a week. Tell me one way the firm benefits from your being here." The young man said, "When I go on vacation, you don't have to hire someone to replace me."

66. If all economists were laid end to end in a straight line, their opinions would still point in all directions.

67. A gang kidnapped the wife of a prominent businessman. The ransom note told him to take $50K to the seventeenth green of the golf course at 8:00 a.m. on Thursday, and they would release his wife. When the husband arrived at the green, it was noon. A masked man stepped from the bushes and demanded, "What took you so long?" "My handicap is 27," the businessman said.

68. I've never been able to figure out how a driver's license tells someone that you have money in the bank.

69. He tells of the rich and rather autocratic employer who believed in telling people what to do and no questions asked. When he asked a new employee where he previously worked, the answer was, "In a barber shop."

    "All right, you can cut my hair," commanded the man of quick decisions as he sent for a comb and scissors. The new worker had been warned by others to do exactly as he was told. When the cutting was over and the employer looked in the mirror and the horrendous haircut, he bellowed, "Just what did you do in the barber shop?"

    "I shined shoes" was the reply.

70. When all is said and nothing done, the committee meeting is over.

71. He claims that a depressed economy, with so many hungry job seekers, brings out the creativity in some. "A well-dressed businessman in Houston jumped into Buffalo Bayou," he says. A bystander hastily dived in after him. The first guy yelled, "Leave me alone . . . I want to die . . . don't save me." "I'm not trying to save you," the other shouted. "I want to know where you work."

72. The guy found a good job with security and a great retirement program.

    He had to take a physical before going to work. Returning home, he told his wife, "Darn, the doctor told me I had to take these little green pills the rest of my life."

    "What's so bad about that?" she asked. "He only gave me six!"

73. A friend commented after the bank failed, "The only real problem in town is that there are not two-story buildings, so everybody is trying to kill themselves by jumping off the curb.

74. This guy was hurt in a factory accident. At the hospital, a doctor told his wife, "I'm sorry to tell you this, but he'll never work again." The wife said, "I'll go in and tell him. It'll cheer him up."

75. The barber at the second chair says that whatever makes him tick needs winding.

76. A company sent me a notice that my bill was a year old, so I sent them a birthday card!"

77. He has an all-electric home—everything's charged.

78. An immigrant came to the United States. Unable to speak a word of English, he found it difficult to find a job. The parish priest mercifully let him act as the church beadle. After a while, it was discovered that he was unable to read or write English. He was dismissed and became a helper in a local grocery. He worked hard for years and saved up enough money to open his own grocery store. It was a success, and he soon had a second. Within ten years he was the owner of a dozen supermarkets. During the holiday season, an official of a large charity group in the city came to him for a donation and showed him the fund-raising brochure. The old man said, "I can't read English. I can't even write it." The official said, "That's amazing. You became a millionaire without being able to read or write English? Do you have any idea of where you'd be today if you could?" The old man said, "Sure, I'd be a beadle in the church!"

79. I make it a point never to hire an electrician with singed eyebrows!

80. A man was fired by his employer. Another employee asked, "When do you plan to fill the vacancy?" The employer answered, "He didn't leave any!"

81. The head of the company called a meeting of all the company brass to discuss firing a female employee. When they were seated, he asked, "How many of you have been dating her?" Seven of the eight men raised their hands. The boss asked the eighth man, "You've never been out with her once? Not once?"

    The eighth man said, "I swear." The boss said, "Good. You fire her!"

82. You can cut down on the number of mistakes you make at work by coming in late.

83. So two businessmen meet. One says, "I'm so sorry about the fire that burned down your plant." The other says, "Shh, it's not until tomorrow!"

84. He tells about the hunchback of Notre Dame who was approached one day by a young man who wanted to take his job as bell ringer away. Given a chance he pulled the rope, and the bell came back plop and hit the kid on the left side of the face. Second try, slap again on the right side of the face goes the bell. One more try and *whippo*, the rope comes back and smacks the kid, knocking him down the bell tower and to the ground below. A stranger came by, looked at the kid, and asked the hunchback: Anybody know this kid? The hunchback said, "No, I don't, but his face rings a bell.

85. He invented a new game about certain workers and how they feel at the end of the day. For instance: cop—beat; muffler man—exhausted; gardener—bushed; judge—fine; tailor—sew, sew; dog catcher—pooped.

86. She is married to a guy, and as soon as both of them returned from their honeymoon, they bought them a motel—Abdul's Hideaway. They put on their marquee: "Do your sinnin' on our linen."

87. I know some people who were ready to take an early retirement, but they couldn't. They needed the rubber bands and paper clips.

88. What time is it by your watch? A quarter too Quarter to what? I don't know. Business has been so bad lately I had to lay off one of the hands.

89. Government bureaucrat wanted a list of employees broken down by sex. Employer said, "Booze is the problem here."

90. It's very important to study math. If you don't know math, how will you know if your unemployment check is right?

91. I really don't know much about computers. To me, software always sounds like something you get at Frederick's of Hollywood.

92. Rough year. I made more money than I can afford.

93. Organized crime takes in over forty billion dollars a year and spends very little on office supplies. (Woody Allen)

94. If your business is going to hell, the federal government is probably the travel agent.

95. Once there was an office worker who would leave work each day pushing a wheelbarrow full of sand. The guard at the gate knew that he was stealing something, so he would go through that sand thoroughly. He found nothing so he would let the guy pass. Finally he asked him what he had been stealing. The man said, "Wheelbarrows."

96. The boss paid my creativity a rare compliment today. He said I never made the same mistake twice—I'm always searching out new ones.

97. I've come to the conclusion. It's the one I've long supposed. The boss's door is always open. It's his mind that's always closed.

98. They claimed they had assets of $200 million. When you smoothed it out, it was $1.75 and 3 toasters.

99. Lending money is always risky. You don't know how it feels to see someone sign a promissory note for $2 million and then wipe his fingerprints off the pen.

100. I am bitter. Last week my broker called and said the Dow Jones just broke 10,500. I said, "Yeah I know. I'm one of them."

101. Remember when we took a bath on Saturday night? Now, thanks to the stock market we can do it all week long.

102. I will never forget how quickly the stock market turned around. It was the first time I ever saw a stock broker jump out the window then make a U-turn.

103. During the terrible recession, a distraught man jumped into Buffalo Bayou. He yelled, "Don't save me." The man on the bridge said, "I won't. I just want to know where you worked."

104. Lady: "Can't you find work?" Tramp: "Yes, but everyone wants a reference from my last employer." Lady: "Can't you get one?" Tramp: "No, he's been dead twenty-eight years."

105. Your account has been on our books over a year. I just want to remind you that I have now carried you longer than your mother.

106. One of my first jobs was cleaning the windows on the envelopes. (Rita Radner)

107. I'm so naïve. I thought special interest groups were people who got 6 percent loans.

108. A man without a smile must not open up a shop.

109. I won't say how our company is doing, but it's the first time I ever heard taps played during the annual report.

110. Re: Stock Market. My family was not affected by the crash of '29. They went broke in '28

111. Secretary—take a letter. She picked N.

112. "Do you know enough to be useful in this office?"
    "Know enough? I left the last office because the boss said I knew too much."

113. Businessman on his deathbed named six bankers as his pallbearers. He said since they had taken him this far, they might as well finish the job.

114. I just received this letter from your desk, so I'd like to speak to the desk.

115. When I came in early to work, the boss asked me if I was having trouble at home.

116. Business has been tough. I know this guy who died, went to hell, and never knew the difference.

117. One of the bad things about having all the money in the world is who would you borrow it from.

118. Very effective collection agency: Attila the Dunn

119. If you are thirty-five years old and your job still involves wearing a name tag, you've probably made a serious vocational error in judgment.

120. A man came from East Germany and was offered a job twelve hours a day and six days a week. He said, "Who wants a part-time job?"

121. My boss put the suggestion box on the paper shredder.

122. I won't say how many mistakes he has made in thirty-five years with the company, but as a token of our esteem and admiration, we had his eraser bronzed.

123. The guest of honor at a retirement party is the only one who can yawn after the boss's favorite joke.

124. "I couldn't give you enough work to keep you occupied." Madam: "You'd be surprised how little it takes to keep me occupied."

125. Boss walked up behind the bookkeeper who had his feet on the desk and was reading the newspaper. "Why aren't you working?" asked the boss. Bookkeeper: "Because I didn't hear you coming."

126. Some people are just made for their work—like flat feet for an exterminator.

127. I asked one job applicant what he could do and he said, "Nothing." I didn't hire him. If there is one thing I hate, it's someone who is after my job.

128. Insurance policies always exclude acts of God. What do they think dying is—a recreational pastime?

129. Inflation has created a new economic problem: windfall poverty

130. He put half his money into toilet paper and the other half in revolving doors. I was wiped out before I could turn around.

131. I'm so rich my bank account is named after me.

132. Sign in office: "It is hard to be a Monday person in a Friday world."

133. The personnel department has just brought in a psychologist to raise the level of consciousness in our office from "un" to "semi."

134. He realized he was a failure when the waiter refused to serve him the "businessman's lunch."

135. America is still the land of opportunity where a man can start out digging ditches and wind up behind a desk—if he doesn't mind the financial sacrifice.

136. Capital punishment: where the government sets up business in competition with you and then takes all your profits with taxes to make up its loss.

137. There's one difference between the tax collector and a taxidermist. The taxidermist leaves the hide.

138. You can't smoke the cigar in this drugstore. I bought it here, didn't I? Yes, but I sell ex-lax also.

139. I don't like insurance companies. I get the money when I die, but they get to use those beautiful office buildings while I'm alive.

140. Watch out for the guy who is the insurance agent, financial advisor, estate planner and broker. Right away you are outnumbered 4-1.

141. Wearing heavy black graduation gowns on a hot June afternoon is ideal preparation for the real world. It gets you used to sweating.

142. He was telling about a harrowing experience he had out west. "There were Indians on my right, my left, in front, and in back of me. What did I do? I bought the rug.

143. He puts off until tomorrow what he has no intention of doing.

144. They moved the desk to the men's room because that is the only place where people seem to know what they are doing.

145. The best thing about owning your own business is that it is OK to fool around with the boss's wife.

146. In hiring someone, show each applicant an inkblot, and the one who tries to sell you a new pen gets the job.

147. Terminations will continue until moral improves.

148. I'm getting worried about my bank. Yesterday one of my checks came back marked insufficient funds. Now, what kind of bank is it that doesn't have $25?

149. The boss said I had miniscule command of the English language, was incredibly slow on the uptake, and was completely oblivious of what was going on around me. Fortunately I had an answer. I said, "Huh?"

150. I have a considerate accountant. His office has a recovery room.

151. Classified ads:

    a.   Illiterate? Write today for help.
    b.   Auto repair service: Try us once; you will never go anywhere again.
    c.   Dog for sale: eats anything and is fond of children
    d.   Stock up and save: limit one per customer
    e.   For sale: antique desk suitable for lady with thick legs and large drawers.
    f.   Man wanted to work in dynamite factory. Must be willing to travel
    g.   Three-year-old teacher needed for preschool. Experience preferred.
    h.   Girl wanted to assist magician in cutting off head illusion. Salary and Blue Cross
    i.   We do not tear your clothing with machinery. We do it carefully by hand.
    j.   Tired of cleaning yourself? Let me do it.
    k.   Vacation special; have your home exterminated. Get rid of aunts.
    l.   Toaster: a gift that every member of the family appreciates. Automatically burns toast.
    m.   For rent: six-room hated apartment.
    n.   We will oil your sewing machine and adjust tension in your home for $1.

o.   Man, honest, will take anything.

p.   Used cars: why go elsewhere to be cheated? Come here first.

q.   Our bikinis are exciting. They are simply the tops.

r.   And now, the superstore unequaled in size, unmatched in variety, unrivaled inconvenience

152. Employee evaluations

Exceptionally well qualified: has made no major blunders to date
Active socially: drinks heavily
Quick thinking: offers plausible excuses for errors
Alert to company developments: an office gossip
Spends extra hours on the job: has a miserable home life
Tactful when dealing with superiors: knows when to keep his mouth shut
Judgment is usually sound: lucky
Character above reproach: still one step ahead of the law
Approaches difficult problems with logic: finds someone else to do the job.
Gets along extremely well with superiors and subordinates alike: a coward
Keen sense of humor: has a vast repertoire of questionable jokes

153. Company Signs

Electrician's truck: Let us remove your shorts
Tire shop: Invite us to your next blowout
Taxidermist's office: We really know our stuff
Podiatrist's office: Time wounds all heels.
On plumber's truck: Don't sleep with a drip. Call your plumber
Plumber: We repair what your husband fixed
In yard of funeral home: Drive carefully—we'll wait
On maternity room door: Push, Push, Push
Outside a muffler shop: No appointment needed. We hear you coming.
Towing company: We don't charge an arm and a leg. We want tows.
Plastic surgeon's door: Hello, can we pick your nose?

154. I know a traveling salesman who died and left his family sixty-five thousand towels.

155. Definition: Ulcer—when you mix business with pressure.

156. Team effort: a lot of people doing what I say

157. What a strange economy. My bank has failed, but the toaster is still working

158. We need either less corruption or more chances to participate in it.

159. My brother-in-law is making a big career move; he's transferring to another unemployment office.

160. Money in the bank is like toothpaste in the tube: easy to get out but hard to put back in.

161. Boss to new employee: "I want you to know my door is always open. Please walk by quietly."

162. Anybody can be a loser—like the businessman who got ulcers without being a success.

163. I understand why pregnant executives have it so hard. It isn't easy being management and labor at the same time.

164. I began to sense I had problems at work when I returned from lunch and found pictures of somebody else's kids on my desk.

165. We may still call you occasionally with questions such as, what exactly did you do here?

166. I never worry about what's happening on the New York Stock Exchange or the American Stock Exchange because I have all my money in over-the-counter investments—groceries.

167. He is our youngest executive, but the senior VPs try not to notice, except when he sends them memos in crayons.

168. Death is nature's way of telling you that interest rates were not your biggest problem.

169. Our executives will never get arrested for a first-degree crime. They never premeditated anything in their lives.

170. Executive ability is knowing how to get credit for what others have done.

171. The problem with stock is that when you are rich, you are rich on paper, but when you are broke, you are broke in cash.

172. First law of management: kickbacks should always exceed bribes.

173. I got a letter from my bank. They want their toaster back.

174. Prospective employer: "You say, sir, that you were at your last place for fifteen years. Why did you leave?" Prospective Employee: "I was pardoned."

175. I bought a life insurance policy from Sears, and it is really great. If I die my wife gets ten thousand lug wrenches.

176. Notice that staff makes inexcusable errors while we make justifiable mistakes.

177. I'm lost. I've gone to look for myself, so if I get back before I return, please ask me to wait.

178. New company incentive program: "One mistake and you are through."

179. Somewhere, right now there is a committee deciding your future and you were not invited.

180. Definition: Computer—an accountant with a personality.

181. I am finally at the point where my net income covers my gross habits.

182. Good timing is when you get the mortgage paid off before entering a rest home.

183. Did you ever get the feeling that your sales staff couldn't sell pickles in a maternity ward?

184. Sales confidence is going after Moby Dick with a rowboat, a harpoon, and a jar of tartar sauce.

185. We have Sam's first employee application on file. Under Age, he wrote "nuclear." Under Church Preference he put "Gothic." Under Zip, he wrote "normal for my age." And under Sex, he wrote, "Occasionally."

186. Re: the financial crisis in Rhode Island last year signs were posted around the state, which read, Welcome to Rhode Island. Make us an offer.

187. Bureaucracy only does two things

    A.   Exercises control
    B.   Maintains itself

188. It takes two things to be a consultant—gray hair and hemorrhoids. The gray hair makes you look distinguished and the hemorrhoids is to show you are concerned.

189. Instead of "We are confident our new pricing strategy will be successful." Take a cue from a famous marine hero who told his troops: "The enemy is in front of us, behind us, to the left of us and to the right of us. They can't escape us this time."

CHILDREN/EDUCATION

1. I wish we could keep our kids at that real cute age of four—but I guess taxidermy is out of the question.

2. Man calls, little boy answers:
    "Who is this? My name's Johnny, and I'm four years old."
    "Can I talk to your mother?"
    "She's upstairs. She can't come to the phone right now."
    "Can I talk to your father?"
    "He's out in the garage, he can't come either."
    "Is any one else there? The policemen, where are they?"
    "They're outside in the front yard."
    "Anyone else?"
    "The firemen are here, but they are up in the attic."
    "My goodness. What in the world are they all doing?"
    "They're looking for me. I gotta go now. Bye."

3. I stopped to see my son in college about 2:00 AM on my way from Dallas. I went to his dormitory room and knocked on the door. I said, "Is this where Joe lives?" From inside they said, "Yeah, drag him on in."

4. Father asked his son why he had four Fs and one D on his report card. He said, "Well, I guess I've just been spending too much time on one subject."

5. Boy won prize—most parents at the PTA meeting

6. In kindergarten he flunked sandpile.

7. A lad called to a farmer who was in the yard, "I just had an accident. Our wagonload of hay turned over in the road." "Come in," said the farmer, kindly, "and have a glass of lemonade." "Paw wouldn't like it." "Awe, he wouldn't mind." And the cooling drink was pressed into the boy's hands.

   After he had partaken of the lemonade, the hospitable farmer said, "Wife, set an extra plate at the table, it's about dinnertime." The boy said, "Paw wouldn't like it." But the farmer and his wife insisted, and so he joined them at the table. After the hearty meal, the farmer said, "Soon as I smoke this pipe, I'll go down and help right that load of hay. By the way, where is your paw?" The lad answered, "Paw's under the hay."

8. A child is a creature that stands halfway between an adult human being and a television set.

9. A holiday performance of the Nutcracker was young Jason's first ballet as he watched the dancers move about on their toes, a puzzled look crossed his face. "Mommy," he finally whispered, "why don't they just get taller ladies?"

10. It was my father that gave me my musical background. He used to spank me with a violin.

11. Last month he wrote me a letter: "Dear Dad, haven't heard from you in weeks. Send me a check so I'll know you're all right!"

12. Dirty? After this kid takes a bath, we don't know whether to clean the tub or dredge it.

13. Disagreeable? This boy can make enemies at Dale Carnegie classes.

14. I used to be one of those kids who wrote down the answers to tests on their fingernails. One day I got excited and chewed up half the Declaration of Independence.

15. Those playpens are really marvelous gadgets. I sit inside and the kids can't get near me.

16. Now the kid wants an encyclopedia. Why can't he walk the way I did?

17.   Every baby resembles the relative who has the most money.

18.   Bobby, coming home the back way with two black eyes and a bloody nose, tried to avoid being seen by his mother. "Aha! Fighting again!" she scolded, catching him tiptoeing in through the door. "Didn't I tell you? Whenever you got angry to count to one hundred before you do anything?" "I did," Bobby insisted. "I did count to one hundred. But the other boy's mother told him to count to fifty!"

19.   Daddy was willing to laugh if you told him it was a joke.

20.   First thing a child learns when he gets a drum for Christmas is that it is the last one he'll ever get.

21.   You can always separate an experienced father from the novices. He's the one who, if his child threatens to run away makes the kid put it in writing.

22.   A few years back, kids weren't getting married at all. Now they seem to be getting married and reaching puberty at the same time. Last week I went to a wedding where the bride and groom were so young, Gerber catered the reception.

23.   The little boy was caught by his teacher saying a forbidden four-letter word. "Jimmy," she said, "you shouldn't use that word. Where did you hear it?" "My mommy said it," the child responded. "Well, that doesn't matter," the teacher explained. "You don't even know what it means." "I do too," Jimmy corrected. "It means the car won't start."

24.   Mixed emotions is when your teenage son gets an A+ in sex education.

25.   The first half of our lives is ruined by our parents and the second half by our children.

26.   A research organization, making a study of juvenile delinquency, telephoned fifty homes between nine thirty and ten thirty at night to ask parents if they knew where their children were. Half of the calls were answered by children who had no idea where their parents were.

27.   August was a bad month for my teenager. It's when he learned that all the summer jobs were taken.

28. When he was eighteen, he finally found a direction for his life. Unfortunately, it was toward the refrigerator.

29. One of the greatest mysteries of life is how that idiot your daughter married can be the father of the smartest grandchildren in the whole world.

30. A man visited a fortuneteller and sat down in front of her crystal ball. "I see you are the father of two children," she said. "That's what you think," the man replied. "I'm the father of three children." The fortuneteller smiled and said, "That's what you think."

31. Hostess at dinner party: "I've noticed your little brother standing there during the whole party. He hasn't moved a step." Guest: "Yes, it's the first time he's worn a necktie, and he thinks he's tied to a post.

32. There is one advantage to the way our son wears his hair. In an emergency, he can be treated by either an MD or a vet.

33. A clever teacher asked, "If there were three flies on the table and I swatted one, how many would be left?" An equally clever second-grader replied, "One, the dead one."

34. A home with a six-year-old is a place where you also wash the soap when you clean the bathroom.

35. Two businessmen, meeting at lunch, were discussing their families. "I have six boys," one of them said. "That's a nice family," sighed the other. "I wish to heaven I had six children." "Don't you have any children?" the proud father asked with a touch of sympathy in his voice. "Oh yes," sighed the second man. "Twelve."

36. Teacher: "If you subtract nineteen from forty-six, what is the difference?" Pupil: "Uh, well . . . that's what I say, what's the difference?"

37. Summer camp is where kids go to learn how to start a fire without matches; how to find their way without a compass; how to avoid poison ivy; what to do if they come face-to-face with a bear, a wolf, or a rattlesnake; and all the other things they wouldn't have to know if they hadn't gone to summer camp.

38. We're living in a time when the only truly childproof containers are books.

39. My son was sweet during infancy but started fermenting during childhood.

40. My son has a toy boat that he takes in the bathtub with him. It has done more harm than the real battleship *Missouri*. That's because I have never accidentally sat down on the real battleship *Missouri*.

41. Last week I went into my son's room and found a big hairy clump of dirt. It was a friend helping him with his homework.

42. Let me tell you what hurts. Your kid comes in and tells you what he learned in history class and you remember the day it happened.

43. Whenever your kids are out of control, you can take comfort from the thought that even God's omnipotence did not extend to his kids. After creating heaven and earth, God created Adam and Eve. And the first thing he said to them was "Don't." "Don't what?" Adam replied. "Don't eat the forbidden fruit," God said. "Forbidden fruit? Really? Where is it?" asked the two. "It's over there," said God, wondering why he hadn't stopped after making the elephants. A few minutes later, God saw the kids having an apple break, and he was angry. "Didn't I tell you not to eat that fruit?" the first parent asked. "Uh-huh," Adam replied. "Then why did you?" commanded God. "I dunno," Adam answered. God's punishment was that Adam and Eve should have children of their own. Thus the pattern was set, and it has never changed. But there is reassurance in this story. If you have persistently and lovingly tried to give them wisdom and they haven't taken it, don't be hard on yourself. If God had trouble handling children, what makes you think it would be a piece of cake for you?

44. Hug your kids at home—belt them in the car!

45. I had an uncle who had delusions of grandeur. It was fascinating. You'd say, "Gee, what a beautiful day!" and he'd say, "Thank you."

46. Teacher: "What's a Grecian Urn?" Student: "Oh, about a dollar an hour."

47. I have to admit it. I'm not nearly as smart as I used to be. Then again, you can't be a teenager all your life.

48. My son is into music. In fact, there isn't an instrument he can't play. The guitar—he can't play that. The piano—he can't play that. The trumpet—he can't play that.

49. If you really want to have an endless summer, don't send the kids to camp.

50. I asked my son, "What can you do?" He said, "Nothing." I said, "Good. I'll get you a job in the government. They won't have to break you in."

51. I just figured out why so many teenagers wear sandals. Shoes you have to know how to tie.

52. I cringe when I think of the prom dress my daughter wore. She thinks "prom" is short for "promiscuous."

53. Some radio stations play three songs in a row. Some play five in a row. My son's favorite stations play ten songs simultaneously.

54. If the future belongs to our children, how come my kids spend money like there's no tomorrow?

55. My kids have a warped view of history. They think "BC" means "Before Cable."

56. My kids believe they can turn noise into music simply by raising the volume.

57. I can't understand it. I taught my kid everything I know, and he still acts stupid.

58. It's not easy raising a teenage daughter. Sugar and spice and everything nice has turned into powder and paint and everything that ain't.

59. Over the holiday break, I asked my son how he's doing in college. He said, "Do you mean scholastically or academically?"

60. I keep telling my kids that they have a lot of potential. It's a nice way of saying they sure can't do much now.

61. Of course I make my kids clean their room. We can't afford to hire stable hands.

62. Parenting would be easier if my children were better at childing.

63. It's amazing how a little soap and water can turn a complete stranger into your own child.

64. My kid is attached to a machine that keeps him alive—the refrigerator.

65. Population statistics are changing, namely, the high divorce rate. Sixty years ago, parents had a lot of children. Today children are likely to have a lot of parents.

66. She was a very unusual girl. Won the three-legged race at the picnic. What makes it so unusual—she didn't have a partner!

67. Last year, my mom got angry when I forgot Mother's Day. I told her it was an accident and she said, "So were you!"

68. My aunt and uncle got into a big fight over the weekend, and for once he had the final say. His exact words were "Go ahead, I dare you to pull that trigger."

69. My uncle performed a community service several years ago—he moved out of the community.

70. As a kid, I had trouble finding myself because my parents were always telling me to get lost.

71. Did you ever get the feeling the only tests college kids are taking is blood?

72. Talk about tough neighborhoods. Our school newspaper had an obituary page.

73. His daughter is not very bright. She was thinking of going to UCLA but decided to go to SMU instead "because it's one less letter to remember."

74. A loyal fan was playing Trivia Adventure (the child's version of Trivial Pursuit) with her seven-year-old son. The boy picked the following question: "What are the two major political parties in the United States?" The boy thought carefully, then replied, "Hanukkah and Christmas."

75. While mother was driving her son to kindergarten, he asked, "Where are all the SOBs this morning?" She replied, "They only come out when your father drives."

76. Three little boys were brought into the police station.
    "What did you do?" asked the sergeant to the first boy.
    "I threw peanuts out the school bus window."
    "That's not so bad," said the sergeant. "And what did you do?" he asked the second boy.
    "I helped throw peanuts out the window."
    "And you?" he addressed the third boy.
    "I'm Peanuts, sir."

77. In my neighborhood the kids use barbed wire for dental floss.

78. She was, a lady reports, fixing an early dinner for her fourteen-year-old son who had a touch football game lined up with some friends. Everything was ready when she discovered she was almost out of ketchup. She was thumping away at the end of the nearly empty bottle, trying to get enough out of it for this hamburger and french fries when the telephone rang. "Get that," she yelled at her son. He picked up the phone and told the caller, "She can't come to the phone right now. She's hitting the bottle."

79. I know you're not going to believe this, but one father complains that his teenage daughter wears such tight blue jeans that she has to carry her makeup kit in her mouth.

80. Just recently, a lady tells me she was busy in the kitchen when her little boy came in and announced he had to go to the bathroom. "Well," she said, "go."
    "I want you to go with me," he said.
    "Now you're getting too big for that," his mother said. "You can go by yourself. Besides, Jesus will be with you."

The little boy trailed off alone. In a few moments, he shouted down the stairs in exasperation, "Come up here, Momma. Jesus won't turn on the light."

81. Rebuked by her mother for having been cross and ill-tempered, the teenage daughter retorted, "How come when it's me it's temper and when it's you it's nerves?"

82. A little boy went out to buy mother a birthday present. He thought it would be nice to get her a cookie jar. At the counter, he lifted and replaced the lid on each jar. Finally, after looking at all of them, he asked the clerk, "Don't you have any lids that don't make noise?"

83. A seventeen-year-old beauty gave instructions to her fourteen-year-old sister, "And remember, too much perfume is counterseductive."

84. We asked Santa at a mall what he wanted for Christmas, and he said, "A dry lap."

85. A little girl was asked what she was going to give her brother for Christmas.
"I don't know."
"What did you give him last year?"
"Measles," she replied.

86. The little girl walked angrily away from two small boys. One of the boys muttered, "She broke our engagement. She returned my frog."

87. Two expectant fathers were nervously pacing the floor of the maternity-ward waiting room. "What tough luck," one grumbled. "This had to happen during my vacation." "What are you complaining about?" said the other. "I'm on my honeymoon."

88. The parents were worried about the foul language of their two teenage sons. The husband and wife are talking about it, and they decide they have to do something. So they go down to breakfast the next morning and approach their two boys. The father overheard one boy say, "Where the hell are the cornflakes?"
The father whacks him in the face, knocks him to the floor, punches him, kicks him in the stomach, and stomps on his fingers. Then the father looks up at his other son and asks, "Well, what do you want?"

And the other son answers, "You can bet your sweet ass it isn't the cornflakes!"

89. Small boy: "If I'm noisy they give me a spanking, and if I'm quiet they take my temperature."

90. One of our kids does bird imitations—he eats worms.

91. Parental truth: never change babies in midstream.

92. A granddaughter story: "What's wrong, Melissa?"
    "I had a scary dream."
    "What was the dream about?"
    "You should know. You were in it."

93. You may not believe this, but we were recently told that break dancing was invented by a kid in Cleveland who was stealing hubcaps off of a moving vehicle.

94. But there are exceptions. I know a fellow who's so rich he doesn't know his son is in college.

95. Three-year-old Susie watched curiously as the babysitter changed her baby sister's diaper. When the sitter used the lotion, Susie asked, "What's that for?"
    In a matter-of-fact tone, the sitter answered, "To make her smell better."
    "So," Susie asked, "why don't you put it on her nose?"

96. When the children are home from college, there is usually no food in the refrigerator. You can't get out to buy food because there's no gas in the car. You can't get gas for the car because there's no money in the sugar bowl. And you can't put money in the sugar bowl because the children go to college.

97. A teacher showed a picture of *Whistler's Mother* to her kindergarten class and asked for a description. Raising her hand, one little girl answered, "It shows a nice lady waiting for the repairman to bring back her television set."

98. One of the hardest jobs of a parent is making a child realize that "no" can be a complete sentence.

99. Overheard one father say his son will be able to pass anything at college, except a bar or pizza parlor.

100. Proud mother holding infant: "He's eating solids now . . . keys, sticks, newspapers."

101. The youngster was talked into putting a part of his summer savings into a bank. When opening a savings account he came to the question: Previous bank—the boy filled in "Piggy."

102. A young daughter of a friend was watching her mother put on cold cream. The mother had it all over her face. The girl asked why and was told it was to make her beautiful. Then mommy began wiping the cream off with tissue, and the daughter asked, "What's the matter, Mommy, you giving up?"

103. If your teenager mows the lawn without being told, don't plan on using the car that night.

104. Youngsters will have to learn that if they never learn to write their name, they will have to pay cash for everything when they grow up.

105. Human beings are the only creatures on earth that allow their children to come back home.

106. Money isn't everything, but it's a surefire way of not losing touch with your kids.

107. "I've found a full-time job this summer for my teenage daughter," the mother of four was telling her neighbor. "She's going to clean up her room."

108. The grown-ups thought that little Philip was cute but dumb. People would offer him the choice of a nickel or a dime. He always took the nickel. Another kid asked him one day, "Don't you know a dime's worth more than a nickel?" Phil said, "Yup, but if I took a dime, grown-ups wouldn't keep making the offer!"

109. The only sure cure for delinquency is birth control.

110. Two fathers met on the street. One said, "What am I going to do? My son doesn't know how to drink. He doesn't know how to play poker. What am I going to do?"

    The other father said, "I don't know why you're complaining."

    The first father said, "Because he drinks and he plays poker!"

111. France's Louis XIII lay on his deathbed, he reached out, touched his five-year-old son, and croaked, "Who's that?" The lad's reply, "Louis XIV."

112. To parents who want to make their children do better scholastically is "to adopt more Asian children."

113. The last things my kids did to earn money was lose their baby teeth."

114. Freedom is watching your son or daughter receive a college diploma that you paid for and leaving the ceremony hoping your 1978 Impala will start.

115. If all the coeds at Vassar were laid end to end, I wouldn't be surprised.

116. A good wife and mother is the one who tells her preschool son he can't eat dessert unless he eats his bread and vegetables and tells her husband that he can't have the dessert if he does eat the bread and vegetables.

117. There had been several earthquake shocks in a certain district, so a couple sent their little boy to an uncle who lived out of the danger zone. A day or two later, they received a telegram: "Am returning your boy—send earthquake."

118. And there's the story about the lady who was taking a survey. She was questioning another lady who said she had only recently become the mother of triplets. "Triplets!" said the pollster enthusiastically. "Why just think of that! Triplets!

    "Yes," said the mother. "I understand it only happens once every ten thousand times." "Oh my," burbled the pollster. "Ten thousand times! How in the world did you find the time to do your housework?"

119. He is worried about his kid's education. When I asked him if he was taking any calculus, he said, "No, I get enough in the milk I drink."

120. She says that one of her sons was running around in such ratty-looking and tattered clothing that she had a T-shirt made for him saying, "I have good clothes in my closet."

121. We know a father of four teenagers who swears it's been six years since he picked up a phone that was not warm.

122. A mother was asked why she let her small child play in the mud. "Because," she replied, "it's easy to find, it doesn't hurt him, and it doesn't need batteries."

123. My mother-in-laws idea of a matched set of luggage is a pair of shopping bags from the same store.

124. Boy was late turning his quiz in. Teacher didn't like it. Boy asked the teacher if he knew his name. Teacher said no so the boy lifted up the tests, put his in the middle, and walked out.

125. We have two daughters, but they don't live with us. They are not married yet.

126. Teacher said, "An apple a day keeps the doctor away." Boy says, "What do you have for cops?"

127. When the father sees the $83 phone bill his son brought home from college, he said, "Son, tell me again how you have trouble communicating."

128. City has posted signs around town—"Watch out for children, they may be armed."

129. Man at work
    "We're celebrating a blessed event at our house. Aren't you a bit old?"
    "Oh, it's not that kind of an event—our son got a job."

130. Father looked at his daughter's new Madonna outfit and said, "What do you have that on for? It's still two months to Halloween."

131. First boy: "My dad is a doctor, and I can be sick for nothing." Second boy: "Big deal. My dad's a preacher and I can be good for nothing."

132. A little boy wanted to talk to his dad so he rattled the newspaper his dad was reading.
    "Dad, isn't it true God gives us our daily bread?
    "Yes, son."
    "And Santa brought me toys at Christmas?"
    "He sure did."
    "And baby sister came from heaven?"
    "That's right."
    "And Mom takes care of us?"
    "Every day of her life."
    The boy wandered off, apparently satisfied with his dad's answers, then came back in and rattled the newspapers again. His dad interrupted his reading to find out what was on the boy's mind this time. The boy asked, "Dad, what do you do around here?"

133. She told him to change the baby so he went out and got another kid.

134. Children will make you think. My daughter saw pictures of the ten most wanted criminals in the post office. She asked if they were mean. I said yes, and they would be caught someday. Daughter: "Why didn't they keep them the day they took their pictures?"

135. My mother bought all my clothes from the army-navy surplus store. It was kind of embarrassing going to school dressed as a Japanese general.

136. We have three grandchildren. Two are spoiled rotten, and the third hasn't come to visit us yet.

137. We went over our son's college expenses, and it was rather discouraging. I figure that for him to study business, I'd have to sell mine.

138. My son got his BA then he got his master's, and now he's thinking of going for a PhD. I just hope this means he'll soon be ready to decide on a major.

139. I'll say this for my teenager. He always knows where his head is at. So do I. Until noon, it's on a pillow.

140. Let's face it. Some kids are like ketchup bottles. You have to hit them to get them moving.

141. Determining a life goal is a real problem. I met one kid who has a mustache, a full beard, and hair down to his shoulder blades, and he doesn't know what to make of himself. How about a throw rug?

142. I can't understand the way kids dress. Last week my daughter spent $200 just to look poor.

143. When it comes to education, what kids really have to learn is the street value of a diploma.

144. I never really worried about the quality of our educational system until my kid came home with his last report card. He got a C in sauna.

145. Kids today are much more sensitive to gourmet eating than we used to be. For instance, we have a son who always asks if we're going to have meat or fish before deciding on Pepsi or 7 Up.

146. All of our kids came home from summer camp with deep, rich, golden tans. I think they moved the Nintendo outdoors.

147. If I seem a little distracted, I am. This morning one of our kids came up to me and wanted to know what life was like in the old days—before Nintendo.

148. Last year the kids told us to relax, lean back, enjoy, and they'd make dinner on Labor Day. And it was really different. I never even knew you could barbecue Twinkies.

149. But there is a human side to it all. A mortician once told me that working in a funeral home is just like having teenagers. You come downstairs each day, say "Good morning," and nobody answers.

150. I really don't know what there is about kids and school. Sometimes I get the feeling that kids think of school as this big vat of knowledge, and if they fall in, they could smarten to death.

151. I really don't understand the relationship between kids and the Cabbage Patch dolls. Let's face it, they're just blobs with vacant, staring, mindless expressions. I mean, what do the dolls see in them?

152. The father of a teenage boy reports that his son got a job at a fast-food establishment. The father went in to buy a hamburger. "I really don't like the food," the father confided, "but this is the first time since he was twelve that I've given him money and got change back on an order without getting an argument."

153. My neighbor says his kid approached the other day and said, "Here's my report card and one of yours I found in the attic."

154. High school English teacher to class: "Write an autobiography, imagining that you are now twenty-five years old." One student tried to shorten the assignment by saying he had died at nineteen. Didn't work.

155. Five-year-old Amy may have it all figured out. "Your mother and daddy," she explained, "make you eat vegetables so you can grow up and be big and strong enough to make your kids eat theirs. If a child looks like his father, that's heredity. If he looks like a neighbor, that's environment."

156. If money didn't talk, it would be a lot harder to communicate with your children.

157. "What a beautiful child! He has an excellent chance to win the baby contest," said the baby's mother. "At the hospital, they said the baby looked like my husband, then they turned him right side up."

158. Kids no longer play post office. They play Federal Express. It's faster.

159. A lady says she learned she had her first grandchild when her son-in-law called the other morning from the hospital and told her, "Congratulations. You've just become a babysitter."

160. Child, looking from bedroom window at night sky, recites, "Twinkle, twinkle, little X, how I wonder what you'll vex. Orbiting above the world so high, waiting to be told who to fry."

161. We were not like most parents. Our children were totally independent by the time they were fifteen—except financially.

162. My son is a typical American teenager—he's thirty-four.

163. I used to hide my son's presents where he wouldn't find them—in the bathtub.

164. He is so dirty he had two toy boats in the tub that went aground.

165. Cleaning your house before the kids stop growing is like shoveling the walk before it stops snowing.

166. My wife and I didn't have an easy summer. We spent two months trying to communicate with an alien creature sometimes know as an ET—Early Teen.

167. Colleges and universities are unique and irreplaceable institutions in this troubled world. Where else can you postpone reality until a later date?

168. Things I've Learned from My Children (Honest and No Kidding)

If you spray hair spray on dust bunnies and run over them with Rollerblades, they can ignite.
A three-year-old's voice is louder than two hundred adults in a crowded restaurant.
If you hook a dog leash over a ceiling fan, the motor is not strong enough to rotate a forty-two-pound boy wearing a Batman underwear and a Superman cape.
It is strong enough however to spread paint on all four walls of a twenty-by-twenty-foot room.
A ceiling fan can hit a baseball a long way.
The glass in windows (even double pane) doesn't stop a baseball hit by a ceiling fan.
When you hear the toilet flush and the words *uh-oh*, it's already too late.
Brake fluid mixed with Clorox makes smoke, and lots of it.
A six-year-old can start a fire with a flint rock even though a thirty-six-year-old man says they can only do it in the movies.

A magnifying glass can start a fire even on an overcast day.

A king-size waterbed holds enough water to fill a two-thousand-square-foot house four inches deep.

Legos will pass through the digestive tract of a four-year-old.

Play-Dough and Microwave should never be used in the same sentence.

Super Glue is forever.

VCRs do not eject PB and J sandwiches even thought TV commercials show they do.

Garbage bags do not make good parachutes.

Marbles in gas tanks make lots of noise when driving.

You probably do not want to know what that odor is.

Always look in the oven before you turn it on.

The fire department in Houston has a least a five-minute response time.

The spin cycle on the washing machines do not make earthworms dizzy.

It still, however, makes cats dizzy.

Cats throw up twice their body weight when dizzy.

169. On the first day of school, the kindergarten teacher said, "If anyone has to go to the bathroom, just hold up two fingers." A little voice from the rear of the room asked, "How will that help?"

170. A children's book you'll never see is *The Boy Who Died from Eating All His Vegetables*.

171. In California, a Boy Scout can get a merit badge in "weirdo."

172. Two kids said, "Let's play doctor." You operate and I'll sue.

173. Kids are so much more dynamic than they used to be. We used to get married and have our first baby nine months later. Today's young people have cut that time in half.

174. Summer camp is usually staffed with seventeen-year-old counselors you wouldn't trust with your car—but your kids okay.

175. There's nothing wrong with teenagers that reasoning with them won't aggravate. (Ron Howard)

176. Teacher asked, "If you had five apples and I asked for one, how many would you have left?" Johnny answered, "Five."

177. If you want something done by your child, ask him at bedtime.

178. Never lend your car to anyone to whom you have given birth. (Erma Bombeck)

179. Parents want their children to have all the things they never had as youngsters—like five As on their report card.

180. Kids are getting suspicious of all this permissiveness. They're beginning to think it's just a sneaky way to get them to do push-ups.

181. Planned parenthood is a very confusing term. It infers that children have a choice.

182. I won't say what my parents thought of me, but I was an only child.

183. Kid gets a space suit and an atomic ray gun for his birthday. He ran outside, and his buddies were playing cowboys and Indians. They said, "*Bang, bang*, you're dead." He said, "*Zap, zap*, you're sterile."

Closing

1. No one is absolutely worthless; they can always serve as a pitiful example.

2. Learn to laugh at yourself; besides, everyone else has been doing it for years.

3. I wish you good health/continued prosperity/long life, and eventually a measure of respectability.

4. It's better to be called an asshole by a few friends than to be called a friend by a bunch of assholes.

5. After a long speech, say, "If you're taking notes, this is number 1."

6. Isn't it strange that princes and kings, and clowns that caper in sawdust rings, and common people like you and me are builders of eternity. Each is given a book of rules, a shapeless mass, a bag of tools; and each must build ere life has flown, a stumbling block or a stepping stone.

7. And remember to tune in again next week, folks, same time, same station, same jokes.

8. It's later than it's ever been.

9. If you have any other question, comment, or inquiries, please keep them to yourself.

10. I don't know if you know this, but a recent scientific study has shown that the average man speaks twenty-five words a day, and the average woman thirty thousand. Unfortunately, when I come home each day,

I've already spoken my twenty-five thousand, and my wife hasn't started her thirty thousand. Therefore, since I have already used up a week's worth of my words today with you, and lest I be forced to listen to my wife uninterrupted for the next month, I think I had better come to an end of this talk.

11. In conclusion, permit me to paraphrase Shakespeare: "All's well that ends."

12. You know coming at the end of such a splendid and erudite program, I feel like the Apache fire-writer. This poor Indian was in the mountains of New Mexico busily sending smoke signals when they set off a nuclear test at the White Sands Proving Grounds. After watching in awestricken silence for a moment, the Indian clucked his tongue and murmured, "Gee . . . I wish I had said that!"

13. I have time for a few questions, but no answers.

14. On your way home, drive safely. The car you are driving may someday be yours.

15. There's one thing that all great speakers have in common. None of them have been here tonight.

16. Closing a Disastrous Meeting: Well, it's been a wonderful evening. Kind of a shame we spent it here.

17. And so, in conclusion, let us never forget those immortal words of Marcel Marceau.

18. Closing: Live, love, and enjoy. None of us have a warranty, but we all have an expiration date.

19. Closing: This has been such a fantastic evening. Tell me, can you OD on ecstasy?

20. Closing: As any audience knows, there is no better painkiller than "Thank you and good night."

21. Do you know where your treasurer is? (or has been)

22. And now as one schizophrenic said to the other, "Let's split."

23. I've always said actions speak louder than words (then sit down).

DEATH

1. Headstone of a wife: :See I told you I was sick."

2. Here lies Murphy. We buried him today, he lived the life of Murphy while Murphy was away.

3. It's a shame because his brother starved to death last week. He was a pickpocket who got stranded in a nudist colony.

4. Ma'am, your husband has just been run over by a steamroller! I'm in the tub. Slip him under the door.

5. How come the right side of your car is painted yellow and the left side is painted red? I know it doesn't look good, but in case of an accident, you should hear the witnesses contradict each other.

6. Didn't you advertise for a wife the other day? Yes, and I got hundreds of replies, and they all said the same thing. What was that? You can have mine.

7. I hope I look as good as you do when I'm your age. You did.

8. Why don't you go down to the morgue and tell them you're ready?

9. If you think the dead don't come alive, you should be here at closing time.

10. His funeral was the first one where they threw a bouquet to the crowd.

11. A woman offered a brand-new Porsche for sale for a price of $10. A man answered the ad, but he was slightly disbelieving. "What's the gimmick?" he inquired. "No gimmick," the woman answered. "My husband died, and in his will he asked that the car be sold and the money go to his secretary."

12. If you don't go to people's funerals, they won't come to yours. (Yogi Berra)

13. Mike was about to die, and the priest bent over him to give him the last rites of the church. Bending over Mike, the priest said, "Repeat after me, 'I renounce the devil and all his evil deeds.'" But there was no response from Mike. The priest repeated, "Repeat after me, 'I renounce the devil and all his evil deeds,'" and still no response from Mike. After the third try, the priest shook Mike and he opened his eyes. "Didn't you hear me?" asked the priest. "Yes," replied Mike, "but you told me I was going to die, and this is a hell of a time to antagonize anybody.

14. A man, whose father was hanged, when asked how his father met his death, replied that he died at a public function when the platform gave way.

15. With the undertaker standing beside her, the woman looked down at the body of her late husband. "He looks peaceful," the widow sniffed, "but there *is* one thing." "And what is that?" inquired the undertaker. "He . . . he never much liked this blue suit. I think he'd have been much happier in grey, like the gentleman in that casket is wearing." The undertaker looked over and nodded. "I can fix it," he said and asked the woman to excuse him. Less than a minute later, the undertaker entered the waiting room. "Madam, everything is ready." Surprised, the woman walked into the viewing room. Sure enough, her husband was wearing the other man's grey suit, and the other man was in blue. "How . . . how did you ever change them so quickly?" she asked. "I didn't," he replied. "I simply switched the heads."

16. Mr. Benton thought he had had the last word when he presented his ex-wife with an unusual gift for her birthday—a tombstone on which he'd had carved, "Here lies my ex-wife Sonja . . . cold as usual." Much to his surprise, however, his wife one-upped him when, for his birthday, his former spouse presented him with a tombstone of his own on which she'd carved, "Here lies my ex-husband Bennett . . . stiff at last."

17. There's one thing I don't like about undertakers—all they care about is my body.

18. I looked at the obituaries the other day, and I realized something—everybody dies in alphabetical order!"

19. A man lay dying. His voice hardly a whisper, he called over his best friend and said, "I can't go to my Maker without telling you all. I have to confess. Remember that hundred thousand that was missing when we owned the carpet store?" The friend and ex-partner said, "I remember." The man said, "I stole it. I also told your wife that you were fooling around with the blonde at the switchboard. And speaking of your wife, I was her lover for two years. Then—" His friend interrupted, "You don't have to tell me any more. I know everything. That's why I poisoned you."

20. One smoker was buried in a flip-top coffin.

21. Two friends met in the street. One looked forlorn and almost on the verge of tears. The other man said, "Hey, how come you look like the whole world caved in?" The sad gent said, "Let me tell you. Three weeks ago, an uncle died and left me forty thousand dollars."

    "That's not bad."

    "Hold on, I'm just getting started. Two weeks ago, a cousin I never knew kicked the bucket and left me eighty-five thousand free and clear."

    "I'd like that."

    "Last week my grandfather passed away. I inherited almost a quarter of a million."

    "How come you look so glum?"

    "This week—nothing!"

22. Today they hedge on everything. What used to be a cemetery is now a Home for the Terminally Still!

23. A funeral procession is walking by slowly. Behind the hearse is a man holding two leashed pit bulls. Behind the man is an endless line of men, also walking to the slow, funeral pace. A curious passerby asks the man with the dogs who the deceased was. The man explains that his mother-in-law is on the way to be buried. She'd been set upon and killed by the two pit bulls. The passerby nodded and asked, "Would you

consider lending me the pit bulls for a day or two?" The man gestured behind him and said, "Get in line!"

24. Mr. Carling was dying. Downstairs in the kitchen, Mrs. Carling was preparing a roast for the wake. The delicious aroma wafted up to the bedroom. Mr. Carling leaned over to his young daughter and said, "I love your mother's roast. Before I die, I would love one thin slice." The daughter nodded and went down into the kitchen. She returned a moment later, empty-handed, explaining, "Mother says it's for after the funeral!"

25. A number of years ago, so the story goes, there was an old mountaineer, a real despot who ruled his family with an iron fist, who suddenly became ill and appeared to have died.

There were no funeral directors back in the hills then, and embalming wasn't practiced. So as was the custom, the widow and the female relations washed and dressed the body, and it was placed in a coffin. After the service, as the coffin was being carried out of the house, one of the pallbearers stumbled, and one end of the box bumped heavily into a gatepost. The knock somehow revived the "corpse" who sat up, cursing everyone in sight.

The old man lived for more than a year, as mean and tyrannical as ever, then fell ill and died again. Once more the body was prepared for burial. Once more the corpse was placed in the coffin, a service was held, and the pallbearers lifted their burden. As they shuffled by, the long-suffering widow lifted her head and cautioned, "Watch out for that post!"

26. In a cemetery, a visitor noticed a Chinese man placing a bowl of rice on a grave. "What time do you expect your friend to come up to eat the rice?" the visitor asked. The same time, the old Chinese fellow responded, "Your friend comes up to smell the flowers."

27. Don't believe everything you read. Even people who lose at Russian roulette have wills that say, "Being of sound mind."

28. Lady said, "I've had so much trouble handling my husband's estate, I almost wish he hadn't died."

29. When I die, I want to be buried facedown. I want to see where I am going.

30. California nightclubs are the wildest. I went to one that featured the world's most unusual Elvis impersonator. He came out, laid down, and folded his hands across his chest.

31. Epitaph for a waiter—God finally caught his eye. 33. Interesting will: "I, John Jones, being of sound mind, leave all my worldly possessions to my secretary, being of sound body."

32. He's so convinced the world is coming to an end he won't even buy a five-day deodorant pad.

33. If you want him to mourn, you'd best leave him nothing.(Martial)

34. Let those who thoughtfully consider the brevity of life remember the length of eternity. (Bishop Ken)

35. Why did you tell Mrs. Jones her husband was dead when he had only lost all his money? I thought I had better break it to her gently.

36. Tombstone: Dr. John Jones, 1920-1990, Office Upstairs

37. Tombstone for her husband: Rest in peace until we meet again

38. On a cloudy rainy day, the deceased was a little old lady who had devoted her entire life to fussing at her poor husband. When graveside services had no more than terminated, there was a tremendous burst of thunder accompanied by a distant lightning bolt and more rumbling thunder. The little old man looked at the pastor and calmly said, "Well, she's there."

39. Here lies the body of our Anna. Done to death by a banana. It wasn't the fruit that laid her low, but the skin of the thing that made her go.

40. Beneath this stone, a lump of clay, lies uncle Peter Daniels, who, too early in the month of May, took off his winter flannels.

41. Grim death took me without any warning. I was well at night and died in the morning.

42. Weep a bit for ZB Lott; he was lit his lights were not.

43. Here lies the body of Martha Dias, who was always messy and not over pious; she lived to the age of three score and ten and gave that to the worms she refused to men.

44. Here richly, with ridiculous display, the politician's corpse was laid away, which all of his acquaintances sneered and slanged. I wept, for I had longed to see him hanged.

45. Owen Moore has gone away, owing more than he could pay.

46. Re: young person: Came in, looked about, didn't like it went out.

47. He will not, whither he has now gone, find much difference, I believe, either the climate or the company.

48. Dentist: Stranger, approach this spot with gravity. John Brown is filling his last cavity.

49. Soldier: Confined in earth in narrow borders, he rises not until further orders.

50. Western: Here lies Wild Bill Britt, ran for sheriff in '82, ran from sheriff in '83, buried in '84.

51. Fisherman: He angled many a purling brook but lacked the angler's skill. He lied about the fish he took, and here he is lying still.

DEFINITIONS

1. Tuxedo—I won't say where I bought this tuxedo, but every time I lay it down, the arms fold.

2. Well-Bosomed Girl—It'll never work; she'll never get it off the ground.

3. Faculty—the people who get what's left, after the football coach received his salary.

4. Opera—where a guy gets stabbed and instead of bleeding, sings.

5. Hors d' oeuvres—a ham sandwich cut into a hundred pieces.

6. Nuclear waste—domain poisoning

7. What do you call a woman with one leg shorter than the other? Eileen.
    What do you call a Chinese woman with one leg shorter than the other? Irene.

8. What has seven teeth and an IQ of 40? The front row in a Willie Nelson concert.

9. What do you call a Mexican cowboy on a white horse? Roy Rodriguez.

10. Skiers anonymous: you have a craving to go skiing; you call and they send someone over to break your leg.

11. Smokers anonymous—have a craving to smoke; you call and they send someone over and you get drunk together.

12. Parent—a guy with snapshots in his wallet where he used to have money.

13. Bargain—an item you can't use at a price you can't resist.

14. The opera season is starting up again. You know what opera is—Italian vaudeville.

15. Mosquito—the original skin diver.

16. Optimist—someone who goes down to the city hall to find out when his marriage license expires.

17. Phony—someone who sends a post card with the message: "Enclosed please find check."

18. Female auto mechanic—tinker belle.

19. Home Sweet Home—where you can scratch where it itches.

20. This is a nonprofit organization. We didn't plan it that way, but that's the way it turned out.

21. World's Greatest Lie—I'm from the government, and I'm here to help.

22. Patience—losing your temper slowly.

23. Brain—an organ that starts working the moment you get up in the morning and does not stop until you get into the office.

24. Death—nature's way of telling us to slow down.

25. People Who Sell Perfume—people who are always sticking their business in your nose.

26. Temper—the weak person's imitation of strength.

27. Love—game at which two can play and both win.

28. Tennis—probably the only activity in which love means nothing.

29. Lawyer—the only person in whom ignorance of the law goes unpunished.

30. Lawsuit—Something no one wants to have and no one wants to lose.

31. Jury—twelve people who vote on who has the better lawyer.

32. Good Manners—being able to put up with bad ones.

33. Evolution—what Darwin has in common with Eve—making a monkey out of Adam.

34. Man—claims kinship with the apes while the apes make no such claim.

35. True Love—it's when my father takes out the garbage and my mother goes with him!

36. Conceit—God's gift to little men.

37. Old—forget to zip pants up

    Real Old—forget to zip them down.

38. Pessimist—a woman who thinks she can't park her car in a tiny space.

    Optimist—a man who thinks she won't try it.

39. Pessimist—One who doesn't waste time worrying because he knows everything will turn out wrong anyway.

40. Tolerance—the uncomfortable suspicion that the person you're talking to may be right.

41. Expert—a person who can take something you already know and make it sound confusing.

42. Pessimist—one who, when he has the choice of two evils, chooses both.

43. Pessimist—someone who can look at the land of milk and honey and see only calories and cholesterol.

44. Idealist—one who, on noticing that a rose smells better than a cabbage, concludes that it will also make better soup.

45. Classical music is the kind that we keep hoping will turn into a tune.

46. Leadership is not bestowed; it is yours only for as long as it is continuously earned.

47. Dilate: to live long

   Morbid: a higher offer
   Nitrate: lower than the day rate
   Node: was aware of
   Outpatient: a person who has fainted
   Postoperative: a letter carrier
   Urine: the opposite of "you're out"
   Varicose Veins: veins which are very close together

48. Pessimists—optimists with experience

50. "Extra" money is defined as that which you have in your possession just before the car breaks down.

51. "Maintenance free" usually means that when it breaks, it can't be fixed.

52. Lazy is doing so little that when you die, it's considered a lateral move.

53. Difference between asylum and a professional school. You must show measureable progress to be released from an asylum.

54. Opportunist—someone who took the chance while you were still making up your mind.

55. I finally figured out the difference between a *recession* and a *depression*. A recession is when your neighbor loses his job. A depression is when you lose your job.

56. Deja Voo—feeling you've heard that b. s. before.

57. Minister—flock watcher

58. Dieting—a system of starving yourself to death so you can live a little longer!

59. A proctologist stands behind his work.

60. Buffet Dinner—one where the guests outnumber the chairs.

61. Recession—when you get socks and underwear or handkerchiefs for Christmas.

62. Opera is where when somebody gets stabbed, instead of bleeding they sing.

63. A statesman is a politician who doesn't intend to run again.

64. *Potential* is a French word that means you aren't worth a damn yet.

65. Executive ability is a very special talent. It's knowing how to get credit for what others do.

66. Kennel—barking lot

67. Hopeless—like leaving the night-light on for Jimmie Hoffa

68. Cab Drivers—urban transportation specialists

69. Rubbish—postconsumer secondary materials

70. Potholes—pavement deficiencies

71. Afishionado—rod and reel enthusiast

72. Uppity Neighborhood—snub division

73. Patience is the ability to let your light shine after your fuse has blown.

74. Careful planning is what enables a man to put off doing a job until his wife forgets about it.

75. A wink—optical collusion

76. A pessimist mourns that he's over the hill. The optimist looks forward to being able to coast the rest of the way.

77. Nouns are all the things you want in life; verbs are what you have to do to get them.

78. Cross-pollination is what is carried on by ill-tempered bees.

79. Outpatient—a person who has fainted

80. Time's a versatile performer . . . it files, marches on, heals all wounds, runs out and will tell.

81. Bachelor—someone who is dedicated to life, liberty, and the happiness of pursuit.

82. Hammock—yawn and garden furniture

83. Hope has been described as the feeling you have that the feeling you have isn't permanent.

84. Bath mats are those rugs that little boys stand next to.

85. Gambling debt—a better not

86. Sunshine—delight of day

87. Monologue—conversation between husband and wife

88. Barbershop—hair-conditioned relief

89. A diet can be defined as a short period of starvation followed by a gain of five pounds.

90. Heredity might be called hand-me-down genes.

91. Nonchalant—the ability to look like an owl when you have just acted like a jackass.

92. Confidence is what you have before you really understand the problem.

93. A loser is a guy who burns his bridges ahead of him.

94. Habit is something you can do without thinking, which is why most of us have so many of them.

95. An efficiency expert is a man who comes into a company in the morning. On his desk is a molehill. He has to make a mountain out of it by five o'clock!

96. An incompetent interior decorator is rotten to decor.

97. Leadership—ability to hide your pain from others.

98. Politician—a person who gets sworn in and cursed out.

99. Persistence—is when you're willing to try anything twice.

100. An *optimist* is a father who will let his son take the new car on a date. A pessimist is one who won't. A cynic is one who did.

101. Redundancy—an air bag in a politician's car

102. A neurotic is a person who is self-employed and isn't able to get along with his boss.

103. Identity crisis. When you take your three kids to get a haircut and discover two of them are not yours.

104. Smile—sign of love and peace

105. MC—mental case

106. Television—a medium, so called, because it's neither rare nor well done. (Ernie Kovaks)

107. A mistake is just another way of doing things (good outlook).

108. BBC Diet—buy bigger clothes

109. Middle Age—when what sits on your knee isn't girls, it's your stomach.

110. A university is defined as thousands of people gathered around a common parking problem.

111. Square—the type who talks louder on long distance calls.

112. New mother—chief cook and bottom washer.

113. Smile—a carnation in the buttonhole of life.

114. Arrogance—the humility of the insecure.

115. Atheist—a man who has no invisible means of support. (J. Buchannan)

116. Baby—a loud noise on one end and no sense of responsibility on the other. (Ronald Knox)

117. Bachelor—a man who never makes the same mistake once. (Ed Wynn)

118. Bigamy—having one wife too many. Monogamy is the same thing.

119. Bank—a place where they lend you an umbrella in fair weather and ask for it back when it begins to rain. (Robert Frost)

120. Breeding—Good breeding consists in concealing how much we think of ourselves and how little we think of the other person. (Mark Twain)

121. Dancing—a perpendicular expression of a horizontal desire.

122. Democracy—a form of religion. It is the worship of jackals by jackasses. (H. L. Mencken)

123. Economy—cutting down other people's wages. (J.B. Morton)

124. Egotist—a person of low taste, more interested in himself than in me. (Ambrose Bierce)

125. Friendship—more tragic than love because it lasts longer. (O. Wilde)

126. Home—the place where when you have to go there, they have to take you in. (R. Frost)

127. Life—Life is rather like a tin of sardines where all of us is looking for the key. (Alan Bennet)

128. Moral indignation—jealousy with a halo. (H.G. Wells)

129. Optimist—a person who has not had much experience. (Don Marquis)

130. Optimist—a person who gets treed by a lion but enjoys the scenery. (W. Winchell)

131. Optimist—The optimist sees the doughnut, and the pessimist sees the hole.

132. Professor—one who talks in someone else's sleep. (W.H. Auden)

133. Diplomacy—the art of saying, "Nice doggie" till you can find a rock.

134. Wit—intellect on a spree

135. Worry—interest paid on trouble before it falls due. (D. Inge)

136. Divorce—a game played by lawyers. (Cary Grant)

137. Vegetarian—a person who will not eat anything that can have children. (D. Brenner)

138. Deficit—what you've got when you haven't got as much as you had when you had nothing.

139. Reformer—the kind of guy who would have you believe that he gave Eve back her apple.

140. Failure—is under no obligation to tell the truth.

141. Luck—waiting at the airport when your ship comes in.

142. Dead atheist—all dressed up and no place to go.

143. Pessimism means never having to be disappointed.

144. Patience—the ability to let your light shine after your fuse is blown.

145. Opera—the graveyard of melody.

146. Blushing—the complexion of virtue.

147. Optimist—someone who thinks the future is uncertain.

148. Confidence—going after Moby Dick in a rowboat with a harpoon and a jar of tartar sauce.

149. Acquaintance—a person whom we know well enough to borrow from, but not well enough to lend to.

150. Acquaintance—a degree of friendship called slight when its object is poor or obscure, and intimate when he is rich or famous.

151. Admiration—our polite recognition of another's resemblance to ourselves.

152. Alimony—when two people make a mistake and one of them continues to pay for it.

153. Love—an ocean of emotions entirely surrounded by expenses. (Lord Dewar)

154. Diplomat—a man who always remembers a woman's birthday but never her age. (Frost)

155. Eskimo—one of God's frozen children.

156. Matrimony—the process whereby love ripens into vengeance.

157. Professional—a person who can do his job even when he doesn't feel like it. Amateur—a person who can't do his job even if he does feel like it.

158. Education—when you read the fine print
Experience—what you get if you don't

159. Compromise—an arrangement whereby people who can't get what they want make sure nobody else does either.

160. Love—a temporary insanity curable by marriage. (Ambrose Bierce)

161. Flashlight—a case for holding dead batteries.

162. Vegetarian—an old Indian word meaning, "lousy hunter."

163. He believes a friend in need is a friend you stay away from.

164. A pessimist is seasick the entire voyage of life.

165. Sympathy means your pain in my heart.

166. Bravery is being the only one who knows you are afraid.

167. Edifice complex—fear of tall buildings.

168. Practical Nurse—one who marries a rich patient.

169. Square—a circle with corners.

170. Medicine ball—where doctors and nurses get together to dance.

171. Vertical—the same as horizontal, only just the opposite.

172. A fine is a tax for doing wrong. A tax is a fine for doing well.

173. Wedding ring—a one-man band.

174. Egotism—the anesthetic that dulls the pain of stupidity.

175. Counterfeiters—workers who put together kitchen cabinets.

176. Eclipse—what a barber does for a living.

177. Heroes—what a guy in a boat does.

178. Avoidable—what a bullfighter tried to do.

179. Bernadette—the act of torching a mortgage.

180. Arbitrator—a cook that leaves Arby's to work for McDonald's.

181. Synonym—a word you use when you can't spell the word you first thought of. (Burt Bacharach)

182. Monologue—a discussion between a man and wife.

183. Nudists—people who peel first and get sunburned afterward.

184. Tomorrow—the greatest labor-saving device today.

185. Failure—the opportunity to begin again more wisely.

186. Praise—the sweetest of all sounds.

187. Opera—where when a man gets stabbed instead of bleeding he sings.

188. Money—a terrible master but an excellent servant. (PT Barnum)

189. Nanosecond—the time that separates the graduation ceremony from the alumni association's first financial appeal.

190. Gamble—the odds are the same for winning the lottery whether you buy a ticket or not.

191. Alarm clock—a device for waking adults who have no babies.

192. Appeaser—one who feeds a crocodile hoping it will eat him last. (Churchill)

193. Committee—reminds you of a snowstorm—no two flakes alike.

194. Sympathy—what you give someone when you don't want to lend them money.

195. Block grant—a solid mass of money surrounded on all sides by governors.

196. Swan Lake—poultry in motion.

197. A comedian says things funny. A wit says funny things.

198. Dentist—one who owns a filling station.

199. Bureaucracy—the art of making the possible impossible.

200. Neurotic—one who builds a castle in the air. A psychiatrist is the one that collects the rent.

201. Love bird—tweetheart

202. Air pollution—sins of emission

203. Reducing—wishful shrinking

204. Redundancy—an air bag in a politician's car

205. Hatred—self-punishment

206. Committee; a cul-de-sac down which ideas are lured and then quietly strangled. (Sir B. Cocks)

207. Perfect man—a wife's first husband

208. Juvenile delinquent—other people's children

209. True love—friendship set on fire

210. Radical—anyone whose opinion differs radically from mine.

211. Accident—premeditated carelessness

212. Golf bag—an elderly female golfer

213. Convalescence—the period you are still sick after you get well.

214. Honesty—mostly the fear of being caught

215. Compliments—like perfume are to be inhaled, not swallowed

216. Desertion—the poor man's method of divorce.

217. Optimist—he who believes a housefly is looking for a way to get out.

218. Critic—a man who knows the way, but can't drive the car.

219. Death—nature's way of telling you to slow down.

220. Conscience—what makes you tell your wife before someone else does.

221. Conscience—the inner voice that warns us that someone is looking.

222. Middle age—when you start exchanging your emotions for symptoms.

223. Hiccups—messages from departed spirits

224. Avon lady—is a ding-a-ling

225. Hopeless—like rearranging the chairs on the *Titanic.*

226. Socialism—not the equal distribution of wealth, but the equal distribution of poverty

227. Diplomat—a man that can convince his wife she looks fat in a fur coat.

228. Alcoholic—someone you don't like that drinks as much as you do.

229. Crook—a business competitor who is doing well.

230. Minor operation—one that is performed on someone else.

231. Egotism—the art of seeing qualities in yourself, which others cannot see.

232. Inflation—when you are wealthy and can no longer afford the things you could when you were poor.

233. Egotist—a man who thinks he is everything you think you are.

234. High brow—a person educated beyond his own intelligence.

235. Gardener—a woman who loves flowers or a man that hates weeds.

236. Home—where we are treated the best and grumble the most.

237. Soap opera—singing in the bathtub

238. Father—a man who expects his son to be as good a man as he meant to be.

239. Siren—a signal used by police to warn burglars they are approaching.

240. Boy—a noise with some dirt on it.

241. Hollywood—an asylum run by inmates.

242. Hollywood—where the wedding cake outlasts the wedding

243. Mistake—evidence that someone has tried to do something

244. Modesty—The feeling that others will discover how wonderful you are.

245. Love—an ocean of emotion complete with gulls and buoys.

246. Love—the triumph of imagination over intelligence

247. Courage—is often just ignorance of the facts.

248. Goblet—a young turkey

249. Fjord—a Swedish automobile.

250. Autobiography—history of motor vehicles

251. Parasites—the inhabitants of Paris.

252. Selfish—what the owners of seafood stores do.

253. Rubberneck—what you do to relax your wife.

254. Relief—what trees do in the spring.

254. Avoidable—what a bullfighter tries to do.

255. Alimony—man's cash surrender value.

256. America—a country where they lock up the juries and let the defendants out.

257. Bigot—one who is obstinately and zealously attached to an opinion you do not entertain.

258. Budget—a method of worrying before you spend instead of afterward.

259. Collector—a man whom few care to see but many ask to call again.

260. Committee—a body that keeps minutes and wastes hours.

261. Conscience—the voice that tells you not to do something after you have done it.

262. Courtship—the period during which the girl decides whether or not she can do any better.

263. Detour—the roughest distance between two points.

264. Diplomat—a man who convinces his wife that a woman looks stout in a fur coat.

265. Echo—the only thing that can cheat a woman out of the last word.

266. Ego—the only thing that can keep on growing without any nourishment.

267. Egotist—a man who tells you those things about himself, which you intended to tell him about yourself.

268. Engagement—un war, a battle; in love, the salubrious calm that precedes the real hostilities.

269. Fame—chiefly a matter of dying at the right moment.

270. Friend—one who has the same enemies you do.

271. Honesty—fear of being caught.

272. Hug—a roundabout way of expressing affection.

273. Marriage is

   a.   the only sentence that is suspended by bad behavior
   b.   a rest period between romances

274. Matrimony—consists of romance, rice, and rocks.

275. Modern Age—when girls wear less on the street than their grandmother wore to bed.

276. Mosquito—a small insect designed by God to make us think better of flies.

277. Pessimist—an optimist who endeavored to practice what he preached.

278. Pessimist—one who, of two evils, chooses them both.

279. Pessimist—builds slums in the air.

280. Pessimist—one who has been intimately acquainted with an optimist.

281. Pessimist—when smelling flowers looks around for the funeral.

282. Pessimist—is always pulling tomorrow's cloud over today's sunshine,

283. Pessimist—complains about the noise when opportunity knocks.

284. Philanthropist—one who returns to the people publicly a small percentage of the wealth he steals from them privately.

285. Praise—what you receive when you are no longer alive.

286. Promoter—a man who will furnish the ocean if you will furnish the ships.

287. Prune—a plum that has seen better days.

288. Public Speaking—the art of diluting a two-minute idea with a two-hour vocabulary.

289. Radical—anyone whose opinion differs from yours.

290. Reputation—a personal possession frequently not discovered until lost.

291. Self-made man—a horrible example of unskilled labor.

292. Success—the one unpardonable sin against one's fellows.

293. Used car—not what it is jacked up to be.

294. Vulgarity—the conduct of others

295. Yawn—the only time some married men get to open their mouths

296. Wedding—a funeral where you smell your own flowers.

297. Worry—a state of mind that leads some people to fear every time the tide goes out that it won't come in again.

298. Wives—are young men's mistresses, companions for middle age, and old men's nurses. (Francis Bacon)

299. Heroes—what a guy in a boat does.

301. Laughter—the sun that drives winter from the human face. (Jason Kaufmann)

302. Smile—an assurance or a reassurance that everything is going to be OK.
    —will go a long way if you give it a good start. (C. McDonald)
    —the importance of the story is in the telling, not in the reading.

303. Eyedropper—a clumsy ophthalmologist.

304. Heroes—what a guy in a boat does.

305. Polarize—what penguins see with.

306. Relief—what trees do in the spring.

307. Rubberneck—what you do to relax your wife.

308. Selfish—what the owner of a seafood market does.

309. Sudafed—litigation brought against a government official.

310. Neurotic—a person who worries about things that didn't happen in the past—instead of worrying about something that won't happen in the future like normal people.

311. Irreconcilable difference—where she's melting down her wedding ring to cast into a bullet.

312. Affluent Polish family—one that can buy twice as much cockroach powder as the family next door.

313. Problem—the difference between where you are and where you would like to be.

DRINKING/GAMBLING

1. Bum asked the man for money to buy food. Man said, "I don't give money, but I will take you in the bar and buy you a drink." Bum said, "No, thank you I don't drink." So the man says, "Here take this package of cigarettes. I don't give money." Bum said, "No, sir, I don't smoke. I'm just hungry." "Well, the gentleman said, "let's go across the street and shoot some dice I will stake you." Again the bum refused when he told the man he did not gamble. So the gentleman invited him to his home for a huge steak. He said, "I want my wife to see what happens to a person that doesn't drink, smoke, or gamble."

2. He has been drunk only twice in his life. The last time was for eleven years.

3. Drunk walks into a bar and asks the bartender, "Was Ron in here about an hour ago?" Bartender said yes. Drunk said, "Was I with him?"

4. Drunk, quarter in parking meter, said, "My god I won an hour."

5. Bartender—make me a zombie. "I'm sorry I believe you have already beaten me to it."

6. I told my host I wanted something that was tall, cold, and full of booze so he brought out his wife.

7. Two drunks taking a shortcut through a cemetery became separated. One stumbled into a freshly dug grave. Pretty soon his friend came along and heard someone crying, only to discover the voice was coming from a grave.

"I'm cold, so cold, I'm freezing," said the voice.

"Well, no wonder," said the drunk. "You kicked all you dirt off, dummy."

8.   The way he drinks, he should be listed in Booze Who.

9.   I asked why Bob was so lucky at the card table and so unlucky at the races. Jim said, "That's simple—they won't let him shuffle the horses."

10. Tarzan came home in the afternoon and asked Jane for a triple Jack Daniels. He sat down and finished it off quickly and indirectly asked her for another . . . and another. Finally she got on his case about coming home every day and getting sloshed. "Jane, I can't help myself," Tarzan protested. "It's a jungle out there."

11. He knows a fellow who boozes it up somewhat, and what they call his condition around the office is "saloon arthritis." "Every night, he gets stiff in another joint."

12. A bum stops at a house to beg for food. The lady of the house says, "Why don't you go out and get a job?" The bum answers, "What for? To support a bum like me?"

13. A beggar meets another on Broadway. He asks, "Don't you usually go on Park Avenue?" The other answered, "I got married a month ago, and I gave my wife Park Avenue as a wedding present."

14. I've known a few drunks. I even knew one incredible drinker who received an honorary liquor license!

15. A man comes into a cafe and sits down in a corner. Seated at the long bar is another man who is belting pretty steadily. After the third drink, the belter falls backward and ends up on the floor. The man rushes to him, picks him up, and puts him back on the seat. Two sips later, the man falls again, and the Good Samaritan rushes to him again and puts him on the seat. The Good Samaritan does this four times, then says to the man, "You should go home. Tell me where you live and I'll take you." The barfly mumbles an address, but it's obvious that he's in no condition to walk there. The good soul carried him out of the car, puts

him in, and drives him to the house. He rings the bell. The wife opens the door, takes a look, and asks, "Where's his wheelchair?"

16. I have a friend who swears the Bible condones getting plastered: He who sins should be stoned!

17. Two men met at a hotel bar during a convention. Before the end of the night, they were buddies forever. They promised to meet again in the same bar exactly one year from that day. A year passed, and one of the men rushed into the bar to find his buddy there. He asked, "When did you get here?" The other man said, "Who left?"

18. I go in for nutritional drinking. I start each day with the juice from three martinis.

19. One basic difference between a drunk and an alcoholic—the drunk doesn't have to go the meetings!

20. A woman decides to frighten her husband out of drinking. She dresses up like the devil and waits for him at the door. When he pours himself in, she says, "Boo!" The man says, "Who are you?" The woman says, "I am the devil." The man says, "Shake hands. I married your sister!"

21. Two drunks saw a man siphoning gas from a car. One said to the other, "I hope I never get that thirsty!"

22. He drinks to pass the time. Last night he passed 2020!

23. I never knew he drank till I saw him sober!

24. He read about the evils of drinking, so he gave up reading!

25. If you can't drink and drive, why do bars have parking spaces?

26. She can't swim a stroke, but she knows every dive in town.

27. I proposed to Lil on hands and knees. She was under the table at the time.

28. He lights up a room by leaving it.

29. He stays longer in an hour than most people do in a week!

30. Dad never gets his suits cleaned. He has them distilled.

31. One day I was standing by the betting windows at the local racetrack, and I saw one fellow run up four times in a row to place heavy bets on a horse named Lucky Z. As he was coming back for another bet, an onlooker stopped him. "It isn't really any of my business, Mac," he said, "but I wouldn't bet anymore on Lucky Z. He isn't going to win the race." The better looked at him suspiciously and jerked. "What makes you think so?" "Well," the stranger replied, "I happen to own Lucky Z, and I know he isn't going to win the race." The other thought a moment and then said, "Well, maybe you're right, but all I can say is, it's going to be a mighty slow race—I own the other four horses."

32. Well, liquor-mortise has set in.

33. He also told me to drink a gallon of whiskey after a hot bath! Why he must be crazy! I couldn't even finish drinking the hot bath.

34. I drank so much water my stomach goes in and out with the tide.

35. He was asked to leave the bar—said he was getting ahead of the ice machine.

36. Went into a tough bar, asked the bartender, "What do you have on ice?" Bartender said, "Oh, you wouldn't know him".

37. Now they have a low-cal bourbon for fat drunks.

38. Yes, she always steps out as fit as a fiddle and comes home tight as a drum. suddenly drunk . . . suffering from a rare disease called Hague and Hague.

39. That's a wonderful description of martinis: sips that passion the night.

40. Two guys in a bar. One said, "I am really scared . . . got a letter from this man who said he'd break my legs if I didn't stop seeing his wife." Other guy said, "That's easy, just stay away from his wife." First guy said, "The problem is he didn't sign his name."

41. Advice—don't ever play poker with a man who has the first name of any city.

42. I'm not drinking, and unless you are, this is as good as I'm going to sound.

43. Mushroom went into a bar. Bartender said, "We don't serve mushrooms." Mushroom asked, "Why, I'm a fungi?"

44. I run this show with an iron hand. All I have to do is snap my fingers, and all the musicians come running. They think it's a crap game.

45. Did you hear the one about the poor kid who paid five dollars for a booklet called "How to Avoid the Draft?" And all it did was tell him to drink bottled beer.

46. I'll tell you how much he drank. This boy hasn't had a drink for over six months, and he's still got a hangover!

47. But he owes a lot to liquor. Why if it wasn't for martinis he never would have learned to eat olives.

48. Alcohol will preserve anything but a secret.

49. If it wasn't for the onions in the martinis, he'd starve to death.

50. He's going to the party in disguise—sober.

51. Her idea of a balanced diet is a drink in each hand.

52. They call him Cap because he's always attached to a bottle.

53. He thinks Beethoven's "Fifth" is a bottle of booze.

54. It's not true that he does nothing but drink—he also throws up.

55. They're calling him Dill—he's pickled so often.

56. He went to Alcoholics Anonymous because it sounded like a place where he could drink in secret.

57. He's the nicest chap on two feet if he could only stand up.

58. The only thing health means to him is something to drink to.

59. He tries to remain seated while the room is in motion.

60. Suffering from a huge hangover, W. C. Fields recoiled when a friend offered him a Bromo-Seltzer. "Good gods no! exclaimed the comedian. "I couldn't stand the noise."

61. I just had a great new idea for gardening . . . water your garden with whiskey and raise stewed tomatoes.

62. My brother-in-law came home drunk one time and walked into the closet and said, "Third floor, please."

63. Three drunks had a game they played every night at a local bar. They would sit and drink for a good while, then one would get up and leave the room. Then the other two would try to guess who left.

64. I'll never forget my dad's last words . . . "I don't see how they can make this liquor for only a dollar a gallon."

65. The captain of a ship once entered "Mate was drunk today" in the ship's log. When the mate slept it off, he was angry and embarrassed. He pleaded with the captain to strike the entry, saying that it was the first time it had happened, and that it would not happen again. But the captain refused and said, "We must always write the exact truth in the log." The next week the mate kept the log, and the first day, he entered, "Captain was sober today."

66. A man was arrested for feeding straight bourbon to his pet bird. He was charged with contributing to the delinquency of a mynah.

67. A young private watched an old sergeant on his way to the Noncommissioned Officers Club. "There," he observed, "goes a bottle-scarred veteran."

68. Drink? If at this moment he fell into a vat of whiskey, he'd raise its alcoholic content.

69. My aunt has come up with an interesting idea. She thinks they ought to put the pictures of missing husbands on beer cans.

70. Two women met at a health spa. One suggested going into the bar for a glass of wine. The other answered, "Thank you, but no."
"Don't you drink? the first asked.
"Well, not at home because I don't want to drink in front of the children. And when I'm away from them, I don't have to!"

71. A novice bridge player was set two on a contract that he should have made. He turned to the best player in the foursome and said, "How would you have played that last hand?" The man replied, "Under an assumed name."

72. Why beer is better than women: A beer won't get jealous when you grab another beer. When you go into a bar you can always pick up a beer. If you change beers you don't have to pay alimony. Your beer will wait patiently for you in the car when you play football. A beer won't get upset if you come home with another beer on your breath.

73. A little song dedicated to the $48 I lost playing bridge last night: "I Bid It My Way."

74. And then it happened! All I remember before they threw me out was that the girl sitting next to me asked me to hold onto her seat for a moment. "Well," she asked "me!"

75. Remember: If you drink, don't drive. And considering the oil spills, if you swim, don't smoke.

76. Red Adair, the oil rig firefighter, was relaxing at a Las Vegas lounge when a drunk came up to him and told him about the great shows he'd seen there.
"I really like Fig Newton," the drunk said. "You mean Wayne Newton," Adair corrected him.
"Yeah, I guess so," the drunk said. "And John Rivers is good too."
"That's not right," Adair corrected him. "That's Joan Rivers."
"Then there was Harry Lewis," the tipsy fellow intoned. "He was swell."
"You got it wrong, buddy, that's Jerry Lewis."

"By the way, buddy, I like you too. What's your name?"

"Red Adair."

"Really, that's who you are, the famous Red Adair?" the drunk said.

"That's me."

"Say, it really must have been great dancing with Ginger Rogers."

77. It is estimated that Americans spend over seven billion a year on games of chance, and that doesn't include elections and weddings. My friend said gambling brought him and his family closer together. He lost all of his money, and they had to move into one room together.

78. Neighbor lady: "I guess your husband will check the ads for bargains on beer." Wife: "I'm sure he will. He drinks so much beer that when he eats a pretzel you can hear it splash."

79. "One more thing," he said, "if you insist on drinking martinis at lunch, make it gin martinis, not vodka. I want the afternoon customers to know you're drunk, not stupid."

80. Wife reading news headline "Life Evolved from Smelly Bacteria, Scientists Assert" to husband in undershirt, beer in hand, watching TV: "Think of it, Ned, you may be the missing link."

81. I don't go out on New Year's Eve. Why should I spend that kind of money on things I don't even remember?

82. An Egyptian mummy strolled into a cocktail lounge, and the bartender asked what it would have. "Nothing," replied the mummy. "I just came in to unwind."

83. Gambler to another, "I haven't been very lucky at the casinos. Last week, I played twenty-one for eight straight hours and didn't get hit with a blackjack until I got to the parking lot!"

84. And then there was the nightclub so dark, the check was in braille.

85. There is a new kind of wine called post office red. You mail five pounds of grapes in a container and mark it Fragile.

86. I'm pushing a new health drink, a double scotch on the rocks. But you stir it with a celery stick.

87. A man told his friend about a recent dream, "I dreamed that I was gambling at the Lido in Venice. I was breaking the bank." His friend said, "That's a nice dream. Let me tell you about the one I had last night. I was on the Riviera with three stunning women."

    The first man asked, "Why didn't you call me?"

    The friend said, "I did. Your answering service said you were in Venice."

88. He is an outstanding candidate for the alcohol of fame.

89. W. C. Fields said New Year's Eve is amateur's night.

90. Then there's the gent who'd been out all night with the fellows. At dawn, he poured himself into the house and said, "Honey, I hope you didn't pay the ransom!"

91. He experienced a bomb scare last week. He got bombed and was scared to go home.

92. If it wasn't for his red nose, his bloodshot eyes, and his stagger, you would never know he is an alcoholic.

93. Man drank a whole glass of gasoline instead of whisky. Instead of giving him the hiccups, it gave him the honks.

94. Wife, on telephone, to husband: "Fred, I want you to stop in a bar and have a couple of quick ones. I'll tell you why when you get home."

95. George Gobel: "You can get just as drunk on water as you can on land."

96. Two drunks at the Washington Monument. One of them lit a fire. The other one said, "Man, you're never going to get that thing off the ground."

97. A man, obviously in bad condition from the night before, stepped up to the bar and sputtered through trembling lips, "Give me something for a hangover, please . . . something tall, cold, and full of gin."

    "Sir," snapped a drunk, who was standing next to him, "you are referring to the woman I love."

98. Dean Martin doesn't drink liquor anymore. He drinks Windex. It gives him a terrible hangover, but his eyes are so clear.

99. He entered the bar optimistically and left misty optically.

100. Asked why he had raised the price of his corn liquor, the moon shiner replied, "It is a vintage ear."

101. He's been drinking all his life. In college, he was voted the most likely to dissolve.

102. A man and his wife are in Las Vegas. The man is berating his wife. "You lost a $100. How could you be so stupid?" "You lost $200 on the crap tables last night," she answered. He responded, "Yes, but I know how to gamble."

103. For a hangover, take the juice of two quarts of whiskey.

104. Putting money in a slot machine and pulling the handle down is the same motion you use to flush.

105. I don't know how much he spends on whiskey, but it is a staggering amount.

106. Drink? His idea of frozen food is scotch on the rocks.

107. 'Twas a woman who drove me to drink, and I never had the courtesy to thank her for it. (W. C. Fields)

108. Inflation has gone up more than a dollar a quart. (W C Fields)

109. I haven't touched a drop of alcohol since the invention of the funnel. (M McCourt)

110. Re: Drunk—well, if it isn't the Bourbonic plague.

111. He's sort of an alcoholic do-it-yourself man. All day long he wanders around the house fixing things—highballs, martinis, old fashions.

112. Drink? He spends $25 a week on salted peanuts alone.

113. She came in as a lush redhead; she left as a red-headed lush.

114. It's a place with crooked gambling and watered liquor, where the customers will never get as loaded as the dice.

115. My dad is as straight and tall as a rifle and just as loaded.

116. At 3:00 AM, he made a big wide circle into the driveway and knocked the hinges off the garage door—good thing he wasn't driving.

117. Man in a bar noticed peanuts in a bowl next to him. He helped himself several times when he realized the peanuts belonged to an elderly lady sitting next to him. Not realizing they belonged to her, he apologized profusely. The old lady said, "That's all right, sonny. With my teeth the way they are about, all I can do is suck the chocolate off of them."

118. Some contemptible scoundrel stole the cork from my lunch.

119. I went into a tough neighborhood bar and asked them what they had on ice. The bartender said, "Oh, you wouldn't know him."

120. First tramp: "What would you do if you won the lottery?" Second tramp: "I'd have the park benches reupholstered."

121. A skeleton walks into a bar and says, "I'd like a beer and a mop."

122. A baby seal walked into a bar. The bartender asked what he would like to have. The seal said, "Anything but a Canadian club."

123. I wanted to get him a gift he would enjoy, but how do you wrap up a saloon?

124. A drunk walked up to a parking meter and put in a quarter. The dial went to sixty. He said, "How about that? I lost one hundred pounds."

125. It is hard to reevaluate your priorities when the only ones you have are beer and baseball.

126. Bill comes tiptoeing into the house at 4:00 AM. His wife asks, "Is that you Bill?" He mumbles, "It better be."

127. This grasshopper walks into a bar and the bartender says, "Hey, we have a drink named after you." The grasshopper replies, "Really? You have a drink named Steve?"

128. I don't want to say he drinks a lot, but for years he thought the curb was a pillow.

129. There is a drink called summer vacation. Two drinks and school is out.

130. He hasn't had a drink since the invention of the funnel.

131. They had a bomb scare in his office. Actually he got bombed and was scared to go home.

132. His neighbors think he is a detective because the cops are always bringing him home.

133. We knew he had a problem when his doctor gave him a prescription to help him stop drinking, and he used it for a coaster.

134. Definition: Frankenstein—a hot dog and a mug of beer

135. My eight-year-old son saw me getting into my tux and said, "Dad, why do you always wear that suit? It always gives you such a headache in the morning.

136. I don't go out on New Year's Eve. Why should I spend that kind of money on things I don't even remember?

137. The answer to this question will determine whether or not you are drunk. Was Mickey Mouse a cat or a dog?

138. Oh! I can't drink these days. I am allergic to alcohol and narcotics. If I use them I break out in handcuffs. (Martin Downey Jr.)

139. W. C. Fields said if he had his life to live over he'd, live over a saloon.

140. The closest he ever came to a 4.0 in school was his blood/alcohol content.

141. He would give you the floor off his back.

142. He only drinks to forget. Last night he forgot how to stand up.

143. A man and a woman are standing at a cocktail party when the woman remarked, "You know, you look just like my third husband." Really?" he said. How many times have you been married? She said, "Twice."

144. He has pictures of himself plastered all over one wall of his office. He has pictures of himself sober on another wall.

ENTERTAINMENT

Song Titles, Verses, etc.

1. Don't put on your swimsuit, Mom, it's not that kind of dive.

2. I'm so miserable without you; it's almost like having you here.

3. I'm dancing with tears in my eyes 'cause the girl in my arms is my brother.

4. How can I miss you if you won't go away.

5. You're the reason our kids are so ugly, little darling.

6. We were all out of firewood, and Dad came home with a load.

7. If your phone don't ring, you'll know it's me.

8. You spread your love around like peanut butter, and now you're in a jam.

9. You done stomped on my heart and smashed that sucker flat.

10. Seven times married, six times divorced—if this don't work I'll stick to my horse.

11. What do you get when you play a country record backward? You get your girl back, your dog back, and your pickup back.

12. Losing the love of your life can be harder than scraping burnt grits off an old frying pan.

13. You can have my husband, but don't mess with my man.

14. I'm the only hell my mother ever raised.

15. I'm just a Monday person in a Friday world.

16. I bought the shoes that just walked out on me.

17. Get your tongue out of my mouth; I'm kissing you good-bye.

18. Button up your overcoat, someone just stole your pants.

19. Mother, please don't point Father at me; he might be loaded again

20. Go into the roundhouse, Nellie, he can't corner you again.

21. You must have been built in Detroit City 'cause someone recalled your heart.

22. How could a twelve-year-old whiskey wrap a man of thirty-four?

23. If you don't believe I love you, just ask my wife.

24. Egypt must be heaven 'cause my mummy came from there.

25. My whiskey and her perfume formed a deadly combination.

26. I don't like remembering the things I can't forget.

27. I was solo till I met you, but now we duet together.

28. I play the jukebox to remember what I'm drinking to forget.

29. Oh, I can write them country songs I do it all the time. The only thing, my rhythm's off, and they don't always rhyme.

30. You pulled the plug on my bathtub of love. Lines: Your lies were like the hair that you let clog my pipes. Your cheating was like the bathroom mold that grows in the night.

31. She got the gold mine, I got the shaft.

32. My son calls another man "Daddy."

33. I was bred in old Kentucky, but I'm just a crumb up here.

34. You flushed me from the bathroom of your heart.

35. She said she wanted to stroke my hair, but it was really my scalp she was after.

36. She wanted to sow some wild oats, so I started her off on rye.

37. She was going to have her face lifted, but she didn't have the jack.

38. Life is a cow, let's milk it together.

39. If there is a woman for every man, baby, how come I got you?

40. I got to first base with my girlfriend, but they threw me out at home.

41. I had an apartment in front, and she had a flat behind.

42. Don't go in the stable, Grandma, you're too old to be horsing around.

43. Don't throw that clock at Father, Mother. It's only a waste of time.

44. I can't get over a girl like you, so get up and answer the phone.

45. I'd like to be a cake of soap in Betty Grable's bathtub.

46. You can't have your Kate and Edith too.

47. Just makin' love don't make it love.

48. You're going to ruin my bad reputation.

49. Sleeping single in a double bed.

50. The pint of no return.

51. Your negligee has turned to flannel nightgowns.

52. The wife of the party.

53. Would Jesus wear a robe on his television show?

54. I'd rather have a bottle in front of me than a frontal lobotomy.

55. You're out doing what I'm here doing without.

56. You blacked my blue eyes once too often.

57. Now I lay me down to cheat.

58. I've been roped and thrown by Jesus in the Holy Ghost Corral.

59. Get your biscuits in the oven and your buns in the bed.

60. She gave her heart to Jethro and her body to the whole danged world.

61. I've got you on my conscience, but at least you're off my back.

62. Does my ring hurt your finger (When you go out at night?)?

63. The zipper's always open on the trousers of my heart.

64. We used to just kiss on the lips, but now it's all over.

65. I don't know whether to kill myself or go bowling.

66. Get out of the wheat field, brother, you're running against the grain."

67. My wife just ran away with my best friend, and I miss him.

68. My wife stole my mistress, and my girlfriend's upset.

69. Personally, I think the band's improved tremendously. You can tell when they're tuning up now.

70. Did you hear about the rock-and-roll singer who wore a hearing aid for three years then found out he only needed a haircut?

71. Did you ever get the feeling that with some colleges, their team ought to march and their band ought to play?

72. What makes Wyatt Earp?

73. I hit her with my putter 'cause she really teed me off.

74. I'm married to my semi, and semi-married to you.

75. You said bless your heart, but it was my liver that needed help.

76. The marines called her apple 'cause she was good to the corps.

77. It's heaven in your arms, baby, but please put me down or I'll be late for work.

78. Then there was the dumb musician who didn't know his brass from his oboe.

79. How come my dog don't bark when you come around?

80. When my love returns from the ladies' room, will I be too old to care?

81. Millions of dollars are used on opera each year which could be used in abolishing it.

82. The dance scene is getting wilder. At one club, they've had to ban premarital dancing!

83. It's hard to describe today's music, but the other day, I was in a restaurant where a waiter dropped a tray of dishes, and six people got up to dance.

84. Classical music is the kind we keep thinking will turn into a tune. (Kin Hubbard)

85. How do you mend a broken everything?

86. Knock, knock, knockin' on the bathroom door.

87. Nowadays, whatever is not worth saying is sung.

88. I put a nickel in the slot machine of love and got a lemon.

89. Happiness is seeing Lubbock, Texas, in the rearview mirror.

90. Rock music: Hear today, deaf tomorrow. (Leo Rosten)

91. Rock and roll might be summed up as monotony tinged with hysteria. (V. Packard)

92. Rock 'n' roll is the most brutal, ugly, degenerate, vicious form of expression it has been my displeasure to hear. It fosters almost totally negative and destructive reactions in young people. It is sung, played, and written for the most part by cretinous goons; and by means of its almost imbecilic reiterations and sly, lewd—in plain fact—filthy lyrics, it manages to be the martial music of every side-burned delinquent on the face of the earth. (Frank Sinatra)

93. Do you ever paint in the nude? No, I usually wear a smoking jacket.

94. Why did they hang that picture? Probably because they couldn't find the artist.

95. An "impressionist" painter was confined to the insane asylum. To all visitors he says, "Look here at my latest masterpiece." They look and see nothing but a large black canvas. They ask, "What does this represent?"

    "That? Why that represents the passage of the Jews through the Red Sea."

    "But where is the sea?"

    "It has been driven back."

    "And where are the Jews?"

    "They have crossed over."

    "And the Egyptians?"

    "They'll be here soon. That's the sort of painting I like—simple, suggestive, and unpretentious."

96. Now I know why they call it the television ratings war. You turn on your set, and it's one bomb after another.

97. Hollywood may call them X-rated, but I call them crossword puzzle movies. In the first scene, they're vertical, and for the rest of the picture, they come across.

98. I went to one of those new movies last week that was so bloody that it was rated O positive.

99. You won't believe how old my television set is. On the back, there's a little plate that says Made in.

100. There's a new movie called *Silence of the Bran Flakes*. It's about a cereal killer.

101. Time to take seriously a news bulletin: when or if they ever interrupt a commercial to issue it.

102. Soap operas prove it takes some women two years to have a premature baby.

103. This season's new promos remind me that never before has so much been said to so many so often about so.

104. TV soap opera—an alcoholic, murderer, two-timing husband, an embezzler, a bigamist, a teenager on drugs, a rapist, an unfaithful wife, an unmarried mother. It's called "Just Plain Folks."

105. Re: Special newsbreaks on TV networks. They have to preempt their regularly scheduled violence.

106. Movies are a fad. Audiences really want to see live actors. (Charlie Chaplin)

107. Forget it, Louie. No civil war picture ever made a nickel. (Irving Thalberg to Louis B. Mayer in *Gone with the Wind*)

108. The movie *King Kong* has been an awe-inspiring figure for people all over the world except for certain neighborhoods in Chicago where he's considered effeminate.

109. A commercial showed Venus de Milo, and the announcer said, "See what happens when you use too strong a detergent?"

110. For years television programs have been made for twelve-year-olds, but now you have to ask, "A twelve-year-old what?"

111. This may be hard to believe, but I saw a movie on TV that was so old, the girl said no.

112. X-rated movies and westerns have one thing in common—they never have to stop to reload.

113. Calling TV entertainment is like calling falling off a cliff transportation.

114. Lewis Grizzard's book title *Don't Bend over in the Garden, Granny.* Them taters got eyes.

115. Interviewer to Mel Gibson: "You have been accused of vulgarity." Mel: "Bullshit."

116. My wife took everything but the blame.

117. "Now that you have heard my voice, what would you suggest to accompany me?" the singer asked. The impresario replied, "A bodyguard."

118. I'm just a bug on the windshield of life.

119. They may put me in prison, but they can't keep my face from breaking out

120. Sign in a window: Piano for Sale

    Sign in window next door: Hurrah!

121. How do you mend a broken everything?

122. Just because you got to first base don't mean you are home free.

123. "When you're swimming in a creek and an eel bites your cheek, that's a moray!" (Dean Martin)

124. To qualify as a rock-and-roll singer, you have to take a scream test.

125. Did you hear that Willie Nelson got hit by a car? He was playing "On the Road Again."

126. Willie Nelson—on the commode again

127. Discourage inbreeding—ban country music

128. I fell in a pile of you and got love all over me.

129. I know a girl who plays the piano by ear. That's nothing. I know a man that fiddles with his fingers.

130. When I'm alone, I'm in bad company.

131. Mama gets the hammer. There's a fly on Papa's head.

132. Aren't these music videos wonderful? Just think. Now punk rock can do for your eyes what it has done for your ears.

133. The filth they are selling as music today is not really music. It's just a guy with a deep voice saying a lot of dirty words while somebody beats on a barrel with a two iron and somebody else kills a cat in the backyard.

134. Two members of the Wayne State men's choir were discussing the range of the new baritone. "Does he have a loud voice?" one asked. "Well," replied the other, "he's the only baritone around who ever sang 'Chloe' and got an answer."

135. She got the ring and I got the finger.

136. I keep forgetting I forgot about you.

137. I would have written you a letter, but I couldn't spell *yeck*.

138. While I was out getting hammered, she was out getting nailed.

139. It's hard to get you off my mind when you are always in my face.

140. I've got the hungries for your love, and I'm waiting in your welfare line.

141. If I can't be number 1 in your life, then number 2 on you.

142. Drop-kick me Jesus through the goalposts of life.

143. She's got freckles on her, but she is pretty.

144. When you leave, walk out backward so I will think you are walking in.

145. She's looking better after every beer.

146. I still miss you baby, but my aim is getting better.

147. I sold my car to a guy who stole my girl, but it doesn't run, so I guess we are even

148. I haven't gone to bed with an ugly woman, but I've sure woke up with a few.

149. I poured spot remover on my dog. Now he is gone.

150. I'm just a bug on the windshield of life.

151. Revised hymns for the old folks

Blessed Insurance
Just a Slower Walk with Thee
Give Me That Old-Timer's Religion
Nobody Knows the Trouble I Have Seeing
It Is Well with My Soul (But My Back Hurts)
Go Tell It on the Mountain (And Please Speak Up)
Precious, Lord, Take My Hand (And Help Me Get Up)
Count Your Many Birthdays, Name Them One by One
Guide Me Oh Thou Great Jehovah (I've Forgotten Where I Parked)
Amazing Grace (Considering My Age)

152. Hymns for all things

The Dentist's Hymn—Crown Him with Many Crowns
The Weatherman's Hymn—There Shall Be Showers of Blessings
The Contractor's Hymn—The Church's One Foundation
The Tailor's Hymn—Holy, Holy, Holy
The Golfer's Hymn—There's a Green Hill Far Away
The Politician's Hymn—Standing On the Promises
The Optometrist's Hymn—Open My Eyes That I Might See

The IRS Agent's Hymn—I Surrender All
The Gossip's Hymn—Pass It On
The Electrician's Hymn—Send the Light
The Shopper's Hymn—Sweet By and By
The Realtor's Hymn—I've Got a Mansion Just Over the Hilltop
The Massage Therapist's Hymn—He Touched Me
The Doctor's Hymn—The Great Physician
And for those who speed on the highway, here are a few hymns
45mph—God Will Take Care of You
>>>55mph—Guide Me, O Thou Great Jehovah
65mph—Nearer My God to Thee
>>>75mph—Nearer Still Nearer . . .
>>>85mph—This World Is Not My Home
>>>95mph—Lord I'm Coming Home
Over 100 mph—Precious Memories

153. A young American singer making his bow at La Scala was flattered when the discerning Italian audience forced him to return and sing an aria for the fourth time. Completely winded, he finally begged off, saying it was physically impossible to sing it a fifth time. A voice boomed from the gallery: "You'll keep on singing until you sing it right."

154. The Top Country and Western Horror Movies

Achy, Breaky Telltale Heart
Nightmare on Rural Route One, Up Past That There Silo
Ah Seen What Y'all Done Last Summer
The Creature from Clint Black's Spittoon
Don't Tell Me You Love Me If You're Gnawing Off My Leg
Night of the Homosekshual, BMW-Drivin, Neiman Marcus
    Suit-Wearin' Zombies
Jurassic Trailer Park
Psychoklohoma
The Hound Dog of the Baskervilles
All My Axes Are in My Exes
The Expectorist
She Broke My Heart and Then She Ate It

155. Things you would never know without the movies

It is always possible to park directly outside any building you are visiting.

A detective can only solve a case once he has been suspended from duty.

If you start dancing in the street, everyone you bump into will know the steps.

Laptop computers are powerful enough to override the communication systems of any invading alien civilization.

It doesn't matter whether you are heavily outnumbered in a fight involving martial arts; your enemies will wait patiently to attack you one by one by dancing around in a threatening manner until you have knocked out their predecessors.

Police departments give their officers personality tests to make sure they are deliberately assigned a partner who is their total opposite.

You can always find a chainsaw when you need one.

One of a pair of identical twins is evil.

Should you decide to defuse a bomb, don't worry about which wire to cut. You will always choose the right one.

During all crime investigations, it is necessary to visit a strip club at least once.

Honest and hardworking policemen are usually gunned down a day or two before retirement.

Should you wish to pass yourself off as a German officer, it is not necessary to speak the language. A German accent will do.

It is easy to land a plane providing there is someone in the control tower to talk you down.

You are very likely to survive any battle in any war unless you make the mistake of showing someone the picture of your sweetheart back home.

156. A hippie was lying all sprawled out over the seat in the movies. The usher came down and told him he would have to move or he would call the police. The hippie just lay there. Finally, the usher asked, "Where did you come from, fellow?" The hippie looked up and said, "The balcony."

FOOD

1. If you want to look thin, run around with fatter people.

2. Fat man got on a scale and a ticket came out which said, "Come back in fifteen minutes—alone."

3. If you get on an elevator with me, you had better be going down.

4. When I wear a white suit, they use me to show home movies.

5. Caught pneumonia standing in front of the refrigerator door

6. "Mom, I'm trying to find myself."

    Mom: "Look over by the refrigerator."

7. Only thing that loses weight in our house is the refrigerator.

8. Always wear a tie the color of the main course.

9. He loves to eat so much; when he dies he wants to be cremated and his ashes put into a dip.

10. If you think PR doesn't work, think of the millions of people that think yogurt tastes good.

11. Politically correct for fat man: he has an alternative body image.

12. Miss Piggy: "Never eat more than you can lift."

13. Never prepare anything that takes longer to cook than to eat.

14. He's so fat—he's my two best friends.

15. It's time to start a diet when your designer jeans develop stretch marks, you stop running and parts of you keep moving, one-size-fits-all doesn't fit you, a full-length mirror doesn't show the full width, you start hating skinny people, your refrigerator door gets more exercise than you do.

16. My neighbor Wolfgang says he stopped watching golf on TV because his doctor recommended more exercise. Now he watches tennis.

17. He's so fat when he gets a shoe shine he has to take the guy's word for it.

18. She always tried to conceal her height by subtle little devices. She wore flat heels and walked on her knees.

19. When it came to testifying in a divorce court, the judge placed the wife on the stand and started to ask her questions. It went like this:

Judge: "Do you have grounds?"
Wife: "Only a half an acre."
Judge: "Do you have a grudge?"
Wife: "No, sir, a carport.
Judge: "Does your husband beat you up?"
Wife: "No, I'm up a half hour before him."
Judge: "Then why do you want a divorce?"
Wife: "Because we can't communicate."

20. Guy said he just lost 120 pounds sent his wife home to his mother.

21. Have you ever noticed that the second day of a diet is usually easier than the first? Mostly because you're off of it by then.

22. An annoyed lady said, "Are you sure you're the same waiter I gave my order to? Somehow I expected a much older man."

23. Keep your city clean—eat a pigeon.

24. Why don't cannibals eat clowns? Because they taste funny.

25. Service in that restaurant is terrible, but you don't mind the wait cause the food is so poor.

26. I've eaten so many TV dinners, every time I see aluminum foil I get hungry.

27. "Waiter, this coffee tastes like mud."

   "Of course it does, it's fresh ground."

28. Then I worked on a garbage truck for the Department of Sanitation. It's $30 a week and all I could eat.

29. My cooking is not so good; last Christmas my family gave me an oven that flushes.

30. I always eat fish because it's brain food. Of course it's not the only brain food. There's noodle soup.

31. A cattleman from Dallas, Texas, once came up with a solution to end his industry's problems. "Everybody run over a chicken," he said.

32. The turkey tonight is just great. In fact, I'd like to ask the chef just one question. What did you stuff it with—old menus?

33. Did you hear the one about the reducing salon that advertises: REAR TODAY—GONE TOMORROW?

34. Hungry? This kid eats like a babysitter.

35. As the papa cannibal said to the baby cannibal: "How many times have I told you not to talk with someone in your mouth?"

36. Well, feed me garlic and call me Stinky.

37. Crossed a potato with a sponge—tastes terrible but sure holds a lot of gravy.

38. We need each other, we tie each other's shoes.

39. He's so desperate, he shaves before weighing himself on the bathroom scale.

40. African hunters come all the way to her house to dip their arrows in her cooking.

41. His idea of weight lifting is standing up.

42. A waiter approached a diner and said, "May I help you with the soup, sir?"

    "What do you mean, help me," said the diner. "I don't need any help."
    "Oh, pardon me, sir," the waiter replied. "From the sound, I though you might want to be dragged ashore."

43. The headwaiter at a posh New York restaurant was appalled when a diner sat down and wrapped a napkin around his neck. The headwaiter called to a waiter and ordered him to notify the customer of his breach of etiquette. Without batting an eye, the waiter walked over to the offender, bowed, and said quietly, "Sir, will you have a shave or a haircut?"

44. Eat? Last week they had to rush him to a doughnut abuse center.

45. I'm not much of a cook. My way of helping out in the kitchen is to stay in the dining room.

46. I asked a friend if he was going to the luau. He asked, "That's all you can Eat, isn't it? I said yes. He said, "Naw I'm not going I can't eat that much."

47. Don't eat anything that multiplies in your refrigerator.

48. Personally, I'm always a little suspicious of people who spend all their time exercising. I've always had the suspicion that push-ups are nothing but sex without a partner.

49. They had another sign that read, "If you want to put your ashes and cigarette butts in your cup and saucer, let the waiter know, and he will serve the coffee in an ashtray."

50. Made a talk in San Angelo and told the waitress I was tired of beef and asked if she had any fresh seafood. She said, "We sure do—we fly it in from Amarillo every day."

51. Eat? This man has a six-room house, and three of them are kitchens.

52. Tough? We're talking about a man who can overcome, outwit, and outmaneuver any diet.

53. We're talking about the only Harvard man I know who got his letter in the cafeteria.

54. "Don't eat so much," said the father to his spitting image. "You'll make a pig of yourself. Do you know what a pig is?" "Yes, Daddy," replied the son. "It's a hog's little boy."

55. "Doesn't my cooking just melt in your mouth?" the young bride asked her husband. "Yes," he answered, "it does. Maybe you could try thawing it out a little more?"

56. "Do you want these eggs turned over?"
"Yeah, to the Museum of Natural History."

57. "And how did you find your steak, sir?"
"I just moved a potato, and there it was."

58. She has an injunction against her preventing her from wearing stretch pants in the city limits.

59. My wife is overweight because of the Noah problem. Every time she sits down to eat, she takes two of everything.

60. Stop me if I'm wrong, but I always thought fast food was prunes.

61. Out to lunch one day, the immigrants were having a fine time until Hymie began to gag. "I . . . I tink I svallowed a bone," Hymie gasped.

    "Hymie, are you choking?"
    "No, demmit, I'm serious!"

62. Fat? The light of her life was the one in the refrigerator.

63. Eat? One time I took her to a Chinese restaurant, gave her chopsticks, and she started two fires!

64. Sign on Spa: "Are you fat and ugly? Do you want to be just ugly? Memberships available now!"

65. Fat? I'll never forget what she wore on the third finger of her left hand—her watch!

66. Have you tried McDonald's new low-fat burger? The McLean? They left out the McTaste.

67. I'm happy to announce I quit smoking. In fact, this is my anniversary. I gave it up exactly twenty pounds ago.

68. I have to cut down on hot dogs and beer. I'm starting to get a ballpark figure.

69. I don't trust the restaurant at this hotel. While ordering, I asked the waiter, "What would you recommend?" He named three other restaurants.

70. The staff at this restaurant loves a challenge . . . like a request for a clean water glass.

71. I asked the waiter what the specialty of the day was. He said, "The Heimlich Maneuver."

72. I tried Slim Fast. But with my willpower, they should have named it Slim Chance.

73. I don't want to say my mother-in-law's a bad cook, but in her house, "leftovers" doesn't mean food, it means survivors.

74. Too many square meals will give you a round body.

75. He went on a liquid diet. He lost eighty pounds and his driver's license.

76. Diet tips:

a. If no one sees you eat it, it has no calories.
b. If you drink a diet soda with a candy bar, they will cancel each other out.
c. If you eat in the closet, calories don't count.
d. Food taken for medicinal purposes does not count. This includes hot chocolate, brandy toasts, Sara Lee chocolate cakes.

77. A lot of people aren't aware that for the best Chinese cook, two chefs usually work together. One does the ingredient preparation that requires so much careful cutting and chopping while the other does the actual stir-frying. Hence, we have the expression "You'll never wok alone."

78. Buffet Dinner: one where the guests outnumber the chairs.

79. The first thing you have to do on an organized weight-loss program is weigh in on one of those merciless doctor's scales. Let's face it: you have your scale at home pretty much trained. You know exactly where to stand to shave a few pounds. In fact, I find that if you hang onto the shower curtain, you can make that needle come to rest pretty much anywhere you please.

80. To save money in a restaurant, say to her, "What will you have, chubby?"

81. The worse the restaurant, the bigger the pepper mill.

82. Why is it that when someone tastes something bad, they immediately want you to taste it?

83. What do you get when you cross a turkey with a kangaroo? You get a turkey that can be stuffed from the outside.

84. When you reheat TV dinners, it is called reruns.

85. He was so fat he fell down and rocked himself to sleep trying to get up.

86. Two women, having lunch in a fancy restaurant, were presented a menu by a waiter, who said, "Let me recommend our special, the tongue sandwich." One woman said, "Heavens no! I'd never eat anything that came out of the mouth of an animal! Just bring me a soft-boiled egg."

87. During a semester break, a girl invited her boyfriend to a home-cooked meal, an invitation eagerly accepted. At dinner, he was soon into his third large helping while everyone watched in amazement. After the fourth plateful, he complimented the hostess on her cooking. Then noticing the dessert fork next to his plate, he asked, "What's this fork for?" Without hesitation, the girl answered, "That's in case the first one wears out."

88. Diet

    Breakfast:
    1/2 grapefruit, 1 slice whole wheat bread, 8 oz. skim milk

    Lunch:
    4 oz. broiled chicken breast, 1 cup steamed Zucchini, 1 Oreo cookie, tea

    Dinner:
    Rest of Oreo package, One qt. Rocky Road ice cream, large pepperoni pizza, pitcher of beer, 3 candy bars, frozen cheesecake, eaten from freezer

89. His wife cooks religiously. Everything she serves is either a burnt offering or a sacrifice.

90. If a man can't do simple arithmetic, he can always be a waiter in a restaurant.

91. Proper diet—triumph of mind over platter

92. Whoever invented pasta really used their noodle.

93. He was like my uncle Max who stopped drinking coffee because it kept him awake all day.

94. Lil went to Pier 21 and ordered the catch of the day. She got hepatitis (true).

95. Tarzan and Jane were getting along swell. The only thing bothering Jane was the sameness of everything in the jungle. She was getting tired of it. "Tarzan, why don't you run out to one of those new McCoconuts

places for some fast food tonight," Jane said. "I think one just opened not too far from here."

"What Jane wants?" Tarzan says.

"Oh, anything at all, Tarzan. Surprise me."

So Tarzan grabbed a vine and off he went. After a while, she heard his famous yell as he swung through the trees. She went out onto the porch of their tree house, and there was Tarzan. He had a cage full of birds under one arm and a gang of monkeys under the other.

"Oh, Tarzan, not finch and chimps again," Jane asked.

96. He is such a bad cook he won't even lick his own fingers.

97. He was so skinny if he turned sideways he was marked absent.

98. The food here is terrible, and the portions are too small. (Woody Allen)

99. They serve Paul Revere pizza—guaranteed to wake you up in the middle of the night.

100. Most people eat the three basic food groups—canned, frozen, and takeout.

101. Muscles come and go . . . flab lasts.

102. I was so fat I had to have my own zip code.

103. What makes the Tower of Pisa lean? The real reason is it doesn't eat spaghetti.

104. You Know You Need to Lose Some Weight:

   1. When you rent a canoe, and they put large weights at the opposite end of the boat to balance it.
   2. When you take a trip to the zoo and children start throwing peanuts your way.
   3. When the softball coach asks you to be second base instead of playing it.;
   4. When a child asks if he can use the life preserver around your waist and you're not wearing one.

105. Graffiti in men's room of a celebrated eatery: "The food in this place is gross." Written under that: "Wait till you try the restaurant."

106. Said his son has new definition of a balanced meal: a Big Mac in each hand.

107. Staying on a diet has slim possibilities.

108. I never eat between meals because, for me, there are no between meals!

109. How could I omit those who need two glasses of water when they eat—one to drink and one to cool down their knife and fork.

110. The last date she went on, the man had to warn her, "When you get to the white part, that's the tablecloth."

111. Only thing better than taking and early-morning walk with someone you love is to have someone you love take an early-morning walk without you and then wake you up when she gets home.

112. Everything she eats turns to her!

113. His high school picture in the yearbook was on page 41 and 42—and 43!

114. He found a great way to eat his wife's soup. He pretends it's mud.

115. The reason I eat with my knife is because my fork leaks.

116. His family is made up of big eaters. After each meal, they have to count the children!

117. He bought her a carving set—three chisels and a mallet.

118. She's such a bad cook, we pray after we eat!

119. When we have guests, it always presents a problem—what kind of wine goes with heartburn?

120. She always burns the toast so he won't notice the coffee.

121. The handiest appliance in our kitchen is the fire extinguisher.

122. She makes dehydrated food without adding water. The other day I went out in the rain and gained sixty pounds.

123. Fat people are so good-natured. They have to be. They can't fight or run.

124. Never pay attention to a fat lecturer when his subject is self-discipline.

125. Why didn't you ever learn to swim? Because it's never been an hour since I ate.

126. Lil is an imaginative cook. She wraps spaghetti around meatballs and calls them yo-yos.

127. The obese patient complained to his doctor that he couldn't lose any weight. "Have you tried jogging?" the doctor asked. Yes, but I keep running into restaurants!"

128. The hardest kind of diet pill to take is the one who keeps telling you how to do it.

129. We heard about a man who went thirty-two days without food or water. We can't understand why he didn't give his order to another waiter.

130. Help keep the kitchen clean. Eat out.

131. Health nuts are going to feel stupid someday, lying in the hospital dying of nothing.

132. Only Irish coffee provides in a single cup all four essential good groups—alcohol, caffeine, sugar, and fat.

133. Politically correct: fat—horizontally challenged, useless—organizationally dysfunctional, drunk—chemically inconvenienced, liar—ethically disoriented, lazy—motivationally deficient, dead—nonviable.

134. For years I ate with the wrong fingers.

135. This restaurant was so bad I asked the waiter, "What would you recommend?" He said, "Get out while you can."

136. Never eat at a restaurant where the place mats have instructions for the Heimlich Maneuver printed on them.

137. I was told, "You're going to have to get in shape." I answered, "What do you mean? Round is a shape."

138. I asked the waiter, "What would you recommend?" He said, "The restaurant down the street."

139. We make breakfast together; she makes the toast and I scrape it.

140. To her the cooking timer is the smoke alarm.

141. Nothing in the world arouses more false hopes than the first few hours of a diet.

142. Regarding Lil's cooking—I yelled supper and the kids ran for the car.

143. On our fifteenth anniversary I asked Lil, "Where would you like to go?" She said, "Some place I've never been." I said, "How about the kitchen?"

144. Lil went on a prune diet. She didn't lose any weight, but I sure knew where I could find her.

145. Finally I started cooking. For Xmas, the kids gave me an oven that flushes.

146. At least my cooking stopped the dog from begging at the table.

147. I think Lil is trying to tell me something. She wraps my lunch in road maps.

148. Re: our marriage vows, Lil said, "For better or worse but not for lunch."

149. Took Lil out to a fancy dinner; she got so excited she dropped the tray.

150. When we have guests for dinner, its always such a problem choosing a wine that goes with heartburn.

151. She thinks a can opener is the key to the john.

152. Lil doesn't like to go out to the fancy places to eat; she has too much trouble getting the straw thru the lid.

153. In my house when you guess "who's coming to dinner," it's usually the paramedics.

154. Everything she makes is tough. We even have a soup knife.

155. At times I help Lil in the kitchen. I help put out the fires.

156. We now have gas rationing at our house. No one gets more than one bowl of beans.

157. Our neighbor grumps that his spouse passed only one course in cooking school—can opener.

158. Man, looking in refrigerator, says, "Ah, the first sign of spring—we're out of turkey!"

159. Just heard from a guy who tried the Grapefruit 45 diet for a few weeks. He says he didn't lose a lot of weight, but he can pucker up quicker than ever before.

160. I can take a shower without getting my feet wet.

161. If Tony's is such great food, why don't you see more truck drivers eating there?

162. Mother in supermarket. Five-year-old scouting ahead. Boy brought back something and put it in the cart. Mother said, "Take it back. You have to cook that."

163. Is she fat? Her favorite food is second helpings.

164. The most remarkable thing about a mother is that for thirty years she served the family nothing but leftovers. The original meal has never been found. (C. Trillin)

165. The best way to serve spinach is to someone else.

166. It's depressing when you realize Julia Child's garbage disposal eats more than I do.

167. Breaks your heart to see people falling off the diet wagon. One friend showed up under the influence of coconut cream pie and another o.d. on Twinkies.

168. Sad story—a kid was treated for five years for a speech impediment and found out all he had to do was give up peanut butter.

169. We were so poor we did all our shopping at the day-old bakery. I was sixteen before I found out whole wheat isn't green.

170. I stopped complaining about the price of beef when I realized we have a kid in college who's costing us more than $3.40 a pound.

171. Mexico has enormous reserves of natural gas. It's found in three principal locations—tamales, enchiladas, and burritos.

172. I caught pneumonia standing in front of the open refrigerator.

173. You know you're in trouble when your date gets a menu with no prices and you get one that looks like a worksheet from the federal budget.

174. I asked the Chinese waiter what pork almond rice ding meant. He said, "Well, pork almond and rice are what we put in the microwave oven. I said, "And ding?" He said, "That's the timer."

175. Their specialty is Poulet a la Chevrolet. That's chicken that's been run over by a pickup truck.

176. One Thanksgiving I called a butcher in San Francisco. I asked, "What do you have that's plump juicy and tender?" He said, "Thpeaking."

177. What a dump of a restaurant. Flyswatters were on the menu.

178. Never eat at a restaurant that lists "Pepto-Bismol Souffle" as a dessert.

180. It's time to go on a diet when (1) the man from Prudential offers you group insurance, (2) or when you have to let out the shower curtain to

take a shower, or (3) when you're standing next to your car and you get a ticket for double-parking. (Totie Fields)

181. I burned out four refrigerator lights since Thanksgiving. Now have a sign on it that says, "We never close."

182. People hooked on coffee are the only people who can thread a needle while the machine is running.

183. I am now on a very effective diet. I don't eat while my wife is on the phone. 184. Girls today can only thaw foods. Why can't they be like their mothers and open cans?

185. His idea of roughing it is cutting a filet mignon with a dull knife.

186. His idea of patriotism is going to a Chinese restaurant and ordering American food.

187. It must be great to be a teenage girl to be able to lose five pounds by just taking off your makeup.

188. We used to go to a café in Needville. It had flies and no windows. I ordered the ace blank and the double blank. They also served whole frogs, not just the legs. And in Needville, the two places to eat were "restaurant "and "café." (True)

189. My daughter has some balanced diet. One day she cuts herself and bled peanut butter.

190. Logic is when you come to the conclusion that you're either gaining weight or the holes in your belt are healing up.

191. Thanksgiving dinner is equivalent to a Chinese dinner. You eat it, and a year later, you're hungry again.

192. A cannibal is a guy who goes into a restaurant and orders the waiter. (Jack Benny)

193. The best way to cook a cockatoo is to put the bird and an axe head into a pot. Boil them until the axe head is soft. The cockatoo is then ready to eat.

194. Many people order Perrier on the rocks, which is water over ice, and the, ice of course, is made of tap water. These people ride tricycles.

195. Man wanted larger drumsticks, so he crossed a turkey with an ostrich. He came up with a scrawny bird that insisted on hiding his head in the mashed potatoes.

196. My wife was injured yesterday preparing dinner—frostbite.

197. If I had my life to live over, I would live over a Mexican restaurant.

198. Fat men are such good-natured people. They have to be. They can neither fight nor run.

199. I know fish is brain food, but I don't like fish. Is there some other brain food? Yes, there's noodle soup.

200. Diner: "What in the world is this broth made from—water? Surely it isn't chicken.
    Waiter: "It's made out of the water the eggs were boiled in."

201. Diner: "Waiter, the flowers on this table are artificial, aren't they?"
    Waiter: "Yes, sir, that's the worst part about running a vegetarian restaurant. If we use real flowers, the customers will eat them."

202. Waiter to ill-bred customer: "My position, sir, does not allow me to argue with you, but if it ever came to a choice of weapons, I would choose grammar."

203. Man went into a hotel to have dinner. Waiter: "Will you have sausage and toast?
    Guest: "No, not for dinner." Waiter: "In that case, dinner is over."

204. "What's the matter, Joe? You look terrible." Joe: "My wife's on a diet."

205. "Does your new wife feed you well?"
    "She gave me chicken three times this week and chicken three times last week." "Then you have no cause to complain."
    "Yes, I do. It was the same chicken."

206. In the finer restaurants, the chef slices the tomatoes by throwing them through a harp.

207. Her favorite dessert recipe begins: take the juice from one bottle of Pepto-Bismol.

208. His cooking keeps flies away better than a Shell No-Pest strip.

209. I don't mind being served leftovers once in a while, but from World War II?

210. I'm a pretty bad cook. If I'd cooked the first Thanksgiving dinner for the Indians, General Custer might be alive today.

211. The family knows how dangerous my cooking is. Why else would grace last forty-five minutes?

212. In New York, a drunk asked the cabbie to stop for a pizza. A few minutes later, he told the cabbie he had been very nice and asked him if he had room up in front for more pizza. The cabbie said he did, so the drunk leaned over in the front seat and puked.

213. The boss walked in the office one day with an armload of doughnuts The girls said they thought he was on a diet. He said he was, but he told the Lord that if He really wanted the man to have doughnuts, He would find him a parking place right at the front door, and sure enough on the eighth time around there it was.

214. Remark: The German sausage has not arrived, or to put it another way, the wurst is yet to come.

215. We went to an Italian restaurant and they brought us a finger bowl. The trouble was that there were three fingers in it.

216. If I gain any more weight, I'll have to let out the shower curtain.

217. Randalls asked me if I wanted paper or plastic. I said, "It doesn't matter I am bisacksual.

218. Did you notice that when someone tastes something bad, they immediately want you to try it?

219. A new café in town offers a new seven-course dinner. That's a six-pack and a possum.

220. Letter from Hefty Bag: they have no interest in making you another suit.

221. Sign in café: "Try the du jour soup. It tastes different every time you have it."

222. The worse the restaurant, the bigger the pepper mill.

223. A cannibal called Dominos and ordered a pizza with everyone on it.

224. Definition: Buffet is a French word meaning, "get up and get it yourself."

225. Dinner guest: "We hate to eat and run, but we are still hungry."

226. He has such a big mouth he can eat a banana sideways or sing duets by himself.

227. He stepped on a scale that gives fortune cards. The card read, "Come back in fifteen minutes—alone."

228. When I was a kid, we didn't have cholesterol. If we had, we would have fried it.

229. Lil has a sign in the kitchen that says, "You have two choices for dinner—take it or leave it."

230. Re: fat man. It is to a point now that he picks up a menu and orders page 2 medium rare.

231. If people were not meant to have late-night snacks, why did God put a light in the refrigerator?

232. We found a Mexican restaurant so authentic you can't drink the water.

233. If you are a sloppy eater, order food the color of your outfit or something that makes a nice contrast.

234. I got a letter from the Houston Weight Control Center. I got recalled.

235. I am not overweight. I am a nutritionally overachiever.

236. He avoids natural foods because he heard so many people are dying of natural causes.

237. Thou shall not weigh more than thy refrigerator.

238. Man goes to an expensive restaurant and asks, "What's the catch of the day?" The waiter says, "You are."

239. If you think PR doesn't work, think of the millions of people that think yogurt tastes good.

240. Cast your bread upon the water, and it will come back a hundredfold. Big deal. Who wants soggy bread?

241. I can now take a shower without getting my feet wet.

242. Israel is producing a new cheese—called Cheeses of Nazrath.

243. I want two hot dogs, one with mustard and one without. Which one?

244. Aggie omelet—when the cook breaks the shell in with the egg.

245. This coffee tastes like mud. Well, it was ground this morning.

Insults/Heckling

1. He is like crab grass on the lawn of life.

2. He doesn't deserve a testimonial dinner—maybe just a testimonial snack.

3. He'd give you the floor off his back.

4. He's still hoping yesterday will get better (good outlook).

5. What has seven teeth and an IQ of sixty? The front row of a Willy Nelson Concert—don't know why I thought of that.

6. He's the gust of honor.

7. How can he be over the hill when he never reached the top?

8. When they run you out of town, get out in front and make it look like a parade.

9. On his last birthday, he sent his dad a telegram of congratulation.

10. Changes his mind a lot will always give you a definite "maybe."

11. He's never lost an enemy.

12. Has the knack of making strangers immediately.

13. What he lacks in intelligence he makes up in stupidity.

14. Came from such a large family he was married before he ever slept alone.

15. The way he dresses, no one would recognize him but a handful of psychiatrists and a few vice squad officers.

16. Has about as much chance of getting elected as Dolly Parton has of drowning.

17. He went on a seven-day diet, and all he lost was a week.

18. I'm sick of hearing he's such a good communicator so was Typhoid Mary.

19. The only person who has written more books that he has read.

20. Some people have a knack for finishing what they're saying long before they stop talking.

21. His IQ is close to room temperature; also approaches his belt size.

22. Only thing he's ever achieved on his own is dandruff.

23. He's a sex symbol for women who no longer care.

24. Guy so dumb he though Joan of Arc was Noah's wife.

25. His greatest credibility is when he pleads ignorance.

26. I went over to his house one night. He asked me what I wanted. I said bring me something that's tall, cold, and full of booze. He brought out his wife.

27. He's got a lot of polish, but it's all on his toenails.

28. His high school was so bad the valedictorian didn't graduate.

29. No one is absolutely worthless; they can always serve as a pitiful example.

30. Old saying: you are what you eat—he always orders turkey.

31. May your life be filled with lawyers.

32. He's a man of convictions, but the only two I know of are DWI.

33. Still holds the record for the one-hundred-yard stagger.

34. Nothing wrong with being mediocre as long as you're good at it.

35. So old when he went to school they didn't even have history.

36. Leadership ability of a ten-cent-off coupon off the federal budget or (national debt)

    —of a Waterpik on the Chicago fire
    —couldn't lead Smokey the Bear out of a burning forest
    —could screw up a two-car funeral
    —couldn't lead a group in silent prayer

37. Deep philosophical discussion: I asked his wife if he believed in life after death. She said, "Heck no, he doesn't even believe in life after supper."

38. So cheap he goes to a restaurant and orders leftovers.

39. Instead of booze he drinks Windex—gives terrible headache but his eyes sure are clear.

40. He drank gasoline one time; instead of giving him the hiccups, it gave him the honks.

41. Remember success may be fleeting but obscurity is forever.

42. He's a man of few words; some of which he's going to organize into a complete sentence.

43. Head? Hell, he ain't got no head. His neck just grew out and haired off.

44. Speaks two languages—English and profanity.

45. The only "10" he's interested in is the one on his electric blanket.

46. I wouldn't say he's good-looking just won first prize in the Yasur Arafat lookalike contest.

47. Hypochondria—was in bed three days with a bad haircut.

48. Only way he's going to get to heaven is if there's a typographic error in the Ten Commandments.

49. I heard he was fixed for life; does it mean a pension or a vasectomy?

50. So ugly the psychiatrist asked him to lie on the couch facedown.

51. Reads a lot—asked him the title of the last book he read, he said, "I don't know. I haven't gotten that far yet."

52. All some people learn about experience is that they make a mistake.

53. He said it was love at first sight. I looked in the mirror and there I was.

54. He's about half smart and not wrapped too tight.
    Doesn't have both oars in the water
    Bubble off plumb.
    Elevator doesn't go all the way to the top.

55. He's lied so much he had to get someone else to call his dogs.

56. He's living proof that wisdom doesn't come with age.

57. I'm a member of a minority group. I'm one of his friends.

58. His idea of a dinner jacket is carrying a sandwich in his coat pocket.

59. Living proof you don't have to be tall, dark, and handsome to be short.

60. Pillar of the community—the dictionary defines a pillar as something that's thick, immovable, and holds everything up.

61. He has delusions of adequacy.

62. He has halitosis of the intellect.

63. Quit trying to shoot his age in golf—now trying to shoot his area code.

64. Puts olives in martinis 'cause he doesn't like to drink on an empty stomach.

65. Humble, unobtrusive, democratic—no one to call him sir, just kneel.

66. Quit watching porno movies on TV. Said it makes him mad to see people having more fun in an hour than he'd had in a lifetime.

67. Used to like sex, now it's food—even put a mirror over the dining room table.

68. Has ultimate solution to airplane hijacking. Everyone fly naked.

69. Sent a Valentine card. Says, "To the one I love most." Sent it to himself.

70. About as useful as hiccups to a glass blower.

71. Our minister of torture.

72. Let's face it. The man suffers from mental saddle sores.

73. Looks as if he was weaned on a pickle.

74. Build a statue in his honor and let the pigeons speak for us.

75. I thought his name was Hollandaise because he is always on the sauce.

76. There but for the grace of God goes God.

77. Has a characteristic American face. Once seen never remembered.

78. Suffers from verbal hemorrhage.

79. Won a golf tournament—shot his IQ

80. Doesn't have a single redeeming defect

81. The type of guy that gives failures a bad name.

82. Named poster boy for birth control.

83. Not all learning is a good thing. Jim finished four years of college. Put on his graduation gown and found out he liked dresses.

84. The only asset about being tall is that you're the first one who knows when it rains.

85. He's a responsible man. They say whenever anything goes wrong he's responsible.

86. As a student, he flunked second opinion.

87. He was arrested for impersonating a leader.

88. Only person I know that enters a room mouth first.

89. Mouth so big can eat a banana sideways.

90. Jim has a new health drink. Double scotch and water, but stir it with a celery stick.

91. It's a mystery how his head could have grown without any nourishment.

92. Out to dinner he brought Jell-O. I asked if he was going to eat it. He said, "I don't eat anything more nervous than I am."

93. Was in the eighth grade four terms—Roosevelt.

94. Go to work for Maytag as an agitator.

95. His face is living proof that man descended from road maps.

96. He went on a diet—lost forty pounds and his driver's license.

97. He decided to donate his body to medical science. Until they need it, he's preserving it in alcohol.

98. He has a new career. He serves as an inspiration for children who can't afford to see the Goodyear Blimp.

99. His i. q. is a perfect 20/20.

100. He was a great disappointment to his parents—they had expected a boy or a girl.

101. He's a loser—even his answering machine hangs up on him.

102. I've known him as a whining child, petulant teenager, a rebellious young man, and a demanding adult—often on the same day.

103. He is considered the Hindenburg of our group—fat, full of hot air, and a total disaster.

104. If it wasn't for pull tabs on beer cans, he wouldn't get any exercise at all.

105. Do you do anything quickly? Yeah, I get tired.

106. His leadership reminds one of Christopher Columbus. He didn't know where he was going when he started out on his journey. He didn't know where he was when he got there. He didn't know where he had been when he got back, and he did it all with someone else's money.

107. He is so dumb he thinks Abraham Lincoln is a Jewish car agency.

108. He came to work smiling this morning—must've seen a wreck.

109. Well, at least "the battle of the sexes" is no longer your problem.

110. Do you ever get the feeling that some people are educated far beyond their intelligence?

111. He cut himself while shaving this morning, and his eyes almost cleared up.

112. He saw on television where you can support a child in Ethiopia for $10 a month, so he sent his own.

113. He was a bottle-fed baby—even his mother didn't trust him up close.

114. I knew him before he had his personality bypass.

115. He doesn't have to turn the lights off to be totally in the dark.

116. He's a tough guy. He said he has the heart of a small boy—he keeps it in a jar on his desk.

117. Guy so tight wanted a tattoo had *mother* tattooed across his stomach so he could use this navel as the *o*.

118. He does so many things; he's the only man I know who's listed on every one of the Yellow Pages.

119. We're talking about a man of vision, of insight, of foresight. A man who once said to Oliver North, "Who's gonna know?"

120. An intellectual man—he has devoted the last few years to the world of letters and watching Vanna White turn them.

121. In his early years, he was known far and wide as a gifted student. If he got anything higher than a C, it was a gift.

122. A humble man. He knows he couldn't possibly be as wonderful as he thinks he is.

123. A man of infinite creativity, he once told a date that like the captain of a ship, he had the authority to perform a marriage ceremony while afloat—on his waterbed.

124. He is perhaps best known for bringing the practices of major league pitching into our office environment. He works one day and rests three.

125. He's Daniel Boone's brother—Baa.

126. I love Paul Simon's bow ties. It always looks like a bat died on his chest.

127. He's as phony as an undertaker's get-well card.

128. Our guest of honor isn't afraid of anything. He recently engaged in a battle of wits—unarmed.

129. He bought his fiancée a lovely wedding ring. It even has a place for a diamond.

130. One thing about our guest. No one will ever try to bump him off because he knows too much.

131. Roast Introduction: We are very pleased that our guest was able to make it tonight. You know how fickle parole boards can be.

132. It gives me great pleasure to introduce our next guest. Obviously, it doesn't take much to give me great pleasure.

133. This man is too considerate. He avoids praying on the Sabbath because he doesn't want to pester God on his busiest day.

134. We came to praise (name), not to bury him. But the vote was close.

135. If I didn't know him so well, I'd probably like him.

136. He's not exactly a household name. In "Who's Who," he's listed as "Who's He?"

137. She's had so many face-lifts every time she raises her eyebrows she pulls up her panty hose.

138. Man started parting his hair from back to front and quit—people keep whispering in his nose.

139. I knew one egomaniac who actually thought he was humble. He used to say, "Some geniuses are conceited, but I'm not."

140. This late word: Scientist have figured out a new way to measure a blonde's IQ—with a tire gauge.

141. She doesn't have much upstairs, but she has a mezzanine you'll never forget!

142. Cheap? The only time I've ever seen him pick up a tab was on a beer can.

143. George Bernard Shaw had been bored nearly to tears by the long and pedantic discourse of a man who was trying to impress him. "You know," said Shaw to the man, "between the two of us we know all there is to be known." The man was delighted and said, "Really? How is that?" Shaw answered, "You seem to know everything except that you are a bore. And I know that."

144. It's a real gift to be as dumb as he is.

145. What he lacks in intelligence he makes up in stupidity.

146. He's just as smart as he can be—too bad.

147. When he says hello, he tells you all he knows.

148. He's got a one-half-horsepower brain pushing a two-ton mouth.

149. He was young and foolish. Now he's no longer young.

150. If you want a free marble headstone when you die, have them bury you up to your neck.

151. You haven't even gotten the brains you were born without.

152. I enjoy talking to him when my mind needs a rest.

153. He's a self-made man who quit work too soon.

154. He's an old fool. You just can't beat experience.

155. He never acts stupid. It's always the real thing.

156. She says she is not a dumb blonde because she's not blonde.

157. He always said, "If you must say something, make it nasty."

158. His rough exterior covers a heart of stone.

159. He thinks everything is funny so long as it happens to someone else.

160. She may be heavenly looking, but she has no earthly use.

161. He's so conceited he thinks that if he had not been born, people would wonder why.

162. He can hardly ever wait to hear what he's going to say, but he never listens.

163. He's not always right, but he's never wrong.

164. Be careful when you talk about her. You're speaking of the woman she loves.

165. She's all wrapped up in herself. Too bad she makes such a small package.

166. He worships the very ground his head is stuck in.

167. He's so conceited that if you're not talking about him, he's not listening.

168. His mouth is so big when he yawns his face disappears.

169. She has Early American features—she looks like a totem pole.

170. He's like a pie, face like a lemon, brain of meringue.

171. If she were a stripper, they'd yell, "Put it on!"

172. Don't feel bad about your looks. You've suffered enough already.

173. Why don't you give yourself a treat? Paint all of your mirrors.

174. Her glamour washes off with a cloth.

175. Her nose runs more than a tourist in Mexico.

176. He can swat flies with his nose.

177. He could make a good living hiring himself out to scare people with the hiccups.

178. This club is so exclusive they don't even tell you where the meetings are held.

179. Your trouble is that you monopolize the conversation when I have something brilliant to say.

180. Why don't you pretend you're somebody pleasant?

181. He's as useful as a parachute on an ocean liner.

182. Would you want someone like you to marry your daughter?

183. If he ever needs a friend, he'll have to buy a dog.

184. He was weeded out of college. They caught him smoking it.

185. He has the personality of a wart.

186. Understand he's sick. Hope it's nothing trivial.

187. I wish I were as smart as you are stupid.

188. Who makes her dress? The police.

189. He's less exciting than the opening of an umbrella.

190. The only thing that suit does for him is keep him warm.

191. She has a complexion like a peach—yellow and fuzzy.

192. He looks like his pardon came through just after the warden pulled the switch.

193. If you look closely, you can tell he's not dead.

194. They're a nice couple, except for him.

195. They go out twice a week. She goes on Thursday, he goes on Friday.

196. Why be unpleasant—with just a little effort you can be a real stinker.

197. After the husband had been "working late" several nights and called again to say he would not be home till late, she said, "Can I depend on that?"

198. He's not only a bachelor, he's a bachelor's son.

199. In a verbal duel, her choice of weapons is mud.

200. He can stay longer in an hour than others do in a week.

201. He's a confirmed bachelor—what was good enough for his father is good enough for him.

202. She's called the opposite sex because if you want anything, she always wants the opposite.

203. She's a vision in the evening and a sight in the morning.

204. His career is in archaeology—it lies in ruins.

205. He started at the bottom and stayed there.

206. Her kids are so obnoxious, she goes to the PTA under an assumed name.

207. He believes in sharing the credit with the guy who did the work.

208. He has what it takes to take what you have.

209. He isn't working, but at least he's got a job.

210. If you're married to a beautiful girl and a good cook, you must be a bigamist.

211. The only thing they have in common is they were married in the same church.

212. He loves to go fishing so he can sit around doing nothing, which his wife won't let him do at home.

213. He is not lazy. He's just convinced that work is caused by a virus.

214. _____ is the only man I know who put odor eaters in his shoes and disappeared.

215. He is so cheap that to save money on his laundry bill he puts soap flakes in his pockets and walks through a car wash once a week.

216. I passed by your house the other night. Thanks.

217. Know how Jim and Tammy first met: They both dated the same guy in high school.

218. There's one thing you can say about stupidity—you always know it's genuine.

219. I'm not saying he's mean exactly, but I am saying he's the kind of guy who would invite you to a beer party and then lock all of the bathrooms.

220. A fellow says he overheard his son and some high school friends talking the other day, and they referred to someone as a "two-bagger." When the fellow asked for a fuller explanation, his son said, "You've heard about a guy who's so ugly a girl has to put a bag over his head to kiss him. Well, with a two-bagger, the girl not only has to put a bag over his head, she has to put a bag over her head too in case his comes off."

221. He has the same effect on people as a wet holiday.

222. If ignorance is bliss, he's Mr. Happy!

223. He gets up very early but never bright.

224. He'll never be too old to learn new ways of being stupid!

225. He tried to sell Father's Day cards at a home for unwed mothers!

226. He's always me—deep in conversation!

227. He's so vicious, Dial-A-Prayer told him to go to hell.

228. She's vicious. When she dies, she wants to be cremated and thrown in somebody's face!

229. He steals ashes from funeral homes and sells them to cannibals as *instant* people.

230. He's the kind of guy who's get a girl pregnant just to kill a rabbit.

231. Ego? He calls Dial-A-Prayer and asks for his messages.

232. Describing a dimwit person: His belt doesn't go through all the loops.

233. "My mind seems to wander."

"Don't worry it's too weak to go far."

234. Did you hear about the sweet Southern girl who thought a bagel was a bird dog?

235. If he loses any more hair, he'll have to carry his dandruff in his hand.

236. He traded his TV in on a new VCR.

237. He has pictures of himself plastered all over one wall in his home. He has pictures of himself sober on another wall.

238. He's the man whose major contribution is proving that experience, and education can be overrated.

239. On the information highway, he is the exit ramp.

240. He played too much football with his helmet off.

241. If you want him to pay attention, pretend you're a bartender.

242. The filling station called—your inflatable doll is ready.

243. His battery was out in his battery-operated watch. Asked man in store if he had one of those little bitty jumper cables.

244. He doesn't personally have ulcers, but he is a carrier.

245. If it weren't for T-shirts and bumper stickers, he'd have no philosophy at all.

246. I hope I never live to be as old as you look.

247. Bette Davis re a starlet: "There's the good time that was had by all."

248. He as a born loser—he went to an orgy, and all he did was steal the grapes.

249. He has all the charisma of a speed bump.

250. When he gives blood, they don't use it for transfusions; they use it to sterilize the instruments.

251. Sign on his door 10-4. That's not his office hours; it's the odds against finding him at all.

252. In kindergarten, he flunked sandpile.

253. We had planned to have entertainment this evening, but we invited our next guest, instead.

254. The next speaker on our program is a well-suspected lawyer.

255. Our next speaker has encountered many obstacles on the road to success . . . he just hasn't overcome any of them.

256. Our guest is no quitter! Of course, he has been fired six or seven times.

257. He's so lazy, his exercise bike has cruise control.

258. He is a truly absorbing person. In fact, this afternoon he absorbed two six-packs.

259. He puts his foot in his mouth so often, he's developed athlete's throat.

260. We are here tonight to honor a man not for what he has done, but because he has gotten away with doing it.

261. Around the office, this man is a god. He's rarely seen, he has no sense of humor, and if he does anything, it's considered a miracle.

262. When he first came here to work, he started at the bottom and immediately found his niche.

263. Our next guest is one of a kind—which is plenty.

264. As you know, every businessperson today is experiencing a liquidity problem, and he is no exception. Last night alone he had to get up three times.

265. Old? He can remember when if people were "spaced out," they were having trouble with their typewriter.

266. Responses to a Roast: What can I tell you? That was a speech to be remembered. Not repeated. Just remembered.

267. Those of us who are close to him know that he's a world-class pessimist. You can tell that from his resume. Under Hobbies, he lists "filling sandbags."

268. He comes from a poor but honest family. How poor? They were so poor that living in poverty was beyond their means.

269. He comes from a family known for its good works. For instance, who can ever forget the public service performed by his great-grandfather when he drank a quart of booze every day. Said he wanted to keep it out of the hands of drunks.

270. As we all know, he is a relaxed, laid-back sort of person who never lets things get to him. These things have included hard work, long hours, and punctuality.

271. He's a little upset tonight. We went out to the bar for a drink, and he remembered to bring money.

272. In all fairness, he only drinks to forget. Last night what he forgot was how to stand up.

273. Our next guest can only be described as holding down one of the most important jobs in television. You've all seen *60 Minutes*. You've all seen Mike Wallace and Dan Rather on *60 Minutes*. You've all seen Harry Reasoner and Morley Safer on *60 Minutes*. You've all seen that watch on *60 Minutes*. Who do you think winds it up?

274. Mean? Who else do you know would rearrange the chocolates in a Whitman Sampler?

275. Creative? He couldn't ad-lib "Shhhhh!" in a public library.

276. This man is so likable—dogs come up and pet him.

277. Willpower? He could lose weight on a cruise!

278. Responding to Someone Who Has Just Roasted You: "First, I want to thank the previous speaker—a man of many talents. As you can see, humor isn't one of them."

279. Early in life, he was inoculated with a burning desire for hard work. Unfortunately, it didn't take.

280. We knew he had a problem when his doctor gave him a prescription to help him stop drinking, and he used it as a coaster.

281. He's also very much into health. Before, every meal he orders a double martini with a twist of lemon for medicinal purposes. The double martini to avoid stress, anxiety, and tension and the twist of lemon to avoid scurvy.

282. He is a generous man—a man of charity. Last year alone his contribution to the Home for Unwed Mothers was in four figures—Betty, Barbara, Irene, and Agnes.

283. I don't want to put down the previous speakers, but there has to be a reason why the happy hour is the name given to that period of time immediately preceding the program.

284. First, on behalf of the previous speakers, I want to thank you for the enthusiastic and warm reception you gave to their speeches. It's always nice to have an audience that doesn't get out much.

285. I'd like to congratulate the previous speakers on what can only be called a Niagara of words and a Sahara of thought.

286. First, I want to thank you all for those hamburger speeches. I call them hamburger speeches because they contain a lot less meat than we were expecting.

287. I won't comment on the previous speakers. Let's just say I mourn for the two hundred chickens and four thousand string beans that have given their lives to make this dinner possible.

288. Jim has put in a memorable thirty years with this company. Twenty-two years if you subtract coffee breaks.

289. As you all know, he's a hands-on executive. For instance, what he had his hands on today is pretzels, beer, and golf clubs.

290. He is a man who could never be called antiunion. On the other hand, if you added up all of the hours he's spent away from his desk, he is definitely against organized labor.

291. Retirement party: "After all that's been said tonight, there's no doubt that ___ has been able to cut the mustard. Now let's see if he can cut the cake."

292. Rich? When he buys a suit, the only thing he has to let out are the pockets.

293. A trusting man, he once sent away for a cologne they said, was guaranteed to make him smell taller.

294. I won't comment on his physique. Let's just say that if you tried to bury him in the sand, you could run out of beach.

295. For a brief period of time, he was a male stripper but gave it up the night the audience kept yelling, "Take it off! Take it off!" and he already had. 296. This isn't generally known, but he was fired from his very first

job when he suffered from a rare case of executive burnout. He had the hots for the boss's wife.

297. A resourceful man. A man who has made up in apathy what he lacks in drive.

298. I won't comment on his work habits. Suffice it to say that his previous job was with the post office, but he couldn't keep up with the pace.

299. He's an only child proving, once again, that some couples do learn from their mistakes.

300. A fiercely self-sufficient and independent man you can tell it by the determined stride he takes while being walked to work by his mother.

301. Today we honor a man who doesn't know the meaning of the word *dissemble*, who doesn't know the meaning of the word *fear*, who doesn't know the meaning of the word *quit*. And so, we've all chipped in to get him this dictionary.

302. Among his many accomplishments, he has a green thumb. It's from fishing olives out of martinis.

303. Eat? It's the first time I have ever saw a mouth with stretch marks?

304. Uncouth? He still thinks a peer group is people who go to the same urologist.

305. He is a man of strict moral and fiscal standards. Never in his life has he ever grabbed for a drink, a blonde, or a check.

306. Cheap? Who else, on the night before Christmas, tells his kids that Santa is being held hostage in Iran?

307. Jim has one big problem. It takes him an hour and a half to get to work—after he gets there.

308. Lazy? He once got an incomplete on a urine test.

309. I won't comment on his drinking, but last week our guest of honor joined a street band. He plays curb.

310. Before we go any further, I'd also like my spouse to stand up and take a bow. (Lead applause and then look around as no one stands up. Shake your head and comment) You know, after that last gas station, I thought the car was kind of quiet

311. When someone is slow in coming up to the microphone: Isn't that wonderful? I think he has two speeds—slow and stop.

312. About a Guest Who Always Dresses Casually:

You can tell he's taken this occasion rather seriously. His socks match.

313. In conclusion—the two words your bladder has been praying for.

314. Rich? When his daughter got married, they had a money tree at the reception. It was a sequoia.

315. Old? The only thing 38-24-36 reminds him of is his Captain Midnight Decoder Ring.

316. If there were a tooth fairy for hair, can you imagine what (roasted) would be worth today?

317. I once roasted a turkey, and he really took it hard. Kept calling me a no-good baster.

318. You are what you eat, which explains why (name)'s favorite dish is turkey.

319. A man who, when it comes to romance, can only be described as Lincolnesque. His last four scores were seven years ago. 320. One man to another about meeting speaker, "I like this guy. He can talk for two hours on any given subject, four hours if he knows anything about it."

321. Look at him, sex takes a holiday.

322. All the ding-a-lings are not on the ice cream trucks.

323. Tell me, if somebody asks me what I see in you, what should I say?

324. What he doesn't know would make a library anyone would be proud of.

325. He's windier than a sack full of assholes.

326. She's a blue blood alright. It shows right through her tattooing. 327. She was so cold her tooth was chattering.

328. She was so tired she could hardly hold her mouth open.

329. If she married for love, she'd be her own groom. 330. In your opinion, what is the height of stupidity? How tall are you?

331. Did I make myself plain? No, God did that.

332. He's received so many degrees, we call him the human thermometer.

333. I don't like to have my picture taken. They don't do me justice. You don't need justice. You need mercy.

334. I wouldn't say he's dumb, but I think he majored in "Huh?"

335. You're as welcome as a hog caller in a public library.

336. Under that flabby exterior is an enormous lack of character. (Oscar Levant)

337. I'll bet you have no more friends than an alarm clock.-H. Youngman

338. He looks like his hobby is stepping on rakes.

339. I wouldn't call him a liar. Let's just say he lives on the wrong side of the facts.

340. Eat? One time I took him to a Chinese restaurant, gave him chopsticks, and he started two fires.

341. She never gives up. She's now in the twenty-third year of her fourteen-day beauty plan.

342. I was told how to recognize a man I didn't know. If you see two people talking and one of them is yawning, he's the other guy.

343. He couldn't sell Windex to a peeping tom.

344. To a fat man, pull up a couple of chairs and we'll begin.

345. He's so dumb he'd find a cure for nymphomania.

346. Vulgar of manner, overfed, overdressed and underbred, heartless, Godless, hell's delight, rude by day and lewd by night, crazed with avarice lust and rum, New York, thy name's delirium. ("Owed to New York" by Byron Rufus Newton)

347. When they circumcised him, they threw away the wrong bit. (Lloyd George)

348. He's not bald; he's just taller than his hair.

349. He has a good head on his shoulders—no neck, just a good head.

350. He's as important as a parachute in a submarine.

351. She has a voice like a garbage disposal with a butcher knife in it.

352. He has all the characteristics of a dog except loyalty. (Sam Houston)

353. He's not a failure; he's a success that hasn't happened yet.

354. Nerve? He's the kind of guy who would start a Ku Klux Klan chapter in Ghana.

355. I won't say what kind of paper it is, but the only ones who buy it are bird owners.

356. In college, he was honorary chugalug on the highball team.

357. She's been on more laps than a napkin. (Walter Winchell)

358. Did you read my last book? Oh, I hope so.

359. He has been called cold, rude, self-centered, arrogant, and egotistical—but that's just his family's opinion.

360. Boy is he cheap. He is fanatically economical. I once borrowed a vice from him, and it had toothpaste on it.

361. He's dumber than a bag of hammers.

362. Why don't you move closer to the wall? It's plastered already.

363. Oh, hello there, I didn't recognize you with your clothes on.

364. Lady, would you like it if I came over to your house while you were working and put out your red light?

365. She's one of my best friends. Why I've known her ever since we were the same age.

366. I like that hairdo. It looks like an explosion in a mattress factory.

367. He'd give an aspirin a headache.

368. If you were building an idiot, you'd use him for a blueprint.

369. (To a male heckler) You're just bitter because your parents wanted a boy.

370. Wearing a Sport Shirt: I once moved from an apartment because it had wallpaper like that.

371. Obnoxious Heckler: You know what makes this even worse? He's the president of my fan club!

372. Female: Now is that a nice thing to say, after all we've meant to each other: Remember when we took that solemn vow that we'd grow old together? Then you went ahead without me?

373. Why don't you go down to the morgue and tell them you are ready?

374. Female: Say, if you ever become a mother, could I have one of your kittens.

375. Male: What do you do—take ugly pills?

376. Lavender Male Heckler: They named a chewing gum after him. (Juicy Fruit)

377. Why don't you go home? Your cage must be cleaned out by this time.

378. That's a nice haircut you've got there. Where'd you get it? In a pet shop?

379. If he were alive, he'd be a mighty sick man.

380. Don't mind him. He isn't a bad guy until you get to know him.

381. He couldn't ad-lib a belch after a Thanksgiving dinner.

382. Is that your face, or did you block a kick?

383. Another crack out of you and your wife and I are through.

384. Shaking Hands: Remove your ring, shake hands, then replace the ring on your finger.

385. Emaciated Person: Pull up a coffin and lie down.

386. It is comforting seeing people yawning. At least I know they are still awake.

387. He lost his best friend. He broke his mirror.

388. He's as phony as an undertaker trying to look sad at a $5,000 funeral.

389. I'm willing to answer your questions as long as you don't question my answers.

390. Responding to a Difficult Question: Can you rephrase that question? Rephrase it into something I can answer.

391. Sir, feel free to speak your mind . . . we have a few seconds.

392. I'd ask you to repeat the question, but we only have this room till Sunday.

393. That's a two-part question—AM and PM.

394. Was that a question or a miniseries?

395. When Someone Asks a Difficult Question: "That's an excellent question, sir. Any other questions?"

396. Annual Meeting: "As I look out I see many familiar faces though many of the bodies have changed."

397. Folks, be patient. Even Hurricane Hugo ran out of wind eventually.

398. I always enjoy one of Jim's speeches. They are like a big red balloon—99 percent hot air but beautifully packaged.

399. I don't know how that guy does it. Most dummies have to work with a ventriloquist.

400. You know, hecklers are a lot like snow . . . no two flakes are exactly alike.

401. Sir, this conversation . . . it isn't toxic, but it is a waste.

402. Sir, I need you like Blue Cross needs another ski slope.

403. Heckler: My friend, bad manners are like bad teeth. Nobody knows you have them if you keep your mouth shut.

404. Heckler: Sir, I think you're in the early stages of swine flu. You're getting pigheaded.

405. Heckler: Sir, I know this is an open meeting, but that means guests, not mouths.

406. Heckler: Sir, would you mind sitting down? So far you've had all the impact of a Water Pik on the Chicago Fire.

407. When You Garble a Sentence, Push up Your Upper Teeth with Your Thumbs and Comment: You just can't buy these things at a garage sale.

408. When You Commit a Faux Pas: Mouths are like doors. They should only be opened when you know where you're going.

409. Rebuttal in a Debate: Well, once again you're jumping to confusions.

410. If You're Having Trouble with the Microphone: Why don't we use the one that says "Made in America?"

411. Response to a Very Long Question: Would you mind repeating that? I must have dozed off.

412. When Someone Gives a Long Opinion during the Q&A: Sir, your answer, does it come with a question?

413. If People Get up and Leave: Look at that. A moving standing ovation!

414. Delayed Reaction: That's one of those Polaroid jokes. It takes about a minute to get the whole picture.

415. When You Take an Unpopular Position: I feel a little like a guy who's spilled a glass of water on his lap. No matter what he says, nobody is going to believe him!

416. When Someone Offers an Objection to a Popular Plan: Now you know why this club will never have to worry about burning down. In case of fire, we just call Jim, and he'll throw a wet blanket on it.

417. Annual Meeting: As I look out, I see a lot of familiar faces though many of the bodies have changed.

418. Aside: It's comforting to see people yawning. At least I know they're still awake.

419. Accepting an Award: I feel I don't deserve such an honor, but what's one man's opinion when weighed against countless others.

420. After Dinner: Tonight's meal was a lot better than the last place I spoke. The food there was so bad, the ASPCA got an injunction forbidding them to give out doggie bags.

421. Taking a Vote: In a few minutes, we'll be taking a vote. All in favor should raise their hands. All opposed should try to stop the others from raising their hands.

422. Inviting Questions: I'm willing to answer your questions, just so long as you don't question my answers.

423. Annual Meeting: I find it hard to believe that an entire year has gone by. It's also uncanny that everyone has aged but me.

424. Heckler: Sir, if silence is golden, you must be on welfare.

425. When Things Are Going Downhill: We're pioneering a new concept in programs tonight, participatory failure!

426. Why don't you go down to the morgue and tell them you are ready?

427. He is terminally weird.

428. May the sewers of Rangoon back up into your septic tank.

429. He is a hotbed of apathy.

430. He is so lazy he won't even swell.

431. He has been called cold, rude, self-centered, arrogant, and egotistical—but that's just his family's opinion.

432. Trying to converse with Bill is like trying to take a sip from a fire hydrant.

433. He wants to be cremated and have the ashes thrown in somebody's face.

434. He is the Hindenburg of Court 136—fat, full of hot air, and a total disaster.

435. He is a homebody—any home, any body.

436. The sign on his door says 10-4. Those are not his office hours. They are the odds against finding him at all.

437. He says he reads a lot. I asked him what is the title of his favorite one. He said, "I don't know. I haven't gotten that far yet."

438. To her, doing her nails means sorting the ten pennies from the sixteen pennies.

439. She is genetically incapable of keeping a secret.

440. So you want to talk philosophy? OK, tell me why Goofy can talk and Pluto can't.

441. Being Irish means your attention span is so short that . . . oh, forget it.

442. Song: "Polack, Polack! Where does your garden grow?"
Refrain: "Usually under his fingernails."

443. He always says, "When my ship comes in." Hell, he never sent one out.

444. He is Irish, which means he thinks he sings very well.

445. He went to see *The Desert* at the movies and asked for two tickets in the shade.

446. He stood in front of the mirror for an hour trying to remember where he had seen himself before.

447. He was so ugly. I took him to the zoo, and they thanked me for bringing him back.

448. People like you are the reason people like me take pills.

449. She always tried to conceal her height by subtle little devices. She wore flat heels and walked on her knees.

LAW/CRIMINAL

---

1. I had so much trouble handling my husband's estate I almost wish he hadn't died.

2. My lawyer was in an accident—ambulance backed over him.

3. My lawyer and his dog are very close—they met each other chasing the same ambulance.

4. Overheard: "Is he a sneaky lawyer? He's studying the Ten Commandments to find loopholes."

5. What's black and brown and looks good on a lawyer? A Doberman Pinscher.

6. What's waste? A busload of lawyers going over a cliff with two empty seats.

7. What have you got with a lawyer buried up to this neck in the sand? Not enough sand.

8. Show me someone who smiles at trouble, and I'll show you a lawyer.

9. A personal injury attorney told his client, "I will take your case on a contingency." "So what does that mean?" "It means if I lose your case I get nothing. If I win your case, you get nothing."

10. Man found shot, stabbed, poisoned, and hung—police suspect foul play.

11. My lawyer does not encourage his clients to commit perjury. He does that for them. 12. Lawyer—no one likes a crooked lawyer till he needs one; a shyster lawyer is the other man's attorney.

13. Difference between God and attorney? God doesn't think he's an attorney.

14. The lawyer handed the client a check for $1,000 after he had been awarded $5,000 and said, "I've deducted my fee and here's what's left. What's the matter, aren't you satisfied?" "Well," replied the client, "I was just trying to remember who got hit by the truck, you or I?"

15. A New York City divorce lawyer died and came before St. Peter. "What exactly have you done to earn eternal happiness?" St. Peter asked. The lawyer recalled that he had given a panhandler on the street a quarter just the other day. St. Peter looked over to his assistant Gabriel and asked, "Is that in the records?" Gabriel nodded, but St. Peter told the lawyer it wasn't enough. "Wait, wait, there's more," said the lawyer. He told of tripping over a homeless boy the week before and giving the lad a quarter. Gabriel checked the records and confirmed that story too. St. Peter contemplated and then asked Gabriel, "What should we do?" Gabriel shot a sidelong glance at the lawyer and said, "I say we give him back half a buck and tell him to go to hell."

16. A lawyer was heard talking with a friend: "People take an instant dislike to me when they find out I'm a lawyer," she complained. "Why would they do that?" "It saves time," her friend replied.

17. In court a lawyer never asks a question he doesn't know the answer to.

18. What's the difference between a catfish and a lawyer? One is a bottom-dwelling, garbage-eating scavenger. The other is a fish.

19. A man was on trial in Nome. The prosecutor asks, "Where were you on the night of October 21 to May 2?"

20. A plane crashed carrying a priest a doctor and a lawyer. Upon arriving at the Heavenly Gate, St. Peter announced that since the crash was unexpected, they would have to consult Jesus about their eternal rewards. The priest approached Jesus. "What do you want as your reward?" asked

Jesus. "Oh, my Lord, only to sit at your right hand," the priest replied. "Granted," said Jesus. Next the doctor approached the throne. "What do you want as your reward?" asked Jesus. "Oh, Father, only to sit a your left hand," said the doctor. "Granted," said Jesus. The lawyer was the last one to approach the throne. "What do you want as your reward?" Jesus asked. There was a brief pause. Then the lawyer responded, "Get up!"

21. A Mexican bandit make a specialty of crossing the Rio Grande from time to time and robbing banks in Texas. Finally, a reward was offered for his capture, and an enterprising Texas Ranger decided to track him down. After a lengthy search, he traced the bandit to his favorite cantina, tiptoed up behind him, put his trusty six-shooter to the bandit's head, and said, "You're under arrest. Tell me where you hid the loot or I'll blow you brains out." But the bandit didn't speak English, and the Ranger didn't speak Spanish. Fortunately, a bilingual lawyer was in the saloon and translated the Ranger's message. The terrified bandit blurted out, in Spanish, that the loot was buried under the oak tree in back of the cantina. "What did he say?" asked the Ranger. The lawyer answered, "He said, 'Get lost, you turkey. You wouldn't dare shoot me.'"

22. After examining the contents of the employee suggestion box, the senior partner of the law firm complained, "I wish they'd be more specific. What kind of kite? What lake?"

23. Two lawyers when a knotty case was o'er,
Shook hands, and were as friendly as before.
Said the client, "Tell me how
You can be friends, who fought just now."
"Thou fool!" said one. "We lawyers, though so keen,
Like shears, ne'er cut ourselves, but what's between.

24. A doctor, a lawyer, and an anthropologist went on safari. In their travels, they chanced to come upon a group of cannibals. The travelers were taken captive and brought before the chief, who made it clear that the three were to come to dinner that evening. "We intend to boil you and eat you," the chief said. "We also intend to use your skins to cover our canoes. However, as a gesture of goodwill, I am willing to grant each of you one last request." The three, preparing for the worst, began to think about their last request. The doctor, knowing all about pain, said he would like most to have a shot of morphine from this first aid bag.

The anthropologist, being familiar with the medicine and hallucinogenic properties of some of the local plants, asked if he could chew on the leaves of one of the plants growing nearby to take his mind off the impending events. The lawyer requested a sharp stick. His captors were puzzled but felt obliged to grant his last wish. When they gave him the stick, the lawyer quickly turned the point toward himself and proceeded to rapidly puncture the skin all over his body. He then declared with great satisfaction, "So much for your damn canoes."

25. Judge: "And how exactly did the trouble start?" Defendant: "Well, she asked me to play a round, and I didn't know she was a golfer."

26. A Charlotte, North Carolina, man having purchased a case of rare, very expensive cigars, insured them against, get this, fire. Within a month, having smoked his entire stock of fabulous cigars and having yet to make a single premium payment on the policy, the man filed a claim against the insurance company. In his claim, the man stated that he had "lost" the cigars in a series of small fires." The insurance company refused to pay, citing the obvious reason that the man had consumed the cigars in normal fashion. The man sued and won. In delivering his ruling, the judge stated that since the man held a policy from the company in which it had warranted that the cigars were insurable, and also guaranteed that it would insure the cigars against fire, without defining what it considered to be an "unacceptable fire," it was obligated to compensate the insured for his loss. Rather than endure a lengthy and costly appeal process, the insurance company accepted the judge's ruling and paid the man $15,000 for the rare cigars he "lost in the fires." After the man cashed the insurance check, the insurance company had him arrested on twenty-four counts of arson. With his own insurance claim and testimony from the previous case being used as evidence against him, the man was convicted of intentionally burning the rare cigars and sentenced to twenty-four consecutive one-year terms.

27. Three lawyers and three MBAs are traveling by train to a conference. At the station, the three MBAs each buy tickets and watch as the tree lawyers buy only a single ticket. "How are three people going to travel on only one ticket?" asks an MBA. "Watch and you'll see," answers a lawyer. They all board the train. The MBAs take their respective seats, but all three lawyers cram in to a restroom and close the door behind them. Shortly after the train has departed, the conductor comes around collecting tickets. He knocks on the restroom door and says, "Ticket,

please." The door opens just a crack, and a single arm emerges with a ticket in hand. The conductor takes it and moves on. The MBAs see this and agree it was quite a clever idea. So after the conference, the MBAs decide to copy the lawyers on the return trip and save some money (being clever with money, and all that). When they get to the station, they buy a single ticket for the return trip. To their astonishment, the lawyers don't buy a ticket at all. "How are you going to travel without a ticket?" says one perplexed MBA. "Watch and you'll see," answers a lawyer. When they board the train, the three MBAs cram into a restroom, and the tree lawyers cram into another one nearby. The train departs. Shortly afterward, one of the lawyers leaves his restroom and walks over to the restroom where the MBAs are hiding. He knocks on the door and says, "Ticket, please."

28. They finally caught him for stealing a car, but it really wasn't his fault. It was standing in front of a cemetery, and he thought the owner was dead.

29. Yesterday I met my first Gay Lib cop. I mean, I don't mind being frisked but for jaywalking?

30. It's not that there are too many lawyers, there just aren't enough ambulances.

31. Ever wonder how much time you could save by leaving most of your estate to your lawyer?

32. Lawyers can be very practical people. I overheard one lawyer talking to his client in jail. He was saying, "Why didn't you just beat the guy up? You're in no financial position to murder anybody."

33. I often wonder why people resort to crime when there are so many legal ways to be dishonest.

34. Leona Helmsley should be sentenced to twenty-five years in Motel Six.

35. Talk about bad luck. I opened a fortune cookie and found a jury summons.

36. A witness said to the judge, "I swore to tell the truth, but every time I do, a lawyer protests.

37. A good attorney is someone who rescues you money from you enemies . . . and keeps it himself.

38. My friend is such a good attorney, the government named a loophole after him.

39. There is something not quite right with the system of justice that locks the jury up for the night while the defendant is out on bail.

40. I slept like a lawyer last night—you LIE on one side then LIE on the other.

41. A legal type I know tells me he recently asked his client, "After you had poisoned the coffee and your husband sat at the table drinking it, didn't you have the slightest pity for him, a moment of sorrow for what you had done?"

   The woman thought about the question. "Yes, there was a moment when I did," she said.

   "You did?"

   "Yes."

   "When was that?" he asked.

   "That was when he asked for a second cup," she said.

41. There are two kinds of lawyers. Those who know the law, and those who know the judge.

42. A surgeon, an architect, and a politician were arguing as to whose profession was the oldest. Said the surgeon, "Eve was made from Adams' rib, and that surely was a surgical operation."

   "Maybe," said the architect, "but prior to that, order was created out of chaos, and that was an architectural job."

   "But," interrupted the politician, "somebody created the chaos first."

43. Hear about the police chief in the state who ordered his men to take a closer look at pornography?

44. Hell hath no fury like the lawyer of a woman scorned.

45. Washington lawyers would find a loophole in the law of gravity.

46. Cartoon: Jury foreman, "We the jury find the defendant guilty and his lawyer obnoxious."

47. Lawyer campaign themes:

Reach out, reach out, and sue someone.
Please don't squeeze the plaintiff.
You deserve a breakout today.
We make our money the old-fashioned way. We sue people.
A will: Don't leave home without one.
Express bail: When you absolutely have to get out overnight.

48. A bus had been hit by a truck belonging to a major company. Lying about on the ground were a dozen bus passengers. A man asked one of the passengers, "Has anybody from the insurance company been here yet?" The passenger shook his head from side to side. The man went on, "Good, then you don't mind if I lie down here next to you!"

49. Property sign: Believe in life after death? Trespass and find out.

50. New Orleans is the only city in the world where you go in to buy a pair of nylon stockings and the want to know your head size.

51. Lawyer doesn't advertise on TV. He is afraid someone will recognize him and call the police.

52. To lawyer: What do you think about *Rowe vs. Wade*? Lawyer said, "I don't care how the Mexicans get across the river.

53. If we really mean freedom of expression, why is it against the law to moon someone?

54. A cop stopped a man and said, "Your eyes look glassy. Have you been drinking? The man said, "No, but your eyes look glazy. Have you been eating doughnuts?"

55. Yankee told the judge in Louisiana, "The man that has filed charges against me is a Cajun, and every single person on the jury is a Cajun. There's no way I can get a fair trial here." The judge said. "Mon cher, you got yoself a problem, heh?"

56. Hear about the female lawyer who charged a widower $100 to prepare his will? Seems that when the widower handed the lawyer the money, two $100 bills were stuck together. After he left the office, the lawyer realized she was facing an ethical problem: should she share the extra money with her partner?

57. Judge turning to the jury and asking, "Have you reached a decision?" "Yes, Your Honor" is the reply. "And your decision?" "Your Honor," the foreman replies, "we find the defendant not guilty by reason of insanity." And from the incredulous judge, "All twelve of you!"

58. He leaned over the bench and said to the prisoner, "How come you can't get a lawyer to defend you?" The dependent said, "As soon as they find out I didn't steal the money, they won't have anything to do with me."

59. Oxy moron—Christian lawyer

60. In my lawyer's office I overheard, "Get that neck brace off. We're suing over a property line."

61. Bumper Sticker: Lawyers Do It Better in Their Briefs

62. The truly successful lawyer owns his own ambulance.

63. A lawyer is a learned gentleman who rescues your estate from your enemies and keeps it for himself. (Lord Brougham)

64. A jury consists of twelve persons chosen to decide which side has the best lawyer. (Robert Frost)

65. To a drunk, many times in court. The Judge said, "John Jones, you are charged with habitual drunkeness. What have you to offer in your defense?" The drunk said, "Habitual thirst, Your Honor."

66. The pompous judge stared sternly at the tattered prisoner. "Have you ever earned a dollar in your life?" "Yes, Your Honor, I voted for you in the last election."

67. Ignorance of the law does not prevent the losing lawyer from collecting his bill.

68. Some doctors tell their patients to always lie on their right side, declaring it is injurious to health to lie on both sides. Yet lawyers as a class enjoy good health.

69. Photographer trying to get lawyer to smile. "Say fees."

70. If voluntary compliance with the law worked, Moses would come down from Mount Sinai with ten guidelines.

71. This is a very friendly legal office. If you want to shake hands with someone, you must reach into your wallet pocket.

72. Many a crooked scheme has been born on a legal pad.

73. Great flaw in the jury system. It's frightening to know your fate is in the hands of twelve people who weren't smart enough to get excused.

74. Accomplice: One associated with another in a crime having guilty knowledge and complicity, as an attorney, who defends a criminal knowing him guilty. (Bierce)

75. A lawyer had a jury trial in a difficult case. The client was out of town when the decision was made. The decision was a complete victory for the lawyer and his client. Excitedly, he sent him a telegram, which said simply, "Justice has triumphed." The client wired back, "Appeal at once."

76. At the grave of a departed friend was an anthropologist, a doctor, and an attorney. The anthropologist suggested they put some money in the grave as was the custom of some ancient tribes he had studied. The anthropologist put a hundred-dollar bill in the coffin. The doctor, not to be outdone, also dropped a hundred-dollar bill in. Then the lawyer writes a check for $300, puts it in the coffin, and removes the $200 in cash.

77. Laws are funny. You can get fined for spitting on the sidewalk, but you can throw up for nothing.

78. She cried, and the judge wiped her tears with my checkbook. (T. Manville)

79. You don't know a woman till you've met her in court. (Norman Mailer)

80. He reminds me of a man who murdered both his parents and then, when sentence was about to be pronounced, pleaded for mercy on the grounds he was an orphan. (A. Lincoln)

81. Probably all laws are useless: for good men do not need laws at all, and bad men are made no better by them. (Demonax the Cynic)

82. Man is an able creature, but he has made thirty-three million laws and hasn't yet improved on the Ten Commandments.

83. America—where they lock up the jury and let the prisoner go home.

84. I just wanted to be like other ten-year-old boys—play ball, go on hikes, neck with the girls, steal cars, slug cops.

85. Their police force is sometimes referred to the Touchables.

86. A call girl was arrested outside the Pentagon for contributing to the delinquency of a major.

87. Overheard in a market: "Her lawyer is honest, but not enough to hurt her case."

88. An incompetent attorney can delay a trial for months or years. A competent attorney can delay one even longer. (EJ Younger)

89. Judges, as a class, display in the matters of arranging alimony, that reckless generosity which is found only in men who are giving away someone else's money. (Wodehouse)

90. A young lawyer with a large firm spent most of his time trying to give the appearance of a prosperous attorney. One day while leaving for lunch, he left a note that said, "Be back in an hour." When he returned he saw a note that a young rival down the hall had left on his desk. It said, "What for?"

91. A young lawyer showed up at a revival and was asked to give a prayer. Unprepared, he gave a prayer straight from a lawyer's heart. "Stir up much strife amongst thy people, oh LORD, lest thy servant perish." (Sen. Sam Ervin)

92. Cops raided a place. Newspapers said it was sort of a professional building with girls to match.

93. Logical laws: there are more horses' asses than there are horses.

94. Teacher asked each of the students what each of their fathers did for a living. Bobby: "My father runs the bank." Sara: "My father is a chef." Johnnie: "My father plays the piano in a whorehouse." She changed the subject and after school went to Johnnie's house and told his dad what he had said. The father said, "Actually I'm an attorney, but you can't tell that to an eight-year-old."

95. Top five best times and places to tell lawyer jokes:

1. Anytime
2. When lawyers are present
3. When lots of lawyers are present
4. When you're at a party with lots of lawyers
5. Anytime you're in the company of people with a sense of humor

96. Top worst times and places to tell lawyer jokes:

1. In an open court
2. At a lawyer's funeral
3. Around lawyers you don't know
4. When a lawyer is a customer, patient, or client
5. In front of children

97. A man tried to hold up a Japanese tour bus. The police got 1,844 photos of him.

98. A wife was before the judge for stealing a can of peaches. The judge asked why. She said she just wanted a little excitement, and she also liked peaches. The judge told her she would have to be punished, and she said she understood. The judge asked her how many peaches were in the can. She said there were six. He said he would give her six days in jail. Her husband asked the judge if he could say something, and the judge gave his consent. The husband said, "She stole a can of peas too."

99. Law of location—No matter where you go, there you are.

100. Make everything legal then we would have no crime.

101. Law of logical argument—Anything is possible if you don't know what you are talking about.

102. An eighty-year-old woman was arrested for shoplifting. When she was brought before the judge, he asked her, "What did you steal?" She replied, "A can of peaches." The judge then asked her why she had stolen the peaches, and she replied that she liked peaches and wanted to have a little excitement. The judge then asked her how many peaches were in the can, and she replied that there were six. The judge said, "Then I will give you six days in jail." At that time, her husband asked the judge if he could say something. The judge said, "Yes, what is it?" The husband said, "She stole a can of peas too."

103. Let the lawyers work it out. They write the laws for other lawyers to dissect in front of other lawyers called judges so that other lawyers can say the first judges were wrong and the Supreme Court can say the second lot were wrong. Sure there is such a thing as law. We are up to our necks in it. About all it does is make business for lawyers. (From "The Long Goodbye" by Raymond Chandler)

104. The New Orleans Police Department K-9 Unit has announced they are getting rid of their German shepherd police dogs. They will be replaced with coon dogs. Their reasoning is that they are not having any trouble with Germans.

LIL/WIFE

(Lil is Mit's loving wife of 54 years)

1. You know the honeymoon is just about over when you start going out with the boys on Wednesday and so does she.

2. LIL
   Statistically divorce is healthier—one-third of all marriages end in divorce, two-third end in death.

3. LIL
   I'm opposed to divorce; I think they ought to stay together and fight it out like the rest of us.

4. Lil said if I wanted breakfast in bed, I should sleep in the kitchen.

5. She was so sure of getting her own way with me that she used to write her diary four days in advance.

6. Her idea of frozen food is a Daiquiri.

7. I won't say she's lazy, but one day I came home from work and nobody was home. And so I looked around, and there on top of the television set was three eggs, a head of lettuce, a tomato, two onions, some celery, and a note saying, "The recipe for your supper is on channel 4 at six o'clock!

8. Now even our neighbors love her singing. In fact, they broke every window in our house just to hear her better.

9. She was so naive she thought the breaststroke had to do with swimming.

10. I notice you're wearing your wedding ring on the wrong finger. LIL: I married the wrong man.

11. But I took misfortune like a man—blamed it on her. 12. She used to always wear open-toed shoes. It was so convenient. She could pick up cigar butts with her toes.

13. I asked her if she was fond of nuts, and she wanted to know if I was proposing.

14. You can't even call it a purse. It's more like a portable attic.

15. Lil doesn't ask for much out of life. Just a roof over her head and the chance to raise it every now and then.

16. Statistics show no wife ever killed her husband while he was washing the dishes or sweeping the floor or taking out the garbage. So every time Lil gets mad at me, I head for the kitchen sink. You won't believe how many times a day I wash the dishes. From daylight to dark, I carry a broom with me while I am at home.

17. I took Lil out last night—didn't really want to go just wanted to see what she looked like without curlers.

18. The most difficult thing in the world is trying to convince Lil that a bargain costs money.

19. Lil and I were sitting in a high-class restaurant one night when a gorgeous redhead recognized me and started waving. "Don't worry, dear," I said, "I met her professionally." "Oh, really?" said Lil. "Yours or hers?"

20. The honeymoon is over when she complains about the racket I make while I'm fixing my own breakfast.

21. The nice thing about being disorganized is when burglars break in, they can't find anything either.

22. She is always dropping little compliments on me. During our honeymoon, she said the way I make love reminds her of a very famous

food product. I said, "Wheaties, the Breakfast of Champions?" She said, "No, Minute Rice."

23. My wife is very sensitive about her weight. How do you explain to her she caught pneumonia from standing in front of an open refrigerator?

24. This is the time of year when you sit in the backyard and you hear such eerie conversations from over the fence. Like one voice saying, "Where should I put the ashes from the charcoal grill?" And another voice saying, "Put them in the urn with Uncle Charlie. He always did like company."

25. I can pinpoint the exact moment when our marriage went bad. After my wife and I bought a waterbed, we kind of drifted apart.

26. "If you make the toast and coffee, breakfast will be ready." Mit: "What are we having for breakfast?" Lil: "Toast and coffee."

27. "Lil, do you think you could learn to love me?"
"I don't know I learned to eat spinach."

28. Lil yelled at me one day, "Mit, they're coming up with a fat substitute. You can be replaced."

29. Lil was a little conceited at first. When she decided to marry me, she said, "You know a lot of men are going to be miserable when I get married," I said, "Really, how many are you going to marry?"

30. I came home at three in the morning, and there was a burglar trying to pick the lock. I said, "I'll open it if you go in first."

31. Karen asked Lil one day, "Daddy, before you married Mom, who told you how to drive?"

32. Lil doesn't like being called a housewife. She prefers "domestic goddess."

33. Lil said she wants to live in the fast lane, but she married a speed bump.

34. I told Lil that I've decided to be buried in the Wal-Mart parking lot. That way I'll be sure she will visit me.

35. Lil and I were driving down lover's lane in the woods, and in silence when Lil said "Mit, dear, can you drive with one hand?" I said, "Yes my sweet" in ecstasy of anticipation. "Then," said my lovely Lil, "you'd better wipe your nose."

36. Lil said, "Mit, all pills don't come in bottles."

37. I get that low feeling when I recognize Lil's voice on the Dr. Ruth call in show.

38. I quit dancing, can't find any concave women.

39. My advice to men: When you think you've won an argument with your wife, the argument isn't over.

40. Lil asked, "Do you love me, Mit?" I said yes. She said, "Yes what?" I said, "Yes, please."

41. Is Lil home? No, do you want to leave a rumor?

42. Lil called the plumber who asked, "Where's the drip?" Lil answered, "Upstairs fixing the leak."

43. I overheard Lil praying for the Lord to give her the strength to fight just one more day.

44. TV has caused dissension in our house. Lil doesn't understand why I have to put on my glasses to hear Dolly Parton sing.

45. Every time there's a sexy scene, she breathes on my glasses.

46. When we first got married, we got along beautifully, but then on the way out of the church . . .

47. I told Lil I had a cold or something in my head. Lil said, "It must be a cold."

48. I sent her a Valentine card, and she said I was oversexed.

49. A fortune-teller told Lil she would be a widow soon and that I would die of poisoning. Lil asked, "Will I be acquitted?"

50. It all started very innocently. Lil said, "What's on the television?" I said, "Dust."

51. I would have bought life insurance on myself much sooner if I'd realized it would have made her such a great housekeeper. She's even waxing the bathtub now.

52. What to give Lil who has everything: I know what she needs. A husband who can pay for it.

53. You never know how she's going to get her own way.

54. Lil's dad asked me, "Would you marry Lil even if she didn't have a penny?"
    I said, "Yes, sir I would." He said, "Well, you're a lucky boy. You've got the right girl."

55. Re: Successful marriage. The secret—She makes all the minor decisions, and I make all the major ones. So far nothing major has come up.

56. I had a disturbing experience. I bought a used suit at a charity sale and found Lil's name and number in the pocket.

57. I just wish Lil would stop referring to my life insurance as "the big payoff."

58. The only thing we have in common is a difference of opinion.

59. Lil and I were strolling through the art museum, and I paused before a painting of extraordinary beauty. She was covered with only a few leaves. I stood there, admiring the painting for quite some time. Finally Lil nudged me. "Let's go, dear. We can't wait here for autumn."

60. I have never done anything behind Lil's back except zip her up.

61. Don't you just hate it when your wife goes on arguing after you've given up?

62. Marriage is like strong horseradish. You can praise it and still have tears in your eyes.

63. Elizabeth Dole says that getting married to Bob Dole has been a real religious experience . . . (pause) . . . a living hell.

64. Early in our marriage, Lil went to the bank to cash my paycheck, and the teller told her, "It needs your endorsement." Lil thought for a moment, then wrote on the back of the check, "Mit is a wonderful husband."

65. Lil has this sign posted in our kitchen: "Woman's work is never done . . . especially if she is waiting for her husband and kids to help her."

66. I live with my wife and three kids in a four-bedlam house.

67. Lil said to me after examining the family budget, "What we used to save for a rainy day wouldn't get us through a 30 percent chance of showers today."

68. Lil's father objected to our marriage. She said, "Don't worry, Dad, it's not as if it's forever."

69. Your marriage may be in trouble if she addresses your birthday card to "Occupant."

70. I'll always remember my wedding day. It was the last time she walked down the aisle without a shopping cart.

71. Lil said she had a glow-worm marriage. The glow is gone, but the worm remains.

72. Our marriage is on a fifty-fifty basis. I tell it like it is, and she tells me like it will be.

73. I had an argument with Lil recently. She wanted to buy a new living room couch. "I said there was nothing wrong with the old one." We argued all evening, but I had the last word. What was that? I said go ahead and buy the damned thing."

74. I realized I hadn't taken home a gift to Lil in several years. So I stopped on the way home from work to pick up some candy and flowers. When I arrived home, I rang the doorbell and handed her the flowers and candy. She immediately broke into tears. "What's the matter, dear?" I

asked. "I've had a terrible day," she replied. "The sink stopped up, the washer broke down, Kevin fell down the steps, the phone has been ringing all day, and I have a terrible headache . . . and now you come home drunk."

75. I am a soft-spoken person—by marriage.

76. I told Lil my new diet consisted of high fiber and low fat, so she came back with a piece of rope!

77. An experienced husband is one who can tell when his wife comes to the end of one argument and begins another,

78. I read to Lil, "This new survey of Americans sure paints a troubling portrait! For example, 7 percent would kill someone, and 25 percent would abandon their family for $10 million! Nearly everyone lies regularly at home or work . . . half say there's no reason to be married, and 31 percent admit to having an affair!
    Wife: "Well, that certainly doesn't describe me. I'd never kill anyone!"

79. Lil and a friend were having lunch at their favorite restaurant when Mabel Jones told Lil she had a secret to tell her. "I wouldn't want anyone else to know this," Mabel said, "but I am having an affair." "What kind of man is he?" Lil asked. Mabel seemed to drift off for a moment, then smiled. "Well, he really isn't anything to look at, but I just can't help myself," she said. "He's a slob, drinks too much beer, slurps his soup, and would rather spend his time watching sports on TV and bowling instead of being with me." Lil didn't say anything, but she was thinking about what Mabel told her. Lunch over, Lil went home, approached me, and demanded, "What's this I hear about you and Mabel Jones?"

80. "The three little words that set Lil's pulse to racing and her heart to pounding aren't 'I love you'—they're 'Reduced for clearance.'"

81. "My wife had a traumatic experience at our bank. She came home in tears. It seems that she somehow got in the wrong line . . . and made a deposit.

82. Where do mothers learn all the things they tell their daughters not to do?

83. Men have a long way to go to achieve equal rights with women. Do you realize diamonds are a girl's best friend, and man's best friend is a dog?

84. Lil: "You're going to have to choose between me and golf."
"But, Lil, I had 114 today. Do you expect me to quit when I'm at the top of my game?"

85. How we met. I was slopping the hogs, and Lil walked up to me and said there was just something about me that stood out from the crowd.

86. If you want to read about love and marriage, today you have to buy two separate books.

87. Lil complained she didn't have any outside interests, so I bought her a lawn mower.

88. "Lil, I've taken you safely over all the rough spots in life, haven't I?"
Lil: "Yes, and I don't think you've missed a one."

89. "Lil, you wouldn't want to go to the play in that old dress of yours, would you?" Lil said, "Of course not." Mit: "Great that's why I bought only one ticket."

90. After our honeymoon, I told Lil I felt like a new man. Lil said she did too.

91. I went out of town for a week. I wanted to leave Lil here. She said, "I'm going with you." I said, "There's absolutely nothing for you to do. It would be boring, and I couldn't be with you very much." She said, "I could shop all day." I said, "Lil, you can buy all the clothes you want right here in Houston." Lil said, "Have a nice trip. That's all I wanted to hear you say."

92. We run our marriage like a business. I am the silent partner.

93. At almost every party, some wife is sure to ask Lil, "What does your husband want to be when he grows up?"

94. There's one problem with reading *Playboy*. Looking at all those beautiful naked girls gets monotonous. I'll tell you something else my Lil said.

95. I don't like to talk about my wife behind her back. It's just safer that way.

96. My business went bankrupt, but my faithful Lil stood by me. I lost all our savings in the stock market, but my faithful Lil stuck with me. The bank foreclosed the mortgage on our house, but faithful Lil was at my side. And now the finance company has repossessed her new mink coat, but my faithful Lil has stuck by me. Isn't that right, Lil? Lil?

97. She doesn't exactly complain about our love life, but last week she took out a classified ad to sell our old mattress. It read: 1968 Simmons. Low mileage.

98. Mit to Lil as they plan their budget, "Let's start with the basic necessities . . . food, clothing, and shelter. We have a choice of two." 99. Lil to Mit: "If I left you for another man, would you be sorry?" Mit: "Why should I feel sorry for a man I don't even know?"

100. An antique shop always gives me the feeling I'm walking around in my wife's purse.

101. Lil went to a jewelry store and tried on a gold necklace. She told the owner it was nice, but she really wanted something more expensive. The owner said, "No problem. Come back tomorrow."

102. I've eaten so much chicken we've taken the mattress off the bed, and we now roost on the slats.

103. Lil and I always kiss at night before we go to bed. It's like touching gloves before we spend the entire night fighting over the covers.

104. Every night I kiss Lil good night and my covers good-bye. Lil wrote it's the other way around.

105. Lil wanted a foreign convertible for her birthday, so I bought her a rickshaw. (H. Youngman)

106. Mit said he'd clean the house when Sears came out with a riding vacuum cleaner.

107. No plastic in the dishwater, metal in the microwave, or utensils in the garbage disposal. There are so many rules in the kitchen it's safer to eat out.

108. Lil is so fussy, she even exchanges gift certificates

109. Lil is doing her part to bring peace to the world. Yesterday she burned her driver's license.

110. Lil likes to watch the soap operas, and I like to watch the baseball games; but the way the Astros are going, there's a lot more scoring on the soap operas.

111. My clothes really get dirty. Lil won't wash them. Once a week I have to put on all my clothes, put soap in the pockets, and walk thru a car wash. 112. I think Lil has the Hong Kong flu. That's when you get up in the middle of the night and you don't cough—you iron clothes.

113. I'm getting a little suspicious of Lil. Yesterday she got three obscene calls—collect.

114. We've cut down on barbecue expenses. We use Lil's toast as charcoal.

115. I told Lil the truth. I told her I was seeing a psychiatrist. Then she told me the truth that she was seeing a psychiatrist, two plumbers, and a bartender. (R. Daingerfield)

116. I told Lil that radiation might hurt my reproductive organs. She said, in her opinion, it was a small price to pay. (Johnny Carson)

117. I said, "Lil, I want to marry you. I want you to be the mother of my children." Lil asked, "Oh? How many children do you have?"

118. Lil: "How do you like my new suit?" "Lil, it would look better on a nail."

119. LIL: Our best friends ate at our house one night and were so impressed with Lil's cooking that they sent her a carving set. They sent her three chisels and a mallet.

120. LIL: I let Mit have a key to the house. He likes to show people how independent he is, but the key doesn't work.

121. "Lil, my razor doesn't cut at all." Lil: "Don't be silly, your beard can't be tougher than the linoleum."

122. Caller: "Good morning, Mrs. Sorrels. I'm from the gas company. I understand there's something in the house that won't work." Lil: "Yes, he's upstairs in bed."

123. I got up early one morning to let the milkman in and couldn't find my bathrobe so I put on Lil's kimono. When I opened the door, I was greeted with a great big kiss. The only thing I could figure was the milkman's wife must have had a kimono just like the one I had on.

124. "Lil, you promised at the altar you would obey me." Lil: "I know, but I just didn't want to make a scene."

125. "Lil, how did you stop your husband from staying out late?" Lil: "Well, when he came in late I called out, 'Is that you, Jack?' and my husband's name is Mit.

126. She's very nearsighted . . . lost her glasses—now she's knitting me a sweater out of spaghetti.

127. I dress so badly Lil doesn't want other people to know I'm her husband. When I open the car door for her, she gives me a tip.

128. Lil: "This is our fifty-second wedding anniversary. Let's have duck for dinner." Mit: "Why kill the duck for something that happened fifty-two years ago?"

129. Lil is so neat she puts paper under the cuckoo clock. (H. Youngman)

130. Lil said she never knew what to get her father for his birthday. I gave him a $100 and said, "Buy yourself something that will make your life easier." So he bought a present for my mother. (Rita Radner)

131. Comic Relief
Adding a touch of humor to an otherwise serious situation like the word *obey* in the marriage ceremony.

132. A husband is a person who is under the impression that he bosses the house when in reality he only houses the boss.

133. Marriage is the only war in which you sleep with the enemy.

134. Lil said she was married by a judge, but it should have been by a jury. (G Burns)

135. Lil also speaks Italian. For example, Veni, vidi, visa—We came, we saw, we went shopping.

136. Lil complimenting a bride on her old-fashioned domesticity: "You open cans just like your mother."

137. It's dangerous to marry a woman who looks good in black. (Czech proverb)

138. An optimistic husband is one who thinks his wife will be right out because he heard her say good-bye on the telephone.

139. If you want your wife to listen and pay undivided attention to every word you say, talk in your sleep.

140. My wife and I have been married for over fifty years, and my greatest thrill is when she puts on a see-through nightie because it doesn't block out so much of the TV set.

141. They say that you can still enjoy sex even into your later years. I dunno. Did you ever try blowing into someone's hearing aid?

142. Growing up, my mom always claimed to feel bad when a bird would slam headfirst into our breakfast room window. If she "really" felt bad, though, she'd have moved the bird feeder outside.

143. Lil said she wants to make love in back of the car, but she wants me to drive.

144. Lil really knows how to end a day. Last night we were finishing dessert and she said, "Did you hear about that brand-new car that's parked upside down?" I said, "No. I'd sure like to see that." She said, "Come out to the garage."

145. I was thinking about Lil's driving when I invited a friend to dinner and gave him instructions about getting here. "You can't miss our house," I said. "It's the one with all the tire marks on the curb."

146. The proven formula for fifty years of successful marriage. I DON'T TRY TO RUN HER LIFE, AND I DON'T TRY TO RUN MY LIFE.

147. I first met Lil in 1941—that was her room number.

148. We were introduced by a mutual friend—a bellhop.

149. When I first saw Lil, lights flashed and bells rang. She was playing the slot machine at the time.

150. I told my wife's father, "I want your daughter for my wife." He said, "I don't want to trade."

151. He asked me if I could support a family. I said, "Yes, sir, I believe I can." He said, "You know there are five of us."

152. It was our fifteenth anniversary. I asked Lil where she wanted to go. Lil said, "Oh, someplace I have never been." I said, "How about the kitchen?"

153. I took Lil out to eat at one of the finest places in town. She got so excited she dropped the tray.

154. Lil and I had words, but I didn't get to use mine.

155. Insurance salesman told Lil that you never know when someone will put arsenic in his coffee. Lil asked, "How much?"

156. My daughter was looking at family pictures one time. She saw this strong, thin, muscular man and asked Lil who he was. Lil said, "That's your father, dear." My daughter looked over at me and asked, "Then who is he?"

157. Many years ago, I asked Lil if she felt she could love someone like me. Lil asked, "How much like you?"

158. Lil was being instructed by the ladies of the church. They told her not to worry and that sex was just a normal bodily function—like a stroke.

159. I asked Lil how many truly great men were in the world. She said, "I don't know, but there is one less than you think there is."

160. Lil never was a social girl. In fact, she didn't start dating till after we were married.

161. I was sitting on the couch feeling kinda gloomy. Lil asked what was wrong. I said, "Oh, I guess I'm just trying to find myself." She said, "Why don't you go look around the refrigerator?"

162. How do you get your wife's attention? Look comfortable.

163. Husbands should forget their mistakes. There is no need for two people to remember them.

164. I asked Lil, "Why do people take such an instant dislike to me?" She said, "'Cause it saves so much time."

165. Lil gives me credit for bringing religion into her life. She said she never really believed in hell till she married me.

166. "Lil, it seems that nobody likes me." She said, "Don't be silly. Everyone doesn't know you."

167. I told Lil the last time we made love I almost froze, and the time before that I almost burned up. She said that was easy to explain. The last time was December, and the time before that was July.

168. "Mama, Mama, the house is on fire."
"Shut up! You'll wake up your father."

169. I came home with three ice chests full of fish. Lil asked me if I had a good time, and I told her yes but the food was lousy and the beds were dirty and I missed her more than ever before. I said when the guys go next year I don't think I'll go because I just didn't want to be without her. Lil said, "I'm not going to clean those fish!"

170. On our forty-sixth anniversary, Lil met me at the door with a drink in each hand and wearing a beautiful nightgown. The only problem was that she was coming home.

171. I took Lil to a drive-in movie but spent the whole night trying to find which car she was in.

172. She flops into bed in curlers, one-half pound of grease on her face, dressed for an army assault coarse. She comes to the breakfast table looking as if she came in second in a suicide contest. The doorbell rings and she says, "You answer it. I can't let the postman see me like this."

173. She's been mad at me all day. She dreamed last night that Robert Redford and I got in a fight over her and I won.

174. Lil once said, "Stir your coffee real well before you drink it."

175. Lil said, "I'm worried about our bank. Yesterday one of my checks came back marked Insufficient Funds. Now what kind of bank is it that doesn't have twenty-five bucks?"

176. Lil went to the grocery store to buy a chicken, but they never seem to have the size she wants. After picking up a frozen chicken, she asked if they ever got any larger. The clerk said "No, ma'am. They are dead."

177. I had an embarrassing moment, I was rummaging through the attic and came across some of Lil's love letters—and they were dated last week.

178. Life with Lil can sometimes be a little embarrassing. She asked our preacher neighbor what he enjoyed most. He said, "I like to save lost young men. Lil asked him to save her one."

179. Lil doesn't drive the car. She aims it.

180. I have family problems. Lil talks to the plants, she talks to the dog, she talks to the parakeet and to the goldfish. Me—she leaves a note on the refrigerator.

181. Lil had Hong Kong flu last week. That's where you get up at three in the morning. You don't cough, but you iron shirts.

182. She gets twenty-two miles to the fender.

183. Lil says she has absolutely nothing to wear and three closets to keep it in.

184. She is a good mime. She is always giving me the silent treatment.

185. Lisa asked Lil: "So you were married in 1954? Which were the best years?" Lil said, "The ones before that."

186. Lil and I had words, but I didn't get to use mine.

187. She uses a toolbox as one of her purses.

188. It was not unusual for me to have to stay late at the office. But one day I told her that, and she said, "Can I depend on it?"

189. Lil said she and I met in a revolving door and started going around together.

190. Lil's favorite casserole recipe is to combine everything on the left side of the refrigerator: put potato chips on top and bake.

191. To Lil from Mit: "This world was not meant for someone as wonderful as you."

192. My love, you take my breath away.
     What have you stepped in to smell that way?
     What inspired this amorous rhyme?
     Two parts vodka, one part of lime.

Love And Marriage

1. You've been with me twenty-one years? I don't remember breaking three mirrors.

2. You think "loading the dishwasher" means getting your wife drunk.

3. Men who have pierced ears are better prepared for marriage. They've experienced pain and brought jewelry.

4. Do not argue with a spouse who is packing your parachute.

5. I don't want to brag, but I've been married twenty years, and I weigh exactly what I weighed on my wedding night—if you include the wife and bottle of champagne I was carrying across the threshold.

6. A diplomatic husband said to his wife, "How do you expect me to remember your birthday when you never look any older?"

7. A talent scout discovered a girl in North Carolina with measurements 63-24-36 and called his office feeling that he had unearthed a sensational act. "What does she do?" his partner asked. "What does she do?" he repeated. "With a little help, she sits up."

8. There's a famous letter in a women's magazine office: "Sir, my wife was about to divorce me until she read a touching article in your magazine about the evils of a broken home. Now she says she is going to stick to me through thick and thin. Please cancel my subscription."

9.   Kurt was going out with a nice girl and finally popped the question. "Will you marry me, darling?" he asked. Lisa smiled coyly and said, "Yes, if you'll buy me a mink." Kurt thought for a moment and then replied, "Okay, it's a deal, on one condition." "What is that?" Lisa asked. "You'll have to clean the cage," Kurt replied.

10. The prospective father-in-law asked, "Young man, can you support a family?" The surprised groom-to-be replied, "Well, no. I was just planning to support your daughter. The rest of you will have to fend for yourselves."

11. Marital
     Harry says he proposed to his wife because she had a quality he admired: she could tolerate him.

12. Baloney is the unvarnished lie—laid on so thick you hate it. Blarney is flattery—laid on so thin you can love it. To tell a woman who is forty she looks like sixteen is baloney. The blarney way of saying it is, "Tell me how old you are. I should like to know at what age women are most beautiful!"

13. Wife to a friend: "Bill doesn't go to porno movies; he said it upsets him to see someone having more fun in one hour than he's had in a lifetime."

14. Have you noticed that women are a lot more concerned with their appearance before they get married? In merchandising there's a name for this—bait and switch!

15. Middle age creates terrible problems. For instance, my wife has started wearing elastic stockings, and it's very upsetting. All of her life she's worried about getting runs. Now she worries about getting blowouts!

16. A middle-aged fellow reports, "The three little words that set my wife's pulse to racing and her heart to pounding aren't I love you!" They are 'reduced for clearance.'"

17. "You must be sensitive to your wife's emotional needs. Never, ever whistle while you pack!"

18. "If you want to know whether she is honest," he says, "check the zero position on her bathroom scale."

19. "If it wasn't for marriage, husbands and wives would have to fight with strangers."

20. Angie Dickinson explains the divorce bit, "The trouble with most men is a woman marries one for life and then discovers he doesn't have any."

21. Our friendly neighborhood chauvinist surprised everyone by saying there should be more women in high government posts. Then he spoiled everything by saying every cabinet needs a few dishes.

22. February is a very difficult month. The football season is over and the baseball season hasn't begun. What do you use to ignore your wife?

23. The Sage of Sugar Creek says that careful planning is what enables a man to put off doing a job until his wife forgets about it.

24. Love is one long sweet dream, and marriage is the alarm clock.

25. Phyllis Diller told me her man asked for her finger measurements. "I thought he was going to buy me a diamond ring, but he gave me a bowling ball."

26. Couple to marriage counselor: "It seems that the only thing keeping us together is neither one of us had AIDS."

27. A very wise and farseeing man of my acquaintance buys his wife such fine and expensive china that she would never think of letting the clumsy ox help dry the dishes.

28. When asked why she never married, an old lady used to say, "It takes a mighty fine husband to be better than none."

29. I'll say one thing for my wife: she really knows how to praise our kids. Just this morning I heard her telling one of them, "You're getting to be just like your father!"

30. My wife is crazy about the sun. She spends the whole summer trying to get a deep brown luxurious tan. She says it's sexy and it is, if you are that way about briefcases.

31. One man to a group: "My psychiatrist tells me that most of the lying done by men in this world should be blamed on women. They insist on asking questions."

32. We had the cheapest honeymoon you could have—instead of Niagara Falls, we drove thru a car wash.

33. "The redhead (his wife)," Zig Ziglar said with a chuckle, "loves to shop. She was recently elected to the Master Charge Hall of Fame."

34. The bride was a rather untidy housekeeper and knew it. At last, she mustered the energy to give things a thorough cleaning one day. That evening her husband shouted from the hall, in great dismay, "Honey, where's the dust on this table. I had a phone number written in it."

35. We share household chores. I dry the dishes and she sweeps them up.

36. If my wife really loved me, she would have married someone else.

37. I love a man with dishpan hands!

38. Model Husband
He was called that, so he looked up the word. It meant "small imitation of the real thing."

39. A couple drove several miles down a country road, not saying a word. An earlier discussion had led to an argument, and neither wanted to concede their position. As they passed a barnyard of mules and pigs, the wife sarcastically asked, "Relatives of yours?" "Yes," the husband replied, "in-laws."

40. A woman was chatting with her next-door neighbor. "I feel really good today. I started out this morning with an act of unselfish generosity. I gave a twenty-dollar bill to a bum." "You gave a bum twenty whole dollars? That's a lot of money to just give away. What did your husband

say about it?" "Oh, he thought it was the proper thing to do." He said, "Thanks."

41. "Women take clothing much more seriously than men. I've never seen a man walk into a party and say, 'Oh my god, I'm so embarrassed, get me out of here. There's another man wearing a black tuxedo.'"

42. "Do you know what would have happened if it had been three wise women instead of three wise men? They would have asked directions, arrived on time, helped deliver the baby, cleaned the stable, made a casserole, and brought practical gifts."

43. A young man approached his family physician and said, "Doc, I'm afraid you'll have to remove my wife's tonsils one of these days." "My good man," replied the doctor, "I removed them six years ago. Did you ever hear of a woman having two sets of tonsils?" "No," the husband retorted, "but you've heard of a man having two wives, haven't you?"

44. "Honey," said this husband to his wife, "I invited a friend home for supper." "What? Are you crazy? The house is a mess, I didn't go shopping, all the dishes are dirty, and I don't feel like cooking a fancy meal?" "I know all that." "Then why did you invite a friend for supper?" "Because the poor fool's thinking about getting married!"

45. Did you hear the one about the young couple who disagreed about their forthcoming nuptials? She wanted a church wedding, and he didn't want to get married.

46. Women are like guns, keep one around long enough and you're going to want to shoot it.

47. A fantastically henpecked husband finally did something entirely on his own initiative: he dropped dead. His nagging wife mourned his loss and the fact that she had nobody left to badger. A visitor sympathized, "How you must miss dear Wilbur." "Yes," said the widow wistfully, "it seems but yesterday that he stood at that very door, holding it open until two flies got in."

48. The honeymoon is over when a man stops helping his wife with the dishes . . . and starts doing them himself.

49. Widows are not the only ones who have late husbands.

50. One fellow asked another, "Does your wife ever call you sugar?" After a moment's hesitation, the other fellow said, "Well, not exactly. But she came close to it this morning." "Yeah, what did she call you?" "A syrup-sopping, no-good biscuit-eating bum."

51. Wife: "Cedric, that woman next door bought a hat exactly like mine."
Husband: "Now I suppose you want to buy another one?"
Wife: "Well, it would be cheaper than moving."

52. My wife accused me of loving football more than I do her. I said, "Maybe I do, but I love you more than I love basketball."

53. If at first you don't succeed, shouldn't you try doing it like your wife told you to?

54. Memories: For a wedding present, he gave us a fifty-piece set of silver. It was a roll of dimes.

55. Pat is a terrible name for a woman. For instance, she can never wear it on the front of a sweater.

56. I used to be my own worst enemy, then I got married.

57. Until now, I had repressed any bad feelings for Donald and Ivana Trump on the theory their marriage had one redeeming social virtue: by choosing each other, they had saved two other people.

58. A woman who had just given birth to triplets was explaining to a friend that triplets happen just once in fifteen thousand times. "Good heavens!" exclaimed the friend. "When did you ever find time to do housework?"

59. I love being married. It's so great to find that one special person you want to annoy for the rest of your life.

60. Overheard from a distraught husband: "I never take my problems home with me—they're there when I get home."

61. Bernice and Bob were looking over various items for wedding gifts at the department store. Puzzled, Bob asked the saleslady, "What would

you suggest for a couple when it is her second marriage and his third?" Taken aback, but certainly not without a sense of humor, the saleslady replied, "Well, sir, certainly nothing monogrammed."

62. That's the trouble with girls today. All they do is thaw food. Why can't they open cans like their mothers did?

63. Your marriage may be in trouble if she addresses your birthday card to Occupant.

64. On our twenty-fifth anniversary, my husband took me out to dinner. Our teenage daughters said they'd have dessert waiting for us when we returned. After we got home, we saw that the dining room table was beautifully set with china, crystal, and candles, and there was a note that read, "Your dessert is in the refrigerator. We are staying with friends, so go ahead and do something we wouldn't do!" "I suppose," my husband responded, "we could vacuum."

65. "Don't criticize your wife. If she were perfect, she would have married much better than you."

66. Among her other faults, a fellow declares, his ex-wife was a terrible housekeeper. "The only time that woman used a broom," he declared, "was when she flew somewhere."

67. I have learned that if you upset your husband he nags you . . . if you upset him even more you get the silent treatment. Don't you think it's worth the extra effort?

68. A couple had been married for forty-five years and had raised a brood of eleven children and was blessed with twenty-two grandchildren. When asked the secret for staying together all that time, the wife replies, "Many years ago we made a promise to each other. The first one to pack up and leave has to take all the kids."

69. My parents recently retired. Mom always wanted to learn to play the piano, so Dad brought her a piano for her birthday. A few weeks later, I asked how she was doing with it. "Oh, we returned the piano," said my dad. "I persuaded her to switch to a clarinet instead." "How come?" I asked. "Well," he answered, "because with a clarinet, she can't sing."

70. His wife, says a fellow, returned from the beauty parlor the other day and told her husband she wasn't really satisfied with the result of her visit. "Actually," she said, "I haven't been all that pleased the last two or three times although it's the same operator who has worked on me for years. I wonder what the trouble is." "Well," said her husband just before the lights went out, "maybe you've built up immunity."

71. An ardent women's libber said to her husband, "Won't it be strange when women rule the country?" "Only to the bachelors," said the husband.

72. They have something now called Marriage Anonymous. When you feel like getting married, you call somebody and they send over a man in a dirty T-shirt who hasn't shaved in three days, smells like stale beer, and whines at you to make him a snack while he lies on the couch, emits various bodily gases and their accompanying noises, and watches football.

73. Wife reading news headline "Life Evolved from Smelly Bacteria, Scientists Assert" to husband in undershirt, beer in hand, watching TV: "Think of it, Ned, You may be the missing link . . ."

74. Every man should marry. After all, happiness is not the only thing in life.

75. Man in a downtown flower shop: "I want something to go with a weak alibi."

76. My doctor just divorced his wife, and I don't blame him. Every night, just before they got into bed, she gave him an apple.

77. Marriage changes passion . . . suddenly you're in bed with a relative.

78. Newchy's Law of Observation: "The probability of being observed is in direct proportion to the stupidity of your actions."

79. Niebuhr's Law of the Jungle: "Everyone out there is someone else's lunch."

80. I think it's a mistake not letting women go into combat. Why let all those years of marriage go to waste.

81. Husband: "What to you want for your birthday?" Wife: "I want a divorce." Husband: "I hadn't planned on spending that much."

82. Medical experts tell us that we can enjoy sex way past eighty . . . of course, they don't mean as a participant.

83. I saw six men kicking and punching the mother-in-law. My neighbor said, "Are you going to help?" I said, "No, six should be enough."

84. When does a Mexican become a Spaniard? When he marries your daughter.

85. I told my wife, "I've given you the best years of my life." And she said, "Those were the best?"

86. One summer evening during a violent thunderstorm, a mother was tucking her son into bed. She was about to turn off the light when he asked with a tremor in his voice, "Mommy, will you sleep with me tonight?" The mother smiled and gave him a reassuring hug. "I can't dear," she said. "I have to sleep in Daddy's room." A long silence was broken at least by his shaky little voice: "The big sissy."

87. How effete has our society become? Actor Burt Reynolds had it right when he said the average American idea of real hardship is "slow room service."

88. A man has six items in his bathroom: a toothbrush, shaving cream, razor, a bar of soap, and a towel from the Holiday Inn. The average number of items in the typical women's bathroom is 337. A man would not be able to identify most of these items.

89. Wife to best friend: "My husband's so self-centered that when he won a trip for two to Hawaii, he went twice."

90. On his birthday, his wife was feeling generous, and so she said, "My gift to you is that tonight you can do with me whatever you want." He thought it over and then sent her home to her mother.

91. Complete set of Encyclopedia Britannica. Excellent Condition—$1,200 or best offer. No longer needed. Got married last weekend. Wife knows everything.

92. Hear about the never-loving couple who went to see a marriage counselor. "Don't you two have anything in common?" he asked them. "Yes," said the wife. "Neither of us can stand the other."

93. The cheapest guy I ever met was the fellow who got his parents a fifty-piece dinner set for their golden anniversary. A box of fifty toothpicks.

94. "Will you love me when I'm old and gray?" she asked. Art Perlinger quotes the husband: "Why not? I've loved you through six colors already!"

95. That's what I call a loaded question. It's like your wife asking, "How do you feel today?" Which indicates either an interest in how you feel today—or she wants the oak tree transplanted.

96. "Sorry, we don't have potted geraniums," the clerk said, and then added helpfully, "could you use African violets?" "No," replied Ed sadly, "it was geraniums my wife told me to water while she was gone."

97. A couple had been married for twenty-five years and also had celebrated their sixtieth birthdays. During the celebration, a fairy appeared and said that because they had been such a loving couple all those years, she would grant them one wish each. The wife wanted to travel around the world. The fairy waved her wand and boom! She had the tickets in her hand. Next, it was the husband's turn. He paused for a moment, then said shyly, "Well, I'd like to have a woman thirty years younger than I." The fairy picked up her wand and boom! He was ninety. So there!

98. A widow recently married to a widower was accosted by a friend who laughingly remarked, "I suppose, like all men who have been married before, your husband sometimes talks about his first wife?" "Oh, not anymore, he doesn't," the other replied.
    "What stopped him?"
    "I started talking about my next husband."

99. "It's just too hot to wear clothes today," Jack says as he stepped out of the shower. "Honey, what do you think the neighbors would think if I mowed the lawn like this?" "Probably that I married you for your money," she replied.

100. My parents were of different religious beliefs, and they delighted in arguing various points. The morning after a long and lively discussion, I asked my mother who had won. "No one ever wins," she explained. "After all, there are no definite answers. Your father could be as right as I am, or I could be as wrong as he is."

101. Q: The definition of irreconcilable differences?
A: When she's melting down her wedding ring to cast it into a bullet.

102. Never go to bed with your problems. Sleep in different beds.

103. He had an argument with his wife recently, says a fellow. She wanted to buy a new living room couch. "I said there was nothing wrong with the old one," the fellow said.
"We argued all evening, but I had the last word."
"And what was that?"
"I said to go ahead and buy the damned thing."

104. Ermine has a calendar with bright sayings each day by one Blanche and Herb. I like this one best: "Blanche, if you make the toast and coffee, breakfast will be ready." Herb: "What are we having for breakfast?" Blanche: "Toast and Coffee."

105. Once upon a time, two brooms fell in love and decided to get married. Before the ceremony, the bride informed the groom broom that she was expecting a little whisk broom. The groom broom was aghast! "How is this possible?" he asked. "We've never even swept together!"

106. An optimistic husband is one who thinks his wife will be right out because he heard her say good-bye on the telephone.

107. I've always been impressed with television because it's so true to life. For instance, if you see a husband and wife on television and they're deliriously happy—it isn't because he got promoted, she's expecting, or they won the Irish Sweepstakes. They're happy because they've just discovered a new toilet bowl cleaner.

108. Everybody else was doing it, says speaker Doc B of Wharton, so he got some weights in order to go into training. "I should have gone into hiding," he says. "I couldn't pick them up down at the freight office."

"This smart young kid had to show off and throw them in the back of the pickup for me. I hate people like her."

109. "I think bankers get a lot of unfair criticism. My bank is very generous with me. They guaranteed me maximum interest for the next five years, which is more than my husband can do!"

110. A couple was leaving a party where the husband had slightly over caroused. "Dear," said his wife, "did anyone ever tell you that you were the most scintillating, fascinating, handsome, debonair man in the world?" "No, I guess no one ever did," he replied. "Then where did you get the idea?" she wanted to know.

111. A recent pollster in a San Diego mall handed out questionnaires to women shoppers. The question asked was, "Is there anything better than sex with the man you love? If so, what might that be?" Among those who answered yes, the preferences included "Double coupons," "A lifetime supply of chocolates," and "Shopping with the man you love's credit card."

112. I can pinpoint the exact moment when our marriage went bad. After my wife and I bought a waterbed, we kind of drifted apart.

113. I often think about marriage—it keeps my mind off sex.

114. I just wish my wife would stop referring to my life insurance as "the big payoff."

115. A man is getting married and is standing by his bride at the church. Standing by him are his golf clubs and bag. His bride whispers, "What are your golf clubs doing here?" The man said, "This is not going to take all day, is it?"

116. Pointed Story, Heavy Travel

   Harry did eight states in five days. His wife picked him up at the airport Friday and took him to dinner. He didn't say much, had one drink, and almost fell asleep. The waiter asked for their orders. Mrs. Harry said, "A salad with Italian and a small sirloin, medium." The waiter wrote that down and asked, "What about the vegetable?" And Mrs. Harry replied, "He'll have the same."

117. Some modern brides still follow tradition. One such read it was bad luck to see the groom the morning of the wedding, so she threw him out of their apartment the night before.

118. Dick Schimmel says a neighbor told him the wife was complaining. She wanted a job outside the home. "What did you do?" Dick asked. "I got her a new riding lawn mower," the neighbor said.

119. Did you hear about the two antennas that got married? The wedding sucked, but the reception was great!

120. How can you tell if your husband is dead? The sex is the same, but you get the remote.

MEDICAL

1. The doctor told the patient to give up half his sex life. Patient asked, "Which half? Thinking about it or talking about it?"

2. Tell my wife how healthy she looks and you have made a mortal enemy.

3. Lent a guy $2,000 to have plastic surgery, and now he doesn't know what he looks like.

4. Sign in OB Ward: "The first five minutes of life are very risky." Someone had scribbled down below: "The last five are not so hot either."

5. The doctor told the patient to take off all his clothes. He asked him if they couldn't go out a few times first.

6. We quit our physician; he is too pessimistic. In his waiting room, they play taps.

7. A hypochondriac can suffer in many ways but never in silence.

8. Sign in psychiatrist's office: "No one in their right comes to see me."

9. Pity the two corpuscles—they lived in vein.

10. Doctor had to leave the office to move his car. He said to his patients, "Don't anybody get better I'll be right back."

11. Medicare has an old wino burial plan. It is called Elder Bury.

12. Newspaper
    We apologize for accidentally omitting the word *pain* from your add for "pain-free dentistry." We regret any confusion this may have caused.

13. "Mit, take these three pills on an empty stomach, if the occasion ever arises."

14. After my accident, Dr. Franklin told Lil, "Mit may never work again." She said," Let me tell him, Doctor, it will cheer him up."

15. George Burns: "Sex is better than ever when you reach seventy, especially the one in the winter."

16. Now they have a new pill—has nothing but side effects.

17. Patient said she had been married twice but had no other serious illnesses.

18. He spent $3,000 for orthodontic care on his son, and he never smiles.

19. Treated an oriental three and one-half years for yellow jaundice—cured him.

20. If you actually look like your passport, you are not well enough to travel.

21. He spent a small fortune to cure his halitosis only to find out his friends didn't like him anyway.

22. Compassionate man visited an old friend at St. Luke's. The doctor had given him six months to live. He brought him a calendar.

23. Psych: "How long have you been feeling like you are a dog?" "Since I was a pup."

24. A lady continually complained. I said, "I wish I had one hundred patients like you. She asked, "What do you mean?" I said, "I have a thousand."

25. He gives blood—not for transfusion but to sterilize the instruments.

26. Man asked the doctor, "Will I be able to play the piano after my operation? The doctor said, "Sure." Patient, "Funny I couldn't do it before."

27. He has donated his body to medical science, but until they need it, he is going to preserve it in alcohol.

28. When Lil was pregnant, she had a young OB, and he would ask her, "Where does it hurt?"

29. The MD said no more wine or women for you, but you can sing all the songs you want.

30. A lady was going door to door with a survey. At one house she asked the lady how many children she had. The answer was that she had triplets and added that that happened only once in fifteen thousand times. She said, "My lord, how do you find time to do your housework?"

31. Blank form: "Who to call in case of an emergency?" Answer: "A good doctor."

32. Doctor: "I am afraid we will not know the exact nature of your condition until after the autopsy."

33. There are so many malpractice suits brought against doctors these days that now if you want a doctor's opinion on something, you have to talk to his lawyer.

34. My neighbor cried to me, "Last week I ate nothing but $100-a-plate dinners. I was in the hospital."

35. Doctor to hospital patient: "Good news, Mr. Fornsby . . . a team of doctors thinks you're strong enough to see the hospital bill!"

36. A local doctor tells about the fellow who hurried into the office and wanted help for his virility, which he said was too high. When the doctor asked him to explain, the man said, "It's too high because it's all up in my head."

37. In the interest of saving time and confusion, many hospitals are using painted stripes on the floors leading to the most used departments. At one in California, the receptionist told a lady who asked where X-ray was to walk along the yellow line. The lady started out along the line like it was a tightrope and finally turned back to the desk and said, "I think you should know that I'm here because I'm sick, not drunk."

38. A man sat in a doctor's office and kept up a strange litany: "I hope I'm sick. I hope I'm sick." Another waiting patient asked, "Why do you want to be sick?" The man said, "I'd hate to be well and feel like this."

39. The doctor was busy, and it took hours to check all of his patients. Down to Mr. Smith, the doctor apologized to the old man, saying, "I hope you didn't mind waiting so long." Mr. Smith said, "It's a shame you couldn't see my illness in its early stages."

40. A doctor examined an airline pilot, asking him, "When was the last time you had sex?" The pilot answered, "About 1955." The doctor asked, "So long ago?" The pilot said, "That wasn't too long ago." He look at his watch and went on, "It's only 2120!"

41. An old woman went to a gynecologist. When his examination was done, she turned to him and asked, "Doctor, does your mother know how you make your living?"

42. A man went to a woman doctor's office. The doctor told him to go into an examining room and take off his clothes. He did so. After a few minutes, there was a knock on the door. The doctor entered. She proceeded to examine him completely, looking closely at every part of his body. Then she said, "Do you have any questions?" The patient said, "I have one, why did you knock?"

43. Coming out of a restaurant, a man met his dentist on the way in. The man asked, "Listen, what should I do about my yellow teeth?" The dentist said, "Wear brown."

44. A man came into a dentist's office with his wife and said to the dentist, "Look, I want you to pull this bad tooth, but we haven't got a lot of time, so forget the novocaine or the laughing gas." "You've got guts," the dentist said. "Which is the tooth?" The man said, "Marie, show him the tooth that hurts."

45. Do you call a gay dentist a tooth fairy?

46. A man rushes into a drugstore and says, "Do you have a cure for hiccups?"
    Without warning, the druggist hits him in the face with a wet rag. The man says, "What the hell are you doing?" "You don't have the hiccups now," the druggist says. "No, but my wife out in the car does!"

47. A man walked into a drugstore and asked the female clerk if he could talk to a pharmacist. She said that she was a pharmacist and the only one on duty. Bashfully, the man explained, "I have a terrible condition. I'm always thinking of sex. I'm never satisfied. I can keep having sex twenty hours a day. Can you give me something for that?" The clerk excused herself and went into the back of the store. She returned a few minutes later and said, "I just talked it over with my sister. The best we can give you is two hundred cash and the store!"

48. It's not very comforting to know that 50 percent off all dentist and physicians practicing today graduated in the bottom half of their class. 49. After an operation the girl asked, "Doctor, do you think the scar on my stomach will show?" The doctor said, "My dear, that depends entirely on you."

50. Medical experts tell us we can enjoy sex way past eighty years of age—of course that doesn't mean as a participant.

51. Good things about Alzheimer's disease—you meet new people every day, and you can hide your own Easter eggs.

52. Went to the beach last week not to swim—just to pick up medical supplies. 53. It's the kind of medicine you have to be in tip-top condition just to get the cap off.

54. Did you ever run into one of those mothers that think their kids can do no wrong?
    I was in a dentist's office last week, and one of them was saying, "Gregory! Now be a good boy and say ah so the nasty dentist can get his finger out of your mouth."

55. Did you hear the one about the nervous surgeon who was finally discharged from the hospital? It wasn't so much all the patients he lost—it was those deep gashes he makes in the operating table.

56. Even the cows need psychiatry! They have a fodder complex.

57. It's so healthy out there; they had to shoot a guy to start a cemetery.

58. The only culture she exposed her children to was bacteria.

59. Let me reemphasize that for the most part our results have been positive. However, some of the patients who have come to us seeking comic relief have experienced enlargement of the jocular vein. Others complained of jest pains. And a few even developed hemorrhoids.

60. In Czechoslovakia, for example, seriously ill patients are hooked up to laugh support systems, which interject humor (in a light vein, of course) at a rate of about 4.6 millidangerfields an hour. In fact, there's a bit of a problem because sometimes people have trouble staying on these strict joke regimen after they leave the hospital. It's very common to see Czech returned for insufficient funs.

61. "That's right. I was advised that if I want to survive, I'd have to give up wine, women, and song."
    "Sorry to hear that, I didn't know you were so ill."
    "I'm not."
    "But you just said your doctor . . ."
    "Not my doctor. That was my accountant!"

62. I'm not appreciated—received a get-well card from Bob Gravette and said, "Get well soon but not too soon."

63. I went to my doctor last week, and he told me to take a hot bath before retiring, but that's ridiculous. It'll be years before I retire!

64. Insurance is like a hospital gown—you're not sure whether you're covered or not.

65. This department requires no physical fitness program! Everyone gets enough exercise jumping to conclusions, flying off the handle, carrying things too far, dodging responsibilities, and pushing his luck.

66. Man went up north secretly to get new hearing aids. When asked how they were, he said, "Wonderful. I can even hear people talking in the next room."
    "Have you told your family?"
    "Not yet, I've already changed my will three times."

67. It takes guts—like selling cuckoo clocks in psychiatrists' waiting rooms.

68. A man partook generously of food and drink one New Year's Eve and subsequently developed a severe intestinal cramp. He went to the doctor and asked, "Do you think the trouble is with my appendix?" "No," said the doctor, "I think it's with your table of contents."

69. Perhaps the best advice on health ever given was by ageless baseball wonder Satchel Paige, who said, "Avoid fried meats which anger up the blood. If your stomach disputes you, lie down and pacify it with cool thoughts. Keep the juices flowing by jangling around gently as you move. Go very light on the vices, such as carrying on in society. The social ramble ain't restful. Avoid running at all times. And finally, don't look back. Something may be gaining on you."

70. My health and accident insurance isn't all that good. For instance, if I'm run over by a truck, all it pays for is the damage done to the truck.

71. Texas Medical Center is very progressive; they have just invented a cure for which there is no known disease.

72. Viagra

    What is the similarity between Viagra and Disney? You have to wait an hour for a three-minute ride.

    Following the approval of Viagra by the UK's authority, the shipment arrived yesterday at Heathrow Airport; before it reached the depot, it was hijacked. Scotland Yard has warned the public to be on the lookout for *hardened* criminals.

    What do you get when you mix marshmallows and Viagra? Hard candy.

    My doctor says that giving Viagra to an eighty-year-old is like installing a new flagpole on a condemned building.

    Did you hear about the new Viagra cookie mix? It's called Big Newtons.

    Did you know that Viagra has been around for ages, but India had kept it a secret for a long time . . . How do you think they could play a flute and make that rope come out of the basket like that?

73. I told the psychiatrist I keep hearing strange voices in my ear. He said, "Where do you want to hear them?"

74. I'm so worried about swine flu, if I saw the *Three Little Pigs*, I'd root for the wolf.

75. I recently went in for cosmetic surgery—I swallowed a mascara brush.

76. My health insurance is an HMO. That stands for Hand Your Money Over.

77. Another man went to the doctor for the first time in years and watched nervously as the doctor looked at his test results. "Uh-oh," said this doctor, "I'm afraid you have only three minutes to live."
    "Three minutes? Doc, can you do anything for me?"
    "I could boil you an egg."

78. My doctor became annoyed when my stay in the hospital was interrupted by my recovery.

79. My father has a hearing aid and a pacemaker. My kids want to know if Grandpa came with batteries.

80. I used to be a hypochondriac, but then I got sick of it.

81. Medicine is so high-tech now. When I'm not feeling well, I don't know whether to go to a drugstore or RadioShack.

82. My health coverage is good and bad. They'll pay 100 percent of all medical procedures under ten dollars.

83. My doctor is very considerate. He charges inflated fees to help me reach my deductible faster.

84. After years of therapy, I finally found a way to deal with my depression—I cry a lot.

85. Did you hear about the fellow who got a kidney transplant and later found out it came from a bed wetter?

86. Did you hear about the rock-and-roll singer who wore a hearing aid for three years—then found out he only needed a haircut?

87. "But, Dad, if I go to medical school, it will take me five more years, and I'll be twenty-seven years old by then." The wise old father responded,

"Tell me, son, how old will you be in five years if you don't go to medical school?"

88. A proctologist stands behind his work.

89. I admire people who can plan ahead—so far the only things I have put aside for my old age is arthritis, gout, and high blood pressure.

90. Schizophrenia isn't all bad. It beats living alone.

91. He said to his date, "Why don't we go to my apartment. Sex is good for relieving arthritis." She said, "But I don't have arthritis." He said, "What's the matter? You don't believe in preventive medicine?"

92. Many hospitals are advertising their wares these days, and they're all missing a great opportunity. So far, their jingles, testimonials, and other appeals for business have been confined to print, broadcast, and billboard advertising. But there's one great advertising medium that has gone unused for more than two decades—the little roadside signs, planted in series—that amused motorists for thirty-seven years as they sold Burma-Shave. In the true spirit of Burma-Shave's long-gone poets, modern advertisers could resurrect the medium along feeder roads into the city where motorists have ample time to read as they poke or wait in rush hour traffic. If you're sitting in a line of cars calculating whether you'll get through on the second or third change of the light ahead, you'd have ample time to read messages from a hospital emergency service:

Broken Arm Got You in Limbo? Pull Right up to Our Drive-In Window Having Babies, Girl Or Boy? We'll Help Deliver Your Bundle of Joy."

From a psychiatric clinic:

"Don't lose your head from minute to minute. We'll screw it on straight with the brains that are in it."

For a cosmetic clinic:

"Stomach sagging? Interest flagging? We'll save you bucks on your tummy tucks."

"They all laughed at hose-nose Rose. Now Rose has beaus since she trimmed her nose."

For hypnosis services for weight and smoking control:

"If your girth is cause for mirth, try hypnosis for your belly's worth."
"No need for you to stew and pace. If she says, "Butt out, furnace face," try hypnosis."

93. The doctor was busy with a patient when his nurse burst into the room.

"Doctor," she exclaimed, "that man you just gave the clean bill of health to? He was walking out of the office, and he dropped dead. What should we do?"

"Don't worry," the doctor replied. "Just turn him around so he looks like he was walking in."

94. Pick out what does not belong on the following list, and explain why. The items are AIDS, herpes, gonorrhea, a farm in northern Missouri. The answer is gonorrhea because you can get rid of it.

95. Seems a seventy-year-old gent and his sixty-seven-year-old baby doll make an appointment with a doctor, went to his office, and said they were having certain problem and would he please watch them do some smooching. The doctor looked puzzled but agreed. When the couple had finished, the doctor said, Looked OK to me. I didn't see anything wrong." He charged them $32. This happened several weeks in a row. The couple would make an appointment, smooch, pay the doctor, and leave. Finally the doctor, thoroughly puzzled, asked, "Exactly what are you trying to find out?" The old gent said, "We are not trying to find out anything. She's married, and we can't go to her house. I'm married, and we can't go home. The Holiday Inn charges $60, the Hilton charges $78. We do it here for $32, and I get a $28 refund from Medicare."

96. Patient: "Doctor, I'd like something to make me smarter."
Doctor: "Take these pills and come back to see me next week."
Patient (next week): "Doc, I don't think I' m any smarter."
Doctor: "Take these pills and come back to see me next week."
Patient (next week): "Doc, I don't think I've gotten any smarter yet. Are you sure these pills aren't candy?"
Doctor: "Now you're getting smarter."

97. I moved to Detroit for health reasons. I'm very paranoid, and Detroit's the only place my fears are justified.

98. A fellow went to a psychiatrist because he thought he was a sick fox terrier. A friend asked, "Did it do any good?" The fellow said, "It sure did. Feel my nose."

99. It has been proven beyond doubt that smoking is a leading cause of statistics.

100. A study has been made of one hundred Japanese optometrists, and it's found that 40 percent of them have cataracts. The other 60 percent have Datsuns and Toyotas.

101. A psychiatrist was sitting in his office when his receptionist buzzed him and said, "Doctor, there are two people out here wanting to make appointments to see you. One has a fear of Santa Claus and the other is afraid of the entire Christmas season. What shall I tell them?"

    The psychiatrist checked his book, then replied, "I'll see the Santa Claustrophobia this afternoon and the Noel Coward in the morning."

102. What do you call a person who has AIDS, herpes, and syphilis? An incurable romantic.

103. A fellow went to the doctor for a complete checkup. "I look in the mirror, and I'm a complete mess," he said. "My jowls are sagging. I have splotches all over my face, my hair is falling out, and I feel ugly. What is it?" The doctor said, "I don't know what it is, but your eyesight is perfect."

104. "The only jewel Fang ever gave me was a Medic Alert bracelet saying, 'In case of accident, the body looked like this before.'" (That's the same body that has so many liver spots it should come with a side of onions.)

105. Advice—never go to the dentist who has had his office soundproofed.

106. The patient glared morosely at the doctor. "Now, now," said the medical man in a soothing tone, "don't look so glum. I've had the same

illness myself." "Sure," said the patient, "but you didn't have the same doctor."

107. How's this for a security device, spotted by a man at a condo: "This property is protected by a pit bull with AIDS."

108. The common cold is both positive and negative. Sometimes the eyes have it and sometimes the nose.

109. A guy went to a doctor to have his throat checked but objected when the nurse told him to take off his clothes. She insisted it was the doctor's rule, so he complied and sat down on a bench next to another naked guy, who was slightly inebriated. He told the tipsy on, "Helluva rule, isn't it?" The other guy said, "Yeah, I just came here to pay my bill."

110. Reports that doctors are often misunderstood are supported by this recent incident after a man had been examined:
    "I'm sorry, but I can't find any cause for your illness," said the doctor. "Perhaps it is due to drinking."
    "Well, I can understand that," replied the patient. "I'll just come back when you're sober."

111. Doctor to others: "Unfortunately, we doctors can't please everyone. I have a patient who's so cheap, he yelled at me because he got well before his pills were all used."

112. A paranoid person who has low self-esteem thinks nobody important is out to get him.

113. Patient tells her doctor: "I've consulted with a fortune-teller, a palm reader, the tarot cards, and a faith healer. Doctor: "And what stupid advice did they give you?" Patient: "They all told me to go see you."

114. I'm so nearsighted yesterday I tried to dial the pencil sharpener.

115. Doctor to patient: "The bad news is that you have only twenty-four hours to live."
    "And what's the worst news?"
    "I've been trying to reach you for the last twenty-four hours."

116. Why did the dentist examine the computer? He wanted to check its bytes.

117. I've had a chronic medical problem all of my life. I'm allergic to calories. I break out in hips.

118. A young lady came to visit a young man in the hospital. His condition didn't allow too many visitors, but the young lady tried to march right in and was stopped by an older woman exiting. The older woman, who looked like a volunteer "gray lady," said, "There are no outside visitors allowed in this room." The young lady said, "Oh, that's all right. I'm his sister."
The older woman said, "How nice to meet you. I'm his mother."

119. The person who has everything usually sits next to you in the doctor's waiting room.

120. He's got more nerve than a root canal.

121. Doctor treated a child five years for a speech impediment and finally found out it was peanut butter.

122. I told my doctor, "It hurts when I do this." He said, "Don't do that." (Henny Youngman)

123. The doctor explained to the heart patient that he would be able to resume his romantic life as soon as he could climb two flights of stairs without becoming winded. The patient listened attentively and said, "What if I look for women who live on the ground floor?"

124. "Have you heard about the kleptomaniac who gave it up?"
"No, I hadn't."
"Well, he had to. He just couldn't take it anymore."

125. Overheard in doctor's waiting room: "Is he a hypochondriac? His water bed is filled with chicken soup."

126. Doctor to patient: "My suggestion is that you give up the pursuit of happiness and concentrate on the pursuit of survival."

127. I wonder what a cured ham had.

128. Jogging reduces stress—now all you have to worry about is being hit by a car bitten by a dog or mugged.

129. Doctor: "Well, Mrs. Franklin, I'm happy to say I've got good news for you."
Patient: "Pardon me, Doctor, it's Ms. Franklin." Doctor: "Oh . . . in that case I've got bad news for you."

130. I once knew a guy so rich that when he went to a doctor for a pain in his leg, it was diagnosed as Perrier of the knee."

131. Never mistake asthma for passion or vice versa.

132. It's better to be healthy than wise. If you're sick, it costs you money, but you can be stupid for free.

133. Never go to a doctor whose office plants have died. (Erma Bombeck)

134. One time I went to the doctor and told him I had a ringing in my ear. He said, "Don't answer it."

135. The doctor who performed my surgery was at the banquet tonite. I happened to glance over at him during the meal, and his wife was cutting his meat for him.

136. My doctor is very conservative. If he doesn't need the money, he doesn't operate.

137. I told my psychiatrist I thought everyone hated me because I was so good-looking. He said, "You don't need a psychiatrist. You need a mirror."

138. I told my psychiatrist I kept hearing strange voices in my ear. He said, "Where do you want to hear them?"

139. If you exercise daily, you will die healthier.

140. Headline: Impotence Is on the Rise

141. My doctor won't let me watch X-rated movies. He said if you don't blink your eyes every ten seconds, you'll go blind.

142. He is a fool who makes his doctor his heir. (Ben Franklin)

143. Joan Rivers: "My obstetrician was so dumb that when I gave birth he forgot to cut the cord. For a year, that kid followed me everywhere. It was like having a dog on a leash."

144. Skin is like wax paper that holds everything in without dripping. (A. Linkletter)

145. Never entrust your life to a surgeon who has more than three Band-Aids on his fingers.

146. Never go to a plastic surgeon whose favorite artist is Picasso.

147. Because I feel inferior, I try harder. Because I am inferior, it doesn't do any good.

148. I told my doctor that sometimes I feel so inferior I don't think anyone notices me at all. He said, "Next."

149. I asked my doctor, "What do you do for a sprained ankle?" He said, "Limp." (M. Berle)

150. My doctor said, "Have you ever had this pain before?" I said yes. He said, "Well, you've got it again." (H. Youngman)

151. Bug your doctor. When he says strip to the waist, take off your pants.

152. She has Mania Klepts—she's always leaving things.

153. My wife takes so many iron pills in the morning when she gets up and stretches, she turns north.

154. I've just heard about his illness. Let's hope it's nothing trivial.

155. This job has done wonders for my paranoia. Now I really have enemies. (Kissinger)

156. "Doctor, did you ever make a serious mistake?"
"Yes, I once cured a millionaire in only three visits."

157. The biggest challenge facing the post office today is a medical problem. If an employee comes down with sleeping sickness, how can you tell?

158. Psychiatrist shows a man an inkblot.
    "What does this remind you of?"
    "Sex."
    Shows him another inkblot.
    "What does this remind you of?"
    "Sex."
    Still another inkblot and the same answer was sex. The psychiatrist says, "Young man, all you seem to think about is sex." The guy yells, "All I seem to think about is sex? Whose showing all the dirty pictures?"

159. Patient went into a Medicaid clinic and got a blood test, a blood pressure test, EKG, eye test, urine analysis, brain scan, and X-rays, but it didn't work out. When he left, his hangnail was as bad as ever.

160. A frail, tired little man told his doctor that the demands of his two-hundred-pound wife were about to kill him. "I work twelve hours a day in order to support her in a way to which she never was accustomed, and then I have to stay up with her till three or four o'clock in the morning dancing with her in the nightclubs." The doctor said. "No woman can stand a nightly routine like that, so let her have her way absolutely for one year. Give in to her every whim, and you have my assurance that a year from today she'll be dead." The man said, "You give me hope. Can I count on it?" "The doctor said, "You have my guarantee." The scene now shifts to the little man's backyard exactly 364 days later. By this time, he was so weak he had to be wheeled around in a chair, and his hands shook so that he had to use both of them to get a glass of orange juice up to his lips. He sat bundled up in two rugs, shivering and watching his wife, huskier than ever, beating a rug. Every time she followed thru with her beater, the clothesline quivered like a violin string, and the rug flew into the breeze. She packed all the wallop of a giant tank. The little man watched her in wonder and cackled to himself, "And to think by this time tomorrow she'll be dead."

161. The doctor was doing so well in his practice he could occasionally tell a patient there was nothing wrong with him.

162. Doctors are people who prescribe medicine of which they know little, to cure diseases of which they know less in human beings of whom they know nothing. (Voltaire)

163. Physicians say one million women are overweight. These, of course, are round figures.

164. A Scotch doctor had a patient who had a temperature of 108. The doctor put him in the cellar to heat the building.

165. The doctor's work fills six feet of ground, but the dentist's work fills an acher.

166. A farmer brought his son to town to have a wisdom tooth extracted. It was his first time to be in a dentist's office. The doctor started to give him the injection, and the farmer asked, "What is that?" The dentist told him it was medicine and soon the young man wouldn't know a thing. The farmer said, "Forget it, Doc, he don't know nuthin now."

167. Every ten seconds a woman gives birth to a child. She must be found and stopped. (Sam Levenson)

167. The doctor told the man he had three minutes to live. The patient cried out, "Can't you do something, Doctor?" The doctor said, "Well, I can boil you an egg."

168. We quit our doctor, and now we go to a vet. It's not bad if you don't mind being licked by other patients and you get your belly rubbed when you are being examined. You also get a little sweet tart. But you have to be careful because in no time at all they can dip and worm you. We are lucky because our vet is also a taxidermist. On the door, he has a sign that says, "Either way you get your loved one back."

169. I had amnesia once or twice.

170. Doctor to patient: "I have good news and bad news. The good news is that you are not a hypochondriac."

171. Hospital report
Patient did not live up to her wellness potential. (In other words, the sucker died.)

172. Statistics show that three out of four people suffer with hemorrhoids. I guess that means that one out of four enjoys it.

173. My doctor is very considerate. He charges inflated fees so I can reach my deductible quicker.

174. I don't understand. Why don't faith healers do teeth?

175. Man asked the doctor, "Will I be able to play the piano after my operation?" The doctor said, "Sure." The patient said, "Funny, I couldn't do it before."

176. HMO stands for Hand Your Money Over.

177. Three years ago on the east side of town, they built a hospital and named it Our Lady of Malpractice. Three million dollars went to the recovery room, but no one wants to use it. No one!

178. A patient confessed to her physician that she had first consulted with a faith healer, fortune-teller and palm reader. The doctor asked, "And what foolish and idiotic advice did they give to you?" The wry answer: "They all told me to see you."

179. I asked the audiologist how much hearing aids cost. He said, "Anywhere from $2 to $4,000. I said, "Let me see the $2 style. He put the device around my neck and said, "Stick this little button in your ear and run this string down to your pocket. I asked, "How does it work?" "For $2 it doesn't work," he said, "but when people see it on you, they talk louder."

180. Creative merchandising is a ten-thousand-pack carton of cigarettes that when empty converts into a casket.

181. I told my doctor it hurts when I do that. He said, "Don't do that."

182. He is dying of fast women, slow horses, crooked dice, and straight whiskey.

183. A patient is lying on a psychiatrist's couch. The psychiatrist asks him, "Is fruit cake one word or two words?"

184. When I was in the hospital after my accident, the doctor said I might have to have brain surgery, and it could leave me with permanent brain damage. Lil asked, "Well, how will we know?"

185. Doctor's office sign in treatment room: Medical School Equivalency Diploma

186. No you don't have to floss them all. Just floss the ones you want to save.

187. Polish woman (standing in middle of the street): "Officer, can you tell me how to get to the hospital from here?" Policeman: "Just stand right where you are."

188. Q: What will happen when the government takes over health care? A: Your coverage will have the efficiency of the post office and the bedside manner of the IRS.

Men/Husband

1. "You told me if I rubbed grease on my chest I would become taller like you, but it didn't work."
   "What did you use?"
   "Crisco."
   "Stupid, that's shortening."

2. She: "What's the difference in a man and government bonds?"
   Her answer: "The bonds mature."

3. I asked the cute manicurist, "How about a date?" She said, "I'm married." I said, "Just call up your husband and tell him you are going to meet a girl friend." She said, "You tell him. He's shaving you."

4. Women astronauts are better because they don't have to stop and ask for directions.

5. Feminist slogan: "A woman without a man is like a fish without a bicycle."

6. One man to another: "My wife thinks I should become more fashion conscious and start dressing better. It's embarrassing to her when we eat in a restaurant, and people who walk past our table drop coins in my coffee cup."

7. A yawn is nature's way of letting a married man open his mouth.

8. Lazy? He's the kind who gets in a revolving door and waits.

9. I won't say I'm an experienced kisser, but they don't call me Lava Lips for nothing.

10. He's as innocent as a chorus girl with three mink coats.

11. I don't have any trouble at costume balls. I just turn up the sides of my toupee and go as a bird's nest.

12. He wears the pants in his family, but there's always an apron over them.

13. I wouldn't say he's effeminate. Let's say he's sort of a near miss.

14. There's just one thing I don't understand. If you're a self-made man, why did you give yourself such a big mouth?

15. I guess fate is against me. People just don't laugh at handsome, virilemen.16. I became a leader of men—an usher in a burlesque show.

17. Life today is made for women, not men. Let's face it, when he's born, people ask about the mother. When he's married, his wife gets all the presents. And when he dies, who goes to Florida on the insurance money?

18. I won't say he cheats, but he won't go bowling anymore. Who can tilt an alley?

19. He's so cheap he uses his old dental floss for wrapping packages.

20. His friends call him Bacon because somebody is always bringing him home. 21. Husband said, "What did I say to offend you, dear? It might come in useful again sometime."

22. These are my golf socks. There's a hole in one.

23. An old woman who had supported her lazy husband all her life was asked why she put up with the bum. The old woman smiled and said, "True, I make the living, but he makes the living worthwhile."

24. While at a banquet, Lady Astor once stated that men were far vainer than women. As all the men vehemently disagreed, she set out to prove her point. She skillfully maneuvered the conversation to men's fashions and said in a loud voice, "It's a pity that the most intelligent and learned men attach least importance to the way they dress. Why, right at this table the most cultivated man is wearing the most clumsily knotted tie!" As if on cue, every man in the room immediately began to adjust his tie. 25. Men are irrational. They want home service in a hotel and hotel service at home.

26. Sometimes it's better not to overhear conversations. Our neighbors were telling my wife they went all the way to Arizona on their vacation, and standing at the rim of the Grand Canyon, they could realize just how insignificant man is. My wife said she could realize it without ever leaving the living room.

27. Cheap? Who do you know makes their own paper clips?

28. I certainly was popular at that party. When I got there, only one person said hello. When I left, everybody said good-bye.

29. I know I've put on a few pounds, but that's no reason for the photographer to say he'd have to use a telefatso lens.

30. I weighed six pounds, eight ounces when I was born. I eat more than that now for lunch.

31. Every time I look in a mirror, I'm amazed. I still can't figure out how that bold young warrior turned into a bald old worrier.

32. Why do they call mothers who work "working mothers?" They don't call fathers who work "working fathers?"

33. I hate egotists. They all think they're as good as I am.

34. I'm so naive I thought kinky sex is when the girl wears curlers.

35. I can remember when every New Year's Eve I used to ring out the old! Ring in the new! Ding, dong! Ding, dong! Now I just tinkle a little and go home.

36. I'll tell you how nearsighted I am. Yesterday I tried to dial a pencil sharpener. 37. I found a way to cut my commuting time in half—I bought an ambulance. 38. I'm a man who works hard, plays hard—and recovers slowly.

39. My father never paid much attention to me. When I came home after three years in the service, he said, "So how was the movie?" 4

0. I've never been much of a swinger. When I tried to sow wild oats, I had crop failure.

41. If a man is talking in the forest and his wife is not there, is he still wrong?

42. It is not a disgrace to be poor. In fact, it's proof you're an honest tax-paying citizen.

43. I hate to advocate drugs, alcohol, violence, or insanity to anyone, but they've always worked for me."

44. Cheapest guy in the world bought his parents a fifty-piece dinner set for their golden anniversary—a box of toothpicks.

45. This is some suit I got . . . yesterday it shrunk four inches . . . and it was only partly cloudy.

46. How do you scare men? You sneak up behind them and start throwing rice. 47. A very wise and farseeing man of my acquaintance buys his wife such fine and expensive china that she would never think of letting the clumsy ox help dry the dishes.

48. A man wearing a dirty raincoat sidled up to a businessman on the street corner and asked, Got any pictures of your wife naked?"
    "Certainly not," huffed the businessman.
    The other man inquired, "Wanna buy some?"

49. He's so henpecked, he still takes orders from his first wife. He never knows what they're arguing about—she won't tell him. 50. Graffiti in ladies' room
    If they can send one man to the moon, why can't they send all of them?

51. Upon entering the theater, ushers hand the women in the crowd a printed questionnaire to fill out. The question: "Is there anything better than sex with the man you love? If yes, what might that be?" Answers: Double coupons. It's been so long, how would I know? Swimming naked in lukewarm cherry Jell-O. Shopping with the man you love's credit cards. Nachos come close. A lifetime supply of chocolate. A good sale. Diamonds. Killing snails in the garbage disposal.

52. Some men get so enthusiastic over getting married that you would think it was their idea. 53. A lady was asked by a friend, "Is your husband hard to please?" "I don't know," said the wife. "I've never tried."

54. An American is a man who knows the lineups of all the baseball teams and about half the words of "The Star-Spangled Banner."

55. Restaurant very, very expensive. I asked the waiter, "What's the catch of the day?" He said, "You are."

56. Lil says the only way she can get me to exercise is to put the remote control between my feet.

57. "Mama, tell me a story."
    "Wait just a few minutes till your daddy gets home and he'll tell us both one."

58. Lil: "Would you mind escorting me out to the garbage cans, Mit?"
    Mit: "Sure but why?"
    Lil: "I want to be able to tell the neighbors that we go out together once in a while." 59. How many men does it take to change a role of toilet paper? We don't know. It's never been done.

60. My life is an open book, and my wife is the editor.

61. Happiness is seeing your ex-husband on a milk carton.

62. How the heck can you blame me for our problems? I'm never home!

63. One way a husband might cure his wife of nervousness is to tell her it's a symptom of advancing age.

64. "I know you guys don't believe me all I tell you about my wife being cold," a fellow said. "But when she walked by a thermostat the other night on her way to bed, the furnace kicked on."

65. Why don't men like cats? They don't know how to cook them. 66. The probability of a young man meeting a desirable and receptive young female increases by pyramidal progression when he is already in the company of (1) a date, (2) his wife, (3) a better-looking and richer male friend.

67. Man in supermarket, pushing a cart with a screaming baby in it. He kept repeating softly, "Keep calm, George. Don't get excited, George. Don't yell, George." An admiring woman said, "You are certainly to be commended for your patience in trying to quiet little George. "Lady," he said, "I'm George."

68. I hate housework. You make the beds, you do the dishes, and six months later you have to start all over again. (Joan Rivers)

69. He solved the mystery of the socks that always disappear when the wash is done. Male ballet dancers stuff them in their tights.

70. Then there's the guy who no longer patronizes a certain elegant men's store because he got tired of having his inseam measured when all he went in for was a tie.

71. Because I'm a guy, I must hold the television remote control in my hand while I watch TV. If the thing has been misplaced, I'll miss a whole show looking for it, though one time I was able to survive by holding a calculator. Because I'm a guy, when I lock my keys in the car I will fiddle with a wire clothes hanger and ignore your suggestions that we call road service until long after hypothermia has set in. Oh, and when the car isn't running very well, I will pop the hood and stare at the engine as if I know what I'm looking at. If another guy shows up, one of us will say to the other, "I used to be able to fix these things, but now with all these computers and everything, I wouldn't know where to start." We will then drink beer. Because I'm a guy, when I catch a cold I need someone to bring me soup and take care of me while I lie in bed and moan. You never get as sick as I do, so for you this isn't an issue. Because I'm a guy, I can be relied upon to purchase basic groceries at the store like milk or

bread. I cannot be expected to find exotic items like cumin or tofu. For all I know these are the same thing. And never, under any circumstances, expect me to pick up anything for which "feminine hygiene product" is a euphemism. Because I'm a guy, when one of our appliances stops working, I will insist on taking it apart despite evidence that this will just cost me twice as much once the repair person gets here and has to put it back together. Because I'm a guy, I don't think we're all that lost, and no, I don't think we should stop and ask someone. Why would you listen to a complete stranger? How the heck could *he* know where we're going? Because I'm a guy, there is no need to ask me what I'm thinking about. The answer is always either sex or football, though I have to make up something else when you ask, so don't. Because I'm a guy, I do not want to visit your mother, or have your mother come visit us or talk to her when she calls or think about her anymore than I have to. Whatever you got her for Mother's Day is okay, I don't need to see it. Did you remember to pick up something for my mom too? Because I'm a guy, you don't have to ask me if I liked the movie. Chances are, if you're crying at the end of it, I didn't. Because I'm a guy, I think what you're wearing is fine. I thought what you were wearing five minutes ago was fine too. Either pair of shoes is fine. With the belt or without it looks fine. Your hair is fine. You look fine. Can we just go now? Because I'm a guy and this is, after all, the '90s, I will share equally in the housework. You do the laundry, the cooking, the cleaning, and the dishes. I'll do the rest.

72. If they could put one man on the moon, why couldn't they put them all?

73. A man's ear was bleeding like a stuck pig. "I bit myself," he explained to the doctor. Doctor said, "That's impossible. How could a man bite himself on the ear?" The man said, "I was standing on a chair."

74. Customer: "Do you have the book *Man the Master of Woman?*" Salesgirl: "Sir, the fiction department is downstairs."

75. Son: "Father, didn't Edison make the first talking machine?" Father: "No, my son, God made the first talking machine. Edison made the first one you can cut off."

76. Mit: "I heard a new one the other day. Have I told it to you?" Charles: "Is it funny?" Mit: "Yes." Charles: "Then you haven't."

77. Women's faults are many man has only two, every thing they say and every thing they do. 78. After I was born, the doctor sent my father a bill for $500. I don't know why. Mom and I did all the work.

79. I don't care how secure a man is; he has to feel a little uneasy going to a Women's Lib weenie roast.

80. An archeologist is the best husband a woman can have. The older she gets, the more interested he is in her. (Agatha Christie)

81. A man without a woman is like a neck without a pain.

82. Until Eve arrived, this was a man's world.

83. I wasn't in the top half of my class at school, but I was in the group that made the top half possible.

84. "My wife and I don't have a home."
    "Why don't you live with your folks?"
    "We can't, they are still living with their folks."

85. I almost had a psychic girlfriend, but she left me before we met.

86. "Dear sir, I was reading in your magazine of the many ways a troubled marriage can be saved. Please cancel my subscription."

87. You just can't break old habits. I still call a staff meeting for Monday morning, but I don't have any staff, and most of the time I don't go.

88. My school was tough. We even had our own coroner. We used to write essays on "What Am I Going to Do If I Grow Up?"

89. Sales people are so rude. I went to buy a tie, and the salesman held up one for $20. I asked, "Anything less expensive?" He held up one for $10. I said, "Too much, show me something cheaper. He held one up for $5. I said, "Show me the cheapest thing you have in this store." He held up a mirror.

90. Re: Plastic Surgery
    A man ended up marrying his first wife, but he didn't know it till he went in to breakfast and recognized his mother-in-law.

91. A woman said she did not need to get married because she had three pets that served the same purpose. She has a dog that growls every morning, a parrot that swears all afternoon, and a cat that that comes home late at night.

92. The ad I *almost* put in.
Seventy-two-year old man looking for nice home. Can pay moderate rent. Of little value around the house but capable of staying out of the way. Pleasant disposition but subject to infrequent and harmless bursts of temper. Made the mistake in front of wife and three grown children of saying, "Either that dog goes or I go." Call 713-771-5338 or come to small temporary house behind the garage in backyard.

93. Of all the things I've ever lost I miss my mind the most. (S. Tyler)

MILITARY

1. The Chain of Command

Colonel:
Leaps over tall buildings with a single bound, is faster than a speeding bullet, can fly higher than a mighty rocket, more powerful than a locomotive, gives policy guidance to God.

Lieutenant Colonel:
Must take a running start to leap over tall buildings, is just as fast as a speeding bullet; when flying and cannot penetrate the atmosphere, talks to God.

Major:
Can leap over short buildings, not quite as fast as a speeding bullet, only flies as high as transports, loses tug-of-war with locomotive, listens to God.

Captain:
Crashes into buildings when trying to leap over them, can shoot bullets, has trouble flying, gets run over by locomotive, talks with animals.

First Lieutenant:
Stumbles into buildings when attempting to enter, wounds self with bullets when attempting to shoot gun, can barely walk, talks with walls.

Second Lieutenant:
Cannot recognize buildings, gets all wet when playing with a water pistol, still crawling. "Choochoo, Daddy. Choochoo," too busy sucking on pacifier.

First Sergeant:
Lifts buildings, walks under, catches bullets, chews its ass, flies higher than "Champagne Charlie," smashes locomotive, chews caboose, He is God!

2. Terms and Definitions
Have you ever looked over your evaluation report and asked yourself, "I wonder just what he means by this phrase." Well, perhaps the following list will help.

TERMS	DEFINITION
Exceptionally well qualified	Has committed no major blunders to date
Active Socially	Drinks heavily.
Character and integrity above reproach	Still one step ahead of the law.
Wife is active socially	She, too, drinks.
Zealous attitude	Opinionated
Unlimited potential	Will retire or be kicked out shortly.
Quick thinking	Offers plausible excuses for errors.
Takes pride in his work	Conceited.
Takes advantage of every opportunity to progress	Buys drinks for COs and NCOs
Forceful and aggressive	Argumentative.
Outstanding	Frequently in the rain.
Indifferent to instructions	Knows more than superiors.
Tactful in dealings with superiors	Knows when to keep his mouth shut.
Approaches difficult problems with enthusiasm	Finds someone else to do the job.
A keen analyst	Thoroughly confused.
Definitely not a desk man	Did not go to college.
Often spends extra hours on the job	Has a miserable home life.
A true southern gentleman	A hillbilly.
Meticulous in attention to detail	A nitpicker.
Demonstrates qualities of leadership	Has a loud voice.
Judgment is usually sound	Lucky.
Maintains a professional attitude	A snob.
Strong adherence to principles	Stubborn as a mule!

Career minded	Hates reservists.
Gets along extremely well with superiors	
and subordinates alike	A coward.
Average officer or NCO	Not too bright.
Slightly below average	Stupid
A very fine officer of great value to the service	Usually gets to work on time.
Develops a good "team feeling"	Has everybody mad at him.
Outstanding ability to get the maximum out of	
his men and all available resources	A slave driver.
Exceptionally effective in the utilization	
of resources	Cheapskate.
Correctly interprets rather difficult questions	Spell it out for him.
Has mastered all duties with knowledge	
or related positions	Jack of all trades.
Hesitates to ask for clarification	Doesn't speak English too well.
One of the few outstanding airmen I know	In this two-man detachment?
Exceptional flying ability	Hasanequalnumberoftakeoffsandlandings
Independent worker	Nobody knows what he does
Work is his first priority	Too ugly to get a date
Careful thinker	Won't make a decision
Aggressive	Obnoxious
Uses logic on difficult jobs	Gets someone else to do it
Career minded	Backstabber
Loyal	Can't get a job anywhere else
Keen sense of humor	Knows a lot of dirty jokes
Good communication skills	Spends lots of time on the phone
Great presentation skills	Able to BS

3.   Patriotism
Here's to our native land! May we live for it and die in it.

4.   Praise
If with pleasure you are viewing any work a man is doing, and you like him, or you love him, say it now! Don't withhold your approbation till the parson makes oration, and he lies with snowy lilies o'er his brow. For no matter how you shout it, he won't really care about it. He won't know how many teardrops you have shed. If you think some praise is due him, now's the time to hand it to him, for he cannot read his tombstone when he's dead! More than fame and more than money is the comment kind and sunny and the hearty warm approval of a friend.

Oh, it gives to live a savor and strengthens those who waver and gives one heart and courage to the end.

If one earns your praise, bestow it! If you like him, let him know it! Let the words of true encouragement be said! Let's not wait till life is over, and he lies beneath the clover. For he cannot read his tombstone when he's dead!

5. I understand he got a medical discharge from the navy because of a limp—in his wrist.

6. Old soldiers never die, young ones do!

7. The old soldier was up before his commanding officer, charged with failing to keep his rifle clean. "You ought to know better," barked the captain. "It pains me to see such an old campaigner with a dirty rifle. And just look at the ribbons on your chest! You never missed a war, a battle, or skirmish. You should be an example to the younger men. Tell me, is this the first charge against you?" "No, sir," replied the older soldier.

"Uh-huh. And what was it last time?" The veteran shuffled uneasily. "Dirty bow and arrow."

8. All these victory parades remind me of a story my grandfather once told me about a group of West Virginia soldiers marching off to battle in the Civil War. A crowd of people stood on the side of the road cheering as the troops went by. "Who are those people cheering?" one recruit asked. "Them," said the veteran sergeant, "is the people who ain't going."

9. The queen and the prince were giving out medals. They arrived at a ruddy-faced youngster. The prince said, "It is with a sense of deep and eternal gratitude that I award this medal to you, Lance Corporal Stone." The soldier said, "Screw you."

Not sure of what he'd heard, the prince said again, "It is with a sense of deep and eternal gratitude that I award this medal to you, Lance Corporal Stone." "Screw you."

The prince turned to the queen and asked, "What shall I do?" The queen said, "Screw him! Let's not give him the medal!"

10. I think it's a mistake not allowing women to go into combat. Why let all those years of marriage go to waste?

11. Officer: "Soldier, do you have change for a dollar?" Soldier: "Sure, buddy." Officer: "That's no way to address an officer! Now let's try it again. 'Soldier, do you have change for a dollar?" Soldier: "No, sir."

12. The army is so strapped for manpower they may come up with their first gay battalion. I didn't believe it either until I saw that good conduct ankle bracelet.

13. Bob was joining the army, and they were handing out rifles when he arrived, so he got in line. When it got to Bob, they had run out of guns. The man issuing the rifles gave him a broom.

   "This is a magic broom. Point it at anybody and say, 'Bangity bangity bang.' And they will die." Bob was really worried because he didn't think it would work, but he got in line for bayonets, thinking he might stand a chance if he could stab them to death. As luck would have it, Bob's turn came and they had run out. "Don't worry," said the man issuing them out, "I will give you this magic carrot. Point it at somebody and say, 'Stabbity stabbity stab,' and they will die." Now Bob is terrified, going into battle with a broom and a carrot, when the sirens go off, signaling invasion. Bob goes out only to be laughed at by the enemy. One enemy even comes up to him, hoping to get a good shot at him. Well, Bob didn't have anything to lose, so he pointed at him and said, "Bangity bang bang" and the guy fell down dead. He did the same thing with the magic carrot. Amazed at what was happening, he continued to fight. Then a guy came slowly up to him and he would not die. Bob tried to shoot and stab him, but he wouldn't die. The last words poor Bob heard as he was being trampled over were "Tankity, tank, tank."

14. Reminds me of the good old days when arms control meant a deodorant.

15. One young soldier destroyed five bridges, blew up an ammo dump, and wiped out an important military installation. Fortunately, after that they sent him overseas.

16. He owed his life to an Oriental girl who hid him in her cellar for two years. They were in San Francisco at the time.

17. My son asked me what I did during the sexual revolution. I told him I was captured early and spent the duration washing the dishes.

18. Women should be made to register for the draft because they are much healthier than men. When they go for a physical, you never hear them coughing.

19. Obviously, women in the armed forces have brought about some changes. For instance, creamed chipped beef on toast is now called by a rather strange name—creamed chipped beef on toast.

20. An Arab country claims it has a missile that could wipe out Cleveland. It also has some negative effects.

21. To cool his ardor, a soldier was given saltpeter in 1943. It is just beginning to work on him.

22. A soldier writes home to his mother, "Dear Mom, I miss you, I miss Pa, but most of all I miss the little potty under the bed." An answer came, "Don't worry, son. You used to miss it when you were at home too."

23. A young airman landed on an aircraft carrier. He jumped out and exclaimed, "I shot down two zeros, sank a destroyer, and torpedoed a battleship. "Very Good," came the reply, "but you make one 'rittle' mistake.

24. A father didn't know where his son was stationed. After a week, a letter came from his son which said, "I can't tell you where I am, but yesterday I shot a polar bear." A week later another letter said, "I can't tell you where I am, but yesterday I danced with a hula girl. Two weeks later a third letter came, which said, "I can't tell you where I am, but the doctor said I should have danced with the polar bear and shot the hula girl.

25. A small group of marines lost a battle. They gave up all their tomorrows that we might live today.

26. Never tell the platoon sergeant you have nothing to do.

27. Try to look unimportant. The enemy may be low on ammo.

28. My parents were always concerned about their kids. My mother waited up for me one night. When I got home, she yelled, "Where were you? I waited so long." I said, "Ma, I was in the army."

29. An army marksman passed through a small town and saw evidence of amazing shooting. On trees, walls, fences, and barns were numerous bull's-eyes with the bullet hole in the exact center. He asked to meet the remarkable marksman. The man turned out to be the village idiot. "This is the most wonderful marksmanship I have ever seen," said the army man. How in the world do you do it?" "Easy as pie. I shoot first and draw the circle afterward."

30. During navy maneuvers, the captain was pushing his destroyer to the limit when a sailor came to the bridge with a message from the admiral. "Read it aloud," beamed the captain." "Of all the blundering idiots, you nearly rammed the flagship," he read. The captain pursed his lips, then snapped, "Very well, sailor, go below and have it decoded."

31. An American standing at a bar in Hong Kong got into a conversation with the Chinese man standing next to him. When the American asked him what he did, the Chinese said," Oh, I was a Chinese airman and fought in Korea." The American asked him his name and he said, "My name is Chow Mein. I was a kamikaze flier." The American said, "Who are you kidding, Chow Mein? I was a flier too, and I happen to know if you were a kamikaze flier you wouldn't be here right now. That was a suicide squad!" The Chinaman grinned and said, "Oh, me Chicken Chow Mein."

32. During the German occupation of France, a peasant who worked for the underground was captured. Now and then he received a letter from his wife, who complained she was having a difficult time with the farm. She had plenty of seed potatoes, but she couldn't plow the fields by herself. He wrote back, "It is all for the best, my dear. Leave the fields unplowed. That's where the guns are. In four days two truckloads of Gestapo men descended on the farm and dug up all the acreage. Frantically, the wife wrote to her husband telling him what had happened and asking him what to do. He wrote back a brief note, "Now plant the potatoes."

MISCELLANEOUS

1. I don't care if syrup goes to a dollar a sop.

2. I lost a lot of respect for the Lone Ranger when I found out that Kemo Sabe meant Sweetie Pie.

3. What can you say about guys who walk around in high heels?

4. Answer the door. "Hello, door."

5. Why are a wise man and a wise guy opposites?

6. I wonder. Did Lincoln ever walk miles to school through knee-deep snow, only to find out it was closed for his birthday?

7. Telegram: "To hell with you, offensive letter to follow."

8. Let us all now ponder the question, "Do Arab women dance sheik to sheik?"

9. If the number 2 pencil is the most popular, why is it still number 2?

10. It doesn't make sense: like playing strip solitaire.

11. The meek shall inherit the earth—if that's okay with you.

12. "West Virginia: One Million People, Fifteen Last Names."

13. An old railroader told him the reason an engine always "stands" and never "sits" on a track is because it has a tender behind.

14. I'd be willing to take my bike to work, but I can't get it into the trunk of my car.

15. They were digging and digging until they found their bonanza. Then they split it up, and today they have the biggest bonanza split out West.

16. Three men of different occupations looked at the Grand Canyon. The archaeologist said, "What a wonder of science." The clergyman said, "One of the glories of God." The cowboy said, "A heck of a place to lose a cow."

17. "By the way, you saw our bridge game last night. How would you have played that last hand of mine?" The expert said, "Under an assumed name."

18. I know a girl who plays the piano by ear. That's nothing. I know a man who fiddles with his whiskers.

19. You are entering Jonesville: Altitude—1,580, population—3,775, founded—1,873, total—7,192.

20. Sometimes you get, and sometimes you get got.

21. Why isn't eleven pronounced "onety-one?"

22. Which one of us is the opposite sex?

23. Everything is so rushed, there's no longer the chance to enjoy the more cultural aspects of life. I mean, if it weren't for being put on hold, I wouldn't hear any good music at all.

24. I may be slow, but I am ahead of you.

25. My son beat up your honor student.

26. Fire: "Called fire department? Did you put water on it yea. Then we don't need to come 'cause that's all we'd do."

27. I make it a point never to hire an electrician with singed eyebrows!

28. His leadership reminds one of Christopher Columbus. He didn't know where he was going when he started out his journey. He didn't know where he was when he got there. He didn't know where he had been when he got back, and he did it all with someone else's money.

29. A guy in a nudist colony was asked what made the greatest impression on him. He replied, "A cane bottom chair."

30. Ad by real estate company: "Luxury homes everyone can afford. For complete details, call repossession department."

31. I really don't know much about computers. To me, software always sounds like something you get at Frederick's of Hollywood.

32. You can always tell an Arab because when he gets out of bed, he takes the sheet with him.

33. These aren't dances. They're fertility rites with lyrics.

34. Don't be discouraged if you don't get the promotion you wanted. Keep in mind that when King Tut was your age, he had already been dead several years.

35. Everyone can give pleasure in some way. One person may do it by coming into a room, and another by leaving.

36. "Did you lose your wallet?"
"No."
"Then lend me $20."

37. One of the most tactful speeches ever thought up suddenly was spoken by the man who blundered into a bathroom where a woman was bathing and calmly turned and left with the words, "I beg your pardon, sir."

38. Hypochondria is the only disease I haven't got.

39. Many people quit looking for work when they find a job.

40. When I'm not in my right mind, my left mind gets pretty crowded.

41. Everyone has a photographic memory. Some don't have film.

42. Boycott shampoo! Demand the real poo!

43. If you choke a smurf, what color does it turn?

44. Who is General Failure, and why is he reading my hard disk?

45. What happens if you get scared half to death twice?

46. Energizer Bunny arrested charged with battery.

47. I poured Spot remover on my dog. Now he's gone.

48. I used to have an open mind, but my brains kept falling out.

49. I couldn't repair your brakes, so I made your horn louder.

50. It may be the way the cookie crumbles on Madison Avenue, but in Hong Kong, it's the way the egg rolls.

51. Common sense
    What we all have so much of and can't understand why everybody doesn't have any.

52. Things are always better somewhere else until you get there.

53. Like to be a member of a minority group? Try putting in an honest day's work.

54. "What are you thinking of? You look depressed"
    "My future."
    "What makes it so hopeless?"
    "My past."

55. I'm short, fat, ugly, conservative, and I read where we were all created in the image of God. Can you believe that?

56. Save the wetlands—drown a developer.

57. Life is what happens to you while you're busy making other plans.

58. What is matched Mexican luggage? Two shopping bags from the same store.

59. Why did you locate here? Because it's right here in the surrounding territory.

60. A young lady once asked Bob Hope, "What are you wearing that smells so nice?" Hope answered, "Clean socks."

61. If you try to fail—and succeed, which have you done?

62. It doesn't make sense, like putting "Rush" on a letter.

63. If practice makes perfect, and nobody's perfect, why practice?

64. I have a wonderful ear. I can pick up anything that's musical. Let's see you pick up the piano.

65. How much are they asking for your apartment rent now? About twice a day.

66. He solved the mystery of the socks that always disappear when the wash is done. Male ballet dancers stuff them in their tights.

67. Biologists Hear about the biologist who crossed a sponge with a potato? Tastes terrible but it holds lots of gravy.

68. Biologists Hear about the biologist who crossed poison ivy with a four-leaf clover? He came up with a rash of good luck.

69. To the Editor of the Chronicle:
Sir, I have just written you a long letter. On reading it over, I have thrown it in the wastebasket. Hoping this meets with your approval.

70. Who invented the brush they put next to the toilet. That thing hurts!

71. One good thing about cooking outdoors. It keeps the flies out of the house.

72. I argue very well. Ask any of my remaining friends. I can win an argument on any topic, against any opponent. People know this and

steer clear of me at parties. Often, as a sign of their great respect, they don't even invite me.

73. The ax forgets—the tree remembers.

74. A Jewish man calls his mother in Florida. "Mom, how are you?"
     "Not too good," says the mother, "I've been very weak."
     The son says, "Why are you so weak?"
     The mother says, "Because I haven't eaten in thirty-four days, eight hours, and twenty-two minutes."
     The son says, "Why haven't you eaten in so long?"
     The mother answers, "Because I didn't want my mouth to be filled with food if you should call."

75. When someone asks where the bathroom is, your mom says, "Pick a corner . . . any corner."

76. Why do you have to "put your two cents in" . . . but it's only a penny for your thoughts?" Where's that extra penny going?

77. During tough times, Harry says he sleeps like a baby. He wakes up every few hours, cries, and wets his pants.

78. I dialed a wrong number and got the following recording: "I am not available right now, but thank you for caring enough to call. I am making some changes in my life. Please leave a message after the beep. If I do not return your call, you are one of the changes."

79. John Jones reaffirms that everything is relative: As the snail said when he went for a ride on the turtle's back, "Wheeee!"

80. Things in perspective. Gray hair doesn't bother a person who is bald.

81. Maintenance free usually means that when it breaks, it can't be fixed.

82. Humpty Dumpty was pushed.

83. Landlord: I want you to pay your rent.
     Struggling Artist: Let me tell you this. In a few years time, people will look up at this miserable studio and say, "Doakes, the famous artist,

used to work there." Landlord: If you don't pay your rent by tonight, they'll be able to say it tomorrow.

84. Lil and I have a friend that's so fat that when she wears a white dress at our house, we show home movies.

85. He was bowlegged, and she was knock-kneed. When they stood together, they spelled the word ox!

86. If astronauts are so smart, why do they count backward?

87. He has a T-shirt that says cruel, nasty, neurotic, paranoid, mean and antisocial but basically happy.

88. Well, if I called the wrong number, why did you answer the phone?

89. Loves radio—you can reach millions, but they can't reach you.

90. A woman asks a friend how things are going. The lady said, "I'd complain but how long would you listen?"

91. A girl asks artist, "Can you paint me in the nude?" Artist says, "Sure, but I have to keep my socks on. That's where I keep my brushes."

92. An American standing at a bar in Hong Kong got into a conversation with the Chinese standing next to him. When the American asked what he did, the Chinese said, "Oh, I was a Chinese airman. I fought in Korea." The American asked him his name, and he said, "My name is Chow Mein, I was a kamikaze flier." The American said, "Who are you kidding, Chow Mein? I was a flier too, and I happen to know if you were a kamikaze flier you wouldn't be here right now. That was a suicide squad!" The Chinaman grinned and said, "Oh, me Chicken Chow Mein."

93. Plumber's sign: "You don't have to sleep with that drip tonight?"

94. If you do settle in the South and bear children, don't think we will accept them as Southerners. After all, if the cat had kittens in the oven, we wouldn't call 'em biscuits.

95. An ornithologist says there are forty million pigeons in the United States, thirty million are birds and the rest are people who pay $50 for blue jeans.

96. I've learned that life is like a roll of toilet paper. The closer it gets to the end, the faster it goes.

97. Adam had no mother-in-law. That's how we know he lived in paradise.

98. I hate egotists. They all think they're as good as I am.

99. I knew one egomaniac who actually thought he was humble. He used to say, "Some geniuses are conceited, but I'm not."

100. Disloyal: he's the kind who'd spit on the Alamo.

101. Ego
    When you think you're important, try ordering somebody else's dog around.

102. Friendship
    They're friends enough to use the same toothpick.

103. Gullible
    He's so gullible I can play craps with him on the telephone.

104. Ignorant
    If you take ignorance out of the Texas legislature, you'll no longer have a representative government.

105. Stingy
    He'd rather sit in the shade of the tree to save the shade of the porch.

106. Weary
    I feel like I've been ironing all day with a cold in high heels.

107. Waste is a terrible thing to mind.

108. Why do "slow down" and "slow up" mean the same thing?

109. Why do "tug" boats push their barges?

110. On the phone a man was giving instructions on how to get to his birthday party. "You go to Main Street and it's the second house on the left. When you get to the house just ring the bell with your elbow."

"Why my elbow?"

"You wouldn't want to come to a party empty-handed, would you?"

111. Here's a classic tale of absenteeism

George Shaw once invited Winston Churchill to an opening night performance of his play with this note: "Dear Mr. Churchill, enclosed are two tickets to my new play which opens Thursday night. Please come and bring a friend, if you have one." Churchill followed with the following note, "Dear Mr. Shaw, I am sorry I have a previous engagement and cannot attend your opening. However, I will come to the second performance, if there is one."

112. Adjournment: making meets end.

113. Worry is like a rocking chair. It gives you something to do but won't get you anywhere.

114. Patrick Henry shouted, "Give me liberty or give me death." The next generation shouted, "Give me liberty." Then came the generation shouting, "Give me."

115. An additional joy of giving rather than receiving is that you don't have to write thank-you notes.

116. There is one thing about stupidity: you can be fairly sure that it is genuine.

117. Nothing is quite so annoying as to have someone go right on talking when you are interrupting.

118. In my neighborhood, they take out rental ads that read, "Only a short run to the subway!"

119. Sign at a landscape nursery: "A house without a tree isn't fit for a dog."

120. Sign in a brassiere shop: "What God has forgotten, we stuff with cotton."

121. The party that picked up the phone after I dialed told me that I had the wrong number. I asked, "Are you sure?" The party said, "Did I ever lie to you before?"

122. A fellow went to dinner at a friend's apartment on the seventeenth floor of a Manhattan apartment house. While his hostess attended to so me last-minute details in the kitchen, he played with her German shepherd. He threw a rubber bone several times, and the dog went to fetch it. Then throwing harder than he had intended, he threw the bone out the terrace door and over the railing. Incredibly, the dog followed it out to the terrace and bounded over the railing and into the seventeen floors below. Horrified, the young began pondering what to say. When they finally sat down to dinner, he looked at the hostess and said, "Perhaps, it's just my imagination, but your dog seemed rather depressed tonight."

123. So they went out onto a Texas feedlot, took soil samples, and sent them to two leading universities. Their scientists just about went crazy analyzing those samples. Finally, they got together, conferred for an extended time, and announced that "the cow, indeed, did jump over the moon."

124. "How did you find the weather while you were away?"
"Oh, I just went outside and there it was!"

125. A convicted robber, who has maintained a clean record for a period of seven years after released from prison, is entitled to have a credit report that makes no mention of his previous trial or convictions. The injustice is that you can attend a state university for just one semester, and it stays on your record forever.

126. All newspaper editorial writers ever do is come down from the hills after the battle is over and shoot the wounded.

127. This man spent years perfecting a musical instrument. He fashioned it by hand adjusted and readjusted its parts, put it to his lips, and blew. No sound came out. He went back to the drawing board and worked for many more years. He put the instrument to his lips, but still no sound came out. The frustration killed him. When he died, they buried him in a place of honor, and right next to his body they placed his violin.

128. Have you noticed that an optimist is always able to see the bright side of other people's troubles?

129. Before we begin, headquarters has asked me to make this announcement. Until further notice, please do not put anything more into the suggestion box. The handle is broken, and it won't flush.

130. I had to get rid of my pet rock. It was becoming a bad influence on the rest of my family. All it did was lay around all day stoned.

131. Collecting Indian arrowheads is a satisfying and useful hobby. They won't be any good as weapons in the next war, but they'll be just right for the one after that.

132. I make a point never to repeat gossip. So please listen good the first time.

133. Are the cabs in Shanghai Chinese Checkers?

134. I'd talk to my plants, but I'm afraid they'd laugh up their leaves at me.

135. He opened a lingerie shop and became King of the Undie World.

136. I have to admit, a gardener I'm not, who else gets crabgrass in a flowerpot?

137. I bought a second-hand tux. I don't know where it came from, but every time they play soft music, the arms cross.

138. Solutions are not the answer.

139. Three most chilling words to hear: "I'll play these" or "Upon further review."

140. He could sell a double bed to the pope.

141. All those in favor taking a break, please signify by raising your eyelids.

142. It's a little scary to realize that if you had to buy your house today, all you could afford is two closets and a bathroom.

143. I accidentally swallowed a watch. I didn't know what to do, so I ate some prunes just to pass the time.

144. My brother-in-law is making a big career move. He's transferring to a different unemployment office.

MIT IS AN AGGIE

1. Well, I lied on my taxes again. I listed myself as "head of household."

2. It's hard to be nostalgic when you can't remember anything.

3. My father never paid much attention to me. When I came home after three years in the service, he said, "So how was the movie?"

4. People are always picking on me. Yesterday I went to a clothing store, and I asked the clerk what I'd look best in. He said, "A ski mask."

5. I went to a Women's Lib meeting last night. It was necessary. I had to get my mind off sex!

6. I am not very handy. For instance, last year I painted my house, and the assessment was reduced.

7. "What a childhood I had. I was ten years old when I found out Alpo was dog food." (Rodney Dangerfield)

8. Of course I'm against sin, I'm against anything that I'm too old to enjoy.

9. Two men were overheard talking about the infidelities of an office Romeo. "I do not know how he gets away with it," said one fellow. "The only thing I've ever done behind my wife's back is to zip her up."

10. Sam is a sex symbol for women who no longer care.

11. He told me he used to have trouble remembering names till he took the George Carnegie course.

12. My patients are so scared they don't have spit!

13. Steve went to the beach last weekend. "Not to sunbathe . . . just to pick up some medical supplies."

14. Cartoon lines by Don Reber in Reading Times: One man to another, "My wife thinks I should become more fashion conscious and start dressing better. It's embarrassing to her when we eat in a restaurant . . . and people who walk past our table drop coins in my coffee cup."

15. Mack confesses that he was a late bloomer: "I rode a stick horse until I was ten." Mack rode it to school one day, he recalls, and someone stole it. "I had to walk all the way home," he says.

16. Norman overheard two delegates at a convention talking about how the speeches were running long. One recalled the rigid time enforcement at a meeting in Texas. A guest speaker had been given exactly twelve minutes. When his talk ran over fifteen minutes, he heard a click of several guns. "Surely you wouldn't shoot a guest," said the speaker, alarmed. "Why, no," drawled a man in the audience. "That would be downright inhospitable. We're gunning for the guy who invited you."

17. A fellow went to the doctor for a complete checkup. "I look in the mirror, and I'm a complete mess," he said. "My jowls are sagging. I have splotches all over my face, my hair is falling out, and I feel ugly. What is it?" The doctor said, "I don't know what it is, but your eyesight is perfect."

18. When I played hooky from school, they sent my mother a thank-you note. (George Burns)

19. I cried because I had no cash. Till I met a man that had no credit cards.

20. The only reason I'm not famous is that no one has ever heard of me.

21. Home is where you can say anything you like because nobody listens to you anyway.

22. Personally, I'm an incurable optimist. I believe you have to live one miserable, rotten day at a time.

23. I brought her a lovely wedding ring. It even had a place for a diamond.

24. In my high school graduation picture, I was the front row.

25. Rebuttal: I'm at that point in my life where I'm beyond resentments, beyond hatreds, I'm really into revenge.

26. An elderly aunt of his was reminiscing recently about her late husband, a fellow says, "Your uncle Ed," she said, "was a man of very few faults." She paused for a moment in thought. "Of course," she continued, "he made the most of the ones he did have."

27. I have no enemies. My friends just don't like me.

28. It's hard to make a comeback, when you haven't been anywhere.

29. I guess you'd call us friends—we have the same enemies.

30. I have a lot of trouble getting my husband to buy clothes. His idea of a dinner jacket is carrying sandwiches in his pocket.

31. One time I asked Lil if she liked nuts. She asked, "Are you proposing?"

32. Married men should forget their mistakes. There's no use two people remembering the same thing.

33. Incontinence Hotline: "Can you hold please?"

34. When I'm feeling down, I like to whistle. It makes the neighbor's dog run to the end of his chain and gag himself.

35. If God wanted us to see the sunrise, he would have scheduled it later in the day.

36. Myrddin was having a tough day and had stretched himself out on the couch to do a bit of what he thought to be well-deserved complaining and self-pitying. He moaned to his wife, "Nobody loves me . . . the

whole world hates me!" His wife, busily occupied with other things, hardly looked up at him and passed on this encouraging word: "That's not true, Myrddin. Some people don't even know you."

37. There's the story about two women having lunch at their favorite restaurant when Mrs. Jones told Mrs. Smith she had a secret to tell her. "I wouldn't want anyone else to know this," Mrs. Jones said, "but I am having an affair." "What kind of man is he?" she asked. Mrs. Jones seemed to drift off for a moment, and then smiled. "Well, he really isn't anything to look at, but I just can't help myself," she said. "He's a slob, drinks too much beer, slurps his soup, and would rather spend his time watching sports on TV and bowling instead of being with me." Mrs. Smith didn't say anything, but she was thinking about what Mrs. Jones told her. Lunch over, Mrs. Smith went home to her husband and demanded, "What's this I hear about you and Mrs. Jones?"

38. A correspondent informed me he was indulging in a little do-it-yourself home repair recently and went to the hardware store in search of supplies. He asked the clerk for a half-inch pipe plug. "Do you want a male plug or a female plug or both?" the clerk inquired. "Well," replied the fellow, "I just want to stop a leak. I'm not interested in breeding them."

39. Toastmaster to the friendly crowd
If I throw a stick, will you leave?
If I want to hear the patter of little feet, I'll put shoes on my cats.
I'm trying to imagine you with a personality.
Too bad stupidity isn't painful.
A day without sunshine is like night.
He got lost in thought and was in an unfamiliar territory.
Honk if you love peace and quiet.

40. Only thing better than taking an early morning walk with someone you love is to have someone you love take an early morning walk without you and then wake you up when she gets home.

41. My uncle died in the spring and fall. "How did he die in the spring and in the fall?" "Warden pulled the spring, and he died in the fall."

42. You know you're getting old when your children study in history class what you learned in current events.

43. Middle age is when you wish you could have some of the naps you refused to take as a kid.

44. I weighed six pounds, eight ounces when I was born. I eat more than that now for lunch.

Opening/Introduction

1. Cooperation—preplanning

    A hillbilly was walking in to the market. Under one arm, he was carrying a pig, under the other arm a watermelon, in on hand a number 2 washtub, and in the other hand he had a live chicken. There was a shortcut by a beautiful shallow stream where the sun was glistening off the small pebbles. The birds were singing their love songs, the trees had just burst with leaves in all their spring fury, and the flowers were in full bloom. He noticed a pretty hillbilly girl walking along behind, so he asked her if she would like to take the shortcut and walk into market with him. She said, "No, Mama told me about you hillbilly boys, and that you would get me down there and hug me and squeeze me and try to kiss me." The fellow said, "How could I do that?" I have a pig under this arm, a watermelon under my other arm, a number 2 washtub in this hand, and a live chicken in this one?" She said, "Well, you could put the pig on the ground, the tub over the pig, the watermelon on the tub, and I could hold the chicken."

2. I once served as the poster boy for birth control.

3. He fell out of an ugly tree and hit every branch on the way down.

4. I once served as a Preparation H spokesman and also served on its testing panel.

5. I am considered the sex symbol for women who no longer care.

6. "Joe, please stand. What can you say about a man who came from humble beginnings and rose to the very height of his profession, based solely on

grit and the will to push on where others might fall back? A man that has so distinguished himself among his peers that no right-thinking person can say a single word against him? A person loved and admired by all that know him."

"Well, enough about me."

"Joe, you can sit down now."

7. I was talking earlier to the mother of our speaker's three children, and I asked her if Jim had always been so self-confident and assured of himself. She said, "Heavens no!" I was willing to drop it at that, but she kept right on talking. "I remember on our first date I had to slap his face three times." I asked, "Did he try to get a little fresh with you? Hug you and steal a little kiss?" She said, "No, I thought the boy was dead."

8. The last thing I want to do tonight is to *overmotivate* you.

9. A normal fairy tale begins "Once upon a time." A Texas fairy tale begins, "You SOB you ain't going to believe this."

10. I was going to tell some stories that would knock your hair out, but I see that a lot of you have already heard them.

11. This appears to be such a great audience. I wish I had a better talk.

12. When Bob heard I was to be the speaker, he told Bill, "Don't expect nothing too deep."

13. What has seven teeth and an IQ of forty? Answer: The front row of a Willie Nelson concert. Don't know why I thought of that.

14. He won't need an introduction tonight, but he will need a conclusion.

15. Our speaker tonight has no equals—superiors yes but equals—no.

16. Recently I've been writing under a nom de plume—that's French for "Don't give your right name!"

17. I finally had to fire her though. One day she came into the office, and I told her to sit down, and the silly girl looked for a chair!

18. You've heard of Victor Mature. This is his brother Pre. And his sister Emma.

19. He's working under a handicap tonight. He's sober.

20. I want to thank the master of ceremonies for those kind words he said about me. Now I know how a pancake feels when you pour syrup all over it.

21. I heard that Charles makes over two hundred speeches a year. Most of them begin with "Now honey, be reasonable."

22. Why be an MC? Because I like being with smart, successful, and exciting people. I also enjoy being with a group like this.

23. I didn't mind people looking at their watches when I did my talk, but when they shook them, that was too much.

24. Studies have shown that humans can hear and comprehend up to 600 words per minute, but most people speak around 120 words per minute. Therefore, the human mind wanders to fill tin the gaps. The Stanford University Social Studies Center surveyed 10,000 people on what else they were thinking about during a controlled talking/listening experiment. About two-thirds of the people (almost 7,000) were thinking of sex. Therefore, two-thirds of this audience will be smiling and having a good time no matter what I say or do here today.

25. Introducing a Panel of Speakers: "This afternoon, we have a bigger variety than Heinz."

26. I know of but one person in our industry who possesses such an extraordinary combination of vision, common sense, integrity, and commitment to quality. Our speaker tonight once met that person.

27. I'm not here to bore you with a lot of statistics. I'm here to introduce you to the person who will.

28. Our next speaker is the foremost living authority on . . . our next speaker.

29. And now, I would like to introduce a man who has made incompetence an art form.

30. Re: Long-winded previous speaker Art Carney couldn't talk that long about sewers.

31. If joke goes dead: it's not funny but it takes up time. 32. Isn't it great when a speaker is really on the ball? When his words are off-the-cuff instead of off-the-wall?

33. Our next speaker comes to us after thirty years of distinguished achievement in the business community. In fact, he was so highly thought of, when he left the car wash, they retired his rag.

34. I only tell jokes—I don't explain them.

35. Speaker, "Can everyone hear me? I've been in front of more dead mikes recently than an Irish undertaker."

36. Speaker called upon the audience not to be awed by his title and all his degrees. "A thermometer also has degrees, and you know where the nurses put them."

37. A man once told a joke at a dinner, and no one laughed. He quickly added, "The interesting thing about that story is that stupid people never get the point of it." Everyone laughed.

38. Before I begin, I want you to know that I have always been a firm believer in preserving America's wildlife. In fact, at this very moment, I'm standing here with a few dozen butterflies in my stomach.

39. You've just become victims of an old public speaking ploy—bait and switch!

40. Opening after introduction: What a wonderful introduction. It's amazing what things people can say when they're not under oath.

41. Opener: "It's nice to see such a large turnout. You must know something I don't."

42. Introduction: "You all should be pleased this man is with us tonight. Otherwise, he might be at your house."

43. Wiping Your Brow: To me, this is a handkerchief. To Cher, her spring wardrobe.

44. This is a very special evening for our guest of honor. After thirty-three years of retirement, this week he finally made it official.

45. Our weekly meetings remind me of the works of Shakespeare. They're usually Much Ado About Nothing and result in a Comedy of Errors.

46. In a show of hands, how many people here are opposed to audience participation?

47. After Girl Performer: "Wasn't that the best female impersonator you ever saw?"

48. After Tap Dancer: "I won't say how he learned to tap dance like that, but he used to work for an exterminator."

49. When Patron Is Trying to Get to a Seat: "Don't get up, lady. Make him jump over you."

50. An emcee sized up his tough-looking audience and exclaimed, "I'll bet half of you know where Jimmy Hoffa is."

51. A speaker at a men's club rambled on so long that everybody walked out but one guy. The speaker thanked the guy for staying. The fellow answered, "Don't thank me. I'm the next speaker."

52. Thank you for that kind introduction. It proves once again that the truth can be likened to a rubber band. That is, if you can't stretch it a little, it isn't very useful.

53. Re: Leadership. If you think you're confused, think of poor Columbus. He didn't know where he was going when he started out. When he got there, he didn't know where he was, and when he got back, he didn't know where he had been—and he did it all on borrowed money. Today, he's a hero.

54. He told me a commencement speaker is like the body at an Irish wake. It's necessary to have you at the party, but they don't expect you to say a great deal."

55. Why are people who need no introductions always introduced?

56. Man came home drunk. As he put the key in the lock, his wife opened the door, and he fell on the floor and said, "Under the circumstances I'll dispense with my opening remarks. I'll now take questions from the floor."

57. I'm reminded of the story about the Roman emperor centuries ago who gathered thousands of his subjects in the coliseum to witness some executions. When the first victim was thrown to the lions, the crowd roared its approval. But as the lions approached, the prisoner whispered something in their ears, and they just turned around and walked away.

    The emperor was furious. "Throw another one in there," he said. But the same thing happened. The second prisoner whispered something into the lions' ears, and they just turned and walked away. Finally after a few more times, the emperor gave up. He went down to the dungeon and asked the prisoners, "What the heck are you telling those lions?" The first prisoner replied. "I just told them that there would be speeches after lunch."

58. Level-headed Texan—where the tobacco juice runs out of both sides of his mouth at the same time.

59. I've talked on by-laws, legislation, political action, third-party insurance, malpractice, ethics, the history of Galveston, the value of humor, and I have an exciting speech on dental floss and the confessions of a compulsive tooth fairy.

60. When You're Late
    "Sorry I'm late. My company is cutting back and made me travel on United . . . United Van Lines.

61. Returning from a Break
    Either they brought in some empty chairs, or some of you have left.

62. When Introducing a Big Subject

Well, as Roseanne Barr's seamstress says, "We have a lot to cover."

63. Speeches are like babies—easy to conceive, hard to deliver.

64. When a Joke Dies
"I don't understand, everybody laughed when the boss told that joke."

65. Referring to Notes
I hope you don't mind if I refer to my notes. I have a photographic memory, but it no longer offers same-day service.

66. Sorry I'm late, I just came from the hospital with my son, where he had a Nintendo control unit surgically pried from his hand.

67. Opening the Floor for Comments:
"Who would like to cast the first stone?" 68. Announcement:
"I have an announcement to make. For those of you who left your cars with the valets, contact the police. We don't have valets."

69. When your guest of honor is wealthy:
Most of us spend all of our lives trying to keep up with the Joneses. Tonight, it gives me great pleasure to present Jones.

70. Opening:
"Before I begin, I want you to know that the following speech has been edited for television. I cut twenty minutes out of it so we could all get home in time for the game on channel 2."

71. What can you really say about our next speaker? He has two legs and two arms just like anyone else, except in his case, they all touch the floor.

72. I've called you all in front of me because it's the only way I can keep you from talking behind by back.

73. For those of you who have never seen a professional speaker, picture a tongue with a meter.

74. Too often a speech is when your body rises to the occasion, but your mind remains seated.

75. When You Get an Award
"I'm kind of embarrassed getting this honor because I really am a very modest person, an extremely modest person, a tremendously talented and wonderfully deserving modest person."

76. The purpose of this meeting is to address problems and make decisions that will affect the future of our industry for many years to come. And frankly, I'd feel better about that challenge if I hadn't spent five minutes in the breakfast room this morning, watching one of our groups trying to decide between cornflakes and Fruit-Loops.

77. Opening:
We try to run a rather informal type of meeting. For instance, we use Bob's Rules of Order.

78. When a Joke Dies: That went over like Marcel Marceau on radio.

79. The cocktail hour is ending,
The salad is now being tossed.
Please go to your table for dinner.
He who hesitates is sauced!

80. Response to a Needling Introduction
An introduction like that always reminds me of baking an apple pie in a microwave oven. It's short, it's sweet, but it still has a lot of crust.

81. Responding to a Testimonial
Right now I feel like a sled dog in Alaska. It's a lot of mush, but I like it.

82. Delivering a speech is like spelling Mississippi. You're never quite sure when to stop.

83. I feel pretty relaxed up here because I asked the bartender what kind of a group you were. He said you're real middle-of-the—road. I said, "What do you mean middle-of-the-road?" He said, "You drink liberally and tip conservatively."

84. As any parliamentarian will tell you, a yawn is a motion to adjourn.

85. We want to begin the meeting. Will everyone take their seats and put them on the chair.

86. Behind every successful speaker there is a program director hoping he is.

87. One way to keep a speaker's presentation short is to put no water on the speaker's stand, just prune juice.

88. Before you speak, always remember the XYZ of good public speaking—examine your zipper.

89. After a long introduction:
"I'd like to make a few brief remarks. It's all you have time for after _____ introduces you.

90. Mike problem
You have to be very careful what you say while you're doing this. One time I was working with it, I said, "Would someone tell me what to do with this thing?" They did.

91. When you're asked to introduce a speaker as famous as our guest tonite, you feel like a bellboy in a honeymoon hotel. No matter how well you do your job, people can't wait until you leave.

92. Our next speaker is with the government. His brother doesn't work either.

93. Our next speaker is world famous and has been mentioned frequently on the weather report. They say, "A mass of hot air is coming up from the South."

94. Cure for butterflies in your stomach: quit eating caterpillars.

95. Our next speaker is a person who has risen to every occasion. His colleagues are impressed, his competitors are amazed, and his wife is delighted.

96. You can always tell if a speaker is lying by looking into his eyes. So put on dark glasses and begin.

97. When the audience anticipates a punch line: "I think you people are listening faster than I'm talking." 98. A visiting speaker sat down after an obvious failure on his presentation. He noted three grim-faced tough guys heading to the podium and was getting nervous. The president said, "Just sit still, friend. They're coming after the program chairman."

99. They told me not to be witty or intellectual, just be myself.

100. I asked Karyon, "You did tell everyone I was coming, didn't you?" Karyon said, "No, but I'll find out who did."

101. MC job: Try to get a good speaker. If you can't, get a weird one. I have succeeded.

102. My job as MC is to introduce the speaker, not guarantee them.

103. He is not Dunn and Bradstreet; he is not Dow Jones. He's just standard and poor.

104. There are still some things money can't buy. Fortunately, our next speaker is not one of them.

105. Opener (many celebrities in attendance): "Looking around, I think I'm the only person here I've never heard of."

106. And now I would like to introduce a man who has made incompetence an art form.

107. Quiet everyone, it is time for Sam to speak. You can enjoy yourself some other time.

108. Looking over the audience: "I'll bet half of you know where Jimmy Hoffa is."

109. The most difficult thing a speaker has to learn is to is not to nod while the toastmaster is praising him.

110. Our next guest has been called a self-made man. This of course was in the days before quality control.

111. As toastmaster I will try to keep my part of the program to a minimum, which won't be easy. Every toastmaster feels like a eunuch in a harem. He'd like to be the main attraction, but he's not cut out for it.

POEMS

1. There was a little dachshund once,
   So long he had no notion,
   The time it took from head to foot
   To register emotion.
   And so it was that when his face
   Was filled with tears and sadness,
   His little tail kept wagging on
   Because of previous gladness.

2. Margie, I love your golden hair;
   Oh, Margie, I saw it on the chair.
   I love your teeth so pearly and white;
   Just like the stars, they come out every night.
   Margie, I love your wooden leg;
   I love your glass eye too.
   Half a woman, half a tree,
   You're the only one for me.

3. Breathes there a husband so naïve
   Who ever let his ears believe
   These wifely words so soft and pleasant:
   "I don't want any birthday present."

4. The cocktail hour is ending,
   The salad is now being tossed;
   Please go to your table for dinner
   He who hesitates is sauced!

5. Heavenly Father, bless us,
    And keep us all alive;
    There's ten of us to dinner
    And not enough for five.

6. Bring back the good old days
    Things will never be the same
    Till a pansy's just a flower
    And Fanny's just a name.

7. Did you hear about the young poet who sent some verses to the editor
    of a magazine. The verses were entitled, "Why Do I live?" It is reported
    the editor's reply was as follows: "You live just because you happened
    to send your poem by post instead of bringing it in person."

8. I can live with my arthritis,
    My dentures fit just fine,
    My bifocals are wonderful
    But how I miss my mind!

9. I think that I shall never see a billboard lovely as a tree.
    Indeed unless the billboards fall
    I'll never see a tree at all.

10. Here's to life ain't it grand. Just got divorced from my old man.
    I laughed and laughed at the court's decision.
    They gave him the kids, and they ain't even his'n!

11. When I sat next to the duchess at tea, it was just as I knew it would be.
    Her rumblings abdominal were something phenomenal, and everyone
        thought it was me.

12. One night in late October when I was far from sober,
    Returning with my load, with manly pride,
    My feet began to stutter,
    So I lay down in the gutter,
    And a pig came near and lay down by my side;
    A lady passing by was heard to say:
    "You can tell a man who boozes,
    By the company he chooses."
    And the pig got up and slowly walked away.

13. Starkle, starkle, little twink
     Who the hell are you I think
     I'm not under what you call,
     The alcofluence of incohol.
     I'm just a little slort of sheep,
     I'm not drunk like thinkle peep.
     I don't know who is me yet,
     But the drunker I stand here the longer I get.
     So just give me one more drink to fill up my cup,
     'cause I got all day sober to Sunday up.

14. "I pray that I may live to fish
     Until my dying day,
     And when it comes to my last cast,
     I then most humbly pray: When in the Lord's
     Greatest landing net
     And peacefully asleep,
     That in His mercy I be judged
     Big enough to keep."

15. There once was a sculptor named Phidias
     Whose manners in art were indivious:
       He carved Aphrodite
       Without any nightie,
     Which startled the ultrafastidious. A

16. There once was an old man of Lyme
     Who married three wives at a time;
     When asked, "Why a third?"
     He replied, "One's absurd!"
     And bigamy, sir, is a crime.

17. There was a young man from Siberia
     Whose morals were somewhat inferior.
     He did to a nun
     What he should not have done
     And now she's a Mother Superior.

18. Here I lie upon my bed
     Throat so dry and throbbing head

Bloodshot eyes and body sore
The morning after the night before.
Can't eat nothing, got no pep
Lost my money lost my rep.
Can't get up, I feel so bad,
Boy, what a wonderful night I had.
Never felt so bad before,
Even my doggone tongue is sore,
When I sneeze, I still taste gin.
Gosh! What a night it must have been.
Can't remember where I went.
Don't know where the time was spent.
But wow! What a time it must have been,
Look at the hell of a shape I'm in.

19. The next time you open a can of Carnation evaporated milk for your recipes, just smile and think of this. A little old lady from North Carolina had worked in and around her family dairy farms since she was old enough to walk, with hours of hard work and little compensation. When canned Carnation Milk became available in grocery stores, she read an advertisement offering $5,000 for the best slogan/rhyme beginning with "Carnation Milk is best of all." She sent in her entry, and about a week later, a black limo drove up in front of her house. A man got out and said, "Carnation loved your entry so much that even though we will not be able to use it, we are here to award you a consolation prize of $1,000, which we've made available just for the originality of your entry.

Carnation milk is best of all,
No tits to pull, no hay to haul
No buckets to wash, no shit to pitch,
Just poke a hole in the son-of-a-bitch.

20. I made myself a snowball,
As perfect as could be,
I thought I'd keep it as a pet,
And let it sleep with me.
I made it some pajamas,
And a pillow for its head,
Then last night it ran away,
But first it wet the bed.

21. Bless this house, oh Lord, we cry,
    Please keep it cool in mid-July.
    Bless the walls where termites dine,
    While ants and roaches march in time.
    Bless our yard where spiders pass
    Fire ant castle in the grass.
    Bless the garage, a home to please.
    Carpenter beetles, ticks, and fleas.
    Bless the love bugs, two by two,
    The gnats and mosquitoes that feed on you.
    Millions of creatures that fly or crawl,
    In Florida, Lord, you've put them all!
    But this is home, and here we'll stay,
    So thank you, Lord, for insect spray!

22. My appetite is my shepherd:
    I shall always want.
    It leadeth me in the path of Burger King for a
    Whopper;
    It destroyeth my shape.
    Yea, though I knoweth I gaineth, I will not stop
    Eating for the food tasteth so good.
    The ice cream and cookies, they comfort me.
    When the table is spread before me, it excites me, for I knoweth
    That soon I shall dig in.
    As I fillith my plate continuously, my clothes runneth smaller.
    Surely bulges my plate continuously, my clothes runneth smaller.
    Surely bulges and excess weight shall follow me all the days of my life
        and I will be fat forever.

Poems/Short Stories

1. Norman Swarztkoff was walking along the Kuwatie beach, finds an old bottle and rubs it, out pops a genie—one wish. Norman pulled out a map of the Middle East and asked for peace. Genie said, "People have been fighting here for one thousand years. Isn't there something easier you could wish for?"

   "I've always been a Dallas Cowboy fan, restore to former glory . . . America's team . . . put them in the Super Bowl, and let them be champions of the world."

   Genie thought and said, "Let me see that map again."

2. Once there were five tailors who loved on the same block. They were quite competitive and began to advertise as a way of attracting customers. The first tailor hung a sign outside this shop. It said, "Best tailor in the city." The second tailor, upon seeing this sign, did a little bit of one-upmanship as she produced a sign, which said, "Best tailor in the state." Not to be outdone, the third tailor put up a shingle announcing, "Best tailor in the country." Of course, it wasn't long before the fourth tailor had a plaque publicizing, "Best tailor in the world." After all of this, the fifth tailor went into his shop and came out with a sign that read simply, "Best tailor on this block."

3. A junior partner in the firm walked into the senior vice president's office.

   He slumped into a chair, downhearted, disconsolate, his head hanging down.

   "Sid, what's the matter. I've never seen you so down."

   "Bart, I don't know what to do, "Sid breathed heavily. "I'm about to be audited by the IRS, and I'm completely bewildered. I don't know how to approach it. I've talked to my accountant and my brother-in-law, and they've given me conflicting advice."

"What did they tell you?"

"First, my brother-in-law said to go to a used-clothing store and buy a ratty old suit of clothes, a shirt with a frayed collar, and an old stained tie. Then he told me to get a beat-up pair of shoes and rent an old jalopy. I'm supposed to drive down to the IRS office, park in front, and walk in for the meeting. Then throw myself on the mercy and see what they say."

The senior officer leaned forward. "What did your accountant tell you to do?"

"He told me to got to Brooks Brothers and pick out a fifteen-hundred-dollar suit. Buy a nice Turnbull and Asser shirt and a Sulka tie and go out and rent the longest limousine I can find. Finally, I should get a business card, form a partner in the most impressive law firm in the city, go down in the limo, and park in front of the IRS office. Then walk in and slap the card on the desk and say, 'If I get called about this matter one more time, you'll be hearing from my lawyer.'"

Sid sighed, "So you can see, Bart, I don't know which to do. What do you think?"

Bart paused for a moment before replying. "Sid, let me tell you about a young secretary who was in here yesterday with a problem. She's getting married next week and came to me for some advice. 'Mr. Harrison,' she said, 'I don't know what to wear on my wedding night. My sister said that when my husband and I are together in the bedroom for the first time I should come out of the dressing room wearing a floor-length white cotton nightgown with a high collar and long sleeves, and I should be wearing white cotton panties underneath. Then my girlfriend said something quite different. She told me to come out of the dressing room wearing a sheer waist-length black sleeveless negligee cut down to the navel with black lace peekaboo panties underneath.'"

Sid was curious. "So, Bart, what advice did you give her?"

"I gave her the same advice I'm going to give you, Sid, "Bart answered, leaning forward. "It doesn't matter what you wear. Either way you're going to get screwed!"

4. One Christmas when the children were young, I realized that I was several days late in getting our Christmas tree. There was a tree lot about three blocks from our home, so I jumped in the car one night and raced over there to pick up a tree. After selecting one, I had the task of getting it from the lot to the house. I didn't have any rope to

tie it on top of the car, so I thought I'd just put it on top of the car and drive very slowly. I'd hold on with one hand . . . I only had three blocks to go on side streets with little traffic. So I put the tree on top of the car, got in the car, reached up, and got a good grip on the trunk of the tree, and then reached over and closed the door firmly—on my arm.

5.	Paul Newman, Robert Redford, and John Jones went to heaven on the same day. St. Peter showed us to our respective quarters, beginning with Paul Newman. He opened the door to what turned out to be a cell—low ceiling, windowless, drab, water dripping from the walls, just stools, no beds. And seated on one stool in the corner was the fat lady of the circus. And St. Peter turned to Paul Newman and said, "For all your misdeeds on earth, this is where you will stay, and this will be your companion." Then he beckoned to Robert Redford. His room was even smaller, again windowless, low ceiling, poorly ventilated. Seated in one corner was a toothless, cadaverous-looking person with stringy hair. And he said to Robert Redford, "For your misdeeds, this is where you will stay, and this will be your companion." And then St. Peter beckoned to Cousins. He came to a room and opened the door. Sunlight poured through a dozen windows . . . flowers . . . the furnishings were magnificent . . . high ceilings. In the center of the room was a majestic bed with pink sheets. On the bed reposed Bo Derek, unclad. And St. Peter said to Bo Derek, "For all your misdeeds, this is *your* companion."

6.	There was a man whose store had been looted right down to the bare shelves. "Did you lose a great deal?" asked a detective. "Everything," said the storekeeper. "But it could have been worse. I'm lucky they didn't loot the place the night before last." "How come?" said the detective. "Well," said the storekeeper, "yesterday I marked everything down 40 percent."

7.	One night, at the end of his career, Boris Tomashefsky, the greatest star of Yiddish theater, collapsed in his dressing room. Minutes later, the stage manager appeared in front of the curtain and told the packed house, "My friends, Mr. Tomashefsky has had a heart attack and will not appear tonight." "Give him an enema," roared a voice from the audience. "You don't understand," said the stage manager. "Boris Tomashefsky is dead. An enema can't help." "Can't hurt," responded the voice.

8.	A man was accused of stealing a tool kit from someone else's garage. "But I just took it as a joke," he protested before the judge. "How far did you carry the tool kit?" the judge wanted to know. "Just three blocks," replied the defendant. "Thirty days, then," proclaimed for carrying a joke too far. 9. A farmer called his six sons around him and demanded to know which one had pushed the outhouse into the creek. When the villain did not step forward, the farmer told the story of George Washington and the cherry tree and how George's father did not punish him when he admitted his guilt in chopping down the tree.

After hearing the story, one of the boys stepped forward and admitted giving the outhouse a shove. The old man picked up a switch and gave the kid the beating of his life. "But, Pa," said the boy, "you said George Washington's father was proud of him when he admitted cutting down the cherry tree. "He was," said the farmer, "but George Washington's father wasn't sitting in the cherry tree when it went down."

10. A young sailor was in a hurry to get home for the weekend. He wasn't quite sure how the accident happened or who was to blame, but he knew there had been a tremendous collision and much property damage. The other driver, observing the wreckage, said, "Well, it's lucky that neither of us was hurt badly. Let's go get a drink and settle our nerves until the cops come." The seaman concurred, and the two stepped into a nearby pub. Still very nervous, the swabbie quickly downed a double. When he noticed that the other glass was still on the bar, he asked, "Aren't you going to drink yours?" "No," said the other man, "I think I'll wait until after the police check around.

11. The importance of tact in communication is demonstrated by Helen and her brother, Bob. When Helen went out of town on vacation, she asked Bob to come by each day and take care of her prized cat. She called from her hotel the next night and asked how the cat was, to which Bob curtly responded, "Oh, your cat's dead." Helen was aghast at the news and shouted, "Bob, how could you be so insensitive! You know how I loved that cat! At least, you could have broken the news to me gradually. One day, you could say that the cat was stuck on the roof. The next day, you could say that the fire department came and tried to rescue the cat, but it jumped from the roof and injured itself. Then, on the third day, after I was prepared, you could have told me that the vet did everything possible, but the cat passed away." After regaining her composure from the news and having criticized Bob adequately, she asked, "Well, how's Mother?" There was a silence for a moment until Bob replied in a soft voice, "She's on the roof."

12. Four ministers were walking in the park one day before an ecumenical meeting, chatting about the trials and tribulations of being men of the cloth. One of their common problems, they decided, was their inability to have close friends with whom they could share their most personal problems. They decided to confide in one another. The first began by confiding to the others that he had a significant drinking problem. The others showed surprise at this revelation, but it inspired them to also share their innermost secrets. The second clergyman then spoke up, informing his cohorts that he was growing increasingly fond of a married woman in his congregation. The third confided that he had, on occasion, dipped into the collection plate to help support his gambling habit. The fourth minister said nothing. Finally, after urging from the three who had confessed their darkest secrets, he could resist their pressure no longer. "I know my secret vice will be more shocking and disturbing to you than any you have heard so far." The others coaxed him on, assuring him that his secret would be safe with them. "Okay then, here it is—you see, I am an incurable gossip."

13. He who knows not, and knows that he knows not, is a fool. Avoid him.

    He who knows not, and knows not that he knows not, is ignorant. Teach him.

    He who knows, and knows not that he knows, is asleep. Waken him.

    But he who knows, and knows that he knows, is a wise man. Follow him.

    He who knows not whether he knows or knows not anything at all is a politician. Do not trust him. (James Hogan)

14. When Hitler attached the Jews, I was not a Jew; therefore, I was not concerned. And when Hitler attacked the Catholics, I was not a Catholic, and therefore, I was not concerned. And when Hitler attacked the unions and the industrialists, I was not a member of the unions and I was not concerned. Then Hitler attacked me and the Protestant church, and there was nobody left to be concerned. (Martin Niemoller)

15. The archaeologist was thrilled beyond words when after digging in Australia, he found a tablet with symbols carved upon it. Carbon dating placed it at nearly two thousand years old, which make the find even more significant. "If we look at these symbols," said the archaeologist at a press conference, "we can infer several things about the society that carved them." Displaying the tablet, he pointed out the symbols in

turn. "The presence of the cross," said he, "indicated that Christianity had reached Australia not long after its founding. Next, the presence of a shovel suggests that the early Australians were builders. The third symbol, what looks to be a donkey, proves that they had domesticated animals while the fourth picture, a baby fowl, demonstrates that they were farmers." "Bull!" shouted a man in the audience, an archaeologist noted for his outré ideas. "Anyone with half a brain knows that it's really early Australian pornography." "Oh?" the discoverer of the tablets said smugly, "and how do you know that?" "Because," he replied, "what it really says is, 'Christ, dig the ass on that chick!'"

16. Mr. Lawson was sitting at the bar when the fellow perched on the stool next to his slid off. Feeling that there was no way the man would make it home on his own, Mr. Lawson managed to get the man's address from him, and since the house was only a few blocks away, he decided they could walk it. Slipping an arm around his waist, they started toward the door. No sooner had they taken a few steps then the men's legs crumpled, and he dropped. Mr. Lawson patiently helped him up, and he dropped again; once outside he fell again and then a fourth time. The man mumbled something, but Mr. Lawson was in no mood to listen. "Ya drunken bum," he complained. "Why the hell didn't you cut it out before you got so falling down drunk?" When the man took two more steps and fell both times, the Good Samaritan decided that enough was enough. He simply threw his shoulders beneath the man and carried him home. Rapping indignantly, he strode in when a woman answered the door and then unceremoniously dumped the man on the couch. "Here's your husband," Mr. Lawson complained. "And if I were you, I'd have a serious talk to him about his drinking." "I will," the woman promised. "But tell me," she went on, looking outside, "where's his wheelchair?"

17. God was annoyed. Too many people were being admitted to heaven, and he established a new criterion: no one could enter unless they knew what one of their faith's principal holidays were all about. As it happened, three Christians died and were the first ones to have to submit to the new ruling. They approached St. Peter one at a time, and he asked the first, "What is Easter all about?" "Uh . . . err . . . a holiday where we color eggs and . . . and . . ." Shaking his head, St. Peter sent the woman to hell, and the next aspiring angel walked up. St. Peter asked him, "What's Easter all about?" "Well . . . ummm . . . it's about this bunny who goes around . . ." Sighing, St. Peter sent the Christian to hell and motioned for the next one to approach. "What is Easter all about?" The

old man cleared his throat. "That's when Jesus was crucified and, rising from the dead, came from within the cave." "Praise the Lord!" St. Peter said. "A learned and worthy soul!" "And when he saw his shadow," the man went on, "it meant there would be six more weeks of winter."

18. Little Jimmy was a naughty little boy who, as it happened, wanted a bicycle more than anything else in the world. When he asked his mother for one, she told him that he could only have a bike if he learned to behave himself, which he promptly promised to do. Alas, after a week of trying to behave, the boy found it next to impossible. Trying to be helpful, his mother suggested, "Maybe if you write a little note to Jesus, you'll find it easier to be good." Jimmy agreed to try and, rushing upstairs, flopped down on his bed, pencil in hand. "Dear Jesus," he wrote, "if you let me have a bike, I promise to be good for the rest of my life." Realizing he could never do that, Jimmy crumpled the paper and started anew. "Dear Jesus, if you let me have a bike, I promise to be good for a month." Realizing that even that was beyond him, Jimmy decided not to start again. Instead he ran into his mother's room, went to her dresser, removed her statue of the Holy Mother, closed it in a shoe box and hid the shoe box under his bed. Hopping onto the bed, he returned to his pad and pencil. "Dear Jesus," he wrote, "if you ever want to see your mother again . . ."

19. The minister entered the bathroom at the church, and while he was using the urinal, he heard moaning coming from one of the stalls. Entering a stall beside the one whence the sounds were coming, he stood on the toilet seat and discreetly peeked over. There he saw Roger De Leon masturbating. Sneaking from the lavatory, the minister decided to have a chat with the boy. Waiting until he came out, he took Roger aside and, without being harsh or judgmental, said, "I happen to know what you were doing in there, Roger, and I must tell you that the boys whom God truly loves are those who save it until they're married." Nearly a month passed before the minister happened to bump into Roger again. "And how are we doing with our . . . problem?" he asked. "Great!" he answered. "So far I've saved nearly a quart."

POLITICAL/GOVERNMENT

1. There was a legislative bill in Austin to legalize bisexuality. Interested I asked a state representative friend of mine what he was going to do about it. He said, "Oh, I could go either way on it."

2. The taxes of today are the promises of yesterday.

3. I asked a friend what he thought about *Rowe v. Wade*. He said, "Personally I don't care how the Mexicans get across the river."

4. I am a sailor in the United States Navy and have a cousin who is a Democrat. My father has epilepsy, and my mother has syphilis, so neither can work. They are totally dependent on my two sisters, who are prostitutes in Louisville, Kentucky, because my only brother is serving a life term in prison for murder. I am in love with a streetwalker who operates near our house, and she knows nothing about my background and insists that she loves me dearly. We intend to get married as soon as she settles her bigamy case, which is now in court. When I get out of the navy, we intend to move to Detroit, Michigan, and open a small house. "Now, my problem is this. In view of the fact that I intend to make the girl my wife and bring her into the family, should I or should I not tell her about my cousin who is a Democrat?"

5. The practical thing we can do, if we really want to make the world over again, is to try out the word *old* for a while. There are some "old" things that made this country. There is the "old" virtue of religious faith. There are the "old" virtues of complete integrity, loyalty, and truthfulness. There is the "old" virtue of incorruptible service and honor in public office. There are the "old" virtues of economy in government, of self-reliance,

thrift, and individual liberty. There are the "old" virtues of patriotism, real love of country, and willingness to sacrifice for it. These "old" ideas are very inexpensive. They even would help win hot and cold wars. Some of these "old" things are slipping badly in American life. And if they slip too far, the lights will go out of America, even if we win the hot and cold wars. Think about it. (Herbert Hoover)

6. I believe it to be the duty of every citizen to do all within his power to improve the conditions under which men work and live. I believe that that man renders the greatest social service who so cooperates in the organization of industry as to afford the largest number of men the greatest opportunity for self-development, and the enjoyment by every man of those benefits which has own work adds to the wealth of civilization. (John D. Rockefeller Jr.)

7. Nobody knows what's going on. Last week the Statue of Liberty was seen throwing up both hands.

8. To accommodate the Christmas rush this year. The post office put out one million extra This Counter Closed signs

9. One man to another, "After listening to this guy speak for the past hour, I can understand why he's been labeled a political moderate. He makes enemies left and right.

10. Good news and bad news—Russia just saved our men from a sinking ship from their submarine. Bad news—it was from Lake Tahoe.

11. All fairy stories don't begin with "Once upon a time." Sometimes with "When I am elected."

12. I made an open-air speech the other night, and the applause was deafening. Two people applauded, and the rest were swatting mosquitoes.

13. Going to war without France is like going deer hunting without your accordion. (Donald Rumsfeld)

14. Remember what Muriel Humphrey told her late husband, Senator Hubert Humphrey, after a particularly windy speech. She said, "Hubert, you don't have to be eternal to be immortal."

15. On the tax form, where it says Dependents: Can I check off for congressmen and senators?

16. Rules for Congress
If it moves tax it! If it still moves, regulate it! If it stops moving, subsidize it!

17. The mayor is laying off five hundred public works employees—they've invented a shovel that stands by itself.

18. I was standing on the corner in Austin last week, and an empty cab drove up, and Governor Richards got out.

19. The reason the crime bill hasn't passed Congress is because Congress can't figure out how it will affect them.

20. I was going to tell you the story of the forty thieves, but you probably wouldn't be interested in politics.

21. But he finally became a success. Now he's a member of the Ways to Be Mean Committee in Washington.

22. Rule in Politics: anytime you get more than ten people together, ask for money.

23. Foreign aid might be defined as a transfer from poor people in rich countries to rich people in poor countries. (Douglas Casey)

24. The Pledge of Allegiance to the flag was adopted by Congress in the summer of 1892. The pledge is, "I pledge allegiance to the flag of the United States of America and to the Republic for which it stands: one Nation under God, indivisible, with Liberty and Justice for All." The words "under God" were approved by Congress in 1954. When President Eisenhower signed the act, adding the recognition of God, he said, "In this way we are reaffirming the transcendence of religious faith in America's heritage and future. In this way we shall constantly strengthen those spiritual weapons which forever will be our country's most powerful resource in peace and war."

25. Pro is the exact opposite of con, and if you need an illustration, there's progress and there's Congress.

26. America only makes Teflon treaties—those that don't stick.

27. He's the type who's always fighting for unpopular causes—like asking the mayor to build sheltered fire hydrants for bashful dogs.

28. A lobbyist is someone who when push comes to shove depends on pull.

29. The Bureaucrat's Creed:
   I believe in the principles of dynamic inaction, and, henceforth, when I do nothing, I will do it with style.
   I believe that red tape should be cut . . . but only as long as it is cut lengthwise.
   I believe in innovation and creativity but only as long as it is innovation or creativity within established guidelines.
   I believe that all people should profundity simplicity, fuzzify goals, and global issues.
   I believe that bureaucracy is the epoxy that greases the wheels of all institutions.

30. A government is the only known vessel that leaks from the top.

31. Red tape is mightier than the sword.

32. The Ten Commandments contain 297 words. The Bill of Rights is stated in 463 words. Lincoln's Gettysburg Address contains 266 words. A recent federal directive to regulate the price of cabbage contains 26,911 words.

33. Christmas is a time when children ask Santa Claus for what they want and adults pay for it. Deficits are when adults spend what they want and children pay for it.

34. My brother-in-law said that politics in his hometown were so crooked that if a man said he controlled twenty votes, he was just talking about himself.

35. The local election was near, and one old resident asked a relative newcomer what he thought of the two candidates running for mayor. "I'm glad," said the man, "that only one of them can be elected."

36. Some sage once remarked, "If you live in a town that is run by a committee, you had better be on it."

37. In politics, if you're against it, it's a machine; if you're for it, it's a party.

38. "Here's what we do," said the cannibal chief. "We leak word that our government is unstable. The Russians will immediately make overtures. Naturally the Americans will get worried and begin relations. Then the Russians will ask to send ambassadors. The American will ask for equal representation. We invite them both to send emissaries. And when they get here we eat 'em."

39. Most of the Democratic candidates claim they're middle-of-the-road. So are potholes.

40. Like to be a member of a minority group? Try putting in an honest day's work.

41. Education USA—teach the girls to take the pill, pass out condoms, and make prayers illegal.

42. Here's a consoling thought for Mother's Day and Father's Day. If your kids are lazy, selfish, disrespectful, disobedient, and unappreciative, it helps to think of the national debt we're going to stick them with.

43. What do you need to make a small fortune? A large fortune. 44. Discipline without freedom is tyranny; freedom without discipline is chaos. (Cullen Hightower)

45. If you lie to people to get their money, that's fraud. If you lie to people to get their vote, that's politics.

46. When the freedom they wished for was freedom from responsibility, then Athens ceased to be free and was never free again. (Edith Hamilton)

47. Any country with "Democratic" in the title isn't. (Jim Murray, Los Angeles)

48. Religion is set up a little differently in Russia than it is here. For instance, when you go to confession in the United States, you come back out again.

49. No one believes a rumor in Washington until it is officially denied.

50. Do you realize, if Bill Clinton gets elected president again, someday there will be more Bill Clinton Slept Here signs around than George Washington.

51. Have you noticed that ever since November we've had nothing but freezing weather, blizzards, ice and sleet and drought combined? Now this can be explained in two possible ways. It can be explained scientifically: a change in the upper wind currents has brought polar air masses farther south than they ever came before. Or, it can be explained philosophically: God is a Republican!

52. In an era of international tension, natural disasters, pestilence, and terrorism, we should all be very grateful that the biggest question facing Washington today is, what wine goes with grits?

53. Bureaucracy: the process of turning energy into solid waste.

54. The Center for the Study of Social Policy, a liberal think tank in Washington, DC, says more than 20 percent of the nation's kids are now living in hunger and poverty . . . and they have a simple solution too: Eat the rich!

55. What's the difference between your wife and the IRS? If you cheat on the IRS, they still want to do it to you.

56. This just in from Illinois. With six cemeteries still to be heard from—the election is still too close to call.

57. America is a land of freedoms. There is freedom to burn the flag, freedom to sing the national horribly—in short freedom to be a jerk.

58. The difference between Democrats and Republicans? A Democrat looks at half a glass of water and says, "That glass is half empty!" A Republican looks at it and says, "Who stole half my glass of water?"

59. I once had my taxes done by a CPA. I won't say how he did, but I think CPA stood for Couldn't Pass Arithmetic!

60. He's the kind of accountant who can put you into a fantastic tax shelter. (Leavenworth)

61. Instead of higher taxes and more government spending, maybe it's time we got back to Bikini Taxes. That is just enough to cover the essentials.

62. In politics admit nothing, deny everything, and make counter allegations.

63. I don't know if this is good news or bad for Bill Clinton—he's just been endorsed by the Motel Managers Association.

64. To get elected, a politician must be flexible—he must be willing to bend the facts and stretch the truth.

65. Politicians are not dishonest. They're just "ethically challenged."

66. Campaign speeches should come with a warning label: "Caution! Likely to cause drowsiness and or vomiting." And campaign promises should bear the label: "Dangerous if swallowed! Not to be taken internally or seriously."

67. Two tourists visiting Washington sat in the observers' gallery at the Capitol and watched as various senators engaged in shouting matches with one another, gesticulating wildly and turning red in the face. One of the tourists said to the other, "This must be what they mean by political asylum."

68. Congress is introducing a farm bill that contains an alarming and radical provision. It suggests that farmer not be paid unless they grow something.

69. I've been trying to figure out how much national health care would cost. According to my calculations, it would be cheaper for the government to send everyone to medical school.

70. Politically correct: "I am not poverty stricken—I just have an earning disorder."

71. Clinton gives the term *going abroad* a whole new meaning.

72. They say a little education goes a long way. Unfortunately, they don't say how far a lot of education will take you.

73. What would draft dodgers do if we went to war with Canada?

74. The Iraqi army discovered a way to get behind enemy lines—surrendering.

75. To succeed in politics, it is often necessary to rise above your principles.

76. The best way to succeed in politics is to find a mob going somewhere and get in front of it.

77. The British created a civil service job in 1803 calling for a man to stand on the cliffs of Dover with a spyglass. He was supposed to ring a bell if he saw Napoleon coming. The job was abolished in 1945.

78. Senator Dole: "If Jerry Brown is the answer, I want to know what's the question."

79. The Iraqis claim that in ten years they will have the capability to wipe out millions of Americans. That puts them exactly two years behind the IRS.

80. Politicians never promise us a rose garden. They just deliver the fertilizer.

81. Government spending gives you an idea of why laws are called bills.

82. Politicians are like dirty clothes. They only come clean when they're in hot water.

83. It's hard to get politicians to vote more money for education. They know they'll never be elected if voters get too smart.

84. They can't help running for reelection. It's the overwhelming urge to return to the scene of the crime.

85. Strong government is needed . . . by weak people.

86. Money talks, but it is under no obligation to tell the truth.

87. Politically speaking: All Lloyd Bentsen added to last November's campaign was a few new wrinkles. Bentsen was to dull what fat is to obesity.

88. At last a weapons system absolutely impervious to attack: it has components manufactured in all 435 congressional districts.

89. In one of his first campaigns as a young man, Lyndon Johnson was helping a Texas sheriff win reelection. At a strategy meeting, the sheriff suggested they put out a story that his opponent carried on unnaturally with barnyard animals. "But he doesn't," said shocked Johnson. "Yeah," replied the sheriff, "but let's make him deny it."

90. One man to another, "Never mind about the scientists. What scares me is that 90 percent of all bureaucrats who ever existed are alive today!"

91. If the King's English was good enough for Jesus, then it is good enough for me." (Ma Ferguson)

92. Two delegates were talking about how the speeches were running long. One recalled the rigid time enforcement at a meeting in Texas. A guest speaker had been given exactly twelve minutes. When his talk ran over fifteen minutes, he heard a click of several guns. "Surely you wouldn't shoot a guest," said the speaker, alarmed. "Why, no," drawled a man in the audience. "That would be downright inhospitable. We're gunning for the guy who invited you."

93. A Democrat and a Republican were talking about what they did for their respective parties prior to the election. The Democrat said that with Mondale running for election, as a loyal supporter he would go into a restaurant, have a fine meal, and leave a big tip. "I always told the waitress to vote Democratic," he said. The Republican said he did almost the same thing for Bush in his bid for a second term. "I went into a restaurant and had a fine meal but didn't leave a tip," the Republican said. "You didn't leave a tip?" the Democrat said. "No, I didn't," the Republican said, "but I never forgot to tell the waitress to vote Democratic."

94. Advice to voters: don't change turkeys in the middle of the stream.

95. Politicians are like cockroaches. It's not what they eat and carry away; it's what they fall into and mess up."

96. Dan Quayle asked Gorbachev, "What's that on your forehead?" Gorby said, "It's a birthmark." Quayle answered, "Oh yeah? How long have you had it?"

97. Senate rules forbid election campaigning on the senate floor, but that didn't keep Sen. Robert Dole from parading around the other day with a bumper sticker that read: "Honk if Walter Mondale promised you anything."

98. An old-timer can remember when a "bureau" was a piece of furniture.

99. A sign n the window provides the perfect commentary on rumors that the Democrats may drop the donkey as their mascot, "Don't Change the Symbol. Stop Nominating Jackasses."

100. One man to another, "We all agree that he has the drive and determination to become a good politician. Despite the fact he was born poor and honest, he's managed to overcome both difficulties."

101. Somewhere out in his audience may even be someone who will one day follow in my footsteps and preside over the White House as the president's spouse. I wish him well. (Barbara Bush)

102. Noting that the state legislature's interim committees had postponed meetings for six weeks because of turkey hunting season, someone asked, "Are all those legislators hunters?" "No," said someone else, "they just don't want to take a chance and show themselves in public while turkeys are fair game."

103. The difference between politics and baseball is that in baseball, when you get caught stealing, you're out.

104. One day the people of the world will want peace so much that the governments are going to have to get out of their way and let them have it. (Dwight Eisenhower)

105. Democrats think a platform is a place to set the beer kegs.

106. The Democratic convention will be in San Francisco. That's were the restrooms are labeled his, hers, and who knows.

107. Husband to wife, "Mondale finally figured out why Hart is so popular with the female voters. The ladies figure any guy who lies about his age understands their problems.

108. It is interesting that John-John and the Democrats had their convention in the Fleet Center, an arena named after an enema.

109. A fellow who had been in a coma since 1944 recovered and was wheeled out of the hospital. He took one look at the parking lot and said, "Japan and Germany must have won the war."

110. Comment regarding something against your own interests: You wouldn't want that! That would be like a chicken voting for Colonel Sanders.

111. If you want to know what the Department of Agriculture contributes to America as opposed to what our farmers contribute to America—eat a food stamp.

112. Congress doesn't care—members get paid whether the country makes money or not. I say put them on commission.

113. The cow chip throwing contest at the Ohio State Fair was won by a politician. Really, I don't think they ought to let professionals enter those contests.

114. It takes two bureaucrats to install a lightbulb. One to insert it and one to screw it up.

115. Re: the controversy over whether or not Bill Clinton should be disbarred makes one wonder what it means when a society sets a "lower standard" for being president than it does for being a lawyer.

116. So many are vying for president
That candidates have found
There aren't enough good promises
To go around.

117. Some of us can remember when going to our eternal resting place didn't mean getting a job with the U.S. government.

118. Re: a certain politician—he is an indictment waiting to happen.

119. Why it is that if ignorance of the law is no excuse, why are there appeal courts to correct the errors of our judges?

120. David Brinkley, appearing on the Johnny Carson show, discussed our two bland presidential candidates: "If they decided to give a fireside chat, the fire would go out."

121. The Supreme Court reaffirmed the legality of affirmative action. The panel held that discrimination to undo discrimination doesn't discriminate.

122. Rang up Dial-A-Joke recently and got Clinton's campaign headquarters.

123. Voting the straight ticket: voting only for heterosexual candidate.

124. Elections consist of two sides and a fence.

125. She has a Supreme Court figure—no appeal!

126. A fellow in Washington went to a doctor. He seemed anxious and nervous. He looked around furtively and said, "Doc, I'm a congressman and I'm suffering from herpes."
     The doctor said, "What do you want to be treated for?"

127. Man called and wanted to speak to the senator. His secretary said, "I'm sorry he's gone to the United Kingdom." Man said, "I'm sorry. Is it too late to send flowers?"

128. In a gubernatorial election, why isn't the winner called a goober?

129. Tax time is very much like election time—you have to send something to Washington whether you like it or not.

130. The president is having trouble getting his crime bill through Congress. It has to be tough enough to jail criminals, yet lenient enough to let congressmen go free.

131. A lobbyist who had several acrimonious encounters during the legislative session with a legislator who happens to be female complained that "she's the kind of woman who makes a man want to ask for his rib back."

132. One citizen to another as they walk through Beirut rubble: "Actually, the war wasn't so bad it was the cease-fires that got us!"

133. Let me see if I've got this right. I can go to jail for lying to Congress once. But what does Congress get for lying to you and me all these years? A pay raise!

134. It's not very encouraging to know your bank deposits are protected by an agency of a federal government that's $1 trillion in debt.

135. U.S. Representative Phil Gramm has dubiously blessed Tip O'Neill, Speaker of the House. "Speaker Tip O'Neill," Gramm says, "has predicted seven of the last four recessions."

136. I've got nothing against the new tax laws. It's brought poverty within the reach of all of us.

137. A sure sign of bureaucracy is when the first person who answers the phone can't help you.

138. What worries me about a government-run national health insurance: We're liable to end up with a bureaucracy that has all the efficiency of the post office—and all the compassion of the IRS.

139. Spinning political yarns, a former member of Congress told about a hotly contested campaign between two candidates for sheriff in a Southern state. Making an impassioned plea for votes just prior to the election, one of the candidates wound up his oration with his clincher: "I know I ain't much, but why settle for less?"

140. A candidate who came out on the short end in the balloting sighs that nothing's been going right for him lately. "If I called Dial-A-Prayer," he moans, "they'd tell me to go to hell."

141. Most problems don't exist until a government agency is created to solve them

142. Re: the savings and loan problem. Don't worry it will all be covered by the FDIC. That's not the Federal Deposit Insurance Corporation—it's the Foolish, Dumb, Innocent Civilians who are going to have to pay for it.

143. Re: law against prayer in schools—means that if the kids are found on their knees in the classroom, they'd better be shooting craps.

144. Whatever happens anywhere in this world eventually will cost the American taxpayer.

145. I love it. You go to a coin-operated store to wash and dry your clothes. Then you got to a filling station where you pump your own gas. And on to a fast food restaurant where you carry your own tray. And what is it being called? A service economy!

146. Secretary of Education was asked this question by a seventh grader: "How can you tell a *good country* from a bad one?" The secretary replied, "I apply the 'gate' test. When the gates of a country are open, watch which way the people run. Do they run into the country or out of the country?"

147. Frankly, I never realized how much Governor Brown wants to solve the problems of California until he offered to go to Washington.

PUN

1. I wondered why the baseball was getting bigger. Then it hit me.

2. He drove his expensive car into a tree and found how the Mercedes bends.

3. Those who jump off a Paris bridge are in Seine.

4. A cardboard belt would be a waist of paper.

5. He wears glasses during math because it improves division.

6. Two peanuts were walking in a tough neighborhood, and one of them was a-salted.

7. Did you hear about the guy whose left side was cut off? He's all right now.

8. It was an emotional wedding. Even the cake was in tiers.

9. Those who throw dirt are sure to lose ground.

10. When the waiter spilled a drink on his shirt, he said, "This one is on me."

11. Nominee for the all-time worst pun:
    A Polish train was running out of coal late one night, but the engineer knew he could get some more in Danzig. As they pulled into the unlit station, the engineer asked the porter, "Can you tell me where we are?" The porter replied, "It says Danzig, in the dark!" The engineer said, "Buy coal, porter!"

12. I was driving down a lonely country road one cold winter day when it began to sleet pretty heavily. My windows were getting icy, and my wiper blades were badly worn and quickly fell apart under the strain. Unable to drive any further because of the ice building up on my front window, I suddenly had a great idea. I stopped and began to overturn large rocks until I located two very lethargic hibernating rattlesnakes. I grabbed them up, straightened them out flat, and installed them on my blades, and they worked just fine. What! You've never heard of . . . wind-chilled vipers!

13. Once upon a time in the enchanted forest there lived three gnus (pronounced "nooze"). There was a momma gnu. There was a poppa gnu. And there was a baby gnu. Come dinner one day and there was nothing to eat. So the poppa gnu decided to go out into the forest and collect some nuts and berries for dinner. Just then the baby gnu piped up and said, "Bleah! Nuts and berries again!" So the poppa gnu went out into the forest. Little did he know that it was hunting season for gnus. And as he was walking along . . . Blam! Blam! The hunter killed him dead in his tracks. After a while, Momma gnu decided that old pops must be lost out in the forest. So she said, "Baby, you be a good gnu while I go out to look for your old man." She didn't know it was hunting season for gnus either. And as she was walking along . . . Blam! Blam! The hunter killed her dead in her tracks. After a while, baby gnu was getting a little lonely and decided to go out and look for his parents. He didn't know it was hunting season either. And as he was walking along . . . Blam! Blam! The hunter got him too. Assassinated him on the trail. Did him in. Knocked him off. Killed him dead in his tracks. Well . . . that's the gnus. The weather in a moment.

14. An Indian chief was feeling very sick, so he summoned the medicine man. After a brief examination, the medicine man took out a long, thin strip of elk hide and gave it to the chief, instructing him to bite off, chew, and swallow one inch of the leather every day. After a month, the medicine man returned to see how the chief was feeling. The chief shrugged and said, "The thong is ended, but the malady lingers on."

15. The driver of a huge tractor trailer lost control of his rig and plowed into an empty tollbooth and smashed it to pieces. He climbed down from the wreckage and looked around. Within a matter of minutes, another truck pulled up and unloaded a crew of workers. The men picked up

each broken piece of the former tollbooth and spread some kind of creamy substance on it, then they began fitting the pieces together. In less than a half hour, they had the entire tollbooth reconstructed and good as new. "Astonishing!" the truck driver said to the crew chief. "What was that white stuff you used to get all of the pieces together?" The crew chief said, "Oh, that was tollgate booth paste."

16. A recent crime wave has been solved in Israel. For months, this fellow had been committing armed robberies along Israel's coastal cities. The only information that the police were able to get—(1) name: Gomez (2) two composite sketches.

   After weeks of frustration, Israel's intelligence service submitted the above information to "Inter-Pol." Remarkably, Inter-Pol fed back the following info.

   1. First name: Joseph
   2. Traveled incognito as a flautist with several famous orchestras.
   3. He and his twin brother were the illegitimate offspring of a prioress from an obscure abbey in a large metropolitan area along the northeast Mediterranean coast of Sprain.
   4. The brothers were unsuccessful as sharecroppers in their native land.

   With this new information, the Israeli police issued an APB for the immediate arrest of the: "Haifa looting, Fluten tooten, Son of a nun, From Barcelona, One time plowboy Joe"

17. A guy goes into his dentist's office because something is wrong with his mouth. After a brief examination, the dentist exclaims, "Holy smoke! That plate I installed in your mouth about six months ago has nearly completely corroded! What on earth have you been eating?" "Well . . . the only thing I can think of is this . . . my wife made me some asparagus about four months ago with this stuff on it . . . Hollandaise sauce she called it . . . and, Doctor, I'm talkin' delicious! I've never tasted anything like it, and ever since then I've been putting it on everything . . . meat, fish, toast, vegetables . . . you name it!" "That's probably it," replied the dentist. "Hollandaise sauce is made with lemon juice, which is acidic and highly corrosive. It seems as though I'll have to install a new plate but made out of chrome this time." "Why chrome?" the man asked. "Well, everyone knows that there's no plate like chrome for the Hollandaise!"

18. The golfing world is celebrating a new invention that promises to revolutionize the sport. The new device that is receiving so much attention is called the "bee nut." It is a fastening attachment that allows a player to adjust the head on their club to any angle, thus saving the need to carry a bagful of clubs. Thus, for example, a player can use the same club to putt with as they used to get out of the sand trap. Golf clubs with this modification are selling quickly, and players everywhere are taking golfing picnics, so they can try their new "bee-nut putter sand-wedge."

19. There was a man who entered a local paper's pun contest. He sent in ten different puns, in the hope that at least one of the puns would win. Unfortunately, no pun in ten did.

20. A guy goes to a psychiatrist, "Doc, I keep having these alternating recurring dreams. First, I'm a teepee, then I'm a wigwam, then I'm a teepee, then I'm a wigwam. It's driving me crazy. What's wrong with me?" The doctor replies, "It's very simple. You're two tents."

21. Way down upon the Mississippi, two tugboat captains, who had been friends for years, would always cry "Aye!" and blow their whistles whenever they passed each other. A new crewman asked his boat's mate, "What did they do that for?" The mate looked surprised and replied, "You mean that you've never heard of . . . an aye for an aye and a toot for a toot?"

22. A young man was in love with a lovely young lady, but unfortunately she did not feel the same way about him. In desperation he went and visited a group of witches searching for a love potion. They informed him that they no longer provided such an item. It was highly unethical to administer a potion to someone without her permission. They did have an alternate solution however. They sold him a bottle of small white pellets. He was to bury one in her yard every night at midnight for a month. He returned to the witches six weeks later excited and thankful. He and the young lady were to wed in a month. The witch told him "Nothin' says loving like something from a coven, and pills buried say it best."

23. It is believed that the stock markets go up and down with the rise and fall of the hemlines in ladies' skirts and dresses. Proof of this phenomenon is in the following historical facts: Glamour stocks and miniskirts soared

in 1993. Conglomerates and hemlines went down in the spring of 1194. Hot pants led the Dow Jones up in 1971. The advice to the investor then is, "Don't sell until you see the heights of their thighs!"

24. Sitting Bull had three wives who were always quarreling about who should be number 1. One was pretty, one was clever, and one was very strong. Finally, tired of their squabbles he told his medicine man to resolve the issue. The medicine man took the wives to his teepee where he had gathered pelts and hides from all over the world. He told each wife to choose a hide and sit on it in front of the sacred campfire. The clever wife chose a pelt of thick white fur, the strong wife chose a hide of orange-and-black stripes, and the pretty wife chose a hide of rubbery grey leather. The medicine man then pointed to the pretty wife and said, "Behold chief, your number 1 wife." The chief was pleased, but the other two wives demanded an explanation. The medicine man said, "Even the ancient ones knew that the squaw of the hippopotamus is equal to the sum of the squaws on the other two hides."

25. Did you hear about the gardener who always carried his shovel with him because he couldn't leave loam without it?

26. My love, you take my breath away. What have you stepped in to smell this way?

27. Punishing Puns—a calendar's days are numbered.

28. Roses are red, violets are blue, sugar is sweet, and so are you. But the roses are wilting, the violets are dead, the sugar bowl's empty and so is your head.

29. If the number 2 pencil is the most popular, why is it still number 2?

30. If work is so terrific, how come they have to pay you to do it?

31. If you're born again, do you have two belly buttons?

32. If you try to fail, and succeed, which have you done?

33. Did you know that in some fishing communities, in the olden days, people used to use fish as a means of exchange, instead of cash? That's where they first invented the credit cod.

34. An old railroader told him the reason an engine always "stands" and never "sits" on a track is because it has a tender behind.

35. What does an elephant do when he hurts his big toe? He calls the big tow truck.

QUOTES

1. Winning isn't everything but wanting to win is. (Vince Lombardi)

2. To laugh often and much, to win the respect of intelligent people and the affection of children . . . to leave the world a bit better . . . to know even one life had breathed easier because you have lived, that is to have succeeded. (Ralph Waldo Emerson)

3. George Burns: You cant help growing older, but you can help growing old.

4. Yogi B.: If you don't go to others funerals, they won't go to yours.

5. Norman v. Peale: You know that God didn't make junk and that you're okay.

6. Yogi Berra: What time is it? You mean right now?

7. Yogi Berra: When you don't know where you're going, any road will take you there.

8. Yogi Berra: When you come to a fork in the road, take it.

9. Yogi Berra: It's deja vu all over again.

Before they made him, they broke the mold
Way down deep he is shallow
This man's work cannot be underrated
I enjoy your company most when I'm by myself.
People who like this sort of thing will find it just the sort of thing they like.

I feel a lot more like I do now than I did when I came in
For every honest man he names, I can name another that tells the truth
Death is a once-in-a-lifetime experience
You look more like you do now than you used to
Things are more like they used to be than they are now
Reality is an illusion
To distinguish the real from the unreal, one must experience both
If you remember something too long, you'd might as well forget it

10. "Any club that will take me as a member I don't want to join." (Groucho Marx)

11. "You said it was a great horse and it was—it took eleven other horses to beat him. (Joe E. Lewis)

12. The art of medicine consists of amusing the patient while nature cures the disease. (Voltaire)

13. A person without a sense of humor is like a wagon without springs—jolted by every pebble in the road. (Henry Beecher)

14. Woody Allen: Most of the time I don't have much fun. The rest of the time I don't have any fun at all.

15. An optimist laughs to forget; a pessimist forgets to laugh. (Tom Nansbury)

16. When you restrain yourself from relieving your feelings at the expense of somebody else, when you restrain yourself from making somebody else unhappy for the satisfaction of speaking your mind, you prove that you have advanced out of the hair-trigger stage of prehistoric days. Man's earliest ancestors didn't stop to think. Stopping to think is the true test of civilization. (Grover Patterson)

17. Just as there are three Rs there are also three As of business life. They are ability, ambition, and attitude. Ability establishes what a worker does and will bring him a paycheck. Ambition determines how much he does and will get him a raise. Attitude guarantees how well he does. (William Sheer)

18. One man with courage makes a majority. (Andrew Jackson)

19. If God wanted us to be brave, why did he give us legs? (Marvin Kitman)

20. W. C. Fields said that if he could live his life over, he'd live over a saloon.

21. Humor is emotional chaos remembered in tranquility. (James Thurber)

22. To love is to admire with the heart; to admire is to love with the mind. (Ernest Hemingway)

23. Love does not consist in gazing at each other but in looking outward together in the same direction. (Antoine de Saint-Exupery)

24. Always take a job that is too big for you. (Harry Emerson Fosdick)

25. Undermine the entire structure of society by leaving the pay toilet door ajar so the next person can get in free. (Taylor Mead)

26. Happiness is not a state to arrive at, but a manner of traveling. (Margaret Lee Runbeck)

27. If happiness truly consisted in physical ease and freedom from care, then the happiest individual would not be either a man or a woman; it would be, I think, an American cow. (William Phelps)

28. True friendship comes when silence between two people is comfortable. (Dave Gentry)

29. May all your troubles during the coming year be as short-lived as your New Year's resolutions.

30. What a wonderful life I've had! I only wish I'd realized it sooner. (Colette)

31. Love doesn't make the world go round. Love is what makes the ride worthwhile. (Franklin Jones)

32. There is no failure except in no longer trying. (Elbert Hubbard)

33. If a man runs after money, he's money-mad; if he keeps it, he's a capitalist; if he spends it, he's a playboy; if he doesn't get it, he's a ne'er-do-well; if

he doesn't try to get it, he lacks ambition. If he gets it without working for it, he's a parasite; and if he accumulates it after a lifetime of hard work, people call him a fool who never got anything out of life. (Vic Oliver)

34. How much more grievous are the consequences of anger than the causes of it? (Marcus Aurelius)

35. Yogi Berra.: First, I want to thank the people who made this meeting necessary.

36. Sam Goldwyn, famous movie producer, was also famous for his colorful, if not confusing, style of speaking. A few of Sam's more memorable lines include the following:

   A verbal contract isn't worth the paper it's printed on.
   Every Tom, Dick, and Harry is named William.
   Now, gentlemen, listen slowly.
   For your information, I would like to ask a question.
   Include me out.
   Don't talk to me when I'm interrupting.
   I may not always be right, but I'm never wrong.

37. I have but one lamp by which my feet are guided, and that is the lamp of experience. I know of no way of judging the future but by the past. (Patrick Henry)

38. Experience is not what happens to a man. It is what a man does with what happens to him. (Aldus Huxley)

39. M. Twain: We should be careful to get out of an experience only the wisdom that is in it and stop there, lest we be like the cat that sits down on the hot stove lid. She will not sit down on a hot stove lid again, but she also will never sit down on a cold one.

   a. Humor is mankind's greatest blessing.

40. Experience does not err; it is only your judgment that errs in expecting from her what is not in her power. (Leonardo da Vinci)

41. Facts do not cease to exist because they are ignored. (Aldous Huxley)

42. Abe Lincoln: Am I not destroying my enemies when I make friends of them?
    A sentence which is true and appropriate at all times:
    "And this too shall pass."
    "How much it expresses. How chastening in the hour of pride. How consoling in the depth of affliction."

43. Yogi Berra: Nobody goes to that restaurant anymore. It's too crowded.

44. If you give what you do not need, it isn't giving. (Mother Theresa)

45. Will Rogers: Be thankful we're not getting all the government we're paying for

46. G. Burns: Too bad all the people who know how to run the country are busy driving taxicabs and cutting hair.

47. Oscar Wilde:

    a. Some cause happiness wherever they go; others whenever they go.
    b. In America the young are always willing to give to those who are older than themselves, the benefit of their inexperience.

48. No person was ever honored for what he received. Honor has been the reward for what he gave. (Calvin Coolidge)

49. Lord, when we are wrong, make us willing to change. And when we are right, make us easy to live with. (Peter Marshall)

50. M. Twain: There are two times in a man's life when he should not speculate: when he can't afford it and when he can.

51. We judge ourselves by what we feel we are capable of doing while others judge us by what we have already done. (Henry W. Longfellow)

52. Man is an able creature, but he has made 35,643,692 laws and hasn't yet improved on the Ten Commandments. (Jacob Braude)

53. This is a court of law, young man, not a court of justice. (Oliver Homes)

54. Abe Lincoln: No man has good enough memory to make a successful liar.

55. Yogi Berra: You can observe a lot by just watching.

56. Republicans sleep in twin beds—some even in separate rooms. That is why there are more Democrats. (Walt Staton)

57. Greater love hath no man than this, that he lay down his friends for his political life. (Theodore Roosevelt)

58. When they call the roll in the Senate, the senators do not know whether to answer "present" or "not guilty." (Theodore Roosevelt)

59. A people that values its privileges above its principles soon loses both. (Dwight Eisenhower)

60. If all our misfortunes were laid in one common heap, whence everyone must take an equal portion, most people would be contented to take their own and depart. (Socrates)

61. In this era of rapid change, one thing remains constant: it's easier to pray for forgiveness than to resist temptation.

62. Always forgive your enemies; nothing annoys them as much. (Oscar Wilde)

63. Everyone thinks of changing humanity, but no one thinks of changing himself. (Leo Tolstoy)

64. All the wonders you seek are within yourself. (Sir Thomas Browne)

65. No matter where you go you can't get away from yourself, so you'd better make yourself into somebody worthwhile.

66. To thine own self be true, and it must follow, as the night the day, thou canst not then be false to any man. (William Shakespeare)

67. Try not to become a person of success but rather a person of value. (Albert Einstein)

68. Always remember that we pass this way but once. Unless your spouse is reading the road map. (Robert Orben)

69. M. Twain: If you tell the truth, you don't have to remember anything.

70. It is not doing the thing we like to do, but liking the thing we have to do, that makes life blessed. (Johann von Goethe)

71. The quality of a person's life is in direct proportion to their commitment of excellence, regardless of their chosen field of endeavor. (Vince Lombardi)

72. The cinema is little more than a fad. (Charlie Chaplin)

73. *Gone with the Wind* is going to be the biggest flop in Hollywood history. I'm just glad it'll be Clark Gable who's falling flat on his face and not Gary Cooper. (Gary Cooper)

74. I think there is a world market for about five computers. (Thomas Watson, chairman of the board of IBM, 1943)

75. Creditors have better memories than debtors. (Benjamin Franklin)

76. If money is your hope for independence, you will never have it. The only real security that a man can have in this world is a reserve of knowledge, experience, and ability. (Henry Ford)

77. M. Twain: Morals consist of political morals, commercial morals, ecclesiastical morals, and morals.

78. A man who has committed a mistake and doesn't correct it is committing another mistake. (Confucius)

79. M Twain: Statistics are alike ladies of the night. Once you get them down, you can do anything with them.

80. Lead, follow, or get out of the way. (Ted Turner)

81. George Burns: Anybody who at age sixty can still do what he was doing at age twenty wasn't doing much at twenty.

82. Rodney Daingerfield: I was so ugly as a kid, we never had a jack-o-lantern. They just stuck me in the window.

83. The last thing my kids ever did to earn money was lose their baby teeth. (Phyllis Diller)

84. M. Twain: If you pick up a starving dog and make him prosperous, he will not bite you. This is the principal difference between a man and a dog.

85. I have nothing against dogs. I just hate rugs that go squish-squish. (Phyllis Diller)

86. Will Rogers: Everybody is ignorant, only on different subjects.

87. The teacher told my kid, "An apple a day keeps the doctor away." He said, "What do you got for cops?" (Rodney Dangerfield)

RELIGION

1. Lady told the priest she wanted to arrange for a funeral. The priest asked what was the deceased name. She said "Brandy." He said that was a strange name. She said, "Not for a dog." The priest said, "You mean the deceased is a dog?" She said, "Yes." He said, "Lady, we don't do dogs." She said, "What can I do? That dog has been my constant companion ever since my husband died." He said, "Take him to the Church of Christ or some other church. Maybe they will help you." She said, "OK, I will. I will get Brandy a decent funeral if it costs me $50,000. The priest said, "Wait a minute. Did you say Brandy was a Catholic?"

2. A Quaker was having great difficulty with his mule. He said, "Mule thee knows that I cannot curse thee, and thee knows that I can not beat you or harm you in any way but what thee does not know is that I can trade thee to a Baptist."

3. A little boy wanted a bicycle, but his mother told him he was just too naughty. The boy asked what he could do. She said, "I just don't know. I've talked to the principal, the school nurses, and all our neighbors. We are at a loss. Maybe if you write Jesus a letter he will give you the answer." So the boy went to his room, started his first letter, and told Jesus if he would let him have a bicycle he would be good for a solid year. He quickly realized he could never last a year, so he started his second letter, and this time he promised six months of good behavior. He knew this too was hopeless, so he ran into his mother's bedroom and got her little statue of Mother of Mary, put it in a shoe box, put the shoe box under his bed, and started his third letter, "Dear Jesus, if you ever want to see your mother again . . ."

4. Definition of a Presbyterian—a Baptist that started drinking but doesn't have enough money to be an Episcopalian.

5. Before Lil got married, the Catholic sisters told her not to worry about sex and that it was just a normal bodily function—like a stroke.

6. The atheists also have dial-a-prayer. You call this number and no one answers.

7. If Jesus was a Jew, why does he have a Puerto Rican name?

8. There was no room at the inn, and the innkeeper said, "I'm sorry, but it's not my fault." Joseph said," It's not my fault either."

9. *Heck* is where people go who don't believe in *gosh.*

10. He left a loudspeaker to the church in memory of his wife.

11. After old Sherlock Holmes solved his last mystery on earth, he sauntered thought the Pearly gates. And as soon as St. Peter saw him, he rushed over to the great sleuth, exclaiming, "Ah, just the man I need! We have a great mystery here. Adam and Eve are here, but they've disguised themselves and we can't tell who they are. Will you please help us to find them?"

    "Sherlock Holmes, who liked to keep his talents sharp, said, "Of course." And in two days Sherlock showed up with Adam and Eve. St. Peter was overjoyed and asked them, "Why did you try to hide from everybody?"

    Adam said that he and Eve hated being celebrities. "Every angel was always coming up and asking us for autographs, so we disguised ourselves as plain everyday angels."

    St. Peter understood, but he was still amazed that Sherlock Holmes had found them. "We tried everything but failed. How did you do it?"

    Old Sherlock was very modest about it all. "Elementary, my friend. I checked all the angels until I found two without navels."

12. Church schools are now offering sex education classes. They are calling it Begatting 101.

13. Lil doesn't belong to any organized religious group. She's a Methodist.

14. What do John the Baptist and Winnie the Pooh have in common? They have the same middle name. 15 What do you say to an atheist when he sneezes?

16. God has a sense of humor. You don't think I wanted to look like this, do you?

17. Mother Superior's health was failing fast. She had refused all nourishment. Finally one of the sisters found in the pantry a very fine bottle of bourbon that someone had given them many years before. She made a large glass of warm milk and added a huge slug of bourbon. She asked the Mother Superior to please try the warm milk. Mother took a sip and another sip. Finally it was all gone. She was failing fast, and the sisters gathered around her bed and asked her if she had any words of wisdom before she went to her heavenly reward. Mother Superior raised up on one elbow, pointed out the window and said, "Don't sell that cow."

18. Cast your bread upon the water, and it will come back to you a hundredfold. What you're going to do with one hundred loaves of wet bread is your problem?

19. General Douglas MacArthur: Build me a son, O Lord, who will be strong enough to know when he is weak, and brave enough to face himself when he is afraid, one who will be proud and unbending in honest defeat and humble and gentle in victory. Build me a son whose wishes will not take the place of deeds; a son who will know thee—and that to know himself is the foundation stone of knowledge. Lead him, I pray, not in the path of ease and comfort, but under the stress and spur of difficulties and challenge. Here let him learn to stand up in the storm; here let him learn compassion for those who fail. Build me a son whose heart will be clear, whose goal will be high; a son who will master himself before he seeks to master other men; one who will reach into the future, yet never forget the past. And after all these things are his, add, I pray, enough of a sense of humor so that he may always be serious, yet never take himself too seriously. Give him humility so that he may always remember the simplicity of true treat mess, the open mind of true wisdom, and the meekness of true strength. Then, I, his father, will dare to whisper, "I have not lived in vain."

20. During the period when the Israelites were suffering in Egyptian bondage, God traveled over the earth seeking those who might follow his mild law. He came across an Arab and said to him, "Would you like to follow *my* commandments?" The Arab frowned suspiciously. "Like what, for instance?" "One is thou shalt not kill!" The Arab said. "You must be mad. Follow that commandment, indeed! My profession consists of lying in wait for camel trains, slaughtering the merchants when they arrive, and confiscating all their goods. A commandment like that would just about ruin the whole system of private enterprise." God turned away and traveled to Babylon. There he accosted a merchant and said, "Would you like to follow *my* commandments?" The Babylonian said, "For example?" "Thou shalt not steal!" "Friend," said the Babylonian, "I am sorry. My entire living is made up of buying cheap and selling dear of misrepresentations and dishonesty. If I cannot steal, I cannot live." Rather discouraged, God turned westward, and in Egypt, he found a bearded old man haranguing the ruler of the land in an attempt to get him to free certain slaves. God called to him. "Moses," he said, "would you like to follow *my* commandments?" And Moses said, "How much do they cost?" "Why, nothing," said God. "I'm giving them away free." "In that case," said Moses, "I'll take ten."

21. Rabbi Joshua, having lived an exemplary life that had been admired by all died in the fullness of time and went to heaven. There he was greeted with hosannas of delight. Inexplicably, he shrank back, covered his face with his trembling old hands, and refused to participate in the festivities held in his honor. All persuasion having failed, he was ushered respectfully before the high judgment seat of God himself. The tender presence of God bathed the noble rabbi, and the divine voice filled his ears. "My child," said God, "it is on record that you have lived entirely in accord with *my* wishes, and yet you refused the honors that have, most fittingly, been prepared for you. Why is this?" Rabbi Joshua, head bent low and voice meek, said, "Oh, Holy One, I am not deserving. Somehow my life must have taken a wrong turning, for my son, heedless of my example and my precepts, turned Christian." "Alas," came the still voice, sweet with infinite sympathy, "I understand entirely and forgive. After all, *my son* did the same."

22. Pious old Levine was praying with mountain-moving fervor. Tears streamed down his cheeks as he swayed back and forth, beating his chest and mumbling his thoughts to God. "Oh, Holy One," he said, "I come

to You again in my trouble, for surely my life is nothing but trouble. All my life long I have known nothing but poverty, illness, and misery. I have been unable to support my family, unable to bring them happiness. And yet I have prayed to you constantly. I have turned to you morning, noon, and night. I have never forgotten you. "Why, then, oh Holy One, am I so visited by misfortune while that atheist Bloom has nothing but wealth and happiness: I know for a fact, oh Holy One, that Bloom never prays, never as much as enters a synagogue, yet his every move coins gold. Why does he prosper. Why do these good things befall him?" And in the silence that followed, a deep voice suddenly sounded in old Levine's ear. "Because Bloom isn't always bugging me, that's why!"

23. There is a new drive in confessional. It is called "toot and tell."

24. Lord, fill my mouth with worthwhile stuff and nudge me when I have said enough. (Preacher's success)

25. Little goofs from church bulletins everywhere: "The service will close with 'Little Drops of Water.' One of the ladies will start quietly, and the rest of the congregation will join in."

    "On Sunday, a special collection will be taken to defray the expense of the new carpet. All those wishing to do something on the carpet, come forward and get a piece of paper."

26. There is eternal justice, which means when the time comes for post office clerks to be admitted to heaven, there'll be six admitting windows, and five will be closed.

27. Boners from school religion exams: Noah's wife was called Joan of Ark.

    The fifth commandment is humor thy father and mother, holy acrimony is another name for marriage, the pope lives in a vacuum, Christians can have only one wife. This is called monotony. The first commandment was when Eve told Adam to eat the apple.

28. Bob Hope said, "I played golf with Billy Graham, and after he putted, the hole healed up."

29. If Oral Roberts really wants to test his miraculous touch for bringing them back from the dead, let's see him try his hand on the Houston Astros.

30. One lady was talking to a group of youngsters at the church Sunday school. "What can we do for God?" she asked them. "God has done so much for us. He even gave us his son." A small boy eagerly spoke up, "I'll give him my sister."

31. A man approached what was certainly a bad car accident. It seemed that a bus had been hit by a truck belonging to a major company. Lying about on the ground were a dozen bus passengers. The man asked one of the passengers, "Has anybody from the insurance company been here yet?" The passenger shook his head from side to side. The man went on, "Good, then you don't mind if I lie down here next to you!"

32. If they allowed priests to marry, their kids would have to call them Father Daddy. 33. The priest was preparing a man for his long days into the night. Whispering firmly, the priest said, "Denounce the devil! Let him know how little you think of his evil!" The dying man said nothing. The priest repeated his order. Still the dying man said nothing. The priest asked, "Why do you refuse to denounce the devil and his evil?" The dying man said, "Until I know where I'm heading, I don't think I ought to aggravate anybody."

34. I looked at the obituaries the other day, and I realized something—everybody dies in alphabetical order!"

35. A man lay dying. His voice hardly a whisper, he called over his best friend and said, "I can't go to my Maker without telling you all. I have to confess. Remember that hundred thousand that was missing when we owned the carpet store?" The friend and ex-partner said, "I remember." The man said, "I stole it. I also told your wife that you were fooling around with the blonde at the switchboard. And speaking of your wife, I was her lover for two years. Then—" His friend interrupted, "You don't have to tell me anymore. I know everything. That's why I poisoned you."

36. An old man is dying and smells the delicious aroma of fresh-baked cookies.
    He says to his wife, "Can I have one of your cookies?" The wife answers, "Absolutely not. You know they're for the wake!"

37. His four children were gathered around Mr. Staley's deathbed. As the eighty-year-old man seemed to doze off in a blissful sleep, the children

started to discuss the final funeral plans. One wanted to spend a hundred dollars for a coffin, a second thought a plain wooden box would do, and the third was even ready to dump the remains into a paper sack. All agreed there was no reason to spend much money as their father would never know the difference. Mr. Staley stirred. Having heard every word, he thought it was time to set the record straight. "Children," he said, "I've never told you this and never wanted to, but I can't go to my final place with this burden. My darling children, your mother and I were never married." His oldest son was aghast. "You mean we're—" Mr. Staley said, "Yup and cheap ones too!"

38. Four bid on painting church—lowest bidder put water in paint. As soon as he finished a storm came, washed off all the paint. Trying to figure out what to do suddenly the clouds parted and a voice from above said, "Repaint. Repaint and don't ever thin again."

39. Two men in heaven were discussing under what circumstances they arrived there. First man said he had frozen to death. Second man said he was very suspicious of his wife, so he came home early one day so he could catch her. He had a feeling another man was there, so he looked in every room, under the bed, and in every closet. He got so excited he had a heart attack and died. First man said, "It's a shame you didn't look in the freezer. We'd both be alive today."

40. There's only one reason why she hasn't broken all of the Ten Commandments. She doesn't know what a graven image is.

41. Lil gives me credit for bringing religion into her life. She said she never believed in *hell* until she married me.

42. I want to thank you, Lord, for being close to me so far this day. With your help I have not lost my temper, been grouchy, judgmental, or envious of anyone. But I will be getting out of bed in a minute, and I really think I'll need your help then.

43. Attends a very liberal church. No ten commandments. They have five commandments, three recommendations, and two suggestions.

44. The trouble with atheism is that it has no future.

45. Bible—basic instructions before leaving Earth.

46. If I had a ticket to heaven and you didn't have one too, I'd give mine up and go to hell with you.

47. Do you have teeth like the Ten Commandments? All broken?

48. The meek shall inherit the earth—if that's okay with you.

49. Lord, when we are wrong make us willing to change, and when we are right make us easy to live with. (Peter Marshall)

50. What do you say when God sneezes?

51. Prevent truth decay—read your Bible!

52. Forgive, O Lord, my little jokes on thee, and I'll forgive thy great big one on me. (Robert Frost)

53. Church Bulletin: "The young adults will have a bean and taco dinner tonight at seven. Special music will follow."

54. Sign: "God made the world in only seven days, but he didn't have any paperwork."

55. Why didn't they play cards on the ark? Because Noah was standing on the deck . . . ugh.

56. Ye shall know the truth, and the truth shall make you mad.

57. Was it a typographical error when the church bulletin referred to the principal speaker at the annual dinner as "the gust of honor"?

58. Today it is easier to pray for forgiveness than to resist temptation.

59. The average man's idea of a good sermon is one that goes over his head and hits one of his neighbors.

60. Answer to church preference—red brick.

61. I think that we're watching too many football games on TV in my house. Last night I overheard my son saying his good night prayers like this: "God, bless Pa! God bless Ma! God bless me, rah, rah, rah!"

62. Sorrow looks back, worry looks around, faith looks up.

63. All the darkness in the world can't put out the light of one candle.

64. In a sensational court case, the plaintiff, who was all twisted and bent over, won $3 million from the driver of another car. The defendant was sure the "injured party" was faking, so after the trial he followed the guy around everywhere even trailing him to France. "Where do we go now?" the defendant taunted the plaintiff. "Off to Lourdes! If you watch closely, you'll see one of the greatest miracles of all time."

65. A rather famous entertainer was traveling back from a two-week goodwill trip to China. On the same boat was a missionary who had worked with the poor in China for many years. When they docked in New York, the missionary saw a crowd of the entertainer's fans waiting at the pier. "Lord, I don't understand," the missionary said. "I gave forty-two years of my life to China, and he gave only two weeks, yet there are thousands welcoming him home and nobody here to welcome me." And the Lord replied, "Son, you're not home yet."

66. Lord, give us enough temptation to make us tolerant,
enough failure to make us humble,
enough success to make us striving,
enough tears to make us tender, and
enough sorrow to make us sympathetic.

67. Do not ask to have your life's load lightened,
But for courage to endure.
Do not ask for fulfillment in all you life,
But for patience to accept frustration.
Do not ask for perfection in all you do,
But for wisdom not to repeat mistakes.
And finally, do not ask for more,
Before saying "Thank You"
for what you have already received.

68. After a preacher died and went to heaven, he noticed that a New York cab driver had been given a higher place than he had. "I don't understand," he complained to St. Peter. "I devoted my entire life to my congregation." "Our policy is to reward results," explained St. Peter. "Now, what happened, Reverend, whenever you gave a sermon?" The

minister said that some in the congregation fell asleep. "Exactly," said St. Peter. "And when people rode in this man's taxi, they not only stayed awake, they prayed."

69. Being a Baptist doesn't keep you from sinning. It just keeps you from enjoying it. 70. A major flood was devastating a southern town, and all the townspeople were urged to flee their homes. One devoutly religious man refused to leave. As the water rose, a jeep was barely making it through but stopped at the man's house to ask him to get in before the flood worsened. The man declined, insisting that he had faith in the Lord and the Lord would save him. A while later, the water rose even higher, and he was forced to the second story of his home. A boat came by and asked him to get in so they could flee the area. Again, he reiterated his faith in the Lord and stayed. Still later, as the water continued to rise, he was forced to take refuge on the roof of his house. A helicopter came by and lowered a ladder, but again the man refused to leave, citing his faith in the Lord. Not long thereafter, the water rose higher and the man drowned. When he reached his Maker, he immediately blurted out, "Lord, I had complete faith in you to save me, but you didn't! You ignored my prayers for help!"

The Lord looked at the man with a little disbelief and said, "What do you mean I ignored your prayers for help . . . I sent a jeep, a boat, and a helicopter, didn't I?"

71. Lord, whenth young people contracted herpes, I told them it was your punishment for their permissiveness. When they contracted AIDS, I told them it was because of their perversion. Just one question Lord. What are you trying to tell me with these hemorrhoids?

72. It's inspiring the way religion has been brought back into the lives of millions of Americans—like my uncle. Before the pope's visit, the last time my uncle was on his knees was to adjust the flesh tones on the *Playboy* channel.

73. Two bellhops were discussing tippers. One said, "Watch out for the TV evangelists. They show up with the Ten Commandments in one hand and a ten-dollar bill in the other, and when they leave they haven't broken either."

74. Lead me not into temptation. I can find it myself.

75. He has a biblical outlook on life. He's going to raise Cain as long as he possible.

76. After church one of the parishioners told the preacher, "Your sermon was like the peace and mercy of God. I mean it was like the peace of God because it passed all understanding, and it was like the mercy of God because I thought it would endure forever.

77. A priest and a rabbi were having dinner together.
    "Come on, rabbi," said the priest. "When are you going to let yourself go and have a piece of ham?"
    "At your wedding," the rabbi said.

78. Bill, Hillary, and Al were in an airplane that crashed. They're up in heaven, and God's sitting on the great white throne. God addresses Al first. "Al, what do you believe in?" Al replies, "Well, I believe that the combustion engine is evil and that we need to save the world from CFCs and that if any more freon is used, the whole earth will become a greenhouse and we'll all die." God thinks for a second and says, "Okay, I can live with that. Come and sit at my left." God then addresses Bill. "Bill, what do you believe in?" Bill replies, "Well, I believe in power to the people. I think people should be able to make their own choices about things and that no one should ever be able to tell someone else what to do. I also believe in feeling people's pain." God thinks for a second and says, "Okay, that sounds good. Come and sit at my right." God then address Hillary. "Hillary, what do you believe in?" "I believe you're in my chair."

79. Three Catholic women and an older Jewish lady were having coffee. The first Catholic woman tells her friends, "My son is a priest. When he walks into a room, everyone calls him 'Father.'" The second woman chirps, "My son is a bishop. Whenever he walks into a room, people call him 'Your Grace.'" The third old woman says, "My son is a cardinal. Whenever he walks into a room, he's called 'Your Eminence.'" As the little old Jewish lady sips her coffee in silence, then first three give her this subtle, "Well . . . ?" So she says, "My son is six feet five. He has broad, square shoulders, lean hips, and is very muscular. He's terribly handsome, has beautiful hair, dresses very well, and always smells wonderful. Whenever he walks into a room, women say, 'Oh my god . . . !'"

80. The other day I went to the religious bookstore where I saw a "Honk if you love Jesus" bumper sticker. I bought it and put it on the back of my car, and I'm really glad I did. What an uplifting experience followed! I was stopped at the light of a busy intersection, just lost in thought about the Lord and didn't notice that the light had changed. That bumper sticker really worked! I found lots of people who love Jesus. Why, the guy behind me started to honk like crazy. He must really love the Lord because pretty soon he leaned out his window and yelled, "Jesus Christ!" as loud as he could. It was like a football game, with him shouting, "GO, JESUS CHRIST, GO! Everyone else started honking too, so I leaned out of my window and waved and smiled to all those loving people. There must have been a guy from Florida back there because I could hear him yelling something about a Sunny Beach, and I saw him waving in a funny way with only his middle finger stuck up in the air. I had recently asked my two kids what that meant. They kind of squirmed, looked at each other, giggled, and told me that it was the Hawaiian good luck sign. So I leaned out the window and gave him the good luck sign back. A couple of people were so caught up in the joy of the moment that they got out of their cars and were walking toward me. I bet they wanted to pray, but just then I noticed that the light had changed, and I stepped on the gas. It's a good thing I did because I was the only car to get across the intersection. I looked back at them standing there. I leaned out the window, gave them a big smile, and held up the Hawaiian good luck sign as I drove away. Praise the Lord for such wonderful folks.

81. God must be a woman. Why else would the earth get redecorated four times a year?

82. A lion gulped down seven missionaries—each of a different denomination. Not having any Rolaids handy, the only way the lion could get relief was to have an ecumenical movement.

83. Let us now consider one of the greatest challenges facing any American today: what does Tammy Bakker put on for Halloween?

84. When Noah built the ark, why didn't he swat the two files while he had the chance?

85. Our minister is a firm believer in the free enterprise system. You can tell it from his letterhead: Reverend Jones—Soul Proprietor.

86. If you think the Ten Commandments on two stone tablets are hard to follow, be thankful Moses didn't return from the mountain with a couple of floppy disks.

87. My ministerial correspondent says a retired member of the clergy he knows, who no longer drives afar, was outraged recently when bus service to his area was eliminated. The retired preacher kept badgering the transit authority about the situation, but he received little, if any, satisfaction. Finally, on one visit to the bus company, he told an official, "Transportation certainly has declined in the last three thousand year." "Declined?" said the official. "What do you mean? Transportation today is a lot better than it was three thousand years ago." The preacher stood his ground. "If you read your Bible," he told the bus man, "you'll find that in Numbers 22:21, it says that Balaam rode into town on his ass. That's certainly more than I've been able to do for the last two months."

88. Man was created. The Creator told him, "I have given you a sex life of twenty years." Man immediately objected. "I need more than that," he argued. The Creator told him to be satisfied with his allotment. Man sulked. He went among the animals. He spoke to the lion. "You have a sex life of twenty years," man said to the lion, "but you don't need it. Why don't you ask the Creator to give half of that time to me?" He asked the same favor of the donkey and the parrot. So the lion, the donkey, and the parrot went to the Creator and said they each would give up half their sex lives to man.
   And that's why man leads a normal sex life for twenty years, spends the next ten years lying about it, the next ten years making an ass of himself, and the last ten years just talking about it.

89. Two horse players, one an atheist and the other a believer, saw a priest raise his hands over a race horse. The believer bet on the horse while the atheist scoffed. The horse won at fifty to one. Weeks later they saw the same priest raise his hands over the same horse, and the atheist put a wad on the horse while the believer stayed at the rail. The horse dropped dead in the stretch. Atheist: "Why didn't you bet on that horse this time?" Believer: "That's the trouble with you atheists. Don't know the difference between baptism and the last rites."

90. The separation of church and state simply defined as bingo v. lotto.

91. "It pictured a rather traditional church building complete with cross on top," he explained. "In the front lawn was a large billboard with these words: The Lite Church—24 percent fewer commitments. Home of the 7.5 percent tithe. Fifteen minute sermons. Forty-five-minute worship services. Eight commandments—your choice. Just three spiritual laws. An eight-hundred-year millennium. Everything you've wanted in a church and less!

92. A Catholic priest we know recently put the church state separation debate into healthy perspective, telling a group of seminary students: "As you know, politics and religion must be kept totally separate. They do not mix. So for the next few weeks, we're just going to have to forget all about religion."

93. Avner Ziv told the two hundred delegates his favorite Jewish joke was the one in which religious leaders are told the world will end in a flood in three days. The pope tells his flock to repent. The rabbi tells his congregation: "Friends, we have exactly three days to learn to swim."

94. The golfer got to a par 3 hole when his guardian angel appeared on his shoulder. She offered him a hole in one if he would give up sex for ten years. He thought about it and said that would be swell. When he got to the next hole, another par 3, his guardian angel make the same offer. He took that one too. And when he got to the really tough sixth hole, she offered him another hole in one for another ten years of a celibate life. "Now remember, that's a total of thirty years without sex," his guardian angel said. "I'll have three holes in one the same day on the same course," the golfer said. "That's never happened for anyone. I love this game so much I'll take your offer." By this time sportswriters were all over the course trying to interview him. When he finished the round, the TV cameras were on, and he was the center of attention. "Well, sir, you've made golf history here today," a sportswriter said. "Certainly a world record on a difficult course. Could you tell us your name?" "I'm Father O'Connell," the golfer said.

95. Sign on a church marquee reads, "Come in and try our exercise program—knee bends."

96. If your prayers aren't answered, the answer is no. 97. The cannibals found a missionary they couldn't cook. He was a friar. 98. Of course

Solomon was the wisest man who ever lived. He had so many wives to advise him.

99. A little girl in church whispered to her dad that she felt ill. "I think I'm going to throw up," she said. Dad told her to hurry to the restroom in the parish hall. She ran out of the pew and headed for the rear of the church. In less than two minutes, she was back.

"Are you all right?" Dad asked.

"Yes," she said. "And I didn't even have to throw up in the restroom."

"That's good," Dad said.

"Yes, it is," she said. "I found that little box by the door that says For the Sick."

100. The real reason it took so long to build the Oral Roberts University was because every time they dug a hole, it healed.

101. One of the best tests of religion is to find yourself in church with nothing less than a $20 bill when the plate is passed.

102. Funny how a dollar can look so big when you take it to church and so small when you take it to the store.

103. I don't believe in reincarnation, but I did in my last life.

104. There was an old monk of Siberia, whose life grew drearier and drearier. He burst from his cell, gave out a yell, and eloped with the Mother Superior!

105. The priest told the nuns to make up a slogan for meatless Fridays. The winning slogan read, "What a friend we have in cheeses." (Jesus)

106. The sermon went on and on. Finally the preacher paused and asked, "What more can I say?" A man in the back said, "How about Amen?"

107. In recent years, the poor evangelist have been getting their lumps.

Many of their sexual adventures have been page 1 stories, giving new meaning to the term *lay preacher*!

108. As Moses said to God, "Let me see if I have it right—the Arabs get the oil and we get the right to cut off the tips of our what?"

109. What is *clip clop clip clop-bang-clippety clop clippety clop*? An Amish drive-by shooting.

110. Man fell asleep during services. Rabbi said to his wife, "Wake him" She replied, "You put him to sleep, you wake him."

111. Times have been hard. A small Bible publishing company just filed chapter 11 verses 1 through 14.

112. My ministerial correspondent says one of his parishioners told him the story:

 Once, it seems, there was a preacher who was dreadfully henpecked. His wife wouldn't let him preach on anything slightly controversial. For instance, he had prepared what he considered a really powerful and well-thought-out sermon on sex, but she absolutely forbade him even to mention the subject from the pulpit.

 Well, one Sunday morning the minister's wife came down with the twenty-four-hour flu and couldn't go to church. The minister saw this as his great opportunity to give his sex sermon. But as he started to leave, his wife asked from her sickbed, "What are you going to preach about today?"

 The minister dithered, "S-s-sailing" and darted out the door, praying to God to forgive him for the little white lie. He delivered an impassioned sermon on sex.

 A few days later, the minister's wife was in the supermarket and met one of the members of the congregation. "Your husband," the parishioner raved, "preached one of the most marvelous sermons I ever heard last Sunday. He make the subject really come alive. He answered questions I had always had and make everything crystal clear. It was wonderful—wonderful. The depth of his knowledge is tremendous. Even my husband was impressed."

 The minister's wife was amazed. "That's remarkable," she said. "Do you know, he's only done it twice and one of those times he fell overboard."

113. It seems that St. Peter, Jesus, and an old gentleman were golfing early one misty morning. St. Peter was first with a shot that went straight as an arrow for 295 years right in line with the pin.

 Jesus was up next. He sliced one that hit a tree, but it bounced across the fairway, gained momentum, slammed through a clump of rough, and landed four feet from the pin on the par-4, 350 yarder.

The older fellow took a practice swing and then whacked the ball. It sailed 150 yards; and just as it was about to stop, a squirrel dashed out, put the ball in its mouth, and ran across the fairway.

It looked like a lost ball until an eagle swept down, grabbed the squirrel, and started to fly away. But a the moment there was a bolt of lightning. Fur and feathers drifted to earth along with the ball, which plinked right into the cup.

Jesus turned to the third member of the trio and said, "Gee, that was a swell shot, Dad."

114. The most recent account of the invitation to the pope, and his acceptance, to speak at commencement exercises. He was to arrive early in the afternoon. The students were so excited they rented one of those all-white limousines with dark windows for the passenger. They sent the chauffeur and limo to the airport to fetch him to the campus. When the pope arrived and saw the limo, he cornered the chauffeur and said he wanted to drive. The chauffeur wasn't sure, but the pope wouldn't let him get away without saying yes.

"I'll never get this chance again," the pope said.

They took off with the pope behind the wheel and the chauffeur in the backseat.

That's when a motorcycle cop happened to pull alongside and saw the pope at the wheel. He tried to see who was in the backseat, but the dark glass wouldn't let him, and he just about crashed. Back at the station, the motorcycle cop told his captain he passed a limousine at the airport, and someone really important was in town.

"Who?"

"Really big?"

"Donald Trump?"

"Nope. Bigger."

"Supreme Court Justice William Rehnquist?"

"Nope. Bigger."

"The president?"

"Nope. Bigger."

"So who's bigger than the president?"

"I can't really say," the cop replied. "But I'll tell you this much, the pope was driving the limo."

115. The man of the cloth had earned a vacation from his flock. One of his lifetime ambitions was to play a championship golf course, and that's what he decided to do. Arriving in Palm Springs, it was his first day on the course. He was doing rather will, too, and this pleased him. But the

toughest hole was coming up. His ball landed far from the seventeenth green.

"When Arnold Palmer plays this hole, he always says it's best to use a number 3 iron along with a little prayer at the same time," the caddie advised him.

"I think I'll give that a try," he said.

The ball landed in a deep trap.

"Oh my, I guess he didn't hear me," he said, heading for the sand bunker.

The caddie smiled. "I think he probably heard you," he said, "but when Mr. Palmer is here, he always keeps this head down when he prays."

116. A minister announced that his next Sunday's sermon was "How to Drink, Steal, Swear, and Lie Your Way to Success." His message: Drink from the fountain of creativity. Steal a few minutes each day to perform a kindness. Swear to do a better job. Lie awake at night and give thanks for your blessings.

117. Seems that God was holding a news conference. The first question was asked by a polish reporter.

"Lord, I can't tell you how delighted we Poles are that the pope is Catholic. Do you think there's a change that a future pope might also be Polish?" he asked.

"There certainly is a chance," proclaimed the Lord.

"What about an Irish pope? We never have had one," said a reporter form Dublin. "Is there a possibility of that?"

"There's certainly a possibility," said the Lord.

"What about an American pope?" said a reporter from New York.

"Definitely a possibility."

"What about a Jewish pope?" asked still another reporter. "Is there a possibility of that?"

The Lord pondered the question. Finally he replied, "Of course there is a possibility, and I really shouldn't speak for the Catholic Church. But I'd say probably not in m lifetime." 118. Children solidify a marriage by giving a couple someone else to blame things on.

119. One man to another: "Don't get me wrong, Henry, I'm for helping our less fortunate neighbors, but the problem with foreign aid is it enables too many countries to live beyond our means."

120. As smiling mother waves good-bye, her young son says to his sister as they prepare to get on school bus, "How can anyone be so happy on the first day of school?"

121. Have you ever considered that God created heaven and earth in six days—and today we have people who still consider themselves efficiency experts?

122. If God had not wanted a second opinion, he never would have created Eve.

123. For God so loved the world that he waited thousands and thousands of years before sending us Bill Clinton.

124. I go to a very liberal church. A very liberal church. For instance, they never put down hell. They call it an alternative lifestyle.

125. Wouldn't it be great if our current educational standards were extended to religion? We'd still have the Ten Commandments—but six would be passing.

126. Religion is set up a little differently in Russia than it is here. For instance, when you go to confession in the United States, you come back out again.

127. There's one big problem with praying in school. If you consider what's going on in schools these days, you wouldn't want to close your eyes that long.

128. A boy prayed and prayed for a bicycle with no results. He figured that was not how the system works, so he stole the bicycle and prayed for forgiveness.

129. Preacher moved in next door where there was a teenage boy. Preacher noticed he had a mower, so he offered to trade the mower for his bicycle. Each said the mower and bike worked. The teenager was off riding for about an hour when he returned the preacher was pulling on the cord. He said, "I thought you said his mower worked?"

    "Boy, it does, you just have to cuss at it a little bit." Preacher, "It's been thirty years since I've said a cuss word. I doubt I could even remember how." Boy said, "Just keep pulling on that cord, preacher. It'll come back."

130. A driver put a note under his windshield. "I've circled this block for twenty minutes, I'm late for an appointment, and if I don't park here I'll lose my job. Forgive us our trespasses." When he came back, he found a parking ticket with a note, which said, "I've circled this block for twenty years, and if I don't give you a ticket, I'll lose my job. Lead us not into temptation."

131. Inspirational message on bulletin board. "Today is the tomorrow you worried about yesterday." Under it somebody had written, "And now you know why."

132. The way things are going it won't be long before Sodom and Gomorrah will be considered model cities.

133. A pastor was calling on his parishioners. He stopped at one home and rang the bell. He waited. No one answered. However, he could hear someone walking inside the house. He rang the bell again. Still no response. Before he left, he took out one of his business cards and wrote a message on the back: "Revelations 3:20—'Here I am! I stand at the door and knock. If anyone hears my voice and opens the door, I will come in and eat with him, and he with me.'" He forgot about the card until the next Sunday. As the people were leaving the church, a young woman greeted him and gave him a slip of paper. Busy talking to everyone, he slipped it into his pocket. Later, at home, he read the message. It was brief: Genesis 3:10. Puzzled, the pastor went to his study and opened the Bible to check the passage: "I heard you in the garden, and I was afraid because I was naked, so I hid."

134. Definition of a Methodist—a Baptist who learned to read.

135. Definition of a Presbyterian—a Methodist who moved to town.

136. Definition of an Episcopalian—a Presbyterian who got rich.

137. Baptist—an old Greek word for "hold them under till they bubble"

138. My wife doesn't belong to any organized religion—she's a Methodist.

139. Ten little commandments spoiling lots of fun. Along came the younger generation and then there were none.

140. I have often wished Moses were alive today. He could part the retirement land I bought in Florida.

141. The Ten Commandments aren't multiple choice.

142. Our new minister is really making a hit with the congregation. When he prays, he asks the Lord for things the other minister didn't even know God had.

143. Teacher, "Children, why did the pilgrims come to America?" Johnny: "So they could worship in their own way and make other people do the same."

144. During a mining boom, Mark Twain visited Virginia City, Nevada, a place of rampant sin abundant booze and wild women. Mark Twain said, "It was no place for a Presbyterian, and I did not long remain one."

145. Weight lifting team at the church—Brawn-again Christians

146. Public relations go all the way back to the Garden of Eden when Adam asked for a bigger fig leaf.

147. There's a definite return to religion today. A recent poll showed that 62 percent of all Americans believe in miracles. Half are churchgoers and half are Astro fans.

148. The more we count the blessings we have, the less we crave the luxuries we haven't.

149. I once wanted to become an atheist, but I gave it up. Not enough holidays. (H. Youngman)

150. What do you do if you want to go to heaven but you hate harp music? (Mark Twain)

151. The church organist has a special tune for the new brides in their eighth month—"Love in Bloom."

152. Obscene phone caller calls Christian Science and says, "Penicillin, antibiotics, cortisone, aspirin."

153. Everyone should hire ministers. They work to beat hell.

154. Many have lost interest in religion. Today if you mention the Last Supper, they think you are on a diet.

155. If God had meant us to have homosexuals, he would have given us Adam and Bruce.

156. God will not look you over for medals, degrees, or diplomas but for scars. (E. Hubbard)

157. Sir, my concern is not whether God is on our side. My greatest concern is to be on God's side, for God is always right. (A. Lincoln)

158. What if there had been room at the inn? (Linda Festa)

159. Every day people are straying away from the church and going back to God. (Lenny Bruce)

160. To emphasize the festive mood of the occasion, we're going to accentuate the positive and eliminate the negative. Therefore the prayer will be longer, and the treasurer's report will be omitted.

161. As treasurer, you have to think about the cost of everything. If a treasurer had been in charge of the Last Supper, there would have been a cash bar.

162. Every time I look into the mirror, I find it increasingly hard to accept that we were created in God's image. I just can't see God being fat, seventy, and wearing bifocals.

163. Samson had the right idea about advertising. He took two columns and brought down the house.

164. Lord, grant that I may always desire more than I can accomplish. (Michaelangelo)

165. The hands that help are holier than the lips that pray. (La Rochefoncald)

166. "Hey," cried Satan to the new arrival, "you act like you own this place."
"I do. My wife gave it to me."

167. Mother overheard her child's prayer. "Now I lay me down to sleep. I pray the Lord my soul to keep. When he hollers let him go. Eenie, meenie, minee, mo."

168. Girl regarding the Ten Commandments: "They don't tell you what you ought to do, and only put ideas in your head."

169. One priest asked the other, "Don't we know each other?" The priest said, "I don't know, but your faith is familiar."

170. It was Father's Day at church, and the preacher was attempting to demonstrate the depth of love a father has for a son. He put a long plank on the floor and told a father to suppose another man was holding on to his son and dared him to come get the boy. "Would you do it?" The father said yes. "Now," asked the preacher, "if that plank spanned from one building to another twenty stories above the ground and the man told you if you didn't walk over the plank to get your son he would drop him from the building, would you do it?" The father thought for a minute then asked, "Which kid you got?"

171. It is hard to believe we were made in God's image. I can't imagine God being short, fat, deaf, eighty years old, and wearing bifocals.

172. They were having a baptismal service in a water-filled ditch by the side of the road as was the custom many years ago. A drunk was staggering down the road and found himself out in the water. The preacher asked him if he had found Jesus. The drunk said he hadn't, so the preacher proceeded to immerse him in the water. When he let him up he again asked him if he had found Jesus. The drunk still said he hadn't. This went on and on each time the preacher kept him underwater a longer time. Finally the drunk who had almost drowned was asked again if he had found Jesus. The drunk asked, "Are you sure this is where he fell in?"

173. A husband and wife went to church. After it was over, she asked if he had seen that wild hairdo Mary had. He said that he hadn't. She asked, "Did you see that outrageous dress that Betty had on?" He said no. Then she asked if he knew why Lucille showed up with a strange

man. Again he said no. Finally she said, "A lot of good it does you to go to church."

174. An anonymous seventeenth-century man wrote down this prayer:
"Lord, thou knowest better than I know myself that I am growing older and will someday be old. Keep me from the fatal habit of thinking I must say something on every subject and on every occasion. Release me from craving to strengthen out everybody's errors. Make me thoughtful but not moody, helpful but not bossy. With my vast store of wisdom, it seems a pity not to use it all, but thou knowest, Lord, that I want a few friends in the end."

175. In the early twenties when Jews emigrated through Ellis Island, the immigrations officials simplified their complicated names in official records. One of these men was called Taylor. He said his life wasn't so simple. Since his name was Taylor, he opened a clothing store, but it failed. He opened another one and it failed. So he prayed to God, "Oh, Lord, let me prosper. Lord, if you do I promise to give you 50 percent of the profits." Did it work? Taylor, did it work? You ever heard of Lord and Taylor?

176. A farming community had a terrible drought, and the crops were dying. The local preacher commanded the whole community to gather at the edge of the fields and pray for rain. A large crowd gathered, and he said, "Brothers and sisters, you have come here to pray for rain. Do you have sufficient faith?"
"Amen," shouted the crowd. "All right," said the preacher, "but I have one question to ask you." The crowd stood silent, puzzled, and expectant. "Brothers and sisters," shouted the preacher, "where are your umbrellas?"

177. Isaac Goldberg says to God: "You help complete strangers—why not me?"

178. Cats are like Baptists. They raise hell, but you can't catch them at it.

179. Child was asked the moral of the "David and Goliath" story. The boy said, "Duck."

180. A preacher staring at his water glass. He can't decide whether to drink it, part it, or walk on it.

181. A religious college had great academia, but the food was terrible. The menu never changed—tomato soup, creamed chicken, mashed potatoes, green beans, and ice cream with chocolate sauce. One sister said the same grace every evening from Hebrew 13:8, "Jesus Christ, the same yesterday and today and forever."

182. Mother overheard her daughter's prayer: "Dear God, let me do well on my test tomorrow, make my friends be nice to me, tell my brother not to mess up my room, and please get my father to raise my allowance and—" The mother interrupted, "Don't bother to give God instructions. Just report for duty."

183. True Story
I was invited by a Shriner Roy Englebrecht to talk to the women's Sunday school class luncheon of about three hundred. Things were going very well when all of a sudden there was what sounded like an explosion in the basketball court where we were eating. It seems a lady had passed out. Of course I stopped, the paramedics came from next door, and she was revived rather rapidly. I was at a loss of what to do next. I told the ladies that I was sorry it had happened that I felt under the circumstances I should quit but volunteered to return at a later date if they wished. It so happened that one of the ladies down in front was a patient of mine. She said, "Oh, go ahead and finish she's not even a member of our church."

184. A lot of kneeling will keep you in good standing.

185. When you get to your wit's end, you'll find God lives there.

186. The good Lord didn't create anything without a purpose, but mosquitoes come close.

187. Three truths about religion

   a.   Jews don't recognize Jesus as the Messiah.
   b.   Protestants don't recognize the pope.
   c.   Baptists don't recognize each other in a liquor store.

188. Look at the world around you and you will see God's creativity. Look at the dinner table and you'll see God's providence. Look in the mirror and you will see God's sense of humor.

189. Obscene phone caller calls the Christian Scientist and says, "Penicillin, antibiotics, cortisone, aspirin."

190. Rub a dub, dub. Thanks for the grub. Yea Lord! Amen.

191. The Welsh pray on their knees—and everyone else.
The Scotch keep the Sabbath and everything else.
The Irish don't know what they believe but are willing to fight to the death for it.
The British are self-made people, which relieves the Lord of an awesome responsibility.

192. Politically correct Twenty-third Psalm
The Lord and I are in a shepherd-sheep relationship, and I am in a position of negative need.
He prostrates me in a greenbelt grazing area and conducts me into lateral proximity with a nontorrential aqueous accumulation.
He restores to original satisfaction levels of my original makeup.
Notwithstanding that I make ambulatory progress through the nonilluminated geological interstice of mortality, terror sensations shall not be manifested within me due to the proximity of omnipotence.
Your pastoral walking aid and quadruped-restraint module induce in me a pleasurific mood state.
You design and produce a nutrient-bearing support structure in the context of noncooperative elements.
You enact a head-related folk ritual utilizing vegetable extracts, and my beverage container exhibits inadequate volumetric parameters.
Surely it must be an intrinsic nondeductible factor that your interrelational emphatic and nonvengeful attributes will pursue me as their target focus for the duration of the current nondeath period.
And I will possess tenant rights in the residential facility of the Lord on a permanently open-ended time basis.

193. A very poor mother, unable to afford a blanket to shelter her son from the extreme cold which blew through their hut, covered him with boards and driftwood. One night the boy wrapped his arms around her and said contentedly, "Mom, what do poor people do on cold nights like this, who have no boards or driftwood to put over their children?"

194. God is love, and he that dwelleth in love dwelleth in God and God in him. Amen.

195. I saw an image, the face of Christ. Our Lord stood before me, with warmth and love in his eyes. He said, "Every time you gave over your life to me, it became my life, my hardships, and my struggles. Each point of light in your life is when you stepped aside and let me shine through until there was more of me than there was of you."

196. At church Joe was in charge of taking up the offerings. One Sunday after the services, the priest counted the cash and found it was smaller than anticipated, so he questioned Joe. He told him that it did not seem enough for the size of the congregation. Joe said that he did not take any of the offering. The priest said, "Get in the confessional," which Joe did. The priest then asked Joe, "Did you take any of the offering?" and this time Joe said, "I can't hear you." Again the same question with the same answer then the priest yelled out the question only to receive the same answer. By now the priest was pretty angry, so he came out of the confessional and said, "Joe, trade places with me and you can ask me a question." So they traded places and Joe asked, "I hear that you and my wife are having an affair. Is that true?" The preacher answered, "By golly, you can't hear in here."

Sex

1. Remember when girls stayed home because they had nothing to wear?

2. Woman called the police department and said, "I have a sex maniac in my apartment. Pick him up tomorrow morning."

3. What's salmonellosis? Martin Buxbaum defines it as a disease that gives you a frantic desire to swim upstream and spawn.

4. Actually told at the June 27 luncheon: "Do you know how Eskimos have babies? They rub noses and just let the little boogers fall out." (Editor's note: This may explain the drop in attendance.)

5. "Leaving sex to the feminists is like letting your dog vacation at the taxidermist."

6. Omar Sharif takes the stand: "The only premarital thing girls don't do these days is cooking."

7. How do you know Michael Jackson is having a party? There are a bunch of tricycles in front of his house.

8. At the beginning of the grandparents' class I teach, I ask the participants if they would share the very first feelings they had when they learned they were going to be grandparents. Most people say they were happy and excited. During one class, however, an expectant grandmother blurted, "I just hated it! I finally knew for certain that my daughter was having sex."

9. How does a man know when his wife is losing interest? When her favorite sexual position is next door.

10. Everything is terrible. I've been replaced at work with a computer, and I've been replaced at home with a vibrator.

11. It's hard to realize that the woman wearing a bikini is the same one who would be embarrassed if her slip showed.

12. I have one question about bikinis: "How do you know when you're wearing the right size?"

13. And I'm beginning to wonder about my wife. Last night I said we haven't had relations for three weeks, so she invited six of them over for dinner.

14. "When I was seventeen years old, I was going out with a fifty-nine-year old man. Sexually we got along great 'cause the things he couldn't do anymore were the things I didn't know about." (Carol Henry)

15. Quote from Phyllis Diller: "Think of me as a sex symbol for men who don't give a damn."

16. "I'm facing a real midlife crisis—my wife's."

17. Myron's romantic spirit was crushed years ago when a younger woman told him he reminded her of the ocean. "Oh," said Myron, "you mean I'm restless, untamed, and romantic?" She answered, "No, you just make me sick."

18. A new pro-life group has the strictest interpretation of them all. They believe that an unborn baby becomes a human being the moment the drive-in movie begins.

19. Dr. Mark, a dentist who doubles as a stand-up comic, performed at the National Sexuality Symposium. He discussed nasal gratification: "Sneezing is better than sex. It's a mini-instant orgasm. You keep your clothes on, you don't get involved, you can do it in public, and when you're done, perfect strangers bless you."

20. I went through Catholic sex education in the 1950s, and I didn't come out all messed up. The nuns taught us that sex was a normal bodily event. Like a stroke.

21. I tried telephone sex once. I got an ear infection.

22. The girl explained to her boyfriend that they would have difficulty in getting the blessing of her domineering mother. Determined his love for the girl would overcome all obstacles, he took her home and explained his intentions to his potential mother-in-law. The girl's mother was horrified at the thought and screeched, "I wouldn't dream of letting my daughter marry you! Frankly, I think you're effeminate." "Yes," said the fellow thoughtfully as he headed for the door, "compared to you, I probably am."

23. During her annual checkup, the well-constructed miss was asked to disrobe and climb onto the examining table. "Doctor," she replied shyly, "I just can't undress in front of you." "All right," said the physician, "I'll flick off the lights. You undress and tell me when you're through." In a few moments, her voice rang out in the darkness: "Doctor, I've undressed. What shall I do with my clothes?" "Put them on the chair, on top of mine."

24. Lady's Man: He doesn't do too well with the ladies, so he thought he'd try to be more aggressive. He saw an attractive woman in the bar, smiled, winked, and dropped his room key into her purse. He waited an hour for the sake of appearance, and then went back to his room. His luggage was gone.

Small Town/ Redneck

1. Thieves broke into the police station last night and stole all the bathroom facilities. The police are investigating meanwhile they have nothing to go on.

2. Man saw a little girl leading a cow down the road. "Where are you taking that cow, little girl?"
"To the bull."
"Can't your father do that?"
"Nope only the bull."

3. He was bowlegged, and she was knock-kneed. When they stood together, they spelled "OX."

4. I lived in a town so small the exterminator was a guy with a rolled-up magazine.

5. We had a fire in our bathroom last week. Thank goodness it didn't spread to the house.

6. Farmer Brown's twelve pigs are all females, so he asks farmer Jones if he can bring them over to mate with Jones's male pigs. Jones agrees, so Brown loads his sows into his truck and drives them over to spend the day. "I've never raised pigs before," Brown says. "How will I know that piglets are on the way?"
"Just look for unusual behavior," replies Jones. The next morning Farmer Brown looks at his pigs and sees nothing unusual, so he loads them in the truck and brings them back to the Joneses' farm. The third day it's the same, so it's back to the Joneses' place again. Next

morning Brown asks his wife, "Honey, are the pigs doing anything unusual?"

"Well," she says, "eleven of them are in the back of the truck and the twelfth one's honking the horn."

7. I went to the bank and asked them to check my balance. She reached out and pushed me.

8. "I see you've been drinking, Ma. Your lipstick is on the trough."

9. I was lost out in the country. I pulled up to an old man and asked, "How do you get to town from here?" He said, "Well, my son in law usually takes me."

10. Salesman accidentally ran over and killed a dog. Unfortunately it was the farmer's favorite hunting dog. He told the man's wife how sorry he was. Wife said the farmer was out in the field and that the man had better break it to him easy like first tell him it was one of the kids."

11. It's a very quiet resort. Nothing much happens during the day, but at night, all hell breaks loose. Everybody sits around the candy machine and watches the chocolate bars melt.

12. He had to leave town because of some of his beliefs—he got to believing some of his neighbors horses' were his.

13. Man who is old enough to know better wishes to meet girl not quite that old.

14. How can you tell when you are really a Southerner at heart? You think the three major food groups are catfish, hush puppies, and sweetened iced tea. You own two or more cars that don't run. You're concerned over the rising cost of ammunition. Your bass boat is worth more than your house. You drive around in your pickup truck with the air conditioner on and the windows rolled down.

15. My job every night was to turn the chickens—didn't have a henhouse so each night they roosted on the well facing out.

16. Ad in paper. Wanted a good woman who can cook, fish, dig worms, sew and who owns a good fishing boat and motor. Please send photo of boat and motor.

17. You call this a ranch? Why I could get into my car, start early in the morning and still not have reached the end of my spread by sundown. I had a car like that once.

18. There are small towns and there are *small* towns; this one is so small it had a fraction for a zip code.

19. This town is so dull the local newspaper changed the name of the Obituary column. It's now known as "What to Do on Saturday Night."

20. When Dudley, the slow-moving clerk in a small store, was not around one morning, a customer asked, "Where's Dudley? Is he sick?" "He isn't here anymore," came the reply. "That so?" said the customer. "Got anybody in mind for the vacancy?" The response was terse: "Dudley didn't leave no vacancy."

21. This town is so small that the telephone book only lists first names.

22. "What's this town called?" asked the tourist.
    "That depends," replied the native.
    "Depends on what?"
    "On whether you live in this rundown dump, or if you're a traveler who has been attracted by the picturesque scenery and quaint old-world charms."

23. Country talk: In some parts of the rural South and Southwest, you're not likely to hear someone described as ignorant, stupid, or dull even if he is all those things. Instead you'll hear, "If brains were leather, he wouldn't have enough to saddle a flea."
    Is the fried chicken good or is it "so good it'll make you teeth white, your skin tight, and childbirth a pleasure." And the coffee? "It was so weak I had to help it out of the pot."
    The stock market crash left some folks "so broke they couldn't even pay attention.
    He's so ugly that when he was born the doctor slapped his mother.
    She's like a radio station. Anyone can pick her up, especially at night.
    He's so conceited he keeps a mirror on the bathroom ceiling so he can watch himself gargle.
    You're not worth a milk bucket under a bull.

24. A correspondent informed me he was indulging in a little do-it-yourself home repair recently and went to the hardware store in search of supplies. He asked the clerk for a half-inch pipe plug. "Do you want a male plug or a female plug or both?" the clerk inquired. "Well," replied the fellow, "I just want to stop a leak. I'm not interested in breeding them."

25. An old farmer got married, but he told the doctor he was having problems. When the urge came he was out in the field, and by the time he got back in, the urge was gone. The doctor told him not to worry, that she was a young woman and would understand and that he should take his shotgun with him. When he got the urge, he should fire a shot in the air, and his new bride would love to come out and meet him. The farmer saw the doctor a couple of months later and asked him how the system was working. The farmer told him it had worked perfectly until hunting season started but he had not seen her since.

26. A city gent stops and asks a farmer, "Do you know where Dover is?"
    The farmer says, "Nope." The city gent asks, "Can you tell me how to get to Haverford?"
    "Nope," says the farmer.
    Exasperated, the city gent says, "Don't you know anything?" The farmer answers, "I ain't lost!"

27. Two kids in a fancy Connecticut bedroom community met on the way to school. One kid said, "My father can lick your father."
    The other said, "Your father is my father!"

28. There was a fire at a hotel in a nearby city. The city's fire department trucks came, but the flames were roaring so high the firemen couldn't get in close enough to fight it. Then several trucks from neighboring towns came to help but had the same failure. Then with all the bells clanging and the old siren moaning, our town's truck from Oklahoma, where my uncle was fire chief, came barreling down the wide avenue, late as usual. All our volunteer firemen were hanging onto ladders and running boards for dear life. The old truck rattled into the hotel driveway, threading its way hell-bent through the other parked trucks. It went right up to the front door and crashed through the plate glass right into the lobby. Each of our volunteer firemen leaped from the truck, holding a nozzle hooked onto a tank of fire-fighting chemicals, and in five minutes, they had the fire out. The owner of the hotel was so happy about the way they put out the fire that he

wrote them a check for $100. He went into a rhapsody of praise for the firefighters.

"I never saw anything like it in my life!" the hotel owner exclaimed. "While the others chickened out, you went right on in to the heart of it."

Later the hotel owner asked my uncle, "Tell me, Chief, what do you and your fearless men intend to do with the $100?"

"The first thing we will do," said my uncle, "is spend about half of it getting get brakes fixed on that old truck."

29. I once lived in a town so small that the exterminator was a guy with a rolled-up magazine.

30. Farmer: "The new guy I hired doesn't know much about farming."
Friend: "What makes you say that?"
Farmer: "He found some milk bottles behind the barn and told me he'd discovered a cow's nest.

31. Man won the lottery and bought a big ranch out near Marfa. After a while he was getting pretty lonely. Finally one day on the horizon he saw a little cloud of dust heading his way. Sure enough it was his neighbor. They exchanged greetings, and the neighbor invited him to a party at his house. He said there would be all the food he could eat and all he could drink. He said there would be dancing, strip poker, and lots of loving. Wow! "I will be there. What should I wear?" he asked? The neighbor said, "It don't make no difference. It's just going to be you and me."

32. Rookie policeman went out to investigate his first accident. The report went something like this: "Pik up in dich. Body by fince. Head in sp-explaned-splade-xeplidade. Then with a mighty kick he wrote 'Head in dich.'"

33. Lost in the country. A man stopped and asked another one, "Pardon me, but is this the second turn to the left?"

34. A woman was mixing biscuit dough, and as she looked out the kitchen window, the speed of her mixing varied with the actions of the rooster as he chased chickens in the backyard. Her son came in from school and asked where his dad was. She said, "I don't know, but he's never here when I want him." (Extremely rapid stirring movement.)

35. The town is so small the telephone dial has only one hole.

36. A small town is where there is nothing doing all the time.

37. On Saturday night if you really want to have a good time, go downtown to the filling station and watch them check dipsticks.

38. Small Town Vocabulary

    Onced and twiced are words
    Fixin'to is one word
    There is no such thing as lunch. There is dinner and supper
    Jeet is actually a phrase meaning, "Did you eat?"

39. They recently spent $68 to beautify the town square. They bought him a new suit.

40. The all-night restaurant closes at 4:30 PM.

41. He is from Plumnilly, Texas. That's plum out of Dallas and nilly to Fort Worth.

42. Bob Murphy Regarding Motivation
    Man was watching a building going up, and he asked one of the workers what he was doing. The worker said he was laying brick for five dollars an hour. He then asked the second man the same question who responded, "I am expertly laying brick. He then went to the third worker who answered the question by saying, "Sir, I am building a cathedral." Of course he got fired 'cause they were building a filling station. That's what you call overmotivation.

43. Sayings

    Advice

    If you cut your own firewood, it will warm you twice.
    Don't hang your wash on someone else's line.
    The empty gourd rattles the loudest.

Agree—I'd vote for that and lend a hand stuffing the ballot box.
Animal—a worm is the only animal that can't fall down.

Bartender—stays on the sober side of the bar.
Busy—busy as a funeral home fan in July.

He blew in on his own wind.
We have a lot on our plates right now.

Cagey—slicker than a slop jar

More twists than a pretzel factory

Clinging—like a booger you can't shake off
Cold—as a cast-iron commode

As an ex-wife's heart
This is hog killing weather.

Confused—as a goat on Astro Turf

I can explain it to you, but I can't understand it for you.

Crazy—Not knitting with both needles

Overdrawn in the memory bank
Isn't hitting on all cylinders
A few termites in the attic
A couple of sandwiches short of a picnic
One bubble off plumb
He is on a different page from the rest of us.
One brick shy of a load
She has too many cobwebs in her attic.

Dead—he's taking a dirt nap.
Distance—as far as the outhouse on a cold morning
Drinking—Daddy's coming home with a load.

Drunk as Cooter Brown

Dumb—he doesn't know "come here" from "sic him."

If a duck had his brain, it would fly north for the winter.

Dry—drier than a popcorn fart

So dry the trees are bribing the dogs.
So dry the Baptists are sprinkling, the Methodists are spitting, and the
Catholics are giving rain checks.

Fast—he jumped on me like a duck on a June bug.

He's quick out of the chute.
Fast as greased lightning
Fast as small-town gossip
Faster than a scalded cat
Hell-bent for leather
Any faster he'd catch up to yesterday
In a New York minute

Flattery—sweet mouthing
Flood—hub deep to a Ferris wheel
Food—he eats more chicken than a preacher.

Chicken is called the gospel bird 'cause that's when the preacher comes
for dinner.

Black coffee—drinking coffee bareback.
Guests—company's coming, add another cup of water to the soup.

We've howdied, but we haven't shook

Handle—the blister end
Home—they lived so far out in the country that the sun went down between
the their house and town.
Honesty—he is so honest you can shoot craps with him over the phone.
Hot—as a stolen tamale

As a honeymoon hotel
So hot the hens are laying hard-boiled eggs.

Impossible—Like looking for a whisper in the wind

Like scratching your ear with your elbow.

Insult—He is like a blister 'cause he doesn't show up till the work's all done

> Woman you could start a fight in an empty house.
> Her mouth ain't no prayer book even if it does flap like leaves in the Bible.
> He is all hat and no cattle.
> He can strut sitting down.
> He has a body like a sack of doorknobs.
> He is dumber than a barrel of hair.
> She is just naturally horizontal.
> He broke his arm patting himself on the back.
> He thinks the sun comes up just to hear him crow.
> I'd like to buy him for what he thinks he's worth and sell him for what
>   he thinks he'll bring.
> Rough as a cob.
> He wouldn't scratch his own mama's fleas.
> I wonder what she'd charge to haunt a house.
> There are more horses' asses than there are horses.
> She acts like the bride at every wedding and the corpse at every
>   funeral.
> He is as dull as dirt.
> He is as dull as a fishing trip with the game warden.

Knees—prayer bones
Law—as tender as a judge's heart
Leaving—it is time to put the chairs in the wagon.

> That's all she wrote.

Marriage—she has found a new dasher for her churn.

> They ate supper before they said grace.
> They are hitched but not churched.
> She has been storked.

Med—he is so sick he needs two beds.

> I've got the green apple nasties.
> All stove up.
> He healed up and haired over.

Other—As common as cornbread

Old as dirt
Funny as all-get-out
Hot will cool if greedy will let it.
Wash off your war paint.
Don't get your panties in a wad.
Whatever melts your butter.
He was raised on concrete
Anytime you happen to pass my house, I'd sure appreciate it.
I don't care if syrup goes to a dollar a sop.
I'm near about passed going.
You can't beat that with a stick
I could sit still for that.
Might as well. Can't dance, never could sing, and it's too wet to plow.
Nothin' to write home about.
That dog won't hunt.
I don't cotton to it.
One thing at a time: don't worry about the mule, just load the wagon.
Would tickle the tar out of you.
Quick as a minnow in a water dipper.
Rougher than a stucco bathtub.
Like going around your elbow to get to your thumb.
If you can't run with the big dogs, then stay on the porch.

Rolex watch—a Texas Timex.

A used key is the one that shines. Re: staying active

Poor—He hasn't got a pot to pee in or a window to throw it out of
Proud—as swelled up as a newly elected politician.

would bring a tear to a glass eye.

braggart—big hat, no cattle.
Reaction—He really twangs my bow.
Rich—He's riding a gravy train with biscuit wheels.

He has more than he can say grace over
He's running with the big dogs
In tall cotton
So rich they can eat fried chicken all week long.
She's rich enough to eat her laying hens.

Sad—I feel lower than a gopher hole.

He looks like the cheese fell off his cracker.
You look like you were sent for and couldn't go.

Salesman—could sell a double bed to the pope
Small/skinny—Flat as a fritter

Thin as a rake and twice as sexy
Thin as depression soup
He's about as big as the little end of nothing.

Smart—trying to fool him is like trying to hide sunup from a rooster.
Threat—I'm gonna put something on you that Ajax won't take off.
Tired—Looks like she's been chewed up. Spit out and stepped on.

Looks like she was rode hard and put away wet.

Truthful—If I tell you a hen dips snuff, you can look under her wing for the
    Garrett
Ugly—So ugly the tide wouldn't take her out.

He was so ugly his mama had to tie a porkchop around his neck so the
    dogs would play with him.
She can't help being ugly, but she could stay home.
Ugly enough to cause a peeping tom to reach in and pull down the
    shade.
So ugly his mama borrowed a baby to take to church.

Unwelcome—as welcome as an outhouse breeze

As hair in a biscuit.

Useless—as useless as a sewed-up pocket

Not worth spit.
He couldn't organize a pissing contest in a brewery.
As two buggies in a one-horse town
He could screw up a two-car funeral.
He's a day late and a dollar short.
She's itching for something she won't scratch for.

He's got no more chance than a June bug in a chicken coop

Valued—I wouldn't trade her for a farm in Georgia.
Wedding ring—one-man band
Wise—wise as a tree full of owls

$\mathcal{S}$PORTS/GOLF

1. The wife decided she was going deer hunting with her husband come *hell* or high water even though she had never been hunting in her life. After reluctantly agreeing, he showed her where her blind would be and told her if she shot one he would be there soon to help her dress it. Surprisingly in a few minutes a couple of shots rang out; he ran over, and there she was pointing the rifle at another man who said, "Lady, it is your deer. I don't want the deer, just let me get my saddle off of it."

2. Bob Hope played golf with Billy Graham, and after he putted, the hole healed up.

3. A fisherman accidentally left his catch under the seat on the bus. The next issue of the local newspaper had this advertisement. "If the person who left a parcel of fish on the no. 47 bus would care to come down to the depot, he can have the bus."

4. About every five minutes a man would place a bet on number 7 to win. After a while a man went up to him and said, "Fellow, it's none of my business, but I hate to see you placing a bet on a horse that is *not* going to win. The bettor asked, "How do you know that?" The guy said, "Because I own horse number 7." The bettor said, "Well, it's going to be a mighty slow race because I own the other six."

5. A group of deer hunters went out. Two went to the north pasture and two to the south pasture. As dark arrived, the two hunters from the south pasture came back, but there had been nothing seen of the two on the north pasture. Finally about an hour after dark, one of the hunters showed up carrying an absolute trophy buck. They asked, "Where is

Harry?" The hunter said, "I think Harry had a heart attack, and he's about a mile back in the pasture." They said, "You mean you brought a deer back but left Harry out there?" He said, "Yeah, I figured there wasn't anybody going to steal Harry."

6. Golfer was on the first tee. From the inside the pro yelled for him to put his ball between the white markers as the ball was about ten feet ahead. He didn't move the ball and addressed his ball once more. Again the pro yelled, "The rules of the club are to put your ball between the white markers." This went on and on. Finally the golfer said, "Fellow, I've been a member of this snooty club for a year now, and you are the first one who has said a single word to me. For your information, this is my second shot."

7. A fellow belonged to Skiers Anonymous. When you get the urge to go skiing, a couple of guys come over and break your leg.

8. An early-morning hunter went to a café. The waitress asked him what he wanted. He said, "Toast coffee, a couple of fried eggs, and a few kind words." Later he asked her, "What about the kind words?" She said, "Don't eat them eggs."

9. A man was hunting birds. He saw some, but they were across the fence on the neighbor's property. He shot the birds and an argument ensued. Finally the rancher said, "Let's just settle it like we do out here in the country. I will kick you in the groin then you do it to me and finally one of us will give up." The hunter said that was OK with him, so the rancher went first. He kicked the guy so hard he turned pale and fell to the ground. Finally he got back on his feet and said, "OK it's my time now." The rancher said, "Oh shucks you can have the damn birds."

10. My horse would have won the race, but he kept looking back for the plow.

11. A young man killed a whooping crane. The game warden heard about it and gave him a lecture and heavy fine. The game warden asked, "By the way, what does a whooping crane taste like?" The man said, "Oh, about like a bald eagle."

12. If athletes have athletes foot, do astronauts have "missle toe"?

13. Two experienced fishermen went ice fishing. They chopped holes in the ice, put worms on their hooks, and didn't get a nibble. This went on for hours; and about midafternoon, a small boy arrived, went confidently onto the ice, chopped a hole between the two men, and caught fish after fish. The men were amazed and finally asked the boy what his secret was. The boy said, "Mmm, mmm, mmm." "What's that? Say it again, son." The boy said, "Mmm, your mmm, wmm." Man said, "I still can't understand you. Would you speak more clearly?" At that the boy cupped his palms, spit out a large amount of substance, and said clearly, "Keep you worms warm."

14. Rene's son told his dad he was going to turn pro as a tennis player. He said he was tired of throwing tantrums for free.

15. Difference between Kellogg's Rice Krispies and UT? Rice Krispies deserve to be in a bowl.

16. Football Prediction—U of H will be eight and three this year—eight misdemeanors and three felonies.

17. He was the nudist camp athlete. He ran a hundred yards in nothing.

18. To listen to Jon Madden is maddening. His frenetics are oh so saddening.
    When he gets all excited and hyperdelighted, we turn him off, quite gladdening.

19. Sure, mostly daily ball and Wrigley Field are okay, but isn't the best reason

for wanting to be a Cub player is that you never have to worry about anyone stealing your World Series ring.

20. Two men were talking on a street when a funeral procession passed by, and they observed a curious thing. A bag of golf clubs was resting on the coffin in the hearse. "He must have been quite a golfer," observed one soberly. "Must have been?" exclaimed the other. "He is! He's playing this afternoon. That's his wife's funeral."

21. I'm quite an athlete though. I once fought Louis and did I have him worried in the first round! He thought he'd killed me.

22. Advice—don't ever play golf with a man who has a suntan and carries a one iron.

23. If you can't hear a pin drop, something is wrong with your bowling.

24. Lee Trevino: "The older I get the better I used to be." 25. He wanted to have a sex change so he could hit golf balls from the women's tees. 26. Lost my brown and white shoes at the golf course—keep an eye out for the brown one.

27. He quit trying to shoot his age. Now he's trying to shoot his area code.

28. And now this health tip for the month of August: never play golf on any day when the temperature exceeds your score.

29. After three sets of clubs and ten years of lessons, I'm finally getting some fun out of golf. I quit.

30. I have a problem with boxing. I don't understand any sport where a guy who makes eleven million dollars is called "The Loser."

31. Q. Three UT football players were in a car. Who is driving?
A. The Police

32. She: You think so much of your golf game you don't even remember the day we got married.
He: Oh yes, I do. It was the day I made the thirty-foot putt.

33. Ad: One set of Jack Nicklaus golf clubs with bag and cart. Size 16 bowling ball and bag with assorted trophies. Call 771-5338. If a man answers, please hang up.

34. Some football team—they won the coin toss and elected to go home.

35. Golf is a good game for people who think they have their life organized.

36. I'm a lousy golfer. I spend so much time in sand traps, instead of a golf cart they give me a camel. 37. Last night I came the closest I have ever come to bowling a perfect three hundred. I had a sixty-four.

38. Lessons to learn before you ever set foot on a golf course: Lesson 1: Do not be embarrassed on the course because you have never played before. You will find most golfers seldom play the game. In fact, probably nine out of ten golfers you meet will tell you they don't know how long it's been since they played and will reassure you by adding that they've probably forgotten everything they knew anyway. Lesson 2: Do not bet at first, especially with people who don't know how long it's been since they've played. Lesson 3: Before you even pick up your first club, look yourself over (stripped and in a mirror, if necessary) and see if you can find some kind of good, all-around ailment. An ailment is essential in golf. The average sometimes golfer would not think to step on the course without bursitis, a gimpy leg, or least a bandaged thumb. Lesson 4: Do not bet with ailing golfers. Lesson 5: Never pay for lessons. Almost any golfer on the course will give you free advice. Lesson 6: Never underestimate how long it takes to play golf. There is no known case of a golfer ever getting home when he told his wife he would. Lesson 7: Don't take the same penalties Jack Nicklaus takes. He gets to practice every day. Lesson 8: Volunteer to keep score. Lesson 9: If you pick up in a sand trap, guess the score you would have had on the hole. Guess six. Lesson 10: If you lose your ball but find another, play it. Don't brag about good luck. Lesson 11: Do not talk when another player is making a shot. Do not cough. But a golf bag with a loud zipper can be a boon at times. Lesson 12: Learn to give golf advice yourself. Tell a player he is hitting the ball too soon. Let him think about that. Lesson 13: Learn to swear.

    And read articles titled "How to Line up Your Fourth Putt" and "How to Hit a Nike out of the Rough When You Hit a Titelist from the Tee."

39. They have several courses out here that are real close together. You don't know which hole you are going to play until after you tee off. 40. There is so much violence in the world that I hardly noticed that the hockey season had started.

41. His wife remarked that if she was coach, she'd never use a running back with a cold. "He'd be more apt to cough up the ball," his wife explained.

42. Bill Peterson, former Houston Oilers coach, was not blessed with the best memory. Peterson also coached in college at Florida State and Rice. Before a big college game, the player who usually led the team in prayer

could not be found, and Peterson, anxious to get God's blessing and still make the kickoff, decided to do it himself. "Boys, let's kneel and say the Lord's Prayer," Peterson said. "Now I lay me down to sleep . . ."

43. This Cowboy fan shows up in RFK Stadium with a monkey and a paid seat for same. The Cowboys scored in the first quarter of the football game; and nearby spectators were amazed to see the monkey leap into the air, turn a perfect flip, and land in the seat. Moments later, a Cowboy defender intercepted a Joe Theismann pass and returned it to the end zone. The monkey jumped to his feet, saluted, and sang a reedy chorus of "The Eyes of Texas." The onlookers were amazed. "This is a meaningless early season game," said one. "What in the world does the monkey do when the Cowboys win a big game?" The Dallas fan shrugged. "I don't know. I've only had him five years."

44. "You've got to practice every day," the basketball coach said. "One day of practice is like one day of clean living—it ain't gonna help."

45. He said, "We knew every time your team came out of the huddle which back was going to carry the ball because three of them were smiling and the other one was shaking like hell."

46. UH beat Aggies in basketball. UH puts on their pants just like the Aggies do. The only difference is that it takes them a little longer to pull them up.

47. Here I sit nursing a football injury I received while moving the TV set Sunday trying to give the Chargers better field position.

48. They have a gay quarterback that they use in emergencies, There is no one better when it comes to engineering a come-from-behind victory.

49. Harry had been a locker room attendant at the university for twenty-five years. He swept the floors, mopped the shower rooms, washed the dirty socks, chlorinated the pool, threw out the trash, cleaned the lockers. All this without complaint until he came home and bitterly cried to his wife, "Now, there's going to be a girls' football team as well. That means another sixty uniforms to wash and all the extra sweeping, mopping, disinfecting." His wife tried to console him, "If it's that tough, you should quit." "How can I?" he moaned. "You know sports is my life."

50. "Now that you've climbed Mount Everest, you say you want to do it again. May I ask why?" Climber: "I want to take one more peak."

51. He says it could be rushing the hunting season, but it's never too soon to prepare yourself for the possibility of becoming lost in the woods. That's why every hunter should take along a deck of cards. "If you get lost, find a stump and start a game of solitaire," he says. "In a couple of minutes, someone will come along to let you know the six goes on the seven and you can ask them for directions."

52. Willie Nelson bought his own personal golf course, near Austin. "What's par?" he was asked. "Anything I want it to be," said Willie. "For instance, that hole over there is a par 47 and yesterday, I birdied the sucker."

53. "I guess I'm in the wrong game. You finish last in basketball they fire you. You know what they call the guy who finishes last in medical school? They call him doctor." (Abe Lemons)

54. Two hunters were lost in the woods. It was getting dark, and they were afraid they would die before morning. One said he remembered reading that when you're lost, you should shoot into the air three times and help would come. "I'll try that," the other hunter said. An hour passed and no help arrived. "Try it again," his buddy said. He did, but still no help arrived. "Let's give it another try." The hunter who had been shooting into the air said he would. "But we've got to take it easy on this," he said, "because pretty soon we'll be out of arrows."

55. From former Houston Oiler head Bud Adams: "If the Astrodome is the eighth wonder of the world, the rent is the ninth."

56. I've tennis elbow, swimmer's ear, my athlete's foot's pathetic. What makes my suffering severe is that I'm not athletic.

57. Regarding the deliberate methods of our great chess players, we hear that one of them has bequeathed his next move to his grandson.

58. A fellow says he and some buddies were involved in a philosophical discussion in the corner beer joint about athletes using steroids. One old fellow who had been sitting too long at the end of the bar overheard part of what they were saying, and putting down his glass and wiping the

foam from his lips, he declaimed muzzily, "Well, I don't know what all the fuss is about. Hell, if they got steroids, they can't run anyway—them thing is too painful."

59. When asked a football coach which play does he feel has been most difficult for his team to execute this season, might reply, "The one in which the runner passes the ball over to the referee after he crosses the goal line."

60. Before a high school football game, the mother of four asked one of the coaches: "How many quarter backs do you have?" The coach grinned and replied, "Three on the team and about three hundred in the stands."

61. The world's worst golfer hit his ball into a monstrous trap. "What club should I use now?" he wailed to his caddie. "What club you use isn't important," answered the young man. "Just take along plenty of food and water."

62. "I hear your son plays on the football team. What position does he play?" "I'm not sure," the proud father replied, "but I think he said he's one of the drawbacks."

63. They've stopped teaching Latin in school. So how is it they keep putting Roman numerals on Super Bowls?

64. A golfer, like a bowler, can straighten the flight of the ball by yelling at it.

65. Golf was invented so that even the man who is not in politics will have something to lie about.

66. My neighbor Wolfgang says all you need to know about his bowling is that the local lanes name a gutter after him.

67. The general manager of the 76ers commented on his relationship with the team's owner: "I wanted to give him something to symbolize our association, but I couldn't get an ulcer framed."

68. The main reason that comparatively few females play golf is that we women have more important things to lie about, and that also is the reason you don't see too many fishing.

69. Her son came home on his vacation. He told her he was giving up the game of games. "I lost three balls in one day," he said. "That's nothing," the mother told him. "A lot of golfers lose three balls during a round." "Yeah, I know that," he said, "but I'm a bowler."

70. He's finally figured out why mountain climbers rope themselves together—to keep the smart ones from going home.

71. As Cincinnati Reds president lies on couch, psychiatrist comments, "Don't worry, you're not being paranoid, Mr. Wagner . . . everyone really *does* hate you.

72. A farmer, on in years, married a lusty young lady. Soon the wife started to grow pale and act fidgety. The marriage seemed to be in danger. The doctor advised the farmer, "Your wife needs much more affection. She needs some more kissing, hugging, and loving. Those young ones want cuddling even during the daytime." The farmer said, "How can I work that one out? There are times during the day when I'm working land so far-off I couldn't see her getting the urge. I can't keep running back every five minutes to check on her, or I'd never get my plowing done." The doctor pondered the problem and soon came up with a solution. He said, "Carry your shotgun with you. When you feel you can put a smile on her face, pull the trigger, and she'll come running to you." A month went by. On his way to another patient, the doctor passed the farmer at work and stopped to ask him, "How'd my system work out?" The farmer said, "It was kind of like a miracle the first week. Then hunting season opened, and I haven't seen hide nor hair of her since!"

73. One football fan lived and died by his favorite football team in the fall. He had no time for his family or children. He could be found only on the couch, a six-pack or part of one at his side, and his eyes glued to the TV screen. One day his wife marched up on front of the screen, opened her housedress, and said with finality, "Okay, buster, play me or trade me!"

74. An attractive middle-aged woman, dressed in the team colors and obviously a big fan, was sitting in a two-seat box all alone. The usher approached her and asked, "Why is the seat empty, ma'am?" The woman said, "It's my husband's seat." "Where is he?" "He died." "Oh well, couldn't you have given the seat to a friend or somebody in the family? "The woman shook her head. "Oh no, they're all at his funeral!"

75. Man at the racetrack went to the window and placed a bet on Blue Bell in the fourth race. When he showed up for the fourth time, an onlooker said, "Buddy, I guess it isn't any of my business, but if I were you I wouldn't be risking all that money on Blue Bell. He's not going to win the fourth race." First man: "How did you figure that out all by yourself?" Second guy: "Well, if you must know, I own Blue Bell and he's not going to win the race. First guy: "Maybe you're right, but if you are, it's going to be a mighty slow race 'cause I own the other six horses."

76. Wanda said, "Jim, you're going to have to choose between golf or me." Jim said, "But, Wanda, I shot 101 today. Do you expect me to quit when I'm at the top of my game?"

77. Skiing is the best medicine. But watch out for slide effects.

78. He heard that a sporting goods manufacturer is coming out with golf balls the size of hailstones.

79. Baseball's Texas Rangers' miserable start has drawn cruel jokes. "If they don't do something pretty soon," one of their mourners said, "they're liable to lose their reputation as a second-rate team."

80. Taking note of all the golf tournaments played for one disease or another: "I'm putting on a tournament for charity. My charity is natural causes. It's a big killer."

81. Do you ever go camping? No. We just take the screen down.

82. George looks like a golf pro—all dressed in the latest designer golf wear—but he slices his ball way out into the trees. He decides to hit it out, and the ball ricochets off a tree and strikes him on the forehead, killing him. At the Pearly gates, St. Peter greeted him and said, "You look like a golfer. Are you any good?" George said, "I got here in two, didn't I?"

83. Man hit trees on the first eleven holes. The twelfth was a three par, and he knocked it on the green. He told his partner, "Well, I didn't hit a tree on this hole." His partner said, "You haven't putted yet."

84. Man wanted to trade his Astros tickets in. He said, "They are awful tickets—they face the field."

85. Closest I ever came to a hole in one—had a five. 86. Me and my dad use to play tag. He'd drive.

87. Golf isn't a matter of life and death. It's more important than that.

88. Arnold Palmer told me how I could cut twelve strokes off my score—skip one par 3.

89. When you cross a badger and a groundhog, you get six more weeks of bad football.

90. A survey shows that wrestling on TV is taken seriously by 93 percent of the viewers. That's disturbing because some of those must be registered voters.

91. They put their pants on the same way our players do; it just takes them a little longer to pull them up.

92. A visitor at the golf club teed up for the first hole, made a wild swing, and completely missed the ball. "It's a good thing I found out at the start," he said, "this course is at least two inches lower than the course I usually play on."

93. Never fall in love with a tennis player. Just remember that "love" means nothing to him.

94. He said the saddest fishing story he's heard so far concerns a local sport who caught a sixty-pound marlin off the coast of Florida and dislocated both shoulders describing it.

95. Man returned from fishing trip and asked his wife why she didn't pack his silk pajamas. She said, "I did. I put them in your tackle box."

96. A lady in Dallas calls 911. Hysterically, she says, "Someone has broken into my house, and I think he's going to rape me." The police officer says, "I'm sorry, we're awfully busy right now. Just get the guy's jersey number, and we'll get back to you."

97. As one deer said to the other, "Man, I wish I had his doe."

98. One time when I was in Kezar Stadium (San Francisco), they gave me a standing boo. (George Halas)

99. It matters not whether you win or lose. What matters is whether I win or lose. (D. Weinberg) 100. Never believe anything until it's been officially denied. (Claud Cockburn)

101. Ed Wynn, just before going moose hunting, would look in the full-length mirror, gasp with horror, and exclaim, "Thank God I'm out of season."

102. All is fair in love and golf.

103. The difference between a professional and an amateur athlete is that the professional is paid by check.

104. Do you realize that in the last six months the Mafia has had more hits than the Astros? 105. Golf—a wonderful sport. Where else could you spend the afternoon with three hookers, score, and your wife doesn't even get mad?

106. I recently lost my ball. I yelled at the caddy, "Why didn't you keep your eye on the ball?" He said, "I'm sorry, sir, but you caught me off guard when you hit it on the first swing."

107. I just saw something scary—a large print magazine for hunters.

108. I'm very concerned about the growing number of injuries caused by football. Last week I got a shock turning on my TV set, cut my finger opening a beer can, and almost choked on a pretzel.

109. The last duck I shot was a rabbit. It must have weighed six pounds, if it was an inch.

110. Joe said he caught a fish—biggest he ever saw. That doesn't tell much. Show me with your hands how long it was. Joe looked around the room and said, "OK, but we'll have to go outside." 111. Fisherman went to the fish market and said, "Throw me three redfish"
    "Why?"

"I want to tell my wife I caught them."

"Well, you'd better let me throw you three flounder. Your wife came in earlier, said you'd probably be here and she wants flounder."

112. The fish I caught were so big, every time I caught one the water level went down three inches.

113. Bridge club women were admiring a large stuffed shark mounted over the mantle. The hostess said proudly, "My husband and I caught that in Acapulco." "What's it stuffed with?"

"My husband."

114. Boy took his four-year-old sister with him fishing. Later he told his parents he would never take her fishing again. Parents: "If you had just asked her to be quiet, she probably would have." Boy: "That wasn't the problem. She ate all my bait."

115. I made a mistake teaching Lil to play golf. She found out it doesn't take fourteen hours to play eighteen holes.

116. My golf handicap is that I can add.

117. My best golf score is 118, but I've only been playing twenty-five years.

118. He shouts "Fore" when he putts.

119. President of the university: "We are working to develop a university of which the football team can be proud."

120. A man really wanted to buy a boat. His wife said no. He bought it anyway but told her she could name it. She painted on the side, "For Sale."

121. There is a college football team so bad that homecoming is scheduled as an away game.

122. Tommy Bolt when advising young golfers on having tantrums on the golf course: "They throw their clubs backward and that is wrong. You should always throw the club ahead of you so you won't have to walk any extra distance to get it."

123. Rowing coach: So you want to come out for the crew, eh? Ever rowed before? Freshman: Only a horse, sir.

124. The same people who gave us golf and called it a game are the ones that gave us the bagpipe and called it music.

125. Wrong way sportsman: "When he's golfing he hooks them. When he is fishing he doesn't."

126. The duck hunter went through a fence with his gun cocked. He is survived by a wife, three children, and a duck.

127. If people really concentrated on the important things in life, there would be a shortage of fishing poles.

128. Do you want to simulate sailboat racing? Stand naked in a cold shower and tear up $100 bills.

129. Today I consider myself as the world's happiest sailing enthusiast. I just sold my boat.

130. He who has the fastest golf cart never has a bad lie. (Mickey Mantle)

131. Ad in paper: For sale-15 hp. Outboard motor. "Last seen in good running condition. Must have scuba gear to see."

132. Q: What is the Indian word for "lousy hunter"?
     A. Vegetarian

133. Golf is a wonderful game. It provides you with a use for all the bad language you picked up on the street as a kid.

134. My wife played her best round of golf last Tuesday. In the unlikely event you haven't heard about it, please call BR-549 for full details of every shot.

135. I noticed an ad in the paper last weekend. It said: "For sale—one set of Ben Hogan golf clubs with bag and cart, size 16 bowling ball, and bag with assorted trophies. Call BR-549. If a man answers, please hang up."

136. I asked Sam why he has deer heads all over his walls. He said it was because they are such beautiful animals. Well, I think my wife is beautiful, but I only have photographs of her on the walls."

137. Jack Benny: Give me golf clubs, fresh air, and a beautiful girl and you can keep my golf clubs and the fresh air.

138. Lee Trevino: Columbus went around the world in 1492. That's not a lot of strokes when you consider the course.

139. Chi Chi Rodriguez: After all these years it's still embarrassing for me to play on the American golf tour. Like the time I asked my caddie for a sand wedge and he came back ten minutes later with a ham on rye.

140. Tommy Bolt, toward the end of one of his infamous high-volume, temperamental, club-throwing rounds, asked the caddie for a club recommendation for a shot of about 155 yards. His caddie said, "I'd say either a 3 iron or a wedge, sir. "A 3 iron or a wedge?" asked Bolt? "What kind of a stupid #@^&$% choice is that?" "Those are the only two clubs you have left in the bag, sir," said the caddie.

141. Jim Mc. Mahon, professional quarterback, when asked what it was like to go to Brigham Young: "They let us chase girls, but they wouldn't let us catch them."

142. At Georgia Southern, we don't cheat. That costs money, and we don't have any. (Erk Russell/ Georgia Southern)

143. Football is only a game. Spiritual things are eternal. Nevertheless Beat Texas—seen on sign in Arkansas in1969.

144. After you retire, there's only one big event left . . . and I ain't ready for that. (Bobby Bowden, Florida State)

145. The man who complains about the way the ball bounces is likely to be the one who dropped it. (Lou Holtz, Arkansas)

146. Have a plan. Be polite. Be professional. But have a plan to kill everyone you meet.
    Be courteous to everyone, friendly to no one. Have a backup plan because the first one won't work.

Toasts

1. As you slide down the banister of wedded life, may the splinters never point your way.

2. May all your "pains" be champagne and all your "ails" come out of a bottle.

3. I drink to your health when we're together
I drink to your health when I'm alone
I've drunk to your health so often
I've almost ruined my own.

4. Irish toast—let's get down on our knees and thank God we're on our feet.

5. Here's to the busy little bee, whose sex is very hard to see; you cannot tell a he from a she, but she can tell and so can he. The busy bee is never still, she does not have time to take the pill; but that is why in days like these, there are so many sons of b's.

6. May you have enough happiness to keep you sweet; enough trials to keep you strong; enough sorrow to keep you human; enough hope to keep you happy; enough failure to keep you humble; enough success to keep you eager; enough friends to give you comfort; enough faith and courage in yourself, your business and your country to banish depression; enough wealth to meet your needs; enough determination to make each day a better day than yesterday.

7. Let us drink to the health of the bride. Let us drink to the health of the groom.
    Let us drink to the parson who tied them and to every guest in this room.

8. Here's to the man who from morning to night
    Has the vim and the will and the courage to fight—
    The courage to fight and the courage to live—
    The courage to learn and to live and forgive.

9. I wish you health; I wish you wealth,
    And a happy home with freedom;
    And may you always have true friends,
    But never have cause to need them.

10. Here's to the host and hostess;
    We're honored to be here tonight.
    May they both live long and prosper,
    May their hearts be ever light.

11. Toast—I wish you good health, long life, continued prosperity, and eventually a measure of respectability.

12. I wish you an abundance of health and goodness and sweet things and sweet dreams, no nightmares. And I wish you lemonade in the shade in July and all that other jazz and hugging and kissing and peace forever in your time and for your children and their children and their children, and God bless us all! Cheers! Salud! Cent'anni! There, that will hold you till Sunday.

13. May the winds of fortune speed you. May you sail a gentle sea. May it always be the other guy who says, "The drinks are on me."

14. Friends we are today and friends will always be. For I'm wise to you and you can see through me.

15. New years: May your troubles last as long as your resolutions.

16. Here's to all of us. For there's so much good in the worst of us and so much bad in the best of us that it hardly behooves any of us to talk about the rest of us.

17. May you have a Xmas you will never forget and a New Year's you will never remember.

18. May you live as long as you want to and want to as long as you live.

19. Here's to the sum of happiness.
Something to do,
Something to love and
Something to hope for.

20. A toast to every one of you
No matter where you are from.
May the best day in your life so far
Be worst than your worst to come.

21. Here's health to all those whom we love,
And health to all those who love us.
Here's health to all those who love those who love those
Who love those who love those who love us.

22. Let us toast the fools, but for them the rest of us could not succeed. (Mark Twain)

23. During the American Revolutionary War, our forefathers said to the British, "May they have cobweb breeches, a porcupine saddle, a hard-trotting, horse and an eternal journey."

24. May the saddest day of your future be no worse than the happiest day of your past.
    May you have the hindsight to know where you have been, the foresight to know where you are going, and the insight to know when you have gone too far.

25. May peace break into your house and may thieves come to steal your debts. May the pockets of your jeans become a magnet of $200 bills. May love stick to your face like Vaseline, and may laughter assault your lips. May your clothes smell of success like smoking tires, and may happiness slap you across the face, and may your tears be that of joy. May the problems you had forget your home address! In simple words—may this year be the best year of your life!

26. 'Tis better to buy a small bouquet
    And give to your friend this very day
    Than a bushel of roses white and red
    To lay on his coffin after he's dead.

27. Always remember to forget the things that made you sad
    But never forget to remember
    The things that made you glad
    Always remember to forget
    The friends that proved untrue
    But never forget to remember
    Those that have stuck to you.
    Always remember to forget
    The troubles that passed away
    But never forget to remember
    The blessings that come each day.

28. May you have all the happiness
    And luck that life can hold
    And at the end of your rainbows
    May you find a pot of gold.

TRAVEL

1. A sign on a small desert gas station in the middle of nowhere: "Don't ask us for information. If we knew anything we wouldn't be here."

2. I went to a convention one time. I woke up in the hotel room the next morning, and my clothes were strewn all around the room and I was still in them.

3. We stayed in a hotel in the slum district. You could look out the window and see all Ten Commandments broken at the same time.

4. For room service you called 911.

5. We drove up the East Coast and saw a sign that said, "Lobster tails" fifty cents each. That looked like a great deal so we stopped. I handed the young man 50C and told him I wanted one of those lobster tails. He said, "Yes, sir. Once upon a time there were these two lobsters."

6. There is a hotel going up in downtown Moscow. It is called the Comrade Hilton.

7. Sign in a brake shop: "Brakes slipping? Try to stop here for repairs."

8. While on an elevator in Tulsa, a man asked me if anyone had ever mentioned that I looked like Mit Sorrels. Being rather flattered, I said, "Well, as a matter of fact they have." He said, "It makes you mad as hell, doesn't it?"

9. She just got her driver's license. It is the first time she has been in the front seat for ten years.

10. A friend said he was so afraid of flying that he never had put all his weight down.

11. Lil said, "Mit, all pills don't come in bottles."

12. A retired air force officer was trying to get permission fly again. The medic asked him when was the last time he had been with a woman. He said, "It's 1959." The medic said, "That's a long time, isn't it?" The officer said, "I don't know it's just 2116 now."

13. Congestion is getting so bad you can now change a flat without losing your place in traffic.

14. A used car dealer told me that if my car was a horse, he would have to shoot it.

15. There are so many foreign cars in Beverley Hills it has been ten years since anyone has been hit above the knees.

16. Hotel manager announcement re: cars being parked by valets. The hotel has no valet service.

17. Visit the Dolly Parton Museum—it has her first wig and her first training bra. It even has the original wheels on it.

18. A friend heard you can support a child in Ethiopia for $10 a month, so he sent two of his own.

19. My nephew brought a car into the garage for its 5,000 mile inspection. "Is there anything the matter with it?" The serviceman wanted to know. "There's only one part of it that doesn't make a noise," nephew said, "the horn."

20. If four out of five accidents happen at home, why do people live there?

21. And then there is the body shop they've named "Wreck—Amended."

22. A man in his beat-up old car drove up to a tollbooth. The toll collector said, "Two dollars." The owner said, "Sold!"

23. Found on the windshield of a car—"Stupidity is not a handicap. Park elsewhere."

24. Last week she originated a completely new driving maneuver. It's called an O-turn. It's for when you're making a U-turn and you change your mind.

25. You might say he went to a very exclusive trade school on the Hudson Where they taught him to make license plates.

26. What a car! I'm going to call it Flattery 'cause it gets me nowhere!

27. But she caught on quick. In less than two months she learned how to scrape toast, carrots, and fenders.

28. Can this girl drive! She gets twenty-two miles to a fender!

29. Yesterday Lil came in and said, "I don't want to upset, you but I scratched the left rear fender a little." I said, "Oh?" She said, "Yes. If you want to look at it, it's in the trunk.

30. Sign on motorcycle repair shop—Vrooom Service

31. The worst part of this hotel is the place has no toilets. Most uncanny thing I ever heard of.

32. My auto mechanic worked on my car and sent me a bill for $750. Called it open-hood surgery.

33. Salesman Sam registered at a small-town hotel and then went into the dining room for dinner. The waitress began a long spiel about the virtues of the hotel's famed potato soup, and finally, after a long argument, Sam convinced her that he hated potato soup and would have non under any circumstances. Later that night, the man in the room next to Sam suffered severe stomach pains, and his wife telephoned a local doctor and asked him to come quick. The wife met the doctor in the lobby and told him that only an enema would help her husband but that he undoubtedly would make an awful fuss about it. Unwittingly,

the physician went into the wrong room and applied the treatment to Sam. Several weeks later a friend remarked he was going through the same town and asked Sam about the hotel. "A wonderful place," said Sam. "But when they offer you potato soup, take it with the dinner!"

34. I knew a traveling salesman who died and left his family sixty-five thousand towels.

35. A Boise salesman had to go to New York on business, and his wife asked if she could come along. "But I'll be tied up in conference all the time. You wouldn't enjoy it at all." "Oh, that's all right. I can spend all my time shipping for clothes." "That's silly. You can get anything you want right here." "Oh, wonderful. That's what I hoped you would say."

36. Is that plane safe? Sure if it weren't, do you think I would sell you this ticket on a credit card?

37. We had a very small room. When I put the key in the lock, I broke the window.

38. "And I don't even have to worry about changing the oil every thousand miles," said the disgruntled owner of a grade A lemon. "There's never any left."

39. A vacation is when you spend thousands of dollars to see what rain looks like in different parts of the world.

40. Re: tip-conscious bellhops. I ordered a deck of cards from room service, and the bellhop made fifty-two trips.

41. First passenger: "Four hours on the plane and I haven't even gotten airsick." Second passenger: "That's because we haven't left the ground yet."

42. Traffic is getting so bad nowadays that you can now change a flat without losing your place in line.

43. There's no courtesy on the highways today. One man put his arm out the window to signal a lane change and somebody stole his watch.

44. People are afraid of airplanes. I got in the ticket line behind an honest man once. He said to the clerk, "Give me two chances to Pittsburgh."

45. My father runs an artist's supply store in Wisconsin. His shop van has painted on the back, "Watch our Van Gogh!"

46. Hear about the guy who tried to hold up a Japanese tour bus? The police got 1,844 photos of him.

47. I'm staying at a motel downtown that has a fantastic system to stop guests from stealing towels. You shower with the manager.

48. When I finally got to the window of the Department of Motor Vehicles, I asked how to register a vintage car. She asked, "Is your car an antique?" I said, "Yes, but it wasn't when I got in line."

49. My auto mechanic suggested that I rotate my tires. I thought that happens automatically when you drive.

50. The town was so dull, the night life was over before dark.

51. I took my car down to see what I could get for it on a trade-in. The dealer offered me a ballpoint pen.

52. You may think this is wrong, but I always park in handicap spots because my car payments cost me an arm and a leg.

53. The airlines are serious about the smoking ban. Before my flight there this morning, I had to walk through a tobacco detector.

54. Before my plane took off, the stewardess announced that the dinner rolls could be used as a flotation device.

55. I suspected our pilot had a drinking problem when he said we were flying on a Boeing 7&7.

56. You can't win. I was at the airport and received a summons for not smoking in a designated smoking area.

57. Somehow it seems appropriate that the most famous landmark in Washington DC is a gigantic shaft.

58. Recently I had a minor auto accident. I told the judge it was Lil's fault because she fell asleep in the backseat.

59. Handguns are only dangerous when they're loaded. So are most drivers.

60. The hotel I'm in has a lovely closet—a nail.

61. Roads are so bad, trucks have slowed down to 65 mph.

62. I told the attendant I wanted a round-trip ticket. She said, "To where?" I said, "To here."

63. He lives in such a tough neighborhood that you can travel two miles without leaving the scene of the crime.

64. A middle-aged man set three pieces of luggage before an airline clerk in the airport. "I want this brown bag to go to Dallas," the man said. "The black one goes to Milwaukee. And I want you to send the other one to Orlando."

    The clerk blinked. A supervisor who had overheard the customer's demands approached and said, "I'm sorry, but we're not parcel post, sir! We can't do that!"

    In a slightly raised voice, the man said, "Why not? That's what you did with my bags the last time!"

65. A cab driver and an English gentleman were having a nice conversation while driving from the hotel to the airport: The cab driver decided to try a riddle on the Englishman. "The person I'm thinking of has the same mother and father that I have yet is not my brother or sister. Who is it?" The Englishman gave the question long and serious consideration, then confessed that he didn't know the answer. The cab driver said, "It's me." The Englishman slapped his thigh and laughed. "My word, that's a jolly good one! I can't wait till I get back to London to try it on the chaps at my club."

    When back in London, the Englishman gathered his friends around him and posed the riddle: "Now this individual I am thinking about has the same parents that I do, but is not my brother or sister. Who is it?

    The other members were deep in thought for some time; one by one gave up. The last said, "All right, old chap, who is it?"

    The Englishman slapped the table triumphantly and gleefully announced, "It's the taxicab driver in Pittsburgh, Pennsylvania!"

66. Sign you see as you leave California and enter Oregon reads, Leaving California—Resume Normal Behavior.

67. We had a good-looking stewardess. She told me, "Sir, if you'd quit leaning into the aisle, I'd quit bumping into you." "I know," I said.

68. Do you still have concerns about taking a plane? No, I still think it's the safest way to fly.

69. The astronauts are the only people who take off in Florida and don't have to change planes in Atlanta.

70. This one's about a woman who was cold in an upper berth on a train. She asked the stranger in the lower bunk if he had an extra blanket. The man didn't have a blanket. But he asked her if she were married. The woman said that she was single.

   So the man asked if she would like to pretend she was married. The woman agreed to pretend that she was married and then the man told her, "Now that you're married, get up and get your own blanket."

71. Opportunity knocks, but so does Regular Unleaded.

72. Talk about switch. I just heard of an auto dealer that raffled off a church.

73. Truck stop sign: "Eat here and get gas."

74. In view of the earthquakes there, LA hotels now have a slogan: "LA—where you don't need a wake-up call."

75. Vacation agony, says the fellow next door, is a mosquito bite on top of poison ivy on top of sunburn.

76. A frequent transatlantic traveler says the chief advantage of the faster, supersonic flights is that you have a lot more time to hunt for your luggage when you arrive.

77. The potentate of an Eastern kingdom came to New York and checked into the biggest suite of the fanciest hotel. The potentate spoke no English. As he worked with an interpreter on a speech, a noise from the other room diverted their attention. Before they could make a move, two masked bandits stormed in, guns in their hands. They demanded the potentate's famous jewels. The interpreter translated their demands. In his native tongue, the potentate told the bandits to go to hell. "He had no jewels," one of the bandits said. "We know he has jewels. We're

going to count to three. If we don't get the jewels, we're going to shoot him!"

The interpreter conveyed the message to the potentate, who said in his own language, "I don't want to die. Tell them that the jewels are hidden in the chandelier in the outer room." The interpreter said to the bandits, "He said he'd rather die than tell you where the jewels are!"

78. Never buy a used car if the radio buttons are all on hard rock stations.

79. Traveling out of state recently, a fellow reports, he had a truly awful meal at the restaurant of the motel where he spent the night. The next morning as he was leaving, he saw a garbage truck pull in. "Hold on a minute," his wife told him. "I want to see if they're picking up or delivering."

80. The story making the rounds in London concerns the battle over the Falkland Islands: Prime Minister Margaret Thatcher was visited by her military chief on his return from the war zone and he told her, "I have good news and bad news for you."

"The good new first, please."

"I can give you every assurance that we have sunk every Argentine ship."

"And the bad news?"

"They were all insured by Lloyd's of London!"

81. Just bought a car with a $500 rebate. The check is OK, but the car keeps bouncing.

82. It was so dry until recently in Houston, a friend of mine washed his pickup truck three times trying to get it to rain.

83. I think all auto mechanics go to the same school: Shaft U. Let's face it. To you it may be a motor that's knocking—to a mechanic, it's opportunity.

84. No one ever sells a used car because it runs too well.

85. The hotel said they had cable. They do. It's in the elevator shaft.

86. Lil does all the driving. All I have to do is sit there and hold the steering wheel.

87. I had a car phone, but I got rid of it. I got tired of going out to the garage every time it rang.

88. I solved the parking problem. I bought a parked car.

89. Lil complained about a man she met, "From the first minute he screamed and cursed."
    "How did you meet him?"
    "I hit him with the car."

90. Lil said she would rather go with me than kiss me good-bye.

91. Lil said she must have water in the carburetor. I asked where it was. She said, "In the bayou."

92. Lil said she had a wreck but not to worry because it was the old car. I asked, "What did you hit?" She said, "The new car."

93. When the weather channel warns of hazardous driving on the road, you know Lil is out there someplace.

94. Lil said, "I hit a tree but it's not my fault. I honked."

95. To her double-parking means on top of another car.

96. "How did you get the car in the living room?" She said, "I turned left in the kitchen."

97. "She drives like lightning."
    "You mean fast?"
    "No. She hits trees."

98. Lil wanted a mink coat, I wanted a new car We compromised—we bought the mink coat, but we keep it in the garage.

99. Lil dented the fender of a parked car. She filed a report. One question on the report was, "What could the operator of the other vehicle have done to avoid the accident?" She wrote, "Park somewhere else."

100. My wife wanted a foreign convertible, so I bought her a rickshaw.

101. My wife is very good about vacations. Each year she says, "We'll go anywhere you'd like." Then she hands me a list of places I'd like.

102. I've stayed in more hotel rooms than the Gideon Bible.

103. All the auto mechanics now have diplomas and certificates on the walls. My mechanic majored in estimates with minors in head shaking and uh-ohs.

104. A do good organization is now training hookers to become auto mechanics because it's such a logical transition. Same position, same prices, same results.

105. Remember when a supercharger was part of the car? Now it's the guy who makes out the bill.

106. I firmly believe if God had wanted us to have airline seating, he wouldn't have given us knees.

107. It isn't easy buying a tank. Ever try kicking a tread?

108. If you want to irritate a stewardess, when she tells you to put your seat in an upright position, stand on your head.

109. I don't want to complain about the difference between coach and first-class fares, but I once flew first class, and when the stewardess came over, I whispered something in her ear. She just smiled and said, "You got that when you bought the ticket."

110. My auto mechanic gets upset when he watches the Mr. Goodwrench commercial. He doesn't understand why Mr. Goodwrench is always wiping his hands on a rag when there are perfectly good seat covers right in front of him.

111. I have a request from the car parker. Would the owner of the convertible with the pink fenders, tutti-frutti body, feather boa hood ornament, and gold satin seat covers please report to the parking lot. There's nothing wrong. He just wants to see what you look like.

112. Hotels really prepared for this convention. The Gideon Bibles are on a chain. Lil doesn't get it.

113. They say now garbage can be made into gasoline. Why not? It's already being made into TV shows, movies, and books.

114. Auto complaint: "Every time I go uphill, it sounds like castanets. What should I do?" The dealer said, "Hum Malaguena."

115. The problem with self-service is that it's always so bad.

116. What would add another interesting dimension to the Mideast problem? If somebody invented a car that ran on chicken soup.

117. Man had his car painted red on one side and yellow on the other. When he had an accident, the witnesses contradicted each other.

118. An experienced car buyer always picks a dealer within walking distance of home.

119. New cars are coming out with windshield wipers that won't hold parking tickets.

120. Pilot of the jetliner, who forgot to turn off the intercom, said, "All I need is a cup of hot coffee and a beautiful blonde. The stewardess heard the intercom and rushed forward to tell the crew. A little old lady said, "No need to hurry, dearie. He's got to have his coffee first."

121. Aviation instructor re: parachutes: "And in conclusion, if it doesn't open that's what's called jumping to a conclusion."

122. There's no courtesy on the freeways today. One man put his arm out the window to signal a lane change and somebody stole his watch.

123. Travel is very educational I can now say Kaopectate in seven different languages. (Bob Hope)

124. I travel a lot, but I only go to about half as many places as my luggage.

125. A tourist in DC asked, "Pardon me, could you tell me which side the State Department is on?" Washingtonian said, "Ours, I think."

126. I know a spinster who went on a world cruise. I don't know what she did, but every time she sees a label marked Made in Japan, she just smiles.

127. The last car I bought came with a tow truck.

128. In the hotel, we had a double bed with bath. Too bad they were in separate buildings.

129. Show me an airline stewardess and I will show you a "plane Jane."

130. Spaceman gets out of his flying saucer, goes up to a hippie on Times Square, and said, "We are from Mars." The cat looked at him and said, "Man, I dig your candy bars the most."

131. Lil and I never argue—we can't hear each other.

132. Lil doesn't like being called a housewife. She prefers "domestic goddess."

133. Lil and I were driving down lover's lane in the woods and in silence when Lil said, "Mit dear, can you drive with one hand?" I said, "Yes, my sweet" in ecstasy of anticipation. "Then," said my lovely Lil, "you better wipe your nose."

134. An old school teacher dreamed of her retirement. She had never gotten married. She had several opportunities, but she was so very dedicated to her children she always postponed it. The day finally came for her to take a cruise. She wanted to take a diary to record this wonderful trip. She wrote, "Monday: I was so thrilled because the captain of the ship asked me to dine at his table. Tuesday: Today I spent most of the day on the bridge with the captain. Wednesday: Today the captain made some indecent demands of me unbefitting those of a captain and a gentleman. Thursday: The captain said if I did not submit to his demands he would sink the ship. Friday: Today I saved 1,200 lives, two times as a matter of fact."

135. I went to Chicago for a one-day trip—not really long enough to warrant taking Lil. When I returned she told me to go to the backyard to see her new hobby. When I got there she had a chicken coop with five hens and two roosters. I asked, "Is that your hobby?" She said it was and I said, "Lil, you were born on a farm. You know it doesn't take two

roosters to service five hens" She said, "Well, it does when one of them is gone half the time."

136. Lil called and said she had good news and bad news about the car. I asked her what it was. She said, "The airbag works."

137. Personally I am not worried about terrorism. I've been married for fifty-three years.

138. Stewardess to Muhammad Ali: "Mr. Ali, please fasten your seat belt." Ali: "Superman don't need no seat belt." Stewardess: "Superman don't need no plane either."

139. If there were no one to watch them drive how many people would drive a Mercedes?

140. France is the only country where the money falls apart and you can't tear the toilet paper. (Billy Wilder)

141. When we have gasohol, we will have the choice of regular or whole wheat.

142. Airline travel is hours of boredom interrupted by moments of stark terror.

143. It would have helped a lot if the pioneers would have located cities closer to the airports.

144. The ultimate solution to airline hijacking—everyone fly naked.

145. Tourist: What's that statue?
Guide: That's St. Francis of Assisi.
Tourist: How nice the gays have their own patron saint.

146. I've never understood those hotels that feature a mirror on the ceiling over the bed. I mean who's going to shave in bed?

147. A man was flying a no-frills airline and beckoned the beautiful stewardess, leaned over, and whispered something in her ear. She smiled and said, "You got that when you flew this airline."

148. DELTA—Don't Ever Leave the Airport
Three Classes—first class, coach, and charred beyond recognition, 20 percent discount if you submit your dental records. Phone 911

149. Man wrote letter to Houston Transit Company: "I've been riding your bus for two years, and the service gets worse every day I think your service is worse than that enjoyed one thousand years ago."

   Houston Transit wrote back: "You must be somewhat confused in your history. The only transportation offered one thousand years ago was by foot."

   The man wrote back: "You are the one confused about history. In the Bible—book of David verse 9 it says, 'Aaron rode into town on his ass.' That gentlemen is something I have not been able to do for the past year."

150. A passenger in a plane saw a parachutist pass by. "Going to join me?" yelled the parachutist.' "No thanks, I'm very happy where I am." "Just as you like," said the parachutist. "I'm the pilot."

151. A man walked up to the ticket agent and asked for a ticket to the moon.
"Sorry, sir, all flights are cancelled."
"Bad weather?"
"No, the moon is full right now."

152. I can't seem to get my car started. If you will go up there and give it a try, I'll sit here and blow the horn for you.

153. The blue book value of my car goes up and down depending upon how much gas is in it.

154. Traveling is very educational. I can mow say "Kaopectate" in seven different languages.

155. Nice hotel. They said they had cable, and they do. It's in the elevator shaft.

156. Q. Why do Triumphs have such big lights?
A. To light up the tow ropes.

157. I couldn't repair your brakes, so I made your horn louder.

158. Little boy: Dad, I wish you would let Mommy drive. It is more exciting.

159. Salesman: You pay a small deposit, then you make no more payments for six months.
Customer: Who told you about us?

160. There are certain things you should be wary of when buying a used car. For instance, if the hood release is worn out.

161. Pilot: Pilot to tower, pilot to tower. I'm three hundred miles from land, six hundred feet high and running out of gas. Please instruct, over.
      Tower: Tower to pilot, tower to pilot repeat after me. Our Father who art in heaven.

162. Two cowboys came upon an Indian lying on his stomach and his ear to the ground. "Look," said one cowboy, "he's listening to the ground and can hear things for miles away in any direction." The Indian looked up and said, "Covered wagon about two miles away. Have two horses, one brown one white. Man, woman, child, household effects in wagon." "Incredible," said the cowboy. "This Indian knows how far away, how many horses, what color they are, who's in the wagon, and what's in the wagon. Amazing." The Indian looks up and says, "Ran over me about an hour ago."

163. Re: Flying in Small Aircraft on Small Airlines

    a.   There was a luggage rack on the roof and a big screen on the front windshield.
    b.   The aviator wore a scarf and goggles.
    c.   There was no food service, but they did request that we each bring a covered dish.
    d.   They didn't have a movie, but the pilot put on a puppet show and showed slides of his vacation.
    e.   It was really a no-frills flight. They had a coin-operated oxygen mask.
    f.   We did a little crop dusting on the way.
    g.   The plane made four stops en route. Three of them were to ask for directions.
    h.   A sign at the entrance read, "Please have exact change ready."

164. A journey of a thousand miles begins with a single step. It is the one you take when you go back to see if you really did turn off the lights.

165. "Dad, how long does it take to get from New York to Boston?"
Father: "About four hours."
Son: "How long from Boston to New York?"
Father: "The same. You ought to know that."
Son: "Well, it's not the same from Thanksgiving to Christmas as it is from Christmas to Thanksgiving."

WOMAN/WIFE

1. Old man got married. His buddy said, "I'll bet you got married 'cause she's a rich widow."
   "Nope."
   "Well, I'll bet it's because she's a great cook."
   "Nope."
   "Then she probably gives you lots of romancing."
   "Nope."
   "Well, she's gotta be a beauty."
   "Nope."
   "Well, why did you marry her?"
   "'Cause she can drive at night."

2. If homosexuality were normal, God would have created Adam and Bruce. (Anita Bryant)

3. Now every Sunday I visit her grave with that tender inscription upon the headstone: "She Was Just a Communist's Daughter, but Everyone Got His Share."

4. Soon the entrancement of the honeymoon began to wear off and we were soon living what's called a football romance. We both were waiting for the other to kick off.

5. This is the only girl who puts makeup on with a trowel.

6. I won't say the dresses are getting shorter, but I know a kid who had to get elevator shoes just to hide behind his mother's skirt.

7. I once took her to dinner, and I'll never forget it. It's the first time I ever saw a vacuum cleaner with teeth.

8. Yes, I'll never forget the day we were playing checkers, and I tried to jump her.

9. Her eyes were bright and shining, her skin was soft as rain.
She stole my heart, she stole my soul, plus wallet, watch, and chain.

10. First nagging wife put down: "You could have done with a smaller fig leaf."

11. She once took a four-year course in ugliness and finished it in two years.

12. She had a face only Rand McNally could love.

13. There was only one thing smaller than her feet—her shoes.

14. But what eyes she had! They came right down to the bridge of her nose, and when they got to the bridge, they crossed.

15. It was love at second sight. The first time I didn't know she had money.

16. Matrimony is the process whereby love ripens into vengeance.

17. A good home must be made—not bought.

18. But she's got a good job in an office now. Where it said Experience on the application blank, she just put down: "Oh boy!"

19. There is a new perfume that drives women crazy. It smells like credit cards.

20. The fundamental reason that women do not achieve so greatly as men do is that women have no wives.

21. Geraldo Rivera in his book claims to have slept with so many women that he's been named an honorary TV evangelist.

22. I thought it was love at first sight, but now I realize it was just a passing fanny.

23. Mr. Agony: "Two weeks ago my best friend quit his job, drew all his money out of the bank, sold his house, and ran away with my wife. Mr. Agony—here's my problem—should I have warned him?

24. I just discovered a wonderful way to save money. Marry your second wife first.

25. Women are like seagulls. It doesn't pay to look up to them.

26. I'll never forget Easter Egg, the love of my life. I call her Easter Egg because she was painted on the outside and hardboiled on the inside.

27. They say a man had never kissed her good night. Of course not! They never left till morning.

28. I was telling my wife the other day: "You got to look on the bright side of things, honey. Remember all that gold jewelry I gave you for Christmas? Be thankful it turned green in time for St. Patrick's Day.

29. She's the original overnight bag.

30. She's been on more laps than a napkin.

31. The only thing she ever gives is in.

32. She wore that gown in a beauty contest. She didn't win but she showed.

33. The only thing she ever read was an eye—chart.

34. I call her Cold because she's so easy to catch.

35. She's a very educated girl. She can say yes in twenty-three languages.

36. I used to call her Turkey because she was stuffed in all the right places.

37. My mother-in-law just got a job driving a taxi. Doing pretty good at it. Knocks down about sixty a week.

38. I have to meet my mother-in-law today. She's coming in on the three o'clock broom.

39. It was one of those modern marriages. She kept everything but her husband.

40. She has startling red lips and a nose to match.

41. I call her Geranium because she's usually potted. 42. Dumb? She thinks VAT 69 is the pope's phone number.

43. She waves her tail so much everybody calls her Fido.

44. How do you tell the ladies from the men now that they are both wearing pants? The one listening is the man. 45. Woman begins by resisting man's advances and ends by blocking his retreat. 46. Marriage is just like a raffle only sometimes you win in a raffle.

47. Mae West: "When given the choice of two evils I always take the one I never tried before."

48. My wife has a wonderful way of making long stories short. She interrupts.

49. Love is like life insurance—the older you get, the more it costs.

50. Love is the only game that is not called on account of darkness.

51. Her husband had laryngitis for three weeks, and she didn't know it.

52. They call her Flow because she talks in a steady stream.

53. She approaches every problem with an open mouth.

54. Someone should put a sign on her mouth saying, "Open Twenty-four hours."

55. He got married because being single took the fun out of cheating.

56. What do you think of sex on television? Well, you've got to watch out for those antennas—a middle-aged man could hurt his back.

57. Judge: "You say it was an accident that you shot your wife?" Man: "Certainly was. She stepped in front of my mother-in-law just as I pulled the trigger."

58. An author once dedicated one of his books to his wife and daughter thusly: "To my wife and daughter, without whose unfailing help and advice, this book could have been written in half the time."

59. Marriage teaches you such important virtues as commitment, loyalty, dedication, perseverance, meekness, and many other things you wouldn't need if you had stayed single.

60. The most happy marriage I can picture would be the union of a deaf man to a blind woman.

61. I n the heat of an argument, a wife exclaims to her husband, "This just goes to prove that women are smarter than men!" Her husband stared at her for a moment and replied, "You're right, dear, I married you and you married me."

62. Marriage is a journey toward an unknown destination: the discovery that people must share not only what they don't know about each other, but what they don't know about themselves.

63. Of course, if you're on your honeymoon, things like rain really don't matter. The classic story is about a couple in a bridal suite on the very first morning of their honeymoon. He goes over to the window, pulls at the shade cord, the shade goes up, he sees that it's raining and he goes back to bed. On the second morning, he goes over to the window, pulls at the shade cord, the shade goes up, he see that its raining, and he goes back to bed. On the third, fourth, fifth, and sixth mornings, he also goes over to the window, pulls at the shade cord, the shade goes up, he sees that it's still raining, and he goes back to bed. On the seventh morning, he goes over to the window, pulls at the shade cord, the shade goes up—and he goes with it.

64. Seeing several familiar faces here reminds me of the man who, while making love, asked, "Am I the first man you ever loved?" She thought for a minute and replied, "You could be, your face is familiar."

65. I'd like to explain away this cast and also make a public service announcement. If there are any people in the audience who just bought the book *The Joy of Sex*, there is a misprint on page 205—it may break your arm, but it's worth it.

66. A retired manufacturer, who took up oil painting as a hobby, phoned his secretary and asked her to pose for him in the nude. "Positively not!" she retorted. "I'm not a model." "That's all right," he said. "I'm not an artist.

67. "Excuse me, madame. This is the hat in my hands, that's the box you're trying on."

68. She was married to him for forty years, and for forty years he didn't do a lick of work. Then he died. She had him cremated, took the ashes home, and put them in an hourglass. "Now, you worthless bum," she muttered, "at last you're going to work."

69. Wives are not like fishing buffs. They brag about the ones that got away and complain about the one they caught.

70. This chick's been married so many times, they don't play "Here Comes the Bride"—they play "I Love a Parade."

71. Have you noticed that women are a lot more concerned with their appearance before they get married? In merchandising there's a name for this—bait and switch!

72. Just got my first garden catalog of the year, and it's really fascinating. Did you know they had elephant fertilizer—if you want to grow trees with big trunks.

73. Then came that fateful day when mother let the maid go 'cause Father wouldn't.

74. I really don't pay much attention to gardening. You can tell. Up until last week, I thought Peat Moss was one of our neighbors.

75. Outside, on their lawn, they placed a sign that read, "Under Destruction."

76. This is the time of year when you sit in the backyard and you hear such eerie conversations from over the fence. Like one voice saying, "Where should I put the ashes from the charcoal grill?" And another voice saying, "Put them in the urn with Uncle Charlie. He always did like company."

77. If medical science has done so much to add years to our lives, how come you never meet a woman who's past forty?

78. I wonder if Dr. Ruth's husband ever asks, "Just a minute, Ruth, where did you learn all this stuff?"

79. Prescription for a happy marriage: Live each day as if it were your last and each night as if it were your first.

80. Phyllis Diller told me her man asked for her finger measurements. "I thought he was going to buy me a diamond ring, but he gave me a bowling ball."

81. In response to a whim, a man was married in a lion cage. Years later, a man asked him, "Did it feel exciting?" first man said, "It did then, it wouldn't now."

82. At a famous resort, the young man met a young lady, and they got along famously. And prior to what he hoped would be a heated, passionate encounter, she asked, "Have you ever had herpes?" The guy said, "No, of course not." She said, "Gee, that's swell. I wouldn't want to get it again."

83. The pretty girl had make it perfectly clear to the young man that she was willing to marry him, but he had been unable to get the approval of her domineering mother. "You see," the girl explained, "Mother thinks you're effeminate." "Well," the young man sighed, "compared to her, I probably am."

84. She's the original good time that was had by all.

85. Among her other faults, a fellow declares, his ex-wife was a terrible housekeeper. "The only time that woman used a broom," he declared, "was when she flew somewhere."

86. One man to another, "When it comes to using cosmetics, women are shrewd. My daughter uses them to improve on Mother Nature whereas my wife uses them to fool Father Time."

87. I used to like sex. Now I love food. I've even mounted a mirror over my dining room table."

88. A prominent fellow at the courthouse said that he came from such a large family that he was married before he ever slept alone.

89. "Last week I advertised in the paper for a husband," said the spinster, "and I got a lot of replies. They all said, 'You can have mine.'"

90. A father complaining about his daughter's boyfriend. "He's the kind of guy that, when you look at him, you wonder if there were any other survivors."

91. Until now, I had repressed any bad feelings for Donald and Ivana Trump on the theory their marriage had one redeeming social virtue. By choosing each other, they had saved two other people.

92. Many of us have watched TV grow from infancy to adultery.

93. Instead of reading the newspaper at the kitchen table, try talking to your wife. You might learn a few things, like your kids have grown up and moved out.

94. He bought his wife a cookbook. It didn't do much good. Her cooking is so bad—she serves milk of magnesia as an after-dinner drink.

95. "I sent a wedding gift," said friend to friend. "I sent a set of West Virginia matched crystal." "What's that?" the other said. "Six empty jars of the same kind of jelly," he replied

96. A lady friend confessed, "I don't understand bondage." He assured her, "It's easy once you learn the ropes."

97. A henpecked friend says he's never done anything behind his wife's back except zip her up.

98. A rich, crotchety, and disagreeable Charleston old lady walked into an art gallery determined to dislike anything she saw. The first gold frame she encountered obviously gave her a shock: "How ugly and grotesque," she told the director who was accompanying her. "Is this what is known as modern art?" "No, ma'am," said the director, "that's a mirror."

99. "It says here that paying attention to one's mate is a sign of true love," Lil said. "What?" asked Mit.

100. Know what you call a woman who knows where her husband is twenty-four hours a day? A widow.

101. When asked why she never married, an old lady used to say, "It takes a mighty fine husband to be better than none."

102. Stealing a kiss may be petty larceny, but sometimes it's grand.

103. Wife to friend, "Bill doesn't go to porno movies. He said it upsets him to see someone having more fun in one hour than he's had in a lifetime."

104. Bumper sticker re: Clinton—"If his private life doesn't matter, let him date your daughter."

105. Plumbers sign—"You don't have to sleep with that drip tonight."

106. He was out with a different kind of girl the other night. She wasn't at all physical. In fact, if her mind didn't wander, she wouldn't get any exercise at all.

107. The clothes Phyllis Diller's fictional mother-in-law wears "come in three sizes: fat, jumbo, and 'my god, it's moving toward us!'" (That's the same mother-in-law who blew her nose downtown, signaling a construction crew to break for lunch.)

108. Plastic surgeons can do amazing things these days. A friend married his former wife a second time and didn't even know it until he went downstairs to breakfast and recognized his old mother-in-law.

109. It's hard to realize that the woman wearing a bikini is the same one who would be embarrassed if her slip showed.

110. Widows are divided into two classes—the bereaved and the relieved.

111. Husband to wife: "I want our kids to have all the things I never had, but first I want to have all the things I never had."

112. His mother-in-law is widowed, a fellow tells me, and she spends a lot of her time traveling around visiting old friends who live in various parts of the country. But she never spends more than three days in one place. He asked her why she didn't stay longer sometimes. "No," she told him. "Three days is entirely long enough to have to be nicer than you actually are."

113. Then we have the old wives' tale that if your palm itches you may soon get something. The young wives' tale is if you itch all over you probably already have it.

114. The fashion world is going way out this year. One clever Seventh Avenue dress shop designer is doing big business with a line of teenage maternity fashions . . . in school colors.

115. Joan Rivers said, "It's been so long since I had sex, I forget which one gets tied up."

116. Then there was the guy who said marriage was like a cafeteria. You pick out something and pay for it down the line.

117. Then there was the girl who was going to have her face lifted, but she didn't have the jack.

118. Never ask a waitress if she has chicken breasts or frog legs.

119. The man had been invited to go on a cruise by a beautiful young woman. Anticipating nights filled with romance, the man went to a drugstore and asked for a package of contraceptives. Then because he suffered from seasickness, he also requested a bottle of Dramamine tablets. The druggist looked at him curiously and, when he handed him his purchases, said, "Can I ask you a question?" "What is it?" asked the man. "If it makes you nauseous," said the druggist, "why do you do it?"

120. The cruise ship reached warm Jamaican waters, and it was the night when dinner meant formal dress. At one table, a man noticed the woman next to him was wearing a diamond pendant. It was just about the biggest diamond he had ever seen. "I hope you don't mind my saying so, but that diamond is beautiful," he said. She smiled pleasantly.

"I don't mind at all and thank you," she said. "It's the Klopman Diamond." The guy looked puzzled. "I've heard of the Hope diamond and some others," he said, "but the Klopman is a new one to me." The lady explained the Klopman diamond was much like the Hope diamond, though somewhat smaller. However, the cuts were identical, and it was equal in quality. The Klopman even came with a curse, the same as the Hope diamond." "That's astonishing, and it comes with a curse," the man said. The woman nodded. "If you'll forgive my curiosity, what kind of a curse?" he asked. "Mr. Klopman," she said.

121. So far the most memorable response anyone has heard from Dr. Ruth is, "You *what?*"

122. Three well-bred Englishmen, one of them heard of hearing, were sipping drinks slowly in the outer bar of a fine London restaurant as they waited for their dinner reservation to be honored. In walked two middle-aged Americans who had also made reservations. The Americans ordered a drink. As they sopped, one started to reminisce about his war days near Oxford. He started to tell about an English girl named Guineivere, saying, "She had beautiful red hair and a little beauty mark right under her left eye. And she was wild. She loved to tumble all day. They had this big manor house, and she used to sneak me into her bedroom, and, wow, what we did under that canopy! I mean, she would swing from the chandelier and jump down right on me." He paused to take a drink. The hearing Englishmen couldn't avoid his excited description and had started to listen. The deaf Englishman knew he was missing something. He asked impatiently, "What did he say?" One of them spoke directly into his ear. "He knows Mother!"

123. One marriage out of three ends in divorce. The other two fight it out to the bitter end!

124. Winston Churchill was irrepressible. At a dinner he asked his American hostess, "May I have a breast?" She explained that in America one asked either for white meat or dark meat. The next day Churchill sent her an

orchid with this note, "I would be most obliged if you would pin this on your white meat."

125. Joe Blow, who just turned fifty, reporting gloomily that his libido is already down 50 percent: "You know that girl in my office with the fantastic set of hooters? Well, now I'm only interested in one."

126. Sex before marriage isn't bad unless it interferes with the ceremony.

127. On her first day out of bed, the new mother put on her bathrobe and walked down the hospital corridor, to the public telephone books. She was thumbing through on of the directories when her doctor happened by. "And what are you doing out here?" he asked. "I'm looking through the phone book to find a nice name for my baby," she said."
   "You don't have to do that. The hospital supplies a little booklet to all new mothers listing every first name you could possibly think of." "You don't understand," she confided. "The baby already has a first name."

128. Some modern brides still follow tradition. One such read it was bad luck to see the groom the morning of the wedding . . . so she threw him out of their apartment the night before.

129. I'm strictly for marriage. The old-fashion couple used to stay married. Nowadays, the old-fashion couple is the one that bothers to get married. My neighbor's daughter asked her dad what does a woman do when she loses interest in sex. He replied, "She gets married."

130. A mother sent a letter to her son in college. "We still love you, son." It was signed, "Love, Mom and Dad," and the Dad was crossed out.

131. "Why are you bringing my daughter home at six in the morning?" Young man: "I gotta go to work at seven."

132. Guy said his wife was a terrible housekeeper—the only time she used a broom was to fly somewhere.

133. Young man had led a sheltered life got married. On his honeymoon night, his bride reached down and touched him. He turned his head and coughed.

134. He doesn't do well with the ladies, so he decided to be more aggressive. He saw a girl in a hotel bar. He smiled, winked, and dropped his room key in her purse. For the sake of appearance, he waited an hour then went back up to his room and all his luggage was gone.

135. A young couple were going across country on their honeymoon. The wife, in casual clothes, looked even younger than her husband. The motel clerk told them there was only one room available with a double bed. Trying to appear nonchalant, the young husband turned to his wife and asked, "Will that be alright?" Being in a devilish mood, she replied meekly, "Anything you say is alright with me, mister." 136. There are so many mixed marriages on TV now they're working on one between Flipper and Lassie.

137. Did you hear about my wife? She ran off with my best friend. Buddy: "I thought I was your best friend." Husband: "Not anymore."

138. If you want to read about love and marriage, today you have to buy two separate books.

139. If her lips are hot and she trembles in your arms, you had better forget her—she probably has malaria.

140. She is in her early flirties.

141. The marriage between an old farmer and his young wife wasn't going too well, so the old man sought the advice of his doctor. The doctor said, "Show her more affection, a kiss, a hug several times a day will keep reminding her of your love." Farmer said, "It won't work. When I'm plowing in the field and I get the urge, it takes me too long to get back to the house." "Okay," said the doctor, "she's younger than you are, so take a shotgun with you and fire it when you feel romantic. She won't mind. She'll come out to see you. A few months later the doctor saw the old man at church and asked if the plan had worked. The farmer said, "For the first few days it was wonderful, but then hunting season started, and I haven't seen her since."

142. Never marry for money. You can borrow it cheaper.

143. I hear AT&T may merge with *Playboy*. Then we could reach out and really touch something worthwhile.

144. This fellow said he and his wife had a social engagement, and he wasn't sure of its exact nature. "Is this a sit-down dinner or what?" he wanted to know. "Oh no," said the wife. "It's a reception—we'll just drop in and talk to some people, eat a few canapes, have a drink, and leave." "I see," said the husband. "In other words, it's one of those gabble, gobble, gulp, and git affairs."

145. If marriages ever are outlawed, only outlaws will have in-laws.

ADVICE, PHILOSOPHY AND WIT—B

369. If you give what you do not need, it isn't giving. (Mother Teresa)

370. Be thankful we're not getting all the government we're paying for. (W. Rogers.)

371. Form good habits. They are as hard to break as bad ones.

372. Happiness is in the pursuit. (Charles Jarvis)

373. Did you ever get the feeling you were walking up a gangplank and there was no ship?

374. No person was ever honored for what he received. Honor has been the reward for what he gave. (Calvin Coolidge)

375. A youth was questioning a lonely old man. "What is life's heaviest burden?" he asked. The old fellow answered sadly, "To have nothing to carry."

376. The only thing wrong with doing nothing is that you never know when you're finished.

377. Remember, no one can make you feel inferior without your consent. (E. Roosevelt)

378. What you have inherited from your fathers, earn over again for yourselves, or it will not be yours. (J. Wolfgang von Goethe)

379. The only thing of value we can give to our children is what *we are*, not what *we have*.

380. "I must do something" will always solve more problems than "Something must be done."

381. He who knows not and knows that he knows not is a fool. Avoid him. He who knows not and knows not that he knows not is ignorant. Teach him. He who knows and knows not that he knows is asleep. Waken him. But he who knows and knows that he knows is a wise man. Follow him. He who knows not whether he knows or knows not anything at all is a politician. Do not trust him. (James P. Hogan)

382. There are two times in a man's life when he should not speculate: when he can't afford it and when he can. (Mark Twain)

383. We judge ourselves by what we think we are capable of doing while others judge us by what we have already done. (H. W. Longfellow)

384. Laws are like cobwebs, which catch small flies but let wasps and hornets break through. (Jonathan Swift)

385. Man is an able creature, but he has made over thirty-five million laws and hasn't yet improved on the Ten Commandments. (Jacob Braude)

386. This is a court of law, young man, not a court of justice. (O. W. Holmes)

387. You cannot be a leader and expect other people to follow you unless you know how to follow too. (Sam Rayburn)

388. A person who plays follow the leader can never finish better than second. Lead, follow, or get out of the way. (Ted Turner)

389. Leadership is not bestowed—it is yours as long as it is continuously earned.

390. A person who can't lead and won't follow makes a dandy roadblock.

391. All that a man gets by lying is that he is not believed when he speaks the truth.

392. No man has a good enough memory to make a successful liar. (A. Lincoln)

393. Life is what happens to you while you're busy making other plans. (John Lennon)

394. Love is not blind; it sees more, not less. But because it sees more, it is willing to see less.

395. You can't hope to be lucky. You have to prepare to be lucky.

396. The harder you work, the luckier you get. (Gary Player)

397. There is no one luckier than he who thinks himself so. (German Proverb)

398. There is no limit to what can be accomplished if it doesn't matter who gets the credit.

399. Anyone can hold the helm when the sea is calm. (P. Syrus)

400. Today's philosophy—if it ain't tied down take it. If it is tied down, take the rope too.

401. Never tell people how to do things. Tell them what to do and let them surprise you with their ingenuity. (Gen. George Patton)

402. Marriage resembles a pair of scissors, so joined that they cannot be separated, often moving in opposite directions, yet always punishing anyone who comes between them. (Rev. Sydney Smith)

403. Nothing flatters a man as much as the happiness of his wife; he is always proud of himself as the source of it. (Samuel Johnson)

404. A successful marriage requires falling in love many times, always with the same person.

405. Marriage is a journey toward an unknown destination: The discovery that people must share not only what they don't know about each other, but what they don't know about themselves.

406. Maturity is the ability to do a job whether or not you are supervised to carry money without spending it and bear an injustice without wanting to get even. (Ann Landers)

407. Maturity begins when we're content to feel we are right about something, without feeling the necessity to prove someone else wrong.

408. The first step in maturity is when you stop blaming others for your problems.

409. "The young think they will live forever, the old fear they will die at any moment."

410. What you do speaks so loudly that I cannot hear what you say.

411. To disagree, one does not have to be disagreeable. (Barry Goldwater)

412. There are a thousand hacking at the branches of evil to one who is striking at the root. (Henry D. Thoreau)

413. Show me a man who doesn't make mistakes and I'll show you a man who doesn't do anything. (Theodore Roosevelt)

414. The greatest mistake you can make in life is to be continually fearing you will make one.

415. An error doesn't become a mistake until you refuse to correct it.

416. Don't ever be afraid to admit you were wrong. It's like saying you are wiser today than you were yesterday.

417. A man who has committed a mistake and doesn't correct it is committing another mistake. (Confucius)

418. If money is your hope for independence, you will never have it. The only real security that a man can have in this world is a reserve of knowledge, experience, and ability. (Henry Ford)

419. Morals consist of political morals, commercial morals, ecclesiastical morals, and morals. (Mark Twain)

420. The quality of a person's life is in direct proportion to their commitment to excellence, regardless of their chosen field of endeavor. (V. Lombardi)

421. It takes both the sun and the rain to make a rainbow.

422. Pessimist: One who, when he has the choice of two evils, chooses both. (Oscar Wilde)

423. A pessimist is someone who can look at the land of milk and honey and see only calories and cholesterol.

424. An idealist is one who, on noticing that a rose smells better than a cabbage, concludes that it will also make better soup. (H.L. Mencken)

425. By the time we realize our parents were right, we have children who think we're wrong.

426. There are only two lasting bequests we can hope to give to our children. One is roots, the other, wings. (Hodding Carter)

427. The first half of our lives is ruined by our parents and the second half by our children. (Clarence Darrow)

428. The pursuit of excellence is gratifying and healthy; the pursuit of perfection is frustrating, neurotic, and a terrible waste of time.

429. In the memo field of all your checks write "For sexual favors."

430. A compromise is an arrangement whereby people who can't get what they want make sure nobody else does either.

431. Worry is like a rocking chair . . . it gives you something to do but doesn't get you anywhere.

432. No matter how busy you are, you're never too busy to stop and talk about how busy you are.

433. Problems are only opportunities in disguise.

434. If you can't have what you want, change your mind.

435. What you are is more important than what you've got.

435. If you're over the hill, why not enjoy the view?

436. There are only three types of people: those who make things happen, those who watch things happen, and those who say, "What happened?"

437. The more we count the blessings we have, the less we crave the luxuries we haven't.

438. Tell me and I'll forget, teach me and I'll remember, involve me and I'll learn.

439. It's better to sleep on what you intend to do than stay awake all night over what you did!

440. That which you cannot give away, you do not possess. It possesses you.

441. A people that values its privileges above its principles soon loses both. (Dwight Eisenhower)

442. If all our misfortunes were laid in one common heap, whence everyone must take an equal portion, most people would be contented to take their own and depart. (Socrates)

443. Life's disappointments are only speed bumps. They are things you have to get over to enjoy the rest of the journey.

444. All progress is the result of change, but all change is not necessarily progress.

445. Experience is not what happens to a man. It is what a man does with what happens to him. (Aldus Huxley)

446. Lord, when we are wrong, make us willing to change. And when we are right make us easy to live with. (Peter Marshall)

447. In this era of rapid change, one thing remains constant: it's easier to pray for forgiveness than to resist temptation.

448. Santa Claus is the idol of every businessperson who has to make a schedule.

448. Everybody is ignorant, only on different subjects. (Will Rogers)

449. All the wonders you seek are within yourself. (Sir Thomas Browne)

450. No matter where you go you can't get away from yourself, so you'd better make yourself into somebody worthwhile.

451. To thine own self be true, and it must follow, as the night the day, thou canst not then be false to any man. (William Shakespeare)

452. When Hitler attacked the Jews, I was not a Jew; therefore, I was not concerned. And when Hitler attacked the Catholics, I was not a Catholic, and therefore, I was not concerned. And when Hitler attacked the unions and the industrialists, I was not a member of the unions and I was not concerned. Then Hitler attacked me and the Protestant church, and there was nobody left to be concerned. (Martin Niemoller)

453. It is better to be silent and be considered a fool than to speak and remove all doubt.

454. It is important to remember that figures and statistics can be misleading. We all know about the man who drowned trying to cross a lake whose average depth was three feet.

455. Success is getting what you want—happiness is wanting what you get.

456. Success is a journey, not a destination.

457. Try not to become a person of success but rather a person of value. (Albert Einstein)

458. If you tell the truth, you don't have to remember anything. (Mark Twain)

459. The most impressive evidence of tolerance is a golden wedding anniversary.

460. If you can't win, make the one ahead of you break the record.

461. Never mistake knowledge for wisdom. One helps you make a living; the other helps you make a life.

462. Don't be so concerned about making a living that you don't take time to make a life.

463. Take your work seriously but yourself lightly.

464. The biggest mistake you can make is to believe you are working for someone else.

465. Today's mighty oak is just yesterday's nut that held its ground

466. Early bird gets the worm, but the second mouse gets the cheese

467. What's the speed of dark?

468. Ambition is a poor excuse for not having enough sense to be lazy

469. Hard work pays off in the future. Laziness pays off now

470. Boycott shampoo! Demand the real poo!

471. The sooner you fall behind, the more time you'll have to catch up.

472. A clear conscience is usually a sign of a poor memory.

473. Ninety-nine percent of the lawyers give the rest a bad name.

474. Expecting the world to treat you fairly because you are a good person is a little like expecting the bull not to attack you because you are a vegetarian.

475. You become more believable if you preface your remarks with, "As Benjamin Franklin said—."

476. Only those who risk going too far will ever know how far they can go. (Unknown)

477. "I can't do it" never accomplished anything. "I will try" has performed wonders. (George P. Burnam) "I Will do it" has created miracles. (HM) And "I m sorry but I tried" is just an excuse for failure. (HMS and others)

478. Easy terms make it difficult to tell what you can't afford.

479. My neighbor says that instead of opening the door when opportunity knocks, his shiftless brother-in-law complains about the noise.

480. Why is it? Bad times pass slowly and good times quickly? Do people, when you are introduced to them, almost always ask "What do you do?" Hey is what you do more important than what you are? Why not ask instead "What are you anyway? or "What is the meaning of life or "Is there some butter in my hair?"

481. Give some people an inch, and right away they want to be a ruler.

482. If everything in life were logical, it would have been a man who rode sidesaddle.

483. The things I think about are a little strange. Did you ever get a cured ham and wonder what it had?

484. Do acupuncturists tell each other, "Jab well done"?

485. Sign on the side of a plumbing truck: a flush beats a full house.

486. Even Mason and Dixon had to draw the line somewhere.

487. For too many people, today's best labor-saving device is tomorrow.

488. The best way to knock a chip off a fellow's shoulder is by a pat on the back.

489. Talk about crazy, mixed-up things—how about straight pins? They're pointed in one direction and headed in another.

490. People are always asking unnecessary questions—you know what I mean?

491. How different words can convey the same message, i. e., "He was bent on seeing her" or "The sight of her doubled him up."

492. The meek shall inherit the earth . . . if that's okay with you!

493. Apologizing for a nasty remark is like trying to unscramble an egg.

494. Speaking of motivation, as some are these days, there's no need to look for a jumper cable if you don't have a battery.

495. It's not whom you know that matters, it's how your wife found out.

496. You can probably get along in life if you try to see yourself as others see you and not get mad about it.

497. One man to another, I've learned one thing . . . when someone begins by saying there's no need to panic, there usually is."

498. Friends come and go, but enemies accumulate.

499. He who fears to suffer suffers from fear.

500. If it were not for T-shirts and bumper stickers, he would have no philosophy at all.

501. Life is like a roll of toilet paper. The closer you come to the end, the faster it goes.

502. Boy that was fast. It is like reading *Playboy* magazine with your wife turning the pages.

503. A clean house is an indication of a misspent life.

504. The things that come to those that wait may be the things left by those who got there first.

505. Forbidden fruits create many jams.

506. Plan ahead. It wasn't raining when Noah built the ark.

507. If you speak badly of someone who speaks good of you, you are probably both wrong.

508. Never pay attention to a fat man whose lecture is on self-discipline.

509. Stress is not an event, but a perception of an event.

510. Failure is not an event, but a perception of an event.

511. Here is a deep thought. You want to talk philosophy? Tell me why Goofy can talk and Pluto can't.

512. It is a shock when geography students take an airplane and discover there are no pink or blue states.

513. I'm nobody's fool. Cheer up. Maybe someone will adopt you.

514. There is no one harder to shut up than the person who has nothing to say.

515. Easy terms make it hard to tell what you can't afford.

516. Deep thoughts:
Lead me not into temptation. I can find it myself.
Knowledge is power, if you know it about the right people.
Man learns in two ways—by doing and by being done.
Pound for pound, the amoeba is the most vicious animal on earth
Sex is hereditary; if your parents never had it, chances are you won't either.

517. A smile is an inexpensive way to improve your looks.

518. I can't choose how I feel, but I can choose what I do about it.

519. A good laugh is sunshine in the house. (Thackeray)

520. The early bird gets the worm, but no one says anything about the early worm.

521. He who angers you controls you.

522. Going to church does not make you a good person any more than going to McDonald's makes you a hamburger.

523. If things get worse, I might just have to break down and change my attitude.

524. Avoid suspicion: when you are walking through your neighbor's melon patch, don't bend over to tie your shoe. (Chinese)

525. Always cheat, always win. The only unfair fight is the one you lose.

526. Figures can be made to lie, but liars seldom figure.

527. Machines will never be human until they start blaming each other.

528. Andrew Carnegie was asked what he considered most important in industry: labor, capital, or brains. With a laugh Carnegie replied, "Which is the most important leg in a three-legged stool?"

529. There's not a lot of difference between losing your temper and killing somebody.

530. "I did my best" is an excuse for failure. You hire people to do a job, not their best.

531. Happiness is in the pursuit. It is the life we live every day—the journey—while success is the destination.

532. A person reveals his character by nothing so clearly as the jokes he resents. (Lichtenberg)

533. You will soon be going out into the world where you will see many things, which are wrong, and this will tend to discourage you. Nevertheless, always remember when the shadows are the darkest, the sun is the brightest, and it may be that because things are better, the evil side of life seems more distinct and easily seen.

534. From *Sunshine Magazine* in the '60s: Crime and subversion are formidable problems today because of a dangerous flaw in our nation's moral armor. Self-indulgence is practiced across the land: the principle of pleasure before duty. It is undermining those attributes of personal

responsibility and self-discipline essential to our nation's survival. It is creating citizens who reach maturity with a warped sense of values and an undeveloped conscience.

535. Temper gets you into trouble: Pride keeps you there.

536. It is difficult to believe that someone can differ from you and still be right.

537. Funny thing about trouble: it always starts out as being fun.

538. A closed mouth gathers no foot.

539. Some people fall for everything and stand for nothing.

540. Remember the teakettle: when it is up to its neck in hot water, it sings.

541. To be bitter is to waste precious moments of a life that is far short already.

542. As Lady Godiva's horse said, "Well, that's a new one on me."

543. Midas Law: Possession diminishes perception of value immediately.

544. Confucius: "No man who catches large fish goes home in alley."

545. Fortune teller: You will be poor and unhappy until you are fifty. "And then?" Fortune teller: Then you will get used to it.

546. It is not necessary to understand things in order to argue about them.

547. A person's reputation is precious, but a person's character is priceless.

548. Never write when you can talk and never talk when you can listen.

549. In some cultures, what I do would be considered normal.

550. Fatal isn't the worst outcome. Not living is the worst outcome.

551. There is no more terrible sight than ignorance in action.

552. Everyone needs a friend. They're the ones you use and take advantage of.

553. Never trust your wife's judgment. Look who she married.

554. I never tell a lie if the truth will do more damage.

555. Worry is like a rocking chair. It gives you something to do but doesn't get you anywhere.

556. The optimist sees an opportunity in every calamity. The pessimist sees a calamity in every opportunity.

557. Only God is in a position to look down on anyone.

558. Early to bed early to rise makes a man a father.

559. In taking revenge, a man is but even with his enemy; but in passing it over, he is superior.

560. Vice is its own reward: virtue is its own punishment.

561. If you want to get somewhere, you have to show up.

562. Somewhere, right now there is a committee deciding your future and you weren't invited.

563. Strange that all the people who hate the rich are the first ones to buy the lottery tickets

564. No one can't never get nothin' for nothin'—nowhere, no time, nohow.

565. All is well that ends.

566. There is no pleasure in having nothing to do; the fun is having lots to do and not doing it.

567. Marrying a woman for her beauty is like buying a house for its paint.

568. Save time—see it my way.

569. The only indispensible man this world has ever known was Adam.

570. The world is full of men making good livings but poor lives.

571. What is the best thing a girl can give a man who has everything? Encouragement.

572. People who live in glasshouses shouldn't get stoned.

573. May no honest heart ever know distress.

574. If at the end of the day you feel dog tired, maybe it is because you growled too much.

575. Many a man thinks he has an open mind when it is merely vacant.

576. Most parents begin with giving in and end by giving up.

577. Old Eskimo legend: don't eat the yellow snow.

578. It doesn't matter whether you win or lose—until you lose; what really matters is whether I win or lose.

579. Do not resent growing old: many are denied that privilege.

580. A brain is no stronger than its weakest think.

581. One way to avoid excitement is to live within your income.

582. Always sympathize with the underdog, but don't bet on him.

583. When a man's socks and tie match, he's wearing a present.

584. What men prize most is a privilege even if it be that of chief mourner at a funeral.

585. Today, it's a wise father that knows as much as his own son.

586. Life is like an ice cream cone—you've got to learn to lick it.

587. If the best part of waking up is Folgers in your cup, you're sleeping with the wrong person.

588. Never keep up with the Joneses. Drag them down to your level. It's cheaper.

589. The happiest people are those who are too busy to notice.

590. A happy man is never poor: an unhappy man is never rich.

591. If you don't learn to laugh at trouble, you won't have anything to laugh at when you grow old.

592. Nobody who can borrow money easily ever wants it badly.

593. Always borrow from a pessimist; he never expects it back.

594. Life's disappointments are only speed bumps—things you have to get over to enjoy the rest of life's journey.

595. There are two ways to get to the top of an oak tree. One is to climb and the other is to sit on an acorn.

596. If you can't have fun, don't do it. If you are not happier now, what makes you feel you will be happier later?

597. When you are up to your ass in alligators, you may forget the primary purpose was to drain the swamp.

598. You shouldn't worry like that. It doesn't do any good. Ninety percent of the things I worry about never happen.

599. Santa Claus is just like the rest of us. He has the entire world to cover once a year, and he always puts it off till Xmas Eve.

600. Three things are necessary for the salvation of man—to know what he ought to believe, to know what he ought to desire, and to know what he ought to do.

601. The trouble with opportunity is that it comes disguised as hard work.

602. The fellow who's busy pulling on the oars doesn't have time to rock the boat.

603. When life seems like an uphill climb, take comfort in the fact that you are mooning everyone behind you.

604. Money can't buy happiness, but then happiness can't buy groceries.

605. Money, like fertilizer, is no good unless you spread it around.

606. There are three types of gossips: vest button type-always popping off: vacuum cleaner type-always picking up dirt: liniment type-always rubbing it in.

607. The best way to curb high school dropouts would be to require a high school diploma as a prerequisite for obtaining a driver's license.

608. Would you rather be in an explosion or a collision? Answer: A collision because if you are in a collision you are there, but if you are in an explosion, where are you?

609. I never repeat gossip. So please listen good the first time.

610. Conceit is when there is a flash of lightning and you say, "Please, no pictures."

611. At school, she was voted the girl most likely to concede.

612. We try to hide our poverty when we are broke but brag about it afterward.

613. Problems are only opportunities in disguise.

614. What you are is more important than what you've got.

615. It is better to be a has-been than a never was.

616. To be a failure, spend your life pushing doors marked Pull.

617. Hindsight is good, foresight is better, but insight is best of all.

618. The only time you must not fail is the last time you try.

619. When you battle with your conscience and lose, you win.

620. Anyone with a clear conscience probably has a bad memory.

621. Silence is not always golden; sometimes it is guilt.

622. Experience, unfortunately, gives the test first and the lesson later.

623. You become experienced by watching what happens to you when you are not.

624. Experience is what happens to you while you are making other plans.

625. Success comes in cans; failure in can'ts.

626. The secret of success: Don't fail!

627. Success is only a matter of luck. Ask any man who has failed.

628. He was too busy learning the tricks of the trade to learn the trade.

629. Never play poker with a man named Ace.

630. Never borrow money from a finance company whose president is named Nunzio or Vito.

631. Tell your child to lie for you and he will lie to you.

632. If he smiles when things go wrong, it means he has found someone else to blame it on.

633. If you win all your arguments, you will end up with no friends.

634. Truth is not only violated by falsehood; it may be equally outraged by silence.

635. Father to son: My boy, treat everyone with politeness even those who are rude to you. Remember that you show courtesy to others not because they are gentlemen, but because you are one.

636. You think you have troubles? An astrologer just told me the twenty-first century is my unlucky century.

637. Growing older can be great if you remember the word *growing*.

638. When you starve with a tiger, the tiger starves last.

639. When the going gets tough, the smart get lost.

640. We need to teach the highly educated person that it is not a disgrace to fail and that he must always analyze every failure to find its cause. He must learn how to fail intelligently, for failing is one of the greatest arts in the world.

641. The severity of the itch is inversely proportional to the reach.

642. He who has all the answers has not heard all the questions.

643. The difference between gossip and news is whether you tell it or hear it.

644. Never hold a grudge after you have gotten even.

645. Life is like a shower. One wrong turn and you are in hot water.

646. When they run you out of town, get out in front and make it look like a parade.

647. Don't itch for something you are not willing to scratch for.

648. As you climb the ladder of success, make sure it is leaning against the right building.

649. Knowledge without action is like snow on a hot stove.

650. The best way to avoid trouble and ensure safety is to breathe through your nose. It keeps your mouth shut.

651. Almost all of our unhappiness is the result of comparing ourselves to others.

652. Don't brag. It is not the whistle that moves the train.

653. Three things that most inhibit happiness: judgment of others, negative thoughts, and envy.

654. Write the letter, put it in the drawer, then read it again in a couple of days. Do you still want to send it? I've found that anger and piecrust soften in two days.

655. At age twenty, we don't worry about what the world thinks of us. At age thirty, we do worry about what the world is thinking about us, and at age forty, we discover that it wasn't thinking of us at all.

656. "The play ended, happily," wrote a critic. What a difference a comma can make.

657. Before criticizing, praise. Remember the barber always lathers the customer before he applies the razor.

658. We cannot bring prosperity by discouraging thrift.
We cannot strengthen the weak by weakening the strong.
We cannot help small men by tearing down big men.
We cannot help the poor by ignoring the rich.
We cannot lift the wage earner by pulling down the wage payer.
We cannot keep out of trouble by spending more than our income.

659. Never try to teach a pig to sing. It wastes your time and annoys the pig.

660. When someone says, "There is no need to panic," there usually is.

661. Never take a beer to a job interview.

662. It is considered tacky to take a cooler to church.

663. The road to success is always under construction.

664. Even if you are certain you are included in the will, it is still considered tacky to drive a U-Haul to the funeral home.

665. Because I feel inferior, I try harder. Because I am inferior, it doesn't do any good.

666. The main accomplishment of almost all organized protest groups is annoy people who are not in them.

667. Ignore your rights and they will go away.

668. It is no disgrace to be poor. In fact, it is proof that you are an honest, tax-paying citizen.

669. Home is where you can say anything you like because nobody listens to you anyway.

670. The best sermons are lived, not preached.

671. Time slips up on you like a windshield on a bug.

672. I remember the time when a child had more brothers and sisters than fathers.

673. Four words that can win friends for you: you are absolutely right.

674. To be happy, you should do something every day to make other people happy—even if it's merely leaving them alone.

675. Successful people begin where failures leave off. Never settle for just getting the job done. Excel.

676. You cannot unsay a cruel thing.

677. Honesty is the best policy because there is less competition.

678. We will never have great leaders as long as we mistake education for intelligence, ambition for ability, and a winning smile for integrity.

679. The true measure of a man's character is what he says when he drops a ten-pound Bible on his foot.

680. The secret of success is to get through life watching out for number 1 without stepping in number 2.

681. It don't take a very big person to carry a grudge.

682. You can catch more flies with honey than you can with vinegar, assuming you want to catch flies.

683. Don't insult the alligator until you have crossed the river.

684. The nice thing about egotists is that they don't talk about other people.

685. Don't be irreplaceable. If you can't be replaced, you can't be promoted.

686. Never ask a question, you don't really want to know the answer to.

687. If everything is coming your way, you are in the wrong lane.

688. Do not argue with a spouse who is packing your parachute.

689. Ignorance picks up confidence as it goes along.

690. We have enough "youth." How about a fountain of "smart"?

691. Whoever said nothing is impossible never tried to slam a revolving door.

692. Observation: there are no failures at a class reunion.

693. Remember—aim low, reach your goals, and avoid disappointment.

694. A pessimist is someone who complains about the noise when opportunity knocks.

695. I believe in forced cannibalism. If people were made to eat what they kill, there would be no more war.

696. Smart is when you believe half of what you hear. Brilliant is knowing which half.

697. Five years ago, I was just a nobody. Today I am five years older.

698. The best way to help the poor is not to be one.

699. Don't let anyone steal your joy. (negativism)

700. The idea of a man picking a wife is about as absurd as that of an apple picking a farmer.

701. Anybody who thinks this is a man's world is probably not too bright about other things either.

702. If a thing is worth doing, it would have been done already.

703. I've never agreed with the statement "All is fair in love and war." Actually it's more fair in war.

704. Always remember that what is sushi in one establishment is bait in another.

705. Seat belts are not as confining as wheelchairs.

706. Just remember, to other people your side looks greener.

707. The less you know, the less informed you are.

708. I almost had a psychic girlfriend, but she left before we met.

709. Never trust a stockbroker who is married to a travel agent.

710. No matter what goes wrong, there is always somebody who knew it would.

711. January 2 is when most people find it is easier to break a resolution than a habit.

712. Don't pray for the rain if you are going to complain about the mud.

713. "Just say no" prevents teenage pregnancy the way "Have a nice day" cures chronic depression.

714. Golf, sex, and child rearing are proof that practice does not make perfect.

715. Don't ever be the first. Don't ever be the last, and don't ever volunteer to do anything. (military)

716. People say hard work never killed anybody, but did you ever hear of someone who rested to death?

717. When in charge, ponder.
When in trouble, delegate.
When in doubt, mumble.

718. Western's law—assumption is the mother of all screwups.

719. Education is what you get from reading the fine print. Experience is what you get from not reading it.

720. Phyllis Diller: Never go to bed mad—stay up and fight.

721. It's always easier to forgive an enemy after you've gotten even.

722. Begin writing your letter marked Page 2. Then continue on as if you had written page 1. The more unbelievable page 2 is the funnier. This is guaranteed to get a response from the person you wrote.

723. About the only thing you can do today on a shoestring is trip.

724. Before you find your handsome prince, you've got to kiss a lot of frogs.

725. If you can't get people to listen to you any other way, tell them it is confidential.

726. Never go to a class reunion pregnant. They will think that's all you've been doing.

727. Why don't faith healers do teeth?

728. The rule of holes: if you are in one-stop digging.

729. If you try and don't succeed, cheat. Repeat until caught. Then lie.

730. Never buy a car you can't push.

731. Three words of advice: Don't give any.

732. Accept that some days you are the pigeon and some days you are the statue.

733. Have you noticed that an optimist is always able to see the bright side of other people's problems?

734. It is easy to become rich, but it is a challenge to remain poor.

735. On friends and relations: don't ever have a guest room.

736. Everyone is someone else's weirdo.

737. Don't ever take a fence down until you know why it was put up.

738. Do not meddle in the affairs of dragons, for you are crunchy and taste good with ketchup.

739. There are very few personal problems that cannot be solved through a suitable application of high explosives.

740. No one ever sells a used car because it runs too well.

741. If you can help a relative in need, they will remember you the next time they are in need again.

742. Too bad stupidity isn't painful.

743. Never kick a fresh cow chip on a hot day.

744. Life isn't like a box of chocolates. It's more like a jar of jalapenos. What you do today may burn your ass tomorrow.

745. The things that come to those who want are probably the things that are left by those who got there first.

746. If stupidity got me in this mess, then why can't it get me out?

747. Politics: beware of the cat who talks on behalf of the mouse.

748. Never buy a used car if all the radio buttons are tuned to hard rock stations.

749. Never argue with an idiot. He will bring you down to his level and beat you with experience.

750. I've learned that sometimes the people you expect to kick you when you are down will be the ones who do.

751. Just think: if it weren't for marriage, men would go through life thinking they had no faults at all.

752. Speech: When I was young, I thought wealth and power would bring me happiness. Boy was I right.

753. My boss: When I started he said, "I want you to be happy here. If there is something you want that we don't have, just let me know. I'll show you how to get along without it."

754. Expecting the world to treat you fairly because you are a good person is like expecting a bull not to attack you because you are a vegetarian.